Digitisation Perspectives

PAOLA MARCHIONNI

EDUCATIONAL FUTURES
RETHINKING THEORY AND PRACTICE
Volume 46

Scope
This series maps the emergent field of educational futures. It will commission books on the futures of education in relation to the question of globalisation and the knowledge economy. It seeks authors who can demonstrate their understanding of discourses of the knowledge and learning economies. It aspires to build a consistent approach to educational futures in terms of traditional methods, including scenario planning and foresight, as well as imaginative narratives, and it will examine examples of futures research in education, pedagogical experiments, new utopian thinking, and educational policy futures with a strong accent on actual policies and examples.

Digitisation Perspectives

Edited by

Ruth Rikowski
Chandos Publishing, Oxford

SENSE PUBLISHERS
ROTTERDAM/BOSTON/TAIPEI

A C.I.P. record for this book is available from the Library of Congress.

ISBN: 978-94-6091-297-9 (paperback)
ISBN: 978-94-6091-298-6 (hardback)
ISBN: 978-94-6091-299-3 (e-book)

Published by: Sense Publishers,
P.O. Box 21858,
3001 AW Rotterdam,
The Netherlands
http://www.sensepublishers.com

Printed on acid-free paper

Cover designed by Victor Verne Rikowski, June 2010

Chapters 2–3, 6–8 and 12–18 were first published in the ejournal Policy Futures in Education, and are reprinted here with permission from the publisher.

TABLE OF CONTENTS

ACKNOWLEDGEMENT

I would like to thank my husband Glenn John Rikowski for his help in the final stages of the preparation of the manuscript for this book, and for his wonderful support in general.

FOREWORD

Digitisation Perspectives asks and answers some deeply fundamental questions about digitisation. There are 22 contributors and this work takes a wide ranging tour across the sector. It starts by considering a 'Background and Overview to Digitisation and Digital Libraries'. This is followed by 'Digitisation and Higher Education' and considerations of 'Digitisation and Inequalities'. Latter sections cover 'Digital Libraries, Reference Services and Citation Indexing'; the 'Digitisation of Rare, Valued and Scholarly Works' and the 'Futuristic Developments of Digitisation'.

The fundamental questions asked and answered in this work are:

- How do we establish and create digital resources?
- Once created, how do we establish access to those resources online?
- How do we maintain those resources over the long term?
- For whom are we doing all this digital activity, and
- How do we address inequalities?

In overview these seem simple enough questions, but at any level of granularity they become complex, interwoven and deeply faceted.

To illustrate this, consider a quick assay into the world of rare manuscript digitisation. This seems straightforward in its surface justification but becomes more complex as one delves deeper. Rare manuscripts, especially Anglo-Saxon manuscripts, are often works of great intrinsic, intellectual and material value that are a source of fascination to many scholars and often the lay-person as well. And yet, they are fragile, rare and thus should not be handled too often, exposed to rough treatment or large variations in temperature and humidity. So digitisation seems an obvious and sensible solution to providing access to these rare and valued materials. We will digitise them, get the resulting images on to the Web and scholars and the lay-person can have access. In this way we can disseminate their wonder whilst preserving the original. What could be simpler or more straightforward?

As we delve deeper we see that digitisation is not such a neutral act. The process of digitisation, even when done carefully may itself become the harshest treatment the manuscript has ever undergone. Sometimes these items of great rarity have never had every page turned and yet with digitisation we will affect such a handling. Once imaged, there are many questions as to how each image should be labelled, described and indexed. Even something as prosaic as filenaming can become the source of debate and disputation in the effort to seek the best digital preservation policy. This does not even begin to address the complexity of gaining an online Web accessible version of the manuscript and addressing the user centred questions of what mode that access should take. Should it be a fancy page turning facsimile interface, or just plain images in a linear order? And that order in which they are arranged, should it be that established by a venerated scholar, such as M. R. James, or could the order be dictated by the modern physical arrangement of the manuscript pages as digitised? Or should both views be facilitated?

And are digitised versions of rare manuscripts just for post-graduate scholarly use? Maybe, if they were at least calendared then a wider educational purpose might be served? But who will do this and what perspective will that interpretation take? What tools will be maintained and developed for educational use, what virtual learning environments or virtual manuscript study tools exist or could be brought into existence to serve scholarship and education? Further, will the lay-public have access and will that access be supported by guides and translations and tools to help them to engage with the content in meaningful and fulfilling ways? And will access be free or a charge levied?

It is also worth considering whether such a Westernised view of history as might be made available through a digitised Anglo-Saxon manuscript is the most appropriate expenditure of time and resources in a world of information. Would expending effort here reduce or increase the digital divide? Does it help to address the real and burgeoning needs of the developing world to spend more resources on the digitisation of a single manuscript collection than has been spent on digitising the papers and life of Archbishop Desmond Tutu in South Africa? Similarly, more has been spent on manuscripts than on distributing digitised health information on water purity and safety in Bangladesh to reduce the death rate from diseases such as Typhus. There is no neutrality in digitisation, it is beset with ethical choices and moral issues. For instance, should we charge for access to the online resources? Are we making it impossible for some countries to engage in the scholarly debate on an equal footing with their peers if we do not embrace Open Access? And yet, if we do not charge, can the online resource remain sustainable in the long term?

So, no act in this digital domain is neutral and without consequences that as Ted Nelson said "intertwingle". It is a jungle out there, with many ecosystems competing for dominance. At its heart are human desires and these are defining the value we place upon information and the needs for digitisation to be achieved in our time. Digitisation has become a cultural, scholastic, economic and political imperative and raises many important issues for our consideration.

Thus, I welcome this book, *Digitisation Perspectives*, edited with great verve by Ruth Rikowski. It seeks to address and answer some of the big questions of digitisation. It succeeds on many levels, not least because it respects the deeply interlocking nature of the subject area, with high quality insights from so many experts covering so much ground.

Simon Tanner
Director, Digital Consultancy in the Centre for Computing in the Humanities
King's College London

INTRODUCTION

I am pleased and proud to introduce my second edited collection and my third book. The subjects of all three books (globalisation, knowledge management and digitisation) overlap and interweave in many ways. In my single-authored book on globalisation, published with Chandos (2005) I explored and developed my political and theoretical positions and passions and related this to my practical library and information experience. Coupled with my absorbing interest and fascination with complex topics I then placed all this within a global/international framework. In my second book, an edited collection on knowledge management (KM) (also published with Chandos, 2007), I changed tactic. This book housed a collection of different voices and perspectives on KM, all experts in their fields, on a diversity of topics including knowledge management and wisdom; intangible value; leadership in the knowledge revolution; the role of the library in knowledge management; accessibility issues for web-based information systems; culture and knowledge management and thermodynamics and knowledge. I concluded the book with my own clear theoretical and political perspective and position.

This book on digitisation provides yet another slant; it is a collection, once again, of different expert voices and perspectives, on a wide variety of topics, this time within the broad subject matter of digitisation. However, the political dimension is kept lower key in this volume. In fact, in my second chapter in the book (Chapter 4) I end with emphasising the wonder, importance and beauty of art, which if approached in a certain way can, I think, sometimes take us beyond the confines of the political scene (albeit we all still have to work and operate within the political system, of course).

All three of my non-fiction books cover topics that are very important today, both within the library and information profession, within education and also within the wider community in general. We now need to think and operate within a global framework in many ways. Sharing, exchanging and managing knowledge (knowledge management) is very important in this global framework, as of course, is the digitisation of this material.

Digitisation Perspectives covers a wide range of important topics within the broad topic of 'Digitisation'. It is divided into six parts. Part 1 provides a 'Background and Overview to Digitisation and Digital Libraries', Part 2 focuses on 'Digitisation and Higher Education whilst Part 3 is on 'Digitisation and Inequalities'. Part 4 covers 'Digital Libraries, Reference Services and Citation Indexing'; Part 5 examines 'Digitisation of Rare, Valued and Scholarly Works' and Part 6, the final section, explores some of the 'Futuristic Developments of Digitisation'. There are 22 contributors altogether in the book; all experts in their fields. Quite a number of books have now been published on this important topic, but hopefully, this book brings something of a different, interesting and refreshing outlook to the subject matter. The book builds on the special issue on 'Digital Libraries' that I co-edited with Isaac Hunter Dunlap for the refereed international ejournal,

Policy Futures in Education in the first quarter of 2008 (see http://www.wwwords.co.uk/pfie/content/pdfs/6/issue6_1.asp). The book is being published with Sense Publishers at the initial invitation and suggestion of Professor Michael Peters at the University of Illinois. Professor, Educational Policy Studies at Urbana-Champaign.

There are four chapters in the 'Background and Overview' section. The first is by Melissa M. Terras, and is entitled 'The Rise of Digitization: an overview'. Terras considers digitisation within three periods; the early years before the World Wide Web, the 1990s and post 2000. As Terras says, in the 1980's:

> ...interest in the application of digitization and image processing in the arts, humanities, library and archive sector began to grow.

There was a significant growth in digitisation in the 1990s, which was due to a variety of forces, such as the increase in the performance and availability of new networked technologies and in the awareness of the possibilities that the new technologies could bring forth. Whilst in the post 2000 period we have witnessed projects such as the JISC (UK Joint Information Systems Committee) digitization programme, and digitisation work being undertaken by commercial firms, such as Google and Microsoft. Terras concludes by saying that:

> There are interesting times ahead for the information professional in dealing with the wealth of digital information now available, keeping up with the changing nature of Internet technologies, and coping with resulting changes in user expectations and needs, to create digital libraries which can exploit the potential of this groundswell of digital – digitised – content.

This is followed by an overview and critique of digital libraries and digitisation which I have written. I consider topics such as the advantages and costs of digitisation; traditional, digital, hybrid and virtual libraries; the library community and digitisation; ebooks; digital libraries on a global basis; gender issues, IT and digitisation and the social and political implications of digitisation. Some of the advantages of digitisation outlined include the ability to be able to search, browse and compare a variety of material; developing digital surrogates of rare or fragile original objects; bringing collections together in a virtual, digitised form, that might not otherwise be bought together and raising the profile and prestige of an organisation. Various digital projects are considered, such as the Oxford Digital Library project and Alouette-Canada, a Canadian national digital online project. In regard to the social and political implications, as I say this:

> ...includes issues around the digital divide; the exploitation of workers in the developing world; the possible loss of a sense of community; the concept of 'self' in the IT age; ...and potential health risks through over-use of e-reading (backache, eye strain etc.). ...issues related to the likelihood of less face-to-face teaching ... (due to the increase in e-learning, easy access to digitised information, etc) and those related to the ever-changing nature of technology...

I conclude by saying that:

> Digitisation and digital libraries offer many new and exciting ways for us to be able to access material, but we also need to exercise some caution, and not just jump on every digital bandwagon.

The third chapter is by M. Paul Pandian and is entitled 'Digital Knowledge Resources'. Pandian provides an historical digital tour, whilst also demonstrating the fast pace of the digital transformations that have taken place over the last few years. Pandian considers emerging technologies, and how these technologies have changed how librarians, information professionals and researchers organise, search, retrieve and preserve information. Pandian also compares and contrasts the digital library with the traditional library, and the valuable role that the traditional library still plays today. In regard to the global nature of digitisation, Pandian says that:

> Libraries of all types and in all settings are developing a global vision of international networked collections and services. This model views libraries as both providers of worldwide knowledge resources for gateways for users to knowledge which is increasingly electronic in form. This transformation requires recognition of important revolutionary changes, which are transforming collections, information services and the working relationships among libraries.

The last chapter in the first section is another one by me, and is entitled 'Digitisation: research, sophisticated search engines, evaluation – all that and more'. As the title implies, this chapter examines a number of different areas of digitisation, in more depth. It explores topics such as digitisation research and development; electronic theses; 'googlisation' and search engine technology. Also explored are: data mining large digital collections and application programming interfaces; the development of digital libraries for the scientific communities in China; the value of digital preservation; the evaluation of digitisation projects and Arms 'viewpoint analysis' of the digital library.

In regard to sophisticated search engine technology, I focus on the work of Summann and Lossau; Brophy and Bawden; Xie (who compared online database systems, Dialog and Factiva with three different types of web search tools – a search engine, a directory and a meta-search engine), and the 'information model for digital libraries' as outlined by Lagoze, Krafft, Payette and Jesuroga. Whilst application programming interfaces assist with data mining of large digital collections, and Cohen's Syllabus Finder, in particular, is considered. I conclude with Arms 'view-point analysis', which looks at digital libraries from three different viewpoints – the organisational view, the technical view and the view of the user. Arms argues that greater consideration should be given to the users viewpoint. Whilst this might seem rather romantic, I make the point that on one level such an approach can, perhaps, take us beyond the rather limited political and economic scene that we can sometimes find ourselves embroiled in today.

Part 2 examines 'Digitisation and Higher Education'. The first chapter in this section (Chapter 5) is on 'Improving student mental models in a new university information setting' and is by Alan Rosling and Kathryn Littlemore. Their chapter outlines the culture and ethos of the university and the students that they encounter and interact with there within the broad context of digitisation. They ask:

> How well are our students able to make use of the digital resources we provide, and how, as teachers, do we in fact teach information literacy skills in the digital setting?

They comment on the 'Google Generation' and 'Digital Natives' and ask:

> The label 'Google Generation' implies that these individuals have a natural affinity with anything online or digital, that they are completely comfortable with existing and new technologies, and hence, their mental models of digital resources are well developed – and easily translated into digital libraries. Is this a fair and realistic assessment of students?

The chapter focuses in particular on 'mental models' and mental model theories. Craik (1943) was one of the first people to describe these mental models, saying that they are 'small scale models' of reality. Whilst Norman (1983) distinguishes between mental and conceptual models, where the mental model is what the user has in her or his mind and the conceptual model is the model that is given to the user by an outsider, such as by a designer. Rosling and Littlemore reflect on mental models saying:

> So our user comes to their 'user education/information skills/information literacy' class bringing with them their past experiences and prior knowledge of computers and online searching and software. As they sit at the terminal they also bring with them their, often very incomplete, mental models of the information landscape; the Internet, how computers work and how they might search successfully.

Mental models and information literacy teaching is also explored, as well as the role of emotional intelligence within this setting. Rosling and Littlemore conclude by arguing that:

> The digital landscape requires more from the librarian…than it did in the days of the print landscape. Teaching 'search strategy' skills is no longer adequate for the complex environment of the Internet and web-based search tools. Mental model research can help librarians to use more focused teaching strategies like encouraging students to explore (or even play), to target more sophisticated feedback towards specific digital problems (why searches fail, access rights, comparing systems)…If we continue to use current mental model research to make even more sense of the student searching experience then we might establish even clearer learning strategies that will move learners further up the information literacy skills ladder.

Chapter 6 explores 'Electronic Theses and Dissertations: promoting 'hidden' research'. In this chapter Susan Copeland examines the development of e-theses internationally and some of the cooperative ventures that have been undertaken to facilitate scholarly communication and resource and knowledge sharing. This includes the development of the Networked Digital Library of Theses and Dissertations (NDLTD). As Copeland says, her chapter:

> ...highlights key issues associated with the creation, management and use of electronic theses and dissertations and provides information about organisations that are actively working to promote this useful source of research data. Information is provided on topics such as training, technical and administrative requirements, and the issues to address whether adopting a local, institutional, approach or participating in a national level service.

Copeland concludes her chapter on an optimistic note, highlighting the fact that although there are "Differences in terminology, procedures and requirements associated with how theses and dissertations are presented in different countries..." improvements are continually being made in this area. The NDLTD has played a particularly valuable role in this regard.

In Chapter 7 Paul Catherall provides an overview of 'Learning Systems in Post-Statutory Education'. This includes a consideration of the origins and forms of learning systems; technical, educational concepts and approaches used, such as distributed and collaborative learning; the VLE (Virtual Learning Environment) and trends in e-learning including future technologies such as m-learning (mobile learning). Some of the challenges in the delivery of systems and software to facilitate learning in a digital environment are also highlighted. In regard to e-learning systems, Catherall says that:

> Web-based learning systems provide a range of interactive functions, including communication channels, content-publishing and assessment tools. It can be seen that these systems have begun to permeate and impact on many aspects of post-statutory education, with recent web technologies allowing for closer systems integration across institutional systems, including library catalogue, student records and finance systems. In the United Kingdom, this institute-wide computing infrastructure is often considered a holistic learning environment.

Meanwhile, Isaac Hunter Dunlap delves into the realms of 'Going Digital: the transformation of scholarly communication and academic libraries'. As Dunlap says:

> This chapter provides both historical perspective and a forward-looking examination into how academic libraries are transforming themselves to both cope with, and help shape, unprecedented transitions in scholarly research and communication.

He notes that, in general, digital libraries:

> ...have become a complex, interactive and interdependent network of resources, user services, social technology interactions, databases, virtual meetings, gateways, 'real time' online instruction opportunities and content management systems.

University libraries are now embracing the emerging technologies and Dunlap considers how structures and functions within the university library are being re-positioned and transformed so that they can fit more effectively into this digital age.

Within this, he explores a number of different areas including the hybrid library; financial constraints; the Open Access movement; the acquisition of digital collections; social networking technologies and the digitisation of special collections.

There are three chapters in Part 3 'Digitisation and Inequalities'. The first of these (Chapter 9) is entitled 'Hegemony and the Web: the struggle for hegemony in a digital age' and is by Tony Ward. Ward draws on his practical experience as a teacher within a critical pedagogical approach. He considers topics such as the digital divide; the promise of the Internet (the fact, for example, that as Ward says "The Internet is seen as a space where everybody can have a voice, can be heard and can express their own realities…"); scarcity, and the creation and control of knowledge and information systems within this; education as a commodity and the modern media. Ward concludes by saying that it is clear to him that the Digital Divide:

> …will never be "bridged" or "closed" as long as we have an economic system that operates on the basis of exclusions...The modern digital media holds an enormous sway over the public mind and in the hands of powerful groups and individuals poses a formidable obstacle to the emergence of a popular democracy. But there have also been many gains in that time. The struggle for hegemony will be ongoing and endless.

And his final thought is this:

> The question remains whether…shifts in the use of technology will ever provide the access to public voice that the truly oppressed can use for their own emancipation. The movement for open access may be one of the most critical in our age.

Ward's desire for a fairer and a kinder world is self-evident.

This is followed by two chapters that explore digitisation in Africa specifically. Chapter 10 is by Dieu Hack-Polay and is entitled 'Digital libraries: an opportunity for African education' and Chapter 11 is by Leburn Rose and is entitled 'Critical Perspectives on Digitising Africa'. Hack-Polay, considers the many benefits that the development of digital libraries can bring to Africa. These include the fact that digital libraries can "…provide a forum for inter-institution communication and updating on the currency in different subject areas"; that data can be retrieved more easily; and that it provides great opportunities for the dissemination of both unpublished and published material in Africa. Hack-Polay explores some of the digital initiatives that are taking place in Africa, such as the African Online Digital Library (AODL). Furthermore, the variety of sub-cultures and different languages and traditions is emphasised and the helpful role that digitisation can play here. Hack-Polay says:

> …digital libraries could be a platform where the education system makes available notions about country or culture-specific histories, stories, good

> practice models in terms of educational, political, scientific and technological development.

Some of the constraints for the effective development of digitisation are also outlined; such as cost, logistics and manpower constraints. Never-the-less Hack-Polay concludes on an optimistic note, saying that:

> Digital libraries could ultimately, more than any other means before, aid literacy development in Africa and in higher education, foster more quality academic output and research.

Meanwhile, Leburn Rose in Chapter 11 is somewhat more sceptical and concerned about how western approaches to digitisation can and do impact on developing countries in Africa. The infra-structure in Africa is very different to that in the developed countries. He refers to the 'dual nature' of technology (including digitisation itself), arguing that it is both 'instrumental' and 'volitional' at the same time. But as he says, the 'volitional perspective' is western-based.

> The volitional perspective [the will to power] on technology is quintessential Western, and presents a distorted view of technology as something that is being created for and imposed upon.

He says that a framework for 'authentic digitisation' needs to be developed in Africa arguing, for example, that:

> Those that seek to sponsor authentic digitisation should focus on strategies that build upon and engender social well-being and are contextually sensitive to the relevant domains of practice.

He then interestingly applies the 'free-body diagram' (a concept adpated from his engineering background) to the picture, whereby a part of the technology is isolated so that it can be 'subjected to analysis'. As he says:

> The conclusion here it not surprising: that the problems which technology attempts to resolve and the outcomes sought are contingent upon the surroundings of which the technology may be a part. One cannot simply export a technology into an unfamiliar context and assume that it will yield similar results to those achieved in the original setting.

Thus, in essence, western digitisation programmes cannot simply be imposed on Africa, or indeed, on the developing world in general; rather, they need to be adapted to the social and economic conditions within these countries, and to their particular infrastructures.

Part 4, 'Digital Libraries, Reference Services and Citation Indexing' returns to some more traditional library services and approaches, and how these are now being developed and changed through and with digitisation practices. Through this we can aim to retain the quality and worth of the traditional aspects of librarianship and the skills that have been learnt and developed, and then build and develop all this within a digital environment. The first chapter in this section is about digitising the reference service. The chapter is by Jia Liu, and is entitled 'Digital Library and Digital Reference Service: integration and mutual complementarity'. Through a series of case studies, Liu argues for a "three-dimensional integration", operating around the digital reference service, the digital library, and areas of overlap and integration between the two services. She notes the fact that whilst the term the 'digital library' is generally known and widely used, the 'digital reference service' is also known under various other terms, such as the 'virtual reference service'; 'online reference service'; 'electronic reference service' and 'ask a/the librarian service'. Liu argues that:

> It is logical, reasonable and necessary for the digital reference service to take the digital library as part of its reference collection.

Some of the work that has been undertaken on the creation and development of digital reference services is considered. The University of California library, for example, has been a pioneer for providing a remote reference service, and in 1997 the Science Library librarians there implemented a pilot 'telereference' project. This project focused on topics such as desktop videoconferencing for conducting reference interviews with student users at a remote location. Liu concludes by saying that:

> Both the digital library and the digital reference service are products under the networked environment and evolve with the developments of information and communication technology (ICT)...Without any doubt, the digital library and the digital reference service have a close relationship and need each other...

The other chapter (Chapter 13) in this section is a detailed analysis of citation indexing; it is entitled 'The New Generation of Citation Indexing in the Age of Digital Libraries' and is by Mengxiong Liu and Peggy Cabrera. Liu and Cabrera review developments in web-based citation indexing and conduct a case study into three major citation search tools; these being *Web of Science, Scopus* and *Google Scholar*. They found that:

> ...none of the three tools can satisfy all of a researcher's citation tracking records. *Web of Science* showed strength in providing citing references to traditional academic journals while *Scopus* performed better in providing citing literature for more current articles. *Google Scholar* returned a significant number of non-traditional citing references. With its advantage of free availability via the Internet, *Google Scholar* is an important compliment to *WoS* and *Scopus.*

Following on from the various evaluations and comparisons of citing reference services, Liu and Cabrera conclude that

> ...there is no single solution for a complete citing reference search without a Universal Citation Digital Library.

Part 5 explores 'Digitisation of Rare, Valued and Scholarly Works' and there are three chapters in this section. Tatiana Niklova-Houston and Ron Houston have written a fascinating and absorbing chapter about the digitisation of ancient manuscripts, which is entitled 'Building the Virtual Scriptorium'. Whilst digital preservation, in general, is seen to be quite worthwhile as an aim, the work on the digitising of ancient manuscripts proves to be particularly challenging. Niklova-Houston and Houston address some of the major challenges and obstacles for the digitisation of ancient manuscripts. They argue that a clear digitisation programme needs to be adopted, which is very mindful of emerging technologies and evolving industry standards. They say that:

> Manuscripts, archives, and early printed books contain a documentary record of the foundations of human knowledge...On the assumption that the widespread availability of knowledge benefits the human condition more than the restriction of knowledge, elements restrictive to the dissemination of manuscripts, archives, and early printed books should be overcome, and the intellectual content of such items should be available to as wide an audience as possible through the digital library equivalent of the medieval scriptorium, termed here the "virtual scriptorium."

Their chapter includes some lovely photographs of various ancient manuscript material that have been digitised and Niklova-Houston and Houston look at three SlavMan (Slavic Manuscript) websites. One of the obstacles to digitising this material comes from the curators of traditional manuscript collections themselves. Curators ask questions such as: "How will digitizing further our secondary mission: to support the scholar?" Another obstacle, of course, is the financial one. Niklova-Houston and Houston conclude by saying that:

> Knowledge is out there, stored in the pages of manuscripts locked away in dusty archives. It will remain there, unused, unless you take your digital camera, digitize the images, and post them in a web-based virtual scriptorium. You may not create the perfect library; you may not have sufficient permissions; your work soon may require formatting. Yet, whether or not you digitize, these problems will persist. Digitize now, and they may be overcome.

Heather Joseph, Executive Director of the Scholarly Publishing and Academic Resources Coalition (SPARC) outlines the work of SPARC in a chapter entitled 'SPARC: creating innovative models and environments for scholarly research and communication'. She explores some of the main activities of this influential organisation, which takes a leading role in shaping the future of scholarly works and communication. SPARC was founded by the Association of Research Libraries in 1997, and it enhances the access and use of scholarly information and is developing alternate scholarly communication models (such as open access models) that utilises digital technology. Joseph explores three of SPARC's major programme areas; namely, education, incubation and advocacy.

Whilst in Chapter 16, Yehuda E. Kalay, explores the 'Impacts of New Media on Scholarly Publishing'. He considers how these 'new media' (such as blogs, wikis, open source, podcasts and the World Wide Web) have dramatically altered academic scholarship on many different levels. The focus is on scientific publishing and the chapter summarises some of the key results of a workshop that was held in the University of California Berkeley in June 2006 that was organised by the Center for New Media (CNM) and supported by Elsevier, the leading publisher of scholarly journals in the field. This was the first of a number of planned workshops. The workshop asked questions such as: "How will scientific publishing be affected by New Media?" Kalay suggests that the New Media technology transformation should be viewed from a "horseless carriage" point of view:

> ...not merely as a technological revolution, but as a wholesale social reorganization, affecting the very core of human knowledge, the modes of its production, validation, and dissemination, and shifting the locus of knowledge production from institutions to individuals, complete with relocation of authority over knowledge authentication and valuation.

Part 6 moves on to look at 'Futuristic Developments of Digitisation'. Tom Peters contribution here is in a chapter entitled 'Meeting and Serving Users in their New Work (and Play) Spaces'. Peters investigates how the upsurge of personal computing devices and related growing digital information environments are creating new and varied needs and expectations. Peters argues that experimentation, inventiveness and creativity will become increasingly important within library and information services in the future, as people's needs and demands become more and more diverse and complex. Within this remit, Peters examines the public services component of both digital and virtual libraries. He concludes by saying that in the future people:

> ...will be using a wide variety of personal, portable information/communication/entertainment devices. We may be facing a future in which no single portable device or even device type comes to dominate the marketplace. Libraries will be expected to deliver services to them all. [we will be sharing]...information and insights across these multiple worlds. Learning and information seeking may become significantly more participatory.

In Chapter 18 by Lori Bell, Mary-Carol Lindbloom, Tom Peters and Kitty Pope, Bell et al look at 'Virtual Libraries and Education in Virtual Worlds: twenty-first century library services'. This highly futuristic chapter explores the virtual library through the for-profit Second Life electronic community. Second Life is a completely virtual world in cyberspace, and includes a variety of facilities, such as shops, theatres and libraries. People buy space in this virtual world and then interact. Bell et al say that:

> As the use of the Internet and time spent on the Internet by individuals grows, and the use of virtual worlds like Active Worlds and Second Life increases, the library needs to have an interactive place and role in these worlds as well as a bricks and mortar space.

The chapter focuses, in particular, on a collaborative library project in Second Life that was set up by two of the authors (Bell and Pope). As Bell et al say, new participants to Second Life "...discover a vast digital continent, teeming with people, entertainment, and opportunities." There are over 50 libraries in Second Life. The Cullom-Davis Library at Bradley University in Peoria, Illinois has set up a replica of the real-life library, in Second Life, for example. Bell et al note that challenges for libraries in Second Life include staffing, funding and sustainability. They conclude by saying that:

> We believe that virtual worlds such as Second Life are the next phase of the Internet...[libraries] need to create an effective presence in virtual worlds to investigate what kinds of library services will work and how they can work together to benefit and serve users. It is also important that libraries work closely with other educators and collaborate with groups. No one library can do everything themselves – collaboration will be key in establishing virtual world presences for libraries.

It will be interesting to see how virtual libraries progress and shape-up in the future, and what sort of impact they are likely to have/will have on the wider society.

Hopefully, this varied collection of works on the broad topic of 'Digitisation' will encourage thought and reflection as well as being informative, enthusing and engaging. Also, that we can aim to focus on the positives of digitisation and endeavour to make digitisation work for the good and the benefit of the majority, rather than just for a select few.

REFERENCES

Rikowski, R. (2005). *Globalisation, information and libraries: The implications of the World Trade Organisation's GATS and TRIPS Agreements*. Oxford: Chandos Publishing. Retrieved from http://www.woodheadpublishing.com/en/book.aspx?bookID=1669&ChandosTitle=1

Rikowski, R. (Ed.). (2007). *Knowledge management: Social, cultural and theoretical perspectives*. Oxford: Chandos Publishing. Retrieved from http://www.woodheadpublishing.com/en/book.aspx?bookID=1691&ChandosTitle=1

Ruth Rikowski
Chandos Publishing, Oxford
May 2010

PART I: BACKGROUND AND OVERVIEW TO DIGITISATION AND DIGITAL LIBRARIES

MELISSA M. TERRAS

1. THE RISE OF DIGITIZATION

An Overview

> Prior to digitisation, the retrieving and re-filing of the prints consumed staff time. Batches of prints to be re-filed hung round on trolleys like patients in a busy A&E Department. The sight of a pink print request form approaching the Local Studies counter caused the heart to sink - it foretold at least half an hour wrestling with ancient filing cabinets, not to mention the wait for the notorious Central Library lift. And what could be more dispiriting, for staff and customer, to discover that the prints selected from the card index were not what were wanted at all? The idea of digitising the Print Collection was very attractive. It would reduce the wear and tear on the original prints and transform public access by allowing customers to browse the whole collection (Moorhouse 2004, 62).

Digital libraries depend on digital content. There are information objects which are "born digital", having been created by computational technologies and never existing in analogue format, but the majority of holdings offered by digital libraries were created through the process of digitization, "the conversion of an analog signal or code into a digital signal or code" (Lee 2002, 3).

The information, culture, and heritage sectors were quick to embrace digitization technologies as they became available, primarily to facilitate access to items in collections by providing them in electronic format. Producing digital versions of holdings through digitization has become an industry in itself, and there has been much effort devoted to producing guides to best practice for undertaking the digitisation of library and archive material.

This chapter provides an overview of the rise of digitization, demonstrating the phenomenal recent uptake of digital technologies within the library sector, laying the foundations for the digital libraries of the future.

EARLY YEARS: BEFORE THE WWW

Digitization may seem a recent phenomenon in memory institutes, but the current state of affairs where libraries, archives, museums, galleries, and even private collections are expected to make available their holdings in digital form follows a period of experimentation with and appropriation of available digital technologies which dates back almost forty years. Institutions began to utilize computer systems in the 1970s

R. Rikowski (ed.), Digitisation Perspectives, 3–20.

> … with the creation of electronic catalogues. The analogue card catalogues that provided access to the collection items were replaced by databases. The bibliographic information on the catalogue cards was converted into database fields. The electronic catalogue provided automatic access to analogue objects such as books, works or art and documents. In the 1980s the conversion of printed source material, such as books and articles, into digital files started to become widespread. Two types of digital files were created. The first file type represents the storage medium of the original analogue document; this is often called a digital image. The second file type represents the coded content (for instance, characters and figures) of the original document, and, depending on the type of original, can be an electronic text, table, or database (van Horik 2005, 12).

In the 1980s, interest in the application of digitization and image processing in the arts, humanities, library and archive sector began to grow. Small scale, in-house projects of limited scope and interest were undertaken by individual institutions experimenting with the application of the newly available (but still expensive) technologies (González 1992), but towards the end of the decade large scale projects were launched by various institutions, including pilot projects aiming to investigate the appropriation of digital technologies to the handling of large volumes of information.

One of the first digitization projects was launched in 1984 by The National Archives and Records Administration (NARA) in Washington. Their project "Optical Digital Image Storage System (ODISS)" aimed to test the utility of digital image and optical disk technologies for the reproduction, storage and retrieval of archival documents. Digitizing 220,000 pages of documents, the ODISS project found digital representations of their holdings to be easy to use, with significant time saving for searching and retrieving information, improvement of legibility for documents digitised in high resolution, reduction of storage space, reduced handling of original documents; although they were perhaps optimistic with their predictions of the longevity of the digitised material – suggesting 100 years! (see González 1992, 1998, and NARA 1991 for an overview).

Another early adopter of digitization was the "Archivo General de Indias" in Spain, a 200 year old archive of extremely valuable documents illustrating the history of the Spanish empire in the Americas and the Philippines. Started in 1986, the pioneering and ambitious digitization project saw three public and private organizations join forces (The Spanish Ministry of Culture, IBM Spain, and the Ramón Areces Foundation) to develop a computerized information system and undertake large scale digitization of the archive holdings. By 1992 the archive had digitised 7 million pages, with 11 million completed by 1998, halting the deterioration of original papers caused by handling in the research rooms (González 1992 gives a full overview of the system and its architecture, and the processes used for digitization. González 1998 reflects on ten years of the project). Although not without its technical and legal problems, the digitised archive, which now has tens of millions of digital images of manuscript material, and electronic texts, is available for consultation in the archive itself (its online presence is rather minimal, although the database can now be searched: http://www.mcu.es/archivos/MC/AGI/index.html).

In the library sector, various experiments were undertaken on printed library material (which has fundamentally different characteristics to archival material). One of the pioneers was the Library of Congress in Washington, which early in the 1980s launched a pilot project to look at both optical disk (for use in the digitization of general periodicals) and videodisc (for non-printed material such as photographs) – both storage mechanisms which are long since defunct[1] (Price 1984, Parker 1985, Fischer and Swora 1986). The advantages which were found in undertaking the research included the saving in storage space compared to that taken up by the original material, although the process of digitization itself was found to be time consuming.

Another pilot project in the library area was the joint development by Cornell University and Xerox corporation, supported by the Commission on Preservation and Access, which attempted to develop a prototype for digitizing damaged, or "brittle", books and providing high quality laser copies on request from users, at great speed, and fair prices. In December 1991, one thousand "brittle" volumes were digitised and digital editions prepared, ready to print. The project also investigated whether digitizing was a convenient alternative to the production of microfilm: finding that the time taken was actually similar, although the possibilities of access were higher (Council on Library Resources 1986, González 1992, 100). Around the same time, Yale University Library, one of the earliest developers of preservation microfilming practices,

> ...engaged in the first stages of a long-term and comprehensive effort to develop practical systems for the conversion of microfilm to digital image, and thereby to develop an understanding of the appropriate relationship of the two technologies in future preservation practice (Waters 1991, 1).

During this period, interest in imaging technology was also growing in the visual arts sector, with many art galleries and museums beginning to undertake projects using imaging technologies, which were becoming increasingly affordable. An attempt at cataloguing the projects that took place in the 1980s and 1990s was undertaken at the European Visual Arts Centre at Ipswich. In 1990, a meeting was hosted to discuss possible European collaboration in the form of a European Visual Arts Information Network (EVAIN) whose aim was to "maximise the potential development and effective use of image-based interactive multimedia applications within museums and galleries" (Pring 1991, iii). This led to the setting up of a database of projects in order to circulate developments and applications in the visual arts area, and in 1991, EVIAN began to publish the bi-annual database of "Image Technology in European Museums and art galleries: ITEM" (Pring 1991). Concentrating on European projects, ITEM organised a joint exchange of information with the Clearinghouse of Art Documentation and Computerization, based at the Thomas J. Watson Library of the Metropolitan Museum of Art, New York, which had documented imaging projects in art galleries and museums in the USA since the late 1980s (Stam 1987, Barnett 1991, iv). The goal of the Clearinghouse was to "provide a gateway of information concerning relevant automated projects and activities" based on the premise that "a substantial amount of information on computerization can be shared by researchers and systems alike." Before the days of the Internet, "this scattered but crucial information was unavailable in any one place, and required time-consuming, often redundant investigation." (Barnett 1991, iv).

The first ITEM database detailed 112 projects, covering a broad range from inter-institutional projects funded at government level, to individual institutions undertaking digitization of their own holdings. For example, an entry on the Europe Museums Network, details its aims to

> ...demonstrate how new media can be developed, gain experience of multimedia design, gain experience of working with multimedia databases and computer system, and gain ideas for new services using broadband telecommunications network (Pring 1991, 6).

and to "meet the needs of museums and the telecoms industry" in "working to create new paths to art and culture for their visitors, to show that new media cannot replace art, but can lead people to it" – although there is little mention of their actual findings or recommendations. Early individual institutional digitization programmes are also catalogued, such as the Musée d'Orsay's "Galérie des Dates" videodisc project, which produced an interactive video disc programme covering nine events in each year of sixty-eight year period. Completed in 1986, this two videodisc collection contained 15,000 slides and 14 hours of sound, allowing visitors to the gallery to explore the historical events through video clips, stills and textual information (Pring 1991, 41).

Towards the close of the 1980s,

> Federal agencies ...[became] increasingly interested in using digital information technologies to store large amounts of information economically and efficiently. This [was] particularly true of programs designed to provide Federal information to citizens, since a corresponding reduction in the creation of paper records could potentially reduce costs and improve the delivery of services to the public (Peterson 1994).

The National Archives and Records Administration (NARA) of the United States of America, in conjunction with the National Association of Government Archives and Records Administrators, conducted studies into digital imaging and optical media storage technologies at both State and local government levels, recommending image capture, storage, and sustainability models (NARA 1991). By the close of the decade, then, all forms of memory institutions were embracing digital technologies. In particular, imaging solutions were seen as means to make their holdings more accessible, searchable, and available, for both government bodies and the general public.

Even at this early stage, prior to the invention of the World Wide Web, what is surprising about early digitization projects was the volume of material which was digitised. Most entries in the ITEM catalogue contain thousands of digitised images: The Italian government funded "Galleria Spada" project produced more that 5,000 images of the Spada Gallery in Rome by 1986 (Pring 1991, 85). The Arts du Costume du XXé Siècle project, at the Union Française des Arts du Costume, produced a videodisc of 33,000 images of their fashion collections, one containing collections from the 18th and 19th centuries, the other haute couture collections of the 20th Century, in 1987. La Storie dell'Arte Italiana (Pring 1991, 87) had digitised over 45,000 images of art, plus 30 minutes of video, in a project completed in 1988. The Henry Moore Sculpture Trust (UK) produced a "Sculpture Interactive" MediaBase Resource on videodisc containing 5,000 images and 70 minutes of film and radio extracts in 1990 (Pring 1991, 75). A considerable investment in time and effort was necessary to digitise such large collections, even without a ready vehicle for distribution (most digital records were consulted in the institution on stand alone machines, or towards the late 1980s, distributed on floppy disc). There clearly was a passion for, and a belief in, this new technology.

Another interesting point to note regarding many of these early projects, across all of the library, archive, and heritage sectors, is the consideration, at an early stage, of the need to instil "best practice" in the digitization process (or to determine what best practice could actually mean when applied to digitization), and the ramifications for making large amounts of material available to the general public. Many early projects were undertaken at world-leading institutions: being able to attract, or provide, the funding required for such large scale digitization. The focus on the majority of early projects tends to be large scale, with large volumes of material being captured, in the hope that Optical Character Recognition technologies would then turn the resulting images into electronic text. Much of this research was optimistic, but the trial and error approach adopted by pioneering projects, and published as bona-fide research, helped to establish many useful guidelines for subsequent digitization attempts.

However, many institutions were optimistic about the type of activity digitization could allow, and how easy it would be for the user to access these digital surrogates (without home computers, or a networked environment). Much of the rhetoric surrounding early digitization programmes was filled with

> ...hollow pronouncements and promises... when early experimentation with desktop technologies and remotely accessible materials for instruction and research gave senior administrators in libraries and universities, as well as funding agencies and government departments, ideas that new technology would save millions of hours of teaching time and increase academic productivity, based on the assumption that a CD-ROM of a term's course-work could replace instructors and face to face classes. Such claims raised expectations unreasonably, and many enthusiastic "early adopters" of digital technologies discovered at great expense that there are hidden costs and pitfalls to developing and using digital content (Hughes 2004, 7).

It took a while for institutions to realise that digitization is a costly and time consuming exercise, which will not reap financial rewards but provides benefits for users, expanding skills, expertise and services, whilst requiring ongoing maintenance, development, and funding.

It is also interesting to note that many early digitization projects were funded by, or carried out in tandem, with industry. In the early 1980s, Kodak carried out a study with the Geneaological Society of Utah regarding the possibility of digitizing its millions of rolls of microfilm (see González 1992, 101), and IBM was involved in a variety of digitization projects, including those with the Archivo General de Indias (Spain), the lifetime collection of American painter Andrew Wyeth's works (USA), the National Museum of Ethnology in Osaka (Japan), The Hebrew Union College (USA and Israel), Yale Library (USA), The Vatican Library (Italy) and the National Gallery of Art (USA) (Mintzer *et al* 1996, Gladney 1997). Such projects were beneficial to both institution and industry: providing the culture and heritage industry with access to expensive, advanced technology, and providing the industrial partners with real life test cases for research and development, publicity, and often financial benefits such as tax-breaks when working alongside charities, education, or governmental institutions.

However, international and national policy makers and funding bodies were taking notice: for example, "DigiCULT" – the European Commission's programme for undertaking "EU-funded research on digital culture and digital libraries deal[ing] with leading-edge information and communication technologies for expanding access to and use of Europe's rich cultural and scientific resources" (European Commission 2007) – emanated from interest in this early digitization work and was established in the late 1980s. Policy development and funding streams for digital libraries and heritage effectively began at European level at the same time: with the European parliament drawing attention to the importance of the emerging digital environment, and fostering technology-based, applied research programmes for libraries under the Third and Fourth Framework Programmes in the early 1990s (Manson 1998). By the close of the 1980s, funding bodies across the world, lead by the USA and the UK, were beginning to develop programmes to provide funds for institutions to undertake digitization projects.

The excitement in the humanities and heritage sector regarding the possibilities of digitization in the late 1980s and early 1990s was palpable, with much published research emanating from early pilot projects regarding the technicalities and possibilities of digitization. Thaller declared that "image processing in many ways has been the "hottest" topic in Humanities computing in recent years" (1992b, 1) after a series of workshops were held in Glasgow, Tromsø, and Firenze on the topic. The exponential growth of digitization in the arts, cultural and heritage sectors was heralded as

> ...a curious and unprecedented fusion of technology, imagination, necessity, philosophy and production which is continuously creating new images, many of which are changing the culture within which we live (Colson and Hall 1992, 3).

The introduction of the networked global information environment in the early 1990s, the resulting public policy encouraging the production of these resources, and the emergence of funding streams to create online resources, was to further encourage unprecedented investment and development in digitization within the library, heritage and cultural sector.

THE 1990s

The exponential growth of digitization projects being undertaken in the close of the 20th Century meant that "to the librarian at the very least, [the 1990s] could be termed the 'decade of digitisation'" (Lee 2002, 160). The increase in digitization efforts was due to a complex interplay between different forces: the increase in performance and availability of new networked technologies (Naughton 2000), an increase in awareness of the possibilities of these technologies. Additionally, the resulting changes in public policy which increased the availability of funding for memory institutions undertaking technological projects and provided infrastructure to facilitate digitization efforts, and the changing perceptions within memory institutions themselves regarding how technology could be appropriated to meet user needs and offer new possibilities increased digitization efforts further. This culminated in "Countless millions of pounds, dollars, francs and marks [being] ploughed into digital projects that have involved the conversion of library, museum and archive collections" (ibid).

In many ways, the 1990s began as the 1980s had ended, with small scale digitization projects being undertaken of treasured holdings. For example, The British Library's earliest and most prominent project was that of the *Beowulf* manuscript, and shortly afterwards, the Bodleian Library began putting digital surrogates of its Medieval and Celtic manuscript material online. Early projects tended to build on and reinforce research efforts into best practice (the research involved with digitization rarely invented new technologies, but ascertained how technologies invented elsewhere for other purposes could be appropriated in memory institutions). Faced with limited computer storage and network speed, expensive capture technologies which had not yet reached maturity, and software which needed tweaking to fit the needs of memory institutions, these projects were pioneering experiments into what could be done, and how best to attempt it.

However, the development of the World Wide Web in the early 1990s (Naughton 2000), which provided a vehicle for dissemination of digital information, encouraged scoping studies and research to be undertaken to ascertain how the new imaging and networked technologies could be appropriated, such as Peter Robinson's seminal study "The Digitization of Primary Textual Sources" (1993). Growing interest from the research councils themselves led to funding streams which encouraged an exponential growth in the creation of digital surrogates, on a worldwide scale, shifting the emphasis rapidly from small, in-house, projects of limited scope, to large scale, ambitious projects aiming to bring access to a high volume of resources to the masses.

In the early 1990s, following interest and resource provision by centralised sources, digitization of individual items began to gather pace. In 1993 in the UK, the Joint Funding Council's Libraries Review Group published a report known as The Follet Report (after Sir Brian Follet who chaired the investigation) which was a major review of the needs of libraries in the changing digital environment (Joint Funding Council's Libraries Review Group 2003). Following publication of the report, the UK government's Joint Information System's Committee (a centralised initiative funded by all four of the Higher Education funding bodies for Scotland, England, Northern Ireland, and Wales) announced funding of a string of initiatives to encourage the development of Electronic Libraries (or ELib), related resources, and infrastructure and services to support the use of digital content in Higher Education and the institutions which serve it. More than £100 million was spent in this area by JISC by the close of the 1990s. In addition to this, JISC provided over £15 million of funding for the ELib programme (which looked into how digital libraries may be developed, including individual small scale studies into digitising particular content, see Wissenburg 2000 and Rusbridge 2001), £50 million on networks, and £24 million on data services (Rusbridge 1998). Other funding bodies were quick to follow, including the Leverhulme Trust, the British Academy, the National Heritage Fund and its related lottery counterpart the New Opportunities Fund, and the Arts and Humanities Research Board (AHRB). It is difficult to ascertain how much money in total went into digitization initiatives in the UK in the 1990s, but fair to say that it rapidly became an industry in itself, with most major academic, library, and museum institutions bidding for funding in an increasingly competitive funding environment.

To facilitate best practice in the creation of digital resources in the UK, and to provide long term storage facilities for resulting digital artefacts, it became clear that centralised services needed to be provided by the funders of digitization projects to ensure that standards were met, that the resources created were not lost upon the close of individual projects (Burnard and Short 1994), and that resources could be used by as wide a constituency as possible. In the library sector, the Consortium of Research Libraries in the British Isles (CURL, http://www.curl.ac.uk/) was founded in 1992, funded in part by JISC, to provide tools, infrastructure, and leadership, creating a cross-searchable library system to encourage easy access to digital resources by "helping to build the Distributed and Hybrid Research Library of the future" (CURL, n.d). The Arts and Humanities Data Service, formed to "collect, preserve and promote the electronic resources which result from research and teaching in the arts and humanities" (AHDS 2005) was founded in 1996, funded jointly by the JISC and the AHRB, incorporating the existing History Data Service and the Oxford Text Archive (AHDS 2006, http://ahds.ac.uk/index.htm). The Technical Advisory Service for Images, providing advice and guidance to the UK's Further and Higher Education community regarding the creation of digital images, managing digitization projects, and delivering these to users for a variety of educational purposes (TASI 2002), was funded in 1997 by the JISC as a 3 year project, and given full status as a service in 2000 (http://www.tasi.ac.uk). These initiatives, and many others like them, served to provide the infrastructure to ensure that the quality of digital resources produced was high, and that the resulting digital resources would be made available to users.

In addition to creating digital images and surrogates of objects, and digital records of existing physical holdings, it was also necessary to investigate the infrastructure in which these records and digital representations could be hosted, searched, stored, and delivered to the users. The concept of the "Digital Library" as an all encompassing provider, store, and search mechanism emerged throughout the 1990s:

> Digital libraries are organizations that provide the resources, including the specialized staff, to select, structure, offer intellectual access to, interpret,

> distribute, preserve the integrity of, and ensure the persistence over time of collections of digital works so that they are readily and economically available for use by a defined community or set of communities (Digital Library Federation 1998).

Much work was devoted to establishing digital library initiatives and providing digital content for such endeavours from the early 1990s. However, it is still not clear what constitutes a digital library:

> The digital library, the electronic library (generally taken to be synonymous with the digital library), the virtual library, the hybrid library, the library without walls are all concepts that librarians seems to be dealing with all the time. What do they mean? Do they mean the same to everyone who uses the terms? Do they all mean the same thing? Do we all mean the same thing when we talk about a library? ... Every library is different, every digital library is different, and different players are advancing many definitions for the digital library (Deegan and Tanner 2002, 20).

Implementations of digital libraries from the 1990s onward explored the concept, and the various possible interpretations of the term.

In the USA, the National Digital Library Program was initiated by the Library of Congress in 1994, reaching its goal of making 5 million historical American items, from over 90 collections, and various US institutions, available on its American Memory Web site (http://www.loc.gov) by 2001. This public-private partnership resulted in over $130 million being donated to the Library; from government, businesses, and individuals (Library of Congress 2001). Another programme, the Digital Library Initiative, was launched by the United States National Science Foundation with the National Aeronautic and Space Administration (NASA) and the Advanced Research Projects Agency (ARPA) in 1994, giving digital libraries a major boost and allowing exploration of some of the major issues confronting the establishment of digital libraries on a large scale. Phase 1, running from 1994 to 1998, funded six digital library projects with a total of $30 million. Phase 2 (DLI2, http://www.dli2.nsf.gov/) running from 1999, provided $55 million to fund 36 projects which aimed to extend and develop innovative digital library technologies and applications. Clearly, a lot of activity was going into the creation of digital resources, but also investigating the infrastructure necessary to provide them. Other funding bodies in the USA also began to support digital library and digitization initiatives during this phase, such as the Research Libraries Group (Erway 1996), JSTOR (Schonfield 2003), The Getty Institute, the Andrew W. Mellon Foundation, the Coalition for Networked Information, and the Art Museum Image Consortium (AMICO) programme. Some of the funding bodies did not and do not limit their support to the USA, but are active in pursuing international collaboration that builds research collections without regard to their physical location.

The centrally funded infrastructure which underpinned these initiatives in the USA mostly centred around the concept of the Digital Library. Digitization initiatives followed long term attempts to share library catalogue information: founded in 1967, the OCLC (Online Computer Library Center, http://www.oclc.org/) is a "computer library service and research organization dedicated to the public purposes of furthering access to the world's information and reducing information costs" (OCLC 2007) through the sharing of library records, providing services for locating, acquiring, cataloguing, lending and preserving library materials now used by over 60,000 institutions in 112 countries, and funded by a variety of international governments, institutions, and charities. The Coalition for Networked Information (http://www.cni.org/), founded in 1990 by the library and IT Communities to "enhance scholarship and intellectual productivity" (CNI 2006), rapidly grew to a current membership of 200 institutions representing higher education, publishing, network and telecommunications, information technology, and libraries and library organizations. The Digital Libraries Federation (http://www.diglib.org/), founded in 1995, comprises of a consortium of the main academic and public libraries, providing leadership and support for large scale digitization programmes, guidelines, and forums for sharing experiences between members. In addition to such consortia and forums, vehicles for disseminating research and reporting of best practice in digitization were established. D-Lib Magazine, an electronic publication with a focus on digital library research published by the D-Lib Alliance, launched its first issue in July 1995, and is still publishing related research and developments today for a wide international readership (http://www.dlib.org/). The Research Libraries Group (now part of the OCLC) started publishing their newsletter, Diginews, an online newsletter for digital imaging and preservation in April 1997, which ran for 10 years, and is now preserved at http://digitalarchive.oclc.org/. The founding (and funding) of such broad initiatives ensured that the communities undertaking digitization were sharing information and expertise, and working towards common goals.

A similar tale is to be told across most of the developed world. The European Union's Telematics for Libraries Programme, running from 1990 to 1998, (http://cordis.europa.eu/libraries/) provided over €30 million to develop innovative library services and tools as well as bibliographic resources and library networking infrastructures which underpin such services, across Europe. A national programme was started in France in 1992 (Beagrie 2003), with the Bibliothèque Nationale de France undertaking an ambitious digitization programme of material in the national library and associated collections. By 2008 this ongoing digitization effort, one of the costliest and largest in Europe, had succeeded in making 10 billion documents available online (http://gallica.bnf.fr/). National reports for countries involved in the preservation of digital information, including historical information about digitization programmes, and covering Australia, France, the Netherlands, the United Kingdom, and beyond, can be found in Beagrie (2003). A summary report of the digitization efforts of all the EU member states has been produced ever year since 2002 by the Minerva project (MInisterial NEtwoRk for Valorising Activities in digitization, http://www.minervaeurope.org/), which also provides guidelines for best practice in digitization (Minerva 2007). DELOS, a Network of Excellence on Digital Libraries, provides guidance, advice, and forums to encourage the integration of efforts in Digital Library research and development across Europe (http://www.delos.info/), and its records also demonstrates the range and interest in digitization at this period.

The shift in digitization projects in the 1990s from the small scale and focussed, to large scale and all encompassing can be seen in the approach taken by one of the world's largest and finest memory institutions: The British Library. Founded in 1972 by the amalgamation of various UK institutions, with a collection of over 150 million individual items gathered over 250 years which cover all ages of written civilisation, the British Library began to seriously consider digitization in the early 1990s. British Library's digitization projects began with the *Electronic Beowulf* in 1992 (Kiernan 1997, Prescott 1998), a collaboration which

> ...linked access, scholarship and conservation of the fire damaged manuscript. Early concentration on material such as Beowulf which was unique, valuable, at risk (in conservation terms), and of high scholarly importance, was typical of the first steps by major libraries in the early 1990s (Smith 2006, 9).

Initial experience gained through the *Beowulf* project at the British Library "was built upon and improved through rapid advances in and general availability of technology" (ibid), which "saw an important shift in the mid-to-late 1990s from digitization as experiment to digitization as an operational task" (ibid). Since 2000, the BL's digitization strategy has focussed on large scale digitization of textual materials to build a "critical mass" (ibid) of material, such as the major newspaper digitization projects: the digitization of a million pages of the Burney collection of 18th Century British Newspapers (http://www.bl.uk/collections/burney.html), and the digitization of two million pages of 19th Century local, regional, and national newspapers (http://www.bl.uk/collections/earlynewspapers.html). The library's materials are increasingly now produced

> ...primarily – or solely – in digital form, and the Library's digital collections are large and rapidly expanding...For the BL, digitisation offers an important way to open up its unique heritage collections, and make more widely accessible items of national and international appeal (Smith 2006, 5–7).

At the start of the 1990s, then, "In the early days of the Web, museums provided some of the best content and some of the most compelling reasons to go on-line" (Peacock *et al* 2004). Towards the close of the millennium, "A decade of digitisation and documentation for the Web ... created a rich array of cultural and historical information across the museum, library and archive sectors" (ibid). The development of the World Wide Web was the cause of the growth of digitization efforts in the library, cultural, and heritage sector, and its increasing popularity with users fanned the expectation and desire to see digitised material online:

> The internet has stimulated a demand for online access to information. Institutions, like museums and libraries, correctly perceive that digital images – at the same time as they reduce the need for direct access to the originals – can be used to provide improved access to those works in their collections that are considered most important (or most "in demand"). Importantly, such access is location- and time-independent. That is, scholars anywhere in the world can retrieve or view web pages (Grycz 2006, 33).

With the growth of material online in the latter part of the 1990s, it became almost impossible to track and trace all digitization projects. Efforts such as ITEM database switched from being a print publication in 1995 (Pring 1995) to being an online resource, but folded in 2000, given the impossibility of the attempts to keep cataloguing this type of online resources, and the success of the Internet in allowing individuals to search for the type of projects they wanted online. The act of finding relevant material, including digital image material, amongst the host of information available online became the subject of much scholarly effort itself (Terras 2008). Around the same time, the process of digitization, explored and experimented with by early projects, and ratified into procedural and technical guidelines along the way (see Besser and Trant 1994, Kenney and Chapman 1996, Kenney and Reiger 1998, Lee 2002, Deegan and Tanner 2002, Hughes 2004, MacDonald 2006), became less of a scholarly endeavour within itself, and more of a standard means to provide digital information to a wider audience. By the end of the decade,

> Digitisation is not a per-se research issue but is part of a wider context related to the information society and the effective use of the digital content by cultural institutions (Minerva 2003, xxiii).

POST 2000

Much digitization effort accompanied the hype surrounding the millennium celebrations, with many funding programmes in place to provide the resources to create digital content. These efforts continued into the new century: for example, in July 2001, the UK Government's lottery based New Opportunities Fund (NOF) announced the largest single co-ordinated funding initiative in the UK for digitization, with grants totalling £50 million for more than 150 UK local and national organisations to document a wealth of UK achievement and heritage in science, culture, and social diversity under its NOF-digitise programme. Such a wide reaching programme was undertaken to create a "communities bank" of Internet resources, primarily for use in learning, and targeting, in particular, "lifelong learners". For a summary of the scope of these projects, explore http://www.enrichuk.net/. The JISC also announced a large scale digitization programme in 2004 (http://www.jisc.ac.uk/digitisation_home.html), aiming to "change the world of authoritative e-resources through its investment in digitising content from some of the UK's greatest collections" (JISC 2007). The first phase, with funding of £22 million,

> …began in 2004 and included the 18th century parliamentary papers, Archival sound recordings, British Library 19th century newspapers, Medical journals backfiles, NewsFilm Online and Online historical population reports (ibid).

The second phase, with a further £12 million,

> …features projects that will enable all users, regardless of location and time, online access to a range of authoritative digitised e-resources previously

> difficult or impossible to access. Together, the projects represent a diversity of rich and vivid perspectives on the history, culture and landscape of the UK and beyond. They capture a wide variety of aspects of UK life, from Cabinet papers to First World War poetry, radio news to East End music hall, political cartoons to British borders, and in a wide range of media, including sound, film, images, journals, newspapers, maps, theses, pamphlets and cartoons (ibid).

Funding councils, then, are now aiming to create a knowledge base of high quality resources, from established projects, institutions, and repositories, under their watchful eye, demanding observance of strict technical guidelines with aims for reuse in national repositories. The majority of these resources are (but are not exclusively) digital image based.

Around the same time as the launch of large scale, centrally funded initiatives such as the JISC digitization programme came the emergence of proposals from large, commercial firms (namely Google and Microsoft) to digitise holdings of institutions wholesale. By avoiding the "cherry picking" tactics of the funding councils, they aim to digitise everything possible, with the view that searching mechanisms to allow intelligent and useful analysis of large scale digital collections will soon become sophisticated enough to allow users to find their potential needles in the digital haystacks. This is often carried out in co-operation with world leading, large institutions to allow large scale digitization of holdings that they could just not afford to do on their own. However, such digitization programmes are rife with copyright problems, and their restrictive legal conditions can often cause complaint and consternation, and:

> …some libraries and researchers worry that if any one company comes to dominate the digital conversion of these works, it could exploit that dominance for commercial gain (Hafner 2007).

As a result of both the commercial and publicly funded efforts to provide high quality material online, it is now difficult to remember a time when institutions did not provide digitised representations of their holdings, and the results of years of investment of effort and resources by the cultural, heritage, commercial, and voluntary sector provide a rich, online environment for users to browse, analyse, and study:

> Do you want to tread Shakespeare's Hamlet in the first quarto edition of 1603? You have only to go to the British Library site and click on the heading "Treasures in Full". Do you need to consult a Finnish journal for a certain date in 1805? Go to the University of Helsinki Library site and the appropriate issue will appear on your screen. To consult descriptions of monuments in Egypt and Nubia, click on the site of the Maison de L'Orient et de la Méditerranée. And so forth (Jeanneney 2007, 19).

Indeed,

> The possibility of examining rare and unique objects outside the secure, climate-controlled environments of museums and archives liberates collections for study and enjoyment (Besser and Trant 1995, 7).

The shift in digitization projects to the large scale, and the growth in use and user expectations regarding the provision and quality of digitised material, results in a change in research questions that need to be asked by professionals working in the area:

> We're getting pretty good at digitizing material at scale.... If you look at many of the projects ... you will see there are lots and lots of materials being digitized. Our museums, our libraries, our archives, our historical societies, are all running digitisation programs.... We have a wealth of experience and a large number of successful projects (not to mention some highly educational failures) to build upon. With the exception of relatively esoteric materials in specialized formats or that have some really unusual characteristics, this is not really research any more. Or to put it another way, the research questions are less about how to do it at all and more about how to optimize – how to do it more efficiently or effectively, how to be sure that you've chosen the most appropriate strategies and technologies (Lynch 2002).

At the time of writing, research questions remain about use and usefulness of digitised collections, how new and developing technologies, such as those touted as "Web 2.0" can be integrated into digital online collections to be of benefit to users, and how to integrate the vast swathes of online ephemera digitised by amateurs into our thinking about digitization, collections, and corpora (Terras 2008).

Digital imaging technologies have been readily adopted by memory institutions, and, following a period of experimentation, it is now commonplace for libraries, archives, museums, art galleries, and private collections to undertake the costly and time consuming effort of producing digital surrogates of their collection, usually for delivery online, to provide the accessibility and digital coverage of collections that users have now come to expect. There are interesting times ahead for the information professional in dealing with the wealth of digital information now available, keeping up with the changing nature of Internet technologies, and coping with resulting changes in user expectations and needs, to create digital libraries which can exploit the potential of this groundswell of digital – digitised – content.

NOTES

[1] The majority of digitisation projects in the 1980s used videodisc (Philip's LaserDisk) as the delivery media: a technology which was soon superseded by CD-ROM, and eventually the Internet. Videodiscs needed their own players – now unavailable: as a result the majority of the output of these early projects is now unreadable. The most high profile example of this was the British Broadcasting Corporation's Domesday Project, where schools around the UK were asked to survey their areas to produce a database of how Britain looked to the British in 1986, 900 years after the original Domesday book was compiled (Finney 2007). The resulting database of statistics, maps, and photographs were saved onto videodiscs for posterity, but by 2000 the majority of videodisc players were defunct, and a lengthy and costly program of conversion and emulation was begun in 2002 by LongLife Data, taking 16 months to recover the videodisc data and re-create the original application (Darlington *et al* 2003). LongLife Data created a web version of Domesday 1986, which is now available at http://www.domesday1986.com/.

REFERENCES

Arts and Humanities Data Service. (2005, December 16). *About the arts and humanities data service* [website]. Retrieved March 27, 2008, fromhttp://ahds.ac.uk/about/index.htm

Arts and Humanities Data Service. (2006). *AHDS Timeline*. Retrieved March 27, 2008, from http://ahds.ac.uk/about/ahds-timeline.htm

Barnett, P. (1991, January). The clearinghouse on art documentation and computerization. In I. Pring (Ed.), *ITEM: European Visual Art Information Network (EVAIN) Image Technology in European Museum and Art Galleries Database*. European Visual Arts Centre at Ipswich (EVAC), Issue 1.

Beagrie, N. (2003). *National Digital Preservation Initiatives: An overview of developments in Australia, France, the Netherlands, and the United Kingdom and of related international activity*, published online, April, Commissioned for and sponsored by the National Digital Information Infrastructure and Preservation Program, Library of Congress. The Council on Library and Information Resources and the Library of Congress. Retrieved January 12, 2008, from http://www.clir.org/pubs/reports/pub116/contents.html

Besser, H., & Trant, J. (1995). *Introduction to imaging, issues in constructing an image database*. Santa Monica, CA: The Getty Art History Information Program.

Burnard, L., & Short, H. (1994). *An arts and humanities data service. Report of a feasibility study Commissioned by the Information Services Sub-committee of the Joint Information Systems Committee of the Higher Education Funding Councils*, published online 31 October. Oxford: Office for Humanities Communication. Retrieved January 25, 2008, from http://ahds.ac.uk/about/documents/ahds-feasibility-study.pdf

Coalition for Networked Information. (2006). *About CNI*. [website] Retrieved February 2008, 17, from http://www.cni.org/organization.html

Colson, F., & Hall, W. (1992). Pictorial information systems and the teaching imperative. In M. Thaller (Ed.), *Images and manuscripts in historical computing, Proceedings of a workshop at International University Institute, Firenze, November 15th 1991*. Göttingen: Max Planck Institute.

Council on Library Resources. (1986). *Brittle books. Reports of the committee on preservation and access*. Washington, DC: Council on Library Resources. Retrieved January 5, 2008, from http://www.eric.ed.gov/ERICDocs/data/ericdocs2sql/content_storage_01/0000019b/80/1c/04/55.pdf

Consortium of Research Libraries in the British Isles. (n.d.). *CURL* [website]. Retrieved from http://www.curl.ac.uk/

Deegan, M., & Tanner, S. (2002). *Digital futures: Strategies for the information age*. Digital Futures Series. London: Library Association Publishing.

Darlington, J., Finney, A., & Pearce, A. (2003, July). Domesday Redux: The rescue of the BBC Domesday Project videodiscs. *Ariadne, 36*. Retrieved November 13, 2007, from http://www.ariadne.ac.uk/issue36/tna/intro.html

Digital Library Federation. (1998). *A working definition of a digital library*. Retrieved March 23, 2008, from http://www.diglib.org/about/dldefinition.htm

Erway, R. (1996). Digital initiatives of the Research Libraries Group. *D-Lib Magazine* [website]. December issue. Retrieved May 10, 2010, from http://www.dlib.org/dlib/december96/rlg/12erway.html

Finney, A. (2007). *Domesday: The BBC Domesday Project - November 1986*. Retrieved February 15, 2008, http://www.domesday.org.uk/

Fischer, A., & Swora, T. (1986). *Library of Congress Optical Disk Pilot Program, Optical Disk Print Pilot Project*. Washington, DC: Library of Congress.

Gladney, H. M., Mintzer, F., & Schiattarella, F. (1997). Safeguarding digital library contents and users: Digital images of treasured antiquities. *D-Lib Magazine* [website], July/August issue. Retrieved March 28, 2008, from http://www.dlib.org/dlib/july97/vatican/07gladney.html

González, P. (1992). The digital processing of images in archive and libraries, large scale international projects. In M. Thaller (Ed.), *Images and manuscripts in historical computing, proceedings of a workshop at International University Institute, Firenze, November 15th 1991*. Göttingen: Max Planck Institute.

González, P. (1998, September). *Computerization of the Archivo General de Indias: Strategies and results*. Council on Library and Information Resources, Pub.76. Retrieved January 6, 2008, from http://www.clir.org/pubs/reports/gonzalez/contents.html

Grycz, C. J. (2006). Digitising rare books and manuscripts. In L. MacDonald (Ed.), *Digital heritage: Applying digital imaging to cultural heritage*. Oxford: Elsevier.

Hafner, K. (2007, October 22). Libraries shun deals to place books on Web. *New York Times* [website]. Retrieved January 9, 2008, from http://www.nytimes.com/2007/10/22/technology/22library.html

van Horik, R. (2005). *Permanent pixels: Building blocks for the longevity of digital surrogates of historical photographs*. The Hague: DANS Studies in Digital Archiving, 1.

Hughes, L. (2004). *Digitizing collections: Strategic issues for the information manager*. London: Facet Publishing.

Jeanneney, J.-N. (2007). *Google and the myth of universal knowledge: A view from Europe*. London: University of Chicago Press.

Joint Funding Council's Libraries Review Group. (1993). *The Follet Report*. A Report for the Higher Education Funding Council for England, the Scottish Higher Education Funding Council, the Higher Education Funding Council for Wales, and the Department of Education for Northern Ireland. Retrieved January 13, 2008, from http://www.ukoln.ac.uk/services/papers/follett/report/

Joint Information Systems Committee. (2007). *Digitisation programme*. London: JISC, published online June. Retrieved January 13, 2008, from http://www.jisc.ac.uk/digitisation_home.html

Kenney, A. R., & Chapman, S. (Eds.). (1996). *Digital imaging for libraries and archives*. Ithaca, NY: Cornell University Library Press.

Kenney, A. R., & Rieger, O. Y. (1998, April 30). *Using Kodak Photo CD technology for preservation and access, A guide for librarians, archivists, and curators*. Department of Preservation and Conservation, Cornell University Library. Retrieved January 15, 2008, from http://www.library.cornell.edu/preservation/kodak/kodak-htm.htm

Kiernan, K. S. (1997). *Beowulf and the Beowulf Manuscript*. Ann Arbor, MI: The University of Michigan Press.

Lee, S. (2002). *Digital imaging, a practical handbook*. London: Facet Publishing.

Library of Congress. (2001, January 10). National digital library program reaches goal of 5 million items online. *News from the Library of Congress*. Library of Congress [website]. Retrieved January 14, 2008, from http://www.loc.gov/today/pr/2001/01-004.html

Lynch, C. (2002, May). Digital collections, digital libraries and the digitization of cultural heritage information. *First Monday* [website], 7(5). Retrieved December 20, 2003, from http://www.firstmonday.dk/issues/issue7_5/lynch

MacDonald, L. (Ed.). (2006). *Digital heritage, applying digital imaging to cultural heritage*. Oxford: Elsevier.

Manson, P. (1998). *Telematics for libraries: Actions and initiatives of the European Union*. 'Beyond the Beginning: The Global Digital Library' conference, 16–17th June 1997. Retrieved January 13, 2008, from http://www.ukoln.ac.uk/services/papers/bl/blri078/content/repor~14.htm

Minerva. (2003, May 6). *Summary of progress*. Coordinating digitisation in Europe. Progress report of the National Representatives Group: Coordination mechanisms for digitisation policies and programmes 2002, European Commission, The Information Society Directorate-General. Retrieved January 16, 2007, from http://www.minervaeurope.org/publications/globalreport/globalrep2002.htm

Minerva. (2007, July 13). *Coordinating digitisation in Europe: progress report of the National Representatives Group*. Progress report of the National Representatives Group: Coordination mechanisms for digitisation policies and programmes, European Commission, The Information Society Directorate-General. Retrieved January 16, 2008, from http://www.minervaeurope.org/publications/globalreport.htm

Mintzer, F. C., Boyle, L. E., Cazes, A. N., Christian, B. S., Cox, S. C., Giordano, F. P., et al. (1996). Toward on-line, worldwide access to Vatican Library materials. *IBM Journal of Research and Development, 40*(2). Retrieved February 7, 2007, from http://www.research.ibm.com/journal/rd/402/mintzer.html

Moorhouse, P. (2004). The computerised local image collection at Manchester archives and local studies. *Manchester Region History Overview, 17*(1), 62–68. Retrieved February 28, 2007, from http://www.mcrh.mmu.ac.uk/pubs/pdf/mrhr_17i_archives_moorhouse.pdf

NARA. (1991). *Digital imaging and optical media storage systems: Guidelines for state and local government agencies.* Washington, DC: National Archives and Records Administration and National Association of Government Archives and Records Administrators.

Naughton, J. (2000). *A brief history of the future: Origins of the internet.* London: Phoenix Press.

Online Computer Library Center. (2007). About OCLC. *OCLC* [website]. Retrieved November 23, 2007, from http://www.oclc.org/about/default.htm

Parker, E. B. (1985, December). The library of congress non-print optical disk pilot program. *Information Technology and Libraries, 4*(4), 289–299.

Peacock, D., Ellis, D., & Doolan, J. (2004). Searching for meaning: Not just records. 'Museums and the Web Conference 2004'. In D. Bearman & J. Trant (Eds.), *Museums and the Web 2004: Proceedings.* Toronto: Archives & Museum Informatics. Retrieved March 12, 2008, from http://www.archimuse.com/mw2004/papers/peacock/peacock.html

Peterson, T. H. (1994). *Digital-imaging and optical digital data disk storage systems: Long-term access strategies for federal agencies.* The Technology Research Staff, The National Archives at College Park. Retrieved February 22, 2010, from http://www.archives.gov/preservation/technical/imaging-stortage-report.html

Prescott, A. (1998). Constructing electronic beowulf. Towards the digital library: The British library's 'Initiatives for access' programme. In L. Carpenter, S. Shaw, & A. Prescott (Eds.), *Towards the digital library.* London: The British Library.

Price, J. (1984, November-December). The optical disk pilot program at the library of congress. *Videodisc and Optical Disc, 4*(6), 424–432.

Pring, I. (Ed.). (1991, January). *ITEM: European Visual Art Information Network (EVAIN) Image Technology in European Museums and Art Galleries Database*, Issue 1. Ipswich: European Visual Arts Centre at Ipswich (EVAC).

Pring, I. (Ed.). (1995, May). *ITEM: European Visual Art Information Network (EVAIN) Image Technology in European Museums and Art Galleries Database.* European Visual Arts Centre at Ipswich (EVAC), 9.

Robinson, P. (1993). *The digitization of primary textual sources.* Oxford: Oxford University Office for Humanities Communication.

Rusbridge, C. (1998, July/August). Towards the hybrid library. *D-Lib Magazine* [website]. Retrieved December 13, 2007, from http://www.dlib.org/dlib/july98/rusbridge/07rusbridge.html

Rusbridge, C. (2001, January). After eLib. *Ariadne* [website]. *26.* Retrieved December 10, 2007, from http://www.ariadne.ac.uk/issue26/chris/intro.htm

Schonfield, R. C. (2003). *JSTOR, A history.* Princeton, NJ: Princeton University Press.

Smith, N. (2006). Digitising documents for public access. In L. MacDonald (Ed.), *Digital heritage, applying digital imaging to cultural heritage.* Oxford: Elsevier.

Stam, D. S. (1987, June). For data based on art call… A computer information clearinghouse. *Museum News*, pp. 67–74.

Techical Advisory Service for Images (TASI). (2002c). About us. *TASI* [website]. Retrieved November 13, 2007, from http://www.tasi.ac.uk/about_us.html

Terras, M. (2008). *Digital images for the information professional.* London: Ashgate.

Thaller, M. (Ed.). (1992a). *Images and manuscripts in historical computing, Proceedings of a workshop at International University Institute, Firenze, November 15th 1991.* Göttingen: Max Planck Institute.

Thaller, M. (1992b). The processing of manuscripts. In M. Thaller (Ed.), *Images and manuscripts in historical computing, Proceedings of a workshop at International University Institute, Firenze, November 15th 1991.* Göttingen: Max Planck Institute.

Waters, D. J. (1991). *From microfilm to digital imagery*. Washington, DC: Commission on Preservation and Access.

Wissenberg, A. (2000). Digitising Journals and the eLib Programme. In *Proceedings, Digitising Journals: Conference on Future Strategies for European Libraries, 13–14th March 2000, Copenhagen* (pp. 11–18). Copenhagen: Danish National Library Authority. Retrieved January 15, 2008, from http://www.deflink.dk/upload/doc_filer/doc_alle/1113_Digitising%20journals.pdf

Melissa M. Terras
Department of Information Studies
University College London, UK

RUTH RIKOWSKI

2. DIGITAL LIBRARIES AND DIGITISATION

An Overview and Critique

INTRODUCTION

Libraries have been, and continually are, being transformed. I have written a considerable amount about the value of the library, particularly the public library (see Rikowski, 2001a, b, 2002a, b, c, d, e, 2003b, 2005), but with the slant being more towards the traditional library. However, the digitisation programme has expanded rapidly, particularly over the last 10 years or so, and the traditional library has been and still is undergoing much change. The term the 'hybrid library', combining both the traditional library and the digital library, is being referred to more and more today, although obviously it is still not in common usage amongst the general public.

Digitisation offers many new and exciting opportunities, and indeed, it is changing our way of life in many ways. It certainly means that much more information is easily and readily available. Yet, there is no way that it can wholly replace the physical, traditional library, with the opportunities for people to engage in dialogue, and to build a sense of community. Neither can the e-book ever replace the hard copy book, in my view. You cannot take an e-book to bed with you!

This chapter will provide an overview and a critique of digitisation and digital libraries.

DEFINITION OF 'DIGITAL LIBRARIES'

It is always important to define terms, so first of all, let us consider the definition of the 'digital library'. Hughes says that digitisation is 'the process by which analogue content is converted into a sequence of 1s and 0s and put into a binary code to be readable by a computer' (Hughes, 2004, p. 4), whilst Lynch says that the 'digital library' can mean different things to different people and that:

> The field of digital libraries has always been poorly-defined, a 'discipline' of amorphous borders and crossroads, but also of atavistic resonance and unreasonable inspiration. 'Digital libraries': this oxymoronic phrase has attracted dreamers and engineers, visionaries and entrepreneurs, a diversity of social scientists, lawyers, scientists and technicians. (Lynch, 2005, p. 1)

Lesk emphasises how building digital libraries will change our understanding of organisations, and perhaps even change our culture:

> Building digital libraries is not just a question of piling up disk drives: it involves creating an entire organization of machines and people, perhaps even

R. Rikowski (ed.), Digitisation Perspectives, 21–41.

> a culture, in which we are able to find information and use it. The social implications of a world in which information is distributed almost without institutions are not understood; what does this mean for universities, for education and for publishers? (Lesk, 2005, p. 5)

The 'digital library' is also referred to by a variety of other terms, such as the 'electronic library', the 'virtual library', the 'library without walls', the 'online archive' and the 'desktop museum'. The term was originally adopted by the computing science community, whilst librarians, at the time, were still referring to the 'electronic library' and the 'hybrid library'.

Many different types of material can be digitised, including pictures, theses, books, journals, newspaper articles and magazines. As Crane says:

> The digital libraries of the early twenty-first century can be searched and their contents transmitted around the world. They can contain time-based media, images, quantitative data, and a far richer array of content than print, with visualization technologies blurring the boundaries between library and museum. (Crane, 2006, p. 1)

The scale of the increase in digitisation has been very rapid over the last few years. By mid 2003, for example, Google claimed to be indexing over 3 billion web pages, and the Web has over 150 terabytes of text.

Jones et al (2006) argue that there is no consensus in regard to the definition of a 'digital library'. They also highlight the difference between the 'institutional repository' and the 'digital library', arguing that the 'institutional repository' exploits intellectual capital produced by an institution, whilst the 'digital library' is a broader collection, and also includes materials published elsewhere. Furthermore, they suggest that a collection of items is not a digital library just because the items have been digitised. Rather, it is a library first and it cannot just be a commercial project: 'A true digital library has to be organised for its purpose, and must not be randomly heterogeneous and indexed as a commercial by-product' (Jones et al, 2006, p. 4).

But to what extent is it possible, anyway, for non-commercial organisations to be largely responsible for digitising the information and the knowledge of the nation, as it were? Can they afford to do this? On the other hand, can information continue to be made freely available? Of course it can be, if we chose to put our resources into any such project, but in capitalism, that is just not a realistic possibility, in any all-encompassing way. This is because the drive to create value and profit will always override other considerations, including the importance of providing free access to information.

Hughes concludes by referring to digitisation in the following way:

> Digitization of cultural heritage materials is changing the ways in which collections are used and accessed. Many materials are amenable to digitization, including scarce, fragile and ephemeral materials, as well as the whole spectrum of moving image and audio materials. All can be safely used by a wider audience in digital form. (Hughes, 2004, p. 29)

ADVANTAGES OF DIGITISATION

There are many advantages to be gained from digitisation (thereby aiding with the creation and expansion of digital libraries). Hughes usefully outlines a number of them. As Hughes indicates, with digitisation one can 'search, browse and compare materials in useful and creative ways' (2004, p. 10). Hence, there is a much greater and easier access to many different types of material and collections. E-books also can provide very good searching facilities, and they take up less storage space than hard copy books.

Some organisations, such as the National Gallery in London, even create an electronic image of every item in their collection. Or sometimes organisations collect electronic images around themes. One example here is the Arnamagnaean Institute at the University of Copenhagen, which is a project that has a web-accessible catalogue of medieval Icelandic manuscripts, with the aim being to achieve a 'virtual reunification' of the two halves of the Arnamagnaean collection. It is also possible to develop a digital surrogate of a rare or fragile original object. This means that people will have access to the object, helping to ensure that the original is not damaged by a lot of handling.

Sometimes, collections have to be split up, over long distances. This can be quite disappointing and inconvenient for the user. The Management Committee of the Feminist Library in London in 2007, for example, were discussing the possibility of having to break up the feminist collection at some point, if they were not able to attract enough funds to preserve the library intact. But through digitisation, whole collections can be brought together by a virtual means.

Other advantages of digitisation (as outlined by Hughes) include the fact that resources can be put to unforeseen uses in the future; that delivery can be satisfied immediately and that it can bring prestige to and raise the profile of an organisation. Also, detailed records can be created about the collections and staff can develop their knowledge and understanding of the new technologies. New ways of preserving, collecting, organising, accessing and disseminating knowledge and information can be developed with digitisation.

Digitisation provides educational benefits as well. John Unsworth (2000) argues that networked digital information can really encourage, support and enrich the essential elements of scholarship. Material that is digitised can be accessed and read in new, different and improved ways. Material can often be read quickly and easily, but obviously it also has to be undertaken with caution, so as to avoid possible health risks. E-learning is also becoming an important part of education, and the notion of the 'virtual campus' is growing. An example of how digitisation is changing the essentials of scholarship can be seen through the development of an online edition of Chopin's 1st Editions Project, which is based at the Royal Holloway College, University of London. The online edition is being used to analyse the creative history of Chopin's music.

Digitisation is also an important means for preserving our cultural heritage as well as enabling advanced research to be conducted on historical materials. This includes digitising ancient manuscripts (see, for example, Nikolova-Houston & Houston's chapter in this book). However, as Beagrie (2004) says, there is a serious gap between our ability to create digital information and our infrastructure and capacity to manage and preserve it over time. This is sometimes referred to as the 'digital dark ages'. Furthermore, decisions have to be made about what historical material to digitise and what not to digitise. As Hughes notes:

> …most institutions will integrate many different technology-based projects over a long period of time. Some of these projects will overlap, some may ultimately contribute to an institutional 'digital library', while others may become known as 'legacy projects', leaving preservation concerns and headaches for future caretakers. (Hughes, 2004, p. 17)

Overall, then, there are clearly many benefits to be gained from digitisation, a few of which have been outlined here.

COSTS OF DIGITISATION

However, digitisation is also costly and there are indirect as well as direct costs. Certainly, it is not easy to make short-term cost savings. Many questions can be raised here. How concerned do we want to be with getting good returns from our expenditure on digitisation, for example? And how can we measure this anyway? On the other hand, can digitisation cause information to 'lose' some of its value? Lesk (2005), for example, asks us to consider what the value of information is, and who is likely to be willing to pay to preserve digitised information. Yet, as he points out, one cannot put a numerical value on delivering information to the desktop instead of within the traditional library.

Hughes also notes the importance of focusing more on long-term strategies for digitisation, particularly given the fact that budgets are limited. She says that:

> In recent years, a growing understanding of the costs of digitization, in terms of both time and financial resources, has placed a greater focus on developing digitization initiatives and programmes that will realize tangible and strategic benefits for the institution and its users, rather than opportunistic or short term projects that are limited in their scope or focus. (Hughes, 2004, p. 8)

A number of studies have been undertaken exploring the likely costs of digitisation. Shelby Sanett (2002), for example, usefully proposed the development of a cost model for preserving authentic electronic records. Her cost model broke costs down according to capital costs, direct operating costs and indirect operating costs (overhead) for both preservation and use of electronic records. Costs included labour, space, materials and equipment. Mackie-Mason et al (1999) examined different pricing and bundling models of electronic resources in relation to usage and publisher revenues.

Connaway & Lawrence (2003) compared library resource allocation for paper with the digital library. This was an exploratory study that asked 11 Association of Research Libraries (ARL) librarians to identify resources needed in transforming from an all-paper to an all-digital library. Within this, they looked at the selection, acquisition, organisation and dissemination of paper and electronic materials. It was assumed that fewer labour, space and material resources would be needed in an all-digital library, but that equipment resources would be the same. Labour included professional, paraprofessional and technical staff. Space included work, private and public space, whilst equipment included bookshelves, tables, network connectivity equipment, terminals and printers, etc. Librarians had to consider two hypothetical types of libraries; a 'paper' library consisting only of paper books and a 'digital' library consisting only of electronic books. It was concluded that a mixed paper-digital library would probably cost more than having either a completely traditional or a completely digital library. Digitisation might increase costs in the shorter term and it might be some while before the full cost benefits of digital media were fully realised. Yet, the findings suggested that the costs for labour, space and material were likely to be less in an all-digital library compared to an all-paper library.

In sum, quite a lot of useful studies have been undertaken investigating the costs of digital libraries, a few of which have been considered in this section. People and organisations can use such studies, and the cost models derived from them, to help them to decide whether to digitise their stock and if so, which parts of it to digitise, and how much of it to digitise.

JISC

JISC is an important body in the United Kingdom (UK) in regard to promoting and developing digitisation. The UK Joint Information Systems Committee (JISC) is a committee of UK Higher and Further Education Funding Councils and serves about 200 higher education (HE) institutions and over 500 further education (FE) institutions in the UK. Its aim is to promote innovative use of information and communications technology (ICT) in tertiary education.

JISC, Digitisation and Preservation Issues

JISC has had a considerable input into various digitisation projects and digital preservation over the last few years (see Beagrie, 2004). It plays several roles in regard to digital preservation. This includes supporting collective action for the sector and advising institutions. It also includes finding appropriate licensing arrangements for commercial content and building long-term preservation with other agencies. If digital preservation issues are not properly addressed, our cultural heritage could well be under threat. JISC has been developing different toolkits to help institutions with their information-related issues.

In 2000 Beagrie was appointed by JISC to build on the digital preservation work that it had been undertaking. There were three major objectives of the project. The first was to establish and disseminate best practice and guidelines for digital preservation; the second was to encourage different organisations to work together, on digital preservation issues, in order to generate funding on a global basis; and the third was to develop a long-term digital preservation strategy for the FE and HE sector in the UK.

Beagrie emphasises that digital preservation needs to be seen as a means to an end and not as an end in itself: 'Ultimately, digital preservation will be successful when it can be seen not as a stand alone institutional activity but as an activity embedded in how institutions manage and approach digital information and resources on an ongoing basis' (2004, p. 11).

The 'JISC Digitisation Programme Blog' started in April 2006. It highlights significant e-resources from the UK. Following on from this, also in April 2006, JISC called for proposals for digitisation. Proposals submitted included the digitisation of Icelandic manuscripts; all the photographic negatives held by the Scott Polar Research Institute; the Carl Giles newspaper cartoon archive; and rare pamphlets and newspapers from the Anglo-Jewish community; the Bristol University Fossil Record Database; and King's College London: Gramophone Magazine.

In sum, the work that JISC has undertaken and continues to undertake in regard to digitisation and digital preservation is very important and continues to grow.

TRADITIONAL, DIGITAL, HYBRID AND VIRTUAL LIBRARIES

In regard to *traditional* libraries, Lagoze et al indicate that they:

> …are much more than well-organized warehouses of books, maps, serials, etc. In their full expression, they are places where people meet to access, share, and exchange knowledge. The resources they select and services they offer should reflect the character of the communities they serve. (Lagoze et al, 2005, p. 2)

Borgman suggests (1999, 2000, 2003) that *digital* libraries should match and then extend traditional libraries. However, the digital library can surely never completely match and replace the traditional library. Meeting and sharing knowledge virtually, is not the same, and surely never can be the same, as meeting face to face. Lagoze et al point out that digital libraries:

> Like any library ... should feature a high degree of selection of resources that meet criteria relevant to their mission, and they should provide services, including search, that facilitate use of the resources by their target community. But freed of the constraints of physical space and media, digital libraries can be more adaptive and reflective of the communities they serve. (Lagoze et al, 2005, p. 2)

Hence, in this way, they should be able to cater well for the wants and needs of communities. Lagoze et al also say that digital libraries should be collaborative, and enable users to contribute knowledge to the library. Furthermore, they should be contextual and express 'the expanding web of inter-relationships and layers of knowledge that extend among selected primary resources' (Lagoze et al, 2005, p. 2).

Digital libraries can sometimes seem to be a catalogue of metadata records. Yet, as Reeves says, digital libraries are also cognitive tools and not just repositories of information:

> The real power of media and technology to improve education may only be realized when students actively use them as cognitive tools rather than simply

> perceive and interact with them as tutors or repositories of information. (Reeves, 1998)

There are various issues that need to be considered in the future. Will the *hybrid* library (combining both the traditional library and the digital library and which is also referred to in both Pandian's and Dunlap's chapters in this book) develop much further, for example? Or will the digital library increasingly start to replace the traditional library? How will people adapt to all this? And what implications will all of this have for society at large? And now we have a new library 'on the scene' – the *virtual* library (referred to in the chapters by Bell et al and Peters in this book). How will this develop in the future? Will it become a significant part of the library world? Bell et al have clear views on this and they 'believe that libraries do need a presence in virtual spaces where more and more people are gathering' (Bell et al).

THE LIBRARY COMMUNITY AND DIGITISATION

What about the response of the library community, in particular, to digitisation? Pearson argues that there is no shortage of action here, but that, on the other hand, there is no real overall sense of direction. Pearson says:

> I believe there is an urgent need for the library sector to pull its act together and for us to find a mechanism to put digitisation of the documentary heritage, and a strategy for achieving it, high on the agenda. Making it all happen is not something that libraries can achieve single-handedly but inertia will lead to regret in due course. It is one of the great visionary challenges for the present professional generation. (Pearson, 2001, p. 5)

We also need to consider to what extent digitisation is changing the role of the traditional librarian. Hughes (2004) asks whether libraries and other organisations that are digitising content and making it available to many are becoming more like publishers, for example. If so, how will this impact on the work of the traditional librarian?

Lynch (2005) makes the point that some think that digital libraries have little to do with the practice of librarianship. Digitisation actually comes from a technical and engineering basis, from the 1960s. Lynch argues that we can see digital libraries as offering a 'mature set of tools, engineering approaches, and technologies that are now ready to be harnessed in the service of many organizations and many purposes' (2005, p. 4).

On the other hand, if digitisation *is* largely the responsibility of librarians and information professionals and they *do* hold the purse strings, then this raises other questions. Pearson says that various assumptions are made about digitisation in this regard. One is that the technology is now well developed and mature and is worth investing money in. And the other is that libraries will be funded in the same way that they always have been and that free access to documents will still be seen to be worthwhile. But can library budgets be stretched this far and will finance mechanisms in reality remain the same? And to what extent is it possible to have free access to substantial amounts of digital information in capitalism? The cost models outlined above should provide some help and guidance to librarians in this regard.

Various research has been undertaken in regard to digital libraries. An important Digital Libraries initiative took place with organisations such as the National Science Foundation, the National Library of Medicine and the Library of Congress in this regard. In a document outlining Phase 2 of the project (in 1998), it said that the Initiative:

> ...looks to stimulate partnering arrangements necessary to create next-generation operational systems in such areas as education, engineering and design, earth and space sciences, biosciences, geography, economics and the arts and humanities. (Digital Libraries Initiative – Phase 2, 1998, p. 2)

Three specific research areas were being explored: firstly, human-centred research, which 'seeks to further understanding of the impacts and potential of digital libraries to enhance human activities in creating, seeking, and using information and to promote technical research designed to achieve this' (Digital Libraries Initiative – Phase 2, 1998, p. 3); secondly, content and collections-based research; and thirdly, systems-centred research, which focused on the integration of technologies, in order to develop flexible information environments. Clearly, this type of research is important and needs to be developed further in the future.

Obviously, digitisation impacts on many different types of librarians and libraries. Murray (2000), for example, considers the expanding role of the school librarian. Traditionally, the role has included teacher and instructional partners, she says, whereas the new role includes navigator, teacher and collaborator, evaluator, publisher, program administrator and staff developer.

The school librarian will continually be involved with new technologies, including digitisation (as indeed are librarians in general). As Murray says:

> As information access becomes increasingly computerized, the school librarian will be responsible for introducing new technologies to her teaching colleagues and students, enabling and empowering them to adopt information-literacy strategies that will make them independent lifelong learners. (2000, p. 2)

In general, journal articles are obviously of crucial importance for obtaining up-to-date information about digital libraries and digitisation. However, books are also valuable. *Digital Libraries* by Lucy Tedd & Andrew Large (2005), for example, introduces readers to the principles underlying digital libraries, and illustrates the principles by reference to a wide range of digital library practices throughout the world. They also look at the origin of digital libraries and why they have emerged and developed. *Understanding Digital Libraries* by Michael Lesk (2005) includes chapters on topics such as the evolution of libraries, images and knowledge representation schemes. The first few chapters of the book examine how the contents of a digital library are stored and organised. There is a chapter on 'multimedia storage and retrieval', for example, which examines digitisation of sound, video, software, pictures and automatic speech recognition. Lesk also looks at different digital library projects around the world, noting, for example, that US digital library projects have largely been undertaken by the National Science Foundation.

In sum, this section has outlined a few of the key issues in regard to digitisation for the library community. There are clearly many other areas that also need to be considered. Looking to the future though, Lynch says that:

> The next decade for digital libraries may well be characterized most profoundly by the transition from technologies and prototypes to the ubiquitous, immersive, and pervasive information and information technology landscape. (2005, p. 6)

E-BOOKS

Gunter says that 'An e-book, in the broadest sense, comprises any book or monograph-length sequence of text made available in electronic form' (2005, p. 514). Many different types of material are being digitised, including e-books and e-theses (see, for example, Susan Copeland's chapter in this book on electronic theses). This digital material can be made available in the digital library. This section focuses on e-books, by way of illustration, and considers some research that has been undertaken on e-books, the impact of e-books and how this is likely to develop in the future. The growth in e-books over the last few years has certainly been significant.

John Cox (2004) examined e-books, and described a case study from 2001, where Librarians of the Conference of Heads of Irish Universities established a working group to assess the e-book market and its potential for university libraries. It was found (in 2002) that the market was volatile, and that there were problems, in particular, with regard to poor on-screen presentation. It was also found that e-books could support learning well in subjects such as business and law, where information is structured in quite clear and discrete blocks.

As part of the study, the group recommended a one-year subscription to an e-books service, focusing on business and computing. It chose *Safari Tech Books Online*, which is owned by Pearson Education and O'Reilly. This has the full text of 2000 titles and subscribers include over 400 academic libraries. Safari proved to be very popular with users at the Irish universities that were being researched. It was found that where content matched need e-books could support the academic goals of the universities. Thus, the future for e-books was bright, especially if on-screen reading became easier and customer-oriented screens and licensing could be realised.

Gunter (2005) reported on a study of the early market for e-books in the UK. Weekly web surveys were conducted with members of a large online panel, which was established by a leading commercial Internet research company. Questions explored subject areas such as awareness, trialling, purchase and borrowing e-books, frequency of behaviour and types of publications accessed and/or obtained. There were 3916 responses in total. From the survey it was found that 85% of respondents were aware of e-books. Amongst these, about half had made trial use of them,

38% had bought at least one e-book, and 13% had borrowed an e-book from a library. The most frequently accessed e-books were technical books (42%), followed by popular non-fiction books that related to a hobby (32%). The less frequently accessed e-books were specialised research monographs (13%), and popular non-fiction – autobiography/biography (10%). Respondents gave three main motivations for buying e-books: convenience, they were cheaper than conventional books and it was easier to search the contents. Other reasons given included the fact that e-books were easier to store, they offered a multimedia format, were easier to carry around, they could be electronically annotated, and it is easier to make copies of e-books for friends. Early e-book users saw electronic reading largely as being for reference work and 56% preferred not to read long passages on screen. In the study, it was found that, in general, e-book use is fairly specific in type. It concluded that, perhaps, e-publishers should focus more on reference books in the near future.

There have been different and varying predictions about the likely growth of e-books but it is safer to rely on real sales figures. According to Macworld (2004), e-book publishing is growing faster than any other form of publishing. There has been a particularly significant growth in e-books in the USA. The Association of American Publishers highlighted the fact that the e-book segment grew from $211,000 in net sales in January 2002 to just over $3.3 million in January 2003. This represented a 1,447% growth rate, which was the biggest year-on-year increase of any category of publishing (Blough, 2003).

In conclusion, the e-book market and e-book publishing is growing and many new publishing companies are being established that produce e-books and sell and distribute them over the Internet. From various studies that have been undertaken with e-book readers, a number of advantages to e-book reading have been identified; these include convenience, lower cost and being easier to search. E-publishing can, on the whole, move much faster than traditional publishing and it is likely to be an increasingly important part of publishing in the future. E-books certainly form an important part of the whole digitisation programme.

A SELECTION OF DIGITAL LIBRARY PROJECTS ON A GLOBAL BASIS

Many different digital library projects are taking place and a few of them are highlighted in this section. Google, in particular, has been very proactive in regard to taking forward various digital library projects. As Crane (2006) notes, Google has created a consortium of libraries to build a huge digital collection on a global basis and there seems to be a lot of money available to convert books into digital form – Google is in the lead here, with Open Content Alliance (see below) following close behind. As Crane points out though, there have also been various barriers, such as a need for compulsory licensing.

The library of the University of Wisconsin-Madison, USA is one example of a library that has joined the Google project (see: Book Digitisation Project Gathers Pace, 2007). The library will provide access to hundreds of thousands of public and historical books and documents from over 7.2 million holdings at University of Wisconsin-Madison Libraries and Wisconsin-Historical Society Library. The project initially focused on library collections that are free of copyright restrictions. Furthermore, it will target other collections that are used a lot, such as the history of medicine and engineering and patents and discoveries.

Part of the library at the University of Oxford is also being digitised (see Oxford-Google Mass-Digitisation Programme, 2006).

> For most of the Bodleian's long history, of course, the accessibility of the Library's collections has been almost entirely dependent on the ability of its users to come physically to Oxford. But the emergence of the Internet, and the scope for creating digital surrogates of library materials for networked availability, have radically altered the paradigm for access to the Library, opening up a whole new meaning for the Bodleian as a 'library for the world' in the 21st century. (Oxford-Google Mass-Digitisation Programme, 2006, p. 1)

The Oxford Digital Library began five years ago, with the help of the Mellon Foundation. In January 2003, after consultation with Google's senior executives, work began to find a way of making the Oxford material available electronically, so that it could benefit both Google and the Bodleian Library. It was decided, first of all, to digitise printed books that had no copyright restrictions. Printed books were chosen rather than documents such as manuscripts. This was because they wanted to aim for critical mass as they thought this was the best way for making inroads into the vast collections, and secondly, because arrangements were already in place for tackling material not thought to be appropriate for mass-digitisation procedures. Much optimism surrounded the project and they saw themselves as being:

> ...part of a 'giant leap for mankind', in helping to 'bring the world's information to the world'. (Oxford-Google Mass-Digitisation Programme, 2006, p. 3)

Other libraries working with Google to digitise parts of their collections include the New York Public Library, the University of California and Madrid's Complutense University, which is the largest university library in Spain.

Then, there is the mass-digitisation project – the 'Open Content Alliance' (OCA), which was announced in 2005, and led by Brewster Kahle (Young, 2006). Selected out-of-copyright books were being taken from libraries around the world and turned into e-books. This had the backing of Yahoo and Microsoft. Libraries have been working on their own on digital projects, but this project brings together digital content created by many different academic libraries. A specialised document scanner, developed by Internet Archive, called the Scribe, was used, to keep the price of scanning cheap.

The disadvantage of Google compared with Open Content Alliance is that one cannot easily download the data or print the whole book. In regard to OCA, Google said that:

> We welcome efforts to make information accessible to the world. The OCA is focused on collecting out-of-copyright works which constitute a minority

> of the world's books – a valuable minority, but certainly not complete. (Cited in Young, 2006, p. 5)

Meanwhile, AlouetteCanada is a Canadian national digital online project, which brings together various digitisation projects across Canada and makes them accessible to the public (see Carlson, 2006). It is a portal site which can be demonstrated at different colleges and museums focusing on digitised materials about or of interest to Canadians. The institutions involved in the project include the Universities of Alberta, New Brunswick and Toronto. A project like this can be very useful, particularly given the fact that Canada is very large geographically, but has such a relatively small population. Most of the money for the project came from public funds.

Ernie Ingles, Chief Librarian at the University of Alberta, compared the project with the privately funded and secretive Google digitisation projects at institutions such as the University of Michigan, saying that:

> Google is making content available freely, but it is making that content available in a commercial way. The question is, will Google always be there in perpetuity to make that content available? (Ingles, cited in Carlson, 2006)

Another digitisation project is the Glasgow Emblem Digitisation Project (2004). The Glasgow Centre for Emblem Studies was awarded a grant of £163,385 by the Arts and Humanities Research Board for digitisation of the corpus of French sixteenth century emblem books under the Resource Enhancement Scheme. The aim was to have a sophisticated website, including high-quality images of approximately 5500 pages, fully searchable text, and full indexes for both text and images.

The GATT Digital Library: 1947–1994 provides access to documents and information about the General Agreement on Tariffs and Trade (GATT), which promoted trade barriers amongst is member states from 1947 to 1994. The digital library was part of a cooperative project between Stanford University Libraries and Academic Information Resources and the World Trade Organisation. A grant for the project was obtained from the Institute for Museum and Library Services, which is an independent US federal agency supporting a variety of preservation and access programmes. The library has over 30,000 public documents, and 300 publications of GATT are accessible from the site.

There are many other interesting and important digital library projects taking place. Examples include the University of Central England Electronic Library; the Networked Digital Library of Theses and Dissertations; the National Science, Technology, Engineering and Mathematics Digital Library Program; Variations projects for music at Indiana University; and the Library of Congress digital programme. Other national digital programmes are also growing, such as Denmark's Electronic Research Library, which is creating a portal for Danish research libraries.

The concept of the 'global digital library' is also being referred to today. Having free access to digitised information globally is a wonderful idea, although somewhat unrealistic! Petrelli (2006) explores some of the developments and projects around the notion of the 'global digital library'.

One such project is the *Bricks Project* (which can be viewed at: http://www.brickscommunity.org/prj). This is a European 6th Framework-funded project, which aims to integrate existing digital resources (i.e. digital museums, digital archives) into a common digital library, operating as a European collective memory. There is an open collection and the distribution of resources is transparent to users, who access a single source of information.

'Diligent' (Digital Library Infrastructure on Grid Enabled Technology[1]) is another European Union-funded project, which is run by Professor Neuhold. It aims to create a distributed digital library enabling access to distributed digital resources through the use of Grid computing. Professor Neuhold thinks that the digital library community must take a lead on important issues, such as long-term preservation, communities working collaboratively to create and maintain the global digital library and specifying reward systems. As Petrelli says:

> The optimists claimed the Grid makes it possible to create a European-wide multimedia digital library that everyone can access from anywhere in a seamless manner. The Grid supports better access to multimedia (e.g. playing video) of the highest quality, and can virtually integrate material that is located in different countries. (2006, p. 23)

In general, there has been a lot of experimentation and research into digital library development around the globe in the last 15 or so years.

Thus, there are many different and important digital library projects taking place globally, and a few examples have been highlighted here. Clearly, these projects are growing in number. One key question here is the extent to which the commercial digitisation projects are likely to grow in the future.

GENDER ISSUES, I.T. AND DIGITISATION

It is a well-known fact that the computer industry in general is very male-dominated (I have considered this elsewhere – see Rikowski, 2003c). So, what might the implications be for digitisation?

As Leslie Regan Shade succinctly says in regard to female computer scientists, 'The statistics for women in the computer science field are dismal, revealing that only a small percentage of computer scientists and computer professionals are female' (Shade, 1993, p. 2). Butcher also notes that 'You don't have to look hard to realise there are far fewer women in the IT industry than men' (Butcher, 2003, p. 6).

Margolis & Fisher (2002) undertook some detailed research on women in computing. They conducted over 230 interviews with over 100 male and female computer science students (equally divided between the genders) over four years (from 1995 to 1999) at Carnegie Mellon University, USA. Multiple interviews were conducted asking students a variety of questions, such as their early experiences with computers, their home and school environments and their decisions to study computer science. They found that:

> Very early in life, computing is claimed as male territory. At each step from early childhood through college, computing is both actively claimed as 'guy

> stuff' by boys and men and passively ceded by girls and women. The claiming is largely the work of a culture and society that links interests and success with computers to boys and men. (Margolis & Fisher, 2002, p. 4)

Furthermore, many of the women who studied computing at degree level lost confidence through their period of study, and started to doubt their own ability. Thus, women are clearly at a serious disadvantage, in many ways, in this IT age.

In regard to computer software specifically, which is obviously of particular importance for digitisation and the reading of e-material, most software has been programmed and designed by men, which often does not cater adequately for women. Frenkel, for example, talking about computer software in schools, says:

> Any computer science curriculum, whether implemented in a wealthy or disadvantaged school must involve the selection of software. But studies show sex bias in educational software ... Children using software designed for the opposite sex are more anxious after they interact with the program, and that anxiety leads to lowered scores in the subject the program was intended to teach. (1990, pp. 5–6)

Sylge also discusses computer design and emphasises how most of it is undertaken by men, and that programming is a very male-dominated area. Furthermore, Woodward (2001) points out that men account for 79% of computer analysts and programmers. Sylge (1995) notes that this might be disadvantageous for women, as women and men do tend to think differently.

Margolis & Fisher also focus on this subject, emphasising, in particular, how boys tend to invent things (in this case, inventing and designing a computer program), whilst girls just use things that the boys have invented. Once again, girls are socialised into playing this type of role. They say that:

> Today, the world of cyberspace is shaping our environment and our culture. Very little is unaffected by the onslaught of technology. The actual products of computer science change the way we do business, the interaction we expect from work, life, and pleasure, and the way we regard entertainment. If boys invent things, and girls use things boys invent, a cyberspace culture will inevitably reflect the desires and sensibilities of males to the exclusion and often denigration of females. (Margolis & Fisher, 2002, p. 12)

If females start to feel excluded in this way, then this could clearly have very serious consequences. We could find ourselves in a situation where females are focusing more on reading hard copy material, whilst males focus more on reading e-material. Males will then have more information available at their disposal and they will be able to access it all more easily. Information and knowledge brings power, so men are then likely to have even more power and privilege. So, if we are not careful, digitisation could increase the inequalities between the sexes still further. Frenkel warns us about the dangers of women being left behind, saying:

> ...what are the repercussions to our increasingly computer-oriented society, if women – about half the population and professional workforce – are not as prepared in this discipline as are men? (1990, p. 10)

Thus, there is a need for more women to be designing screens and layouts, so that their wants and needs are more adequately reflected, and women need to be more proactive in the IT world in general, I would suggest.

Simon (2006) presents the findings of some empirical research on women and technology which took place in 2001–02 in the UK. The aim of the research was to investigate women's perceptions of technological change in general (and not just related to the library environment specifically), and it used the concept of the information society as a flexible framework. In-depth interviews and focus groups were conducted, grounded theory was used and it was very much a 'grass roots' view. Information was collected from 50 women, aged from 20 to 70+, from a range of backgrounds. Three main areas were addressed in the interviews: the concept of the 'information rich and information poor'; temporal and spatial impacts of the new technologies; and the future of the community in the network age. In general, many of the women interviewed were very positive about the new technologies, although some also expressed doubts and concerns. Their main experience of the Internet had been obtained from a work-based experience. There was also a real sense of concern about being left out, or at least, left behind, in the IT age, although, some were not happy about the need to retrain.

Women account for 70–80% of the workforce in UK and USA libraries, and obviously, technology is becoming an important part of libraries today. And so, as Simon emphasises, women need to be very much a part of this new IT age:

> ...although analyses vary, there is little questioning of the importance of ICT in everyday life, and as such it becomes ever more vital to understand how women think about, and deal with, technology in their everyday lives. (Simon, 2006, p. 478)

Opinions differ as to whether IT will open up new and exciting possibilities for females and overcome some of the barriers, or whether it is and will continue to be just another form of expressing and asserting male domination. Shade & We, for example, highlight many of the problems that need to be overcome but are optimistic that women can play a significant role in cyberspace. They say that we need to make:

> ...the Internet easily accessible to all people; making networking an attractive communications tool for women, by creating tangible and viable information and resources; and by encouraging young girls and women to become involved in the development and deployment of the technology. It also means creating a friendly online environment, one that allows women to speak their thoughts without having to hide their gender. The world of cyberspace is one which is being shaped daily by the millions of interactions on it, and women can contribute much to these exchanges. (Shade & We in Shade, 1993, p. 9)

In conclusion, I would suggest that women should be shaping the new technologies in general, and digitisation projects in particular, rather than letting the new technologies shape them.

SOCIAL AND POLITICAL IMPLICATIONS OF DIGITISATION AND DIGITAL LIBRARIES

There are many social and political implications leading on from digitisation projects and the creation and extension of digital libraries. This includes issues around the digital divide; the exploitation of workers in the developing world; the possible loss of a sense of community; the concept of 'self' in the IT age; the possibility that less physical space will be allocated to libraries and information resources in the future; and potential health risks through over-use of e-reading (backache, eye strain, etc.) There are also issues related to the likelihood of less face-to face teaching and less contact with university tutors (due to the increase in e-learning, easy access to digitised information, etc.) and those related to the ever-changing nature of technology and the fact that technology often becomes quickly outdated. Some of these issues will be considered briefly in this section, but for me, what is important is to maintain an appreciation of the value of Marxism throughout all such deliberations.

Helm (2006) alerts us to the fact that a lot of the digitisation projects are achieved by the exploitation of labourers in the developing world. He says that a new category of work is emerging – the 'digital factory job'. Thousands of people are inputting data and 'These digital bricklayers are in a sense building the new information pyramid' (Helm, 2006, p. 1). Helm reports that in Madras, India, for example, 'editors' making a fifth of US pay work extremely long hours in order to digitize archived American newspapers from the 1700s to the 1980s. In Boston, New York and Palo Alto, California, Google book workers manually turn each page of millions of library books, so that they can be scanned and made available to people that visit the Google website. Helm says that:

> Such menial work with data and information is hardly new. But the growing fruits of such operations – gaining online access to historical papers, for example – have never been so close to the fingertips of the average person. (2006, p. 2)

He also emphasises that 'there are plenty of people willing to work behind the digital curtain one keystroke at a time' (p. 3).

Thus, whilst many of us might reap the benefits of digitisation, many of these benefits have been gained by the exploitation of workers, particularly of those in the developing world. This, then, creates even further divisions between the rich and the poor.

Then, of course, there is the digital divide itself, with the world being divided between those that have access to a computer and those that do not. Clearly, digitisation could make this division worse. Large international companies in the developed world, in particular, can gain huge benefits from free and easy access to digitised information. Meanwhile, for those of us that are living in the digital age, Zizek (2006) asks whether we are actually living in an age of digital democracy or whether it is more a 'new tyranny of cyberspace'. He says:

> Marxists and other critically-disposed thinkers like to point out how cyberspace equality is of course deceptive – it ignores the material disparities (wealth, social position, power or lack of it and so on). (Zizek, 2006, p. 30)

So, how 'liberated' are we by this new IT age? Many talk about being feeling overwhelmed by the amount of emails they receive, for example, as well as feeling inundated by the sheer quantity of information that is 'out there' in cyberspace. Also, how 'empowered' are knowledge workers, in reality? (see, for example, Rikowksi, 2004a).

The concept of 'self' can also take on strange forms in this new digital age, argues Zizek. He says that:

> The fact that I perceive my virtual self-image as mere play thus allows me to suspend the usual hindrances which prevent me from realising my 'dark half' in real life. My electronic id is given wing. (Zizek, 2006, p. 30)

He also makes the point that he never really knows his cyberspace partners and, equally, they never really know him!

Also, the fruits of our intellectual labour are being captured, stored and repackaged more and more, which can lead to further exploitation of labour, and this clearly has implications for society. Crane (2006) makes the point that 'Digital libraries, where books read one another in however a rudimentary fashion, have already begun to separate intelligence and action from the human brain' (2006, p. 4).

Petrelli considers the broader implications of digitisation, saying that 'The digital age is changing not only the way we work, but how we think of ourselves and communicate' (2006, p. 22). Crane also notes that:

> ...we also must consider the consequences not only for digital libraries but also for the intellectual life of the human race as a whole if the record of human experience becomes, in substantial measure, freely available online anytime and anywhere. (2006, p. 3)

However, the most important question to ask is 'what is actually driving this digitisation project forward?' Is it being driven forward by altruistic reasons, that digitisation will bring real and lasting benefits to humankind in general? Well, I do not think that anyone is that naïve! No, instead, it is, once again, the drives embedded within global capitalism itself that are driving this whole programme forward so vigorously. This relates to the theory (from an Open Marxist perspective) that I am developing in my published works (see, for example, Rikowski, 2003a, 2004a, b, 2005, 2007).

Thus, to put it simply, we are now in the knowledge revolution, this being the latest phase of capitalism. As I say in my article, 'Value – the life blood of capitalism': 'in the industrialised/developed world today we are entering into the knowledge revolution, where knowledge is seen to be the key to success' (Rikowski, 2003a, p. 161) and 'value is the life-blood of capitalism. There is no resting place for capital – it seeks out new value everywhere and anywhere and this value is created by labour' (p. 175).

This knowledge revolution depends on the exploitation of intellectual labour and the:

> ...creation of value from intellectual labour, which is then embedded in the commodity becomes necessary, so that intangible commodities can be sold in

> the market-place and profits can be made (and ultimately profits can only ever be derived from value). (Rikowski, 2004b, p. 7)

Digitisation programmes and digital library projects can assist with the effective exploitation of this intellectual labour. With digitisation, effective knowledge management practices can be adopted, for example. By this means, value can be created and extracted from intellectual labour and profits can then be derived from this value. All this ensures the continued success of capitalism, whilst labour continues to be exploited, alienated and objectified, because value can only be created from labour. As Marx indicated: 'the labourer, by virtue of his labour being of a specialised kind ... by the mere act of working, creates each instant an additional or new value' (Marx, 1887, p. 201).

Thus, when we see digital projects gathering pace rapidly, we need to pause, and think and question. What is being gained from any one such project? Is digitisation always worthwhile? Does it necessarily mean that our information resources are being preserved and utilised more effectively? To what extent are commercial digital projects gathering pace and how is this likely to develop in the future (given that profit is the driving factor)? Could digitisation mean that few, if any, hard copies are available in the future? Could it mean that increasing amounts of material will not be available in the future, as technology changes, and the material is not transferred to the new medium? Might it lessen the value of scholarly publications (see, for example, Kalay's chapter in this book). What are the likely health risks of these digitisation programmes? And who is likely to benefit from this digitisation process? As I outlined earlier in this chapter digitisation and digital libraries obviously can and do bring enormous benefits to society, particularly in regard to making information easily and readily available. However, questioning is also necessary, I think.

CONCLUSION

In conclusion, many different issues in regard to digital libraries have been discussed in this chapter. This includes a definition of digital libraries; the advantages of digitisation; the costs of digitisation; the UK Joint Information Systems Committee (JISC), and in particular, its work with digital preservation; traditional, digital, hybrid and virtual libraries; the library community and digitisation; e-books; a selection of different digital library projects on a global basis; gender issues, information technology and digitisation; and the social and political implications of digitisation and digital libraries.

Digitisation and digital libraries offer many new and exciting ways for us to be able to access material, but we also need to exercise some caution, and not just jump on every digital bandwagon.

NOTES

1 http://diligentproject.org/content/view/73/100/

REFERENCES

Beagrie, N. (2004). The continuing access and digital preservation strategy for the UK Joint Information Systems Committee (JISC). *D-Lib Magazine*, *10*(7/8). Retrieved May 11, 2010, from http://dx.doi.org/10.1045/july2004-beagrie

Bell, L., Lindbloom, M.-C., Peters, T., & Pope, K. (2008). Virtual libraries and education in virtual worlds: Twenty-first century library services. *Policy Futures in Education*, *6*(1), 49–58. Retrieved May 11, 2010, from http://dx.doi.org/10.2304/pfie.2008.6.1.49

Blough, K. (2003, March 18). *E-books sales lead off 2003*. Association of American Publishers, press release. Retrieved from http://www.publishers.org/press/releases.cfm?PressReleaseArticleID=138

Book Digitisation Project Gathers Pace. (2007, December/January). *Research information*, *27*, 10.

Borgman, C. (1999). What are digital libraries? Competing visions. *Information Processing and Management*, *35*, 227–243. Retrieve September 4, 2007, from http://portal.acm.org/citation.cfm?id=315055

Borgman, C. (2000). Digital libraries and the continuum of scholarly communication. *Journal of Documentation*, *54*(4), 412–430. Retrieved May 11, 2010, from http://dx.doi.org/10.1108/EUM0000000007121

Borgman, C. (2003). The invisible library: Paradox of the global information infrastructure. *Library Trends*, *51*(4), 652. Retrieved September 4, 2007, from http://findarticles.com/p/articles/mi_m1387/is_4_51/ai_105046545/pg_18

Butcher, M. (2003, March 13). Girls beat the system: A competition aimed at encouraging girls to choose a career in IT has had an enthusiastic reception. *The Guardian Online, Supplement*, p. 6.

Carlson, S. (2006). AlouetteCanada hopes to pluck scattered digitization efforts into a central portal. *Chronicle of Higher Education*. Retrieved September 4, 2007, from http://chronicle.com/daily/2006/06/2006062101t.htm

Connaway, L., & Lawrence, S. (2003). Comparing library resource allocations for the paper and the digital library. *D-Lib Magazine*, *9*(12). Retrieved May 11, 2010, from http://dx.doi.org/10.1045/december2003-connaway

Copeland, S. (2008). Electronic theses and dissertations: Promoting 'hidden' research. *Policy Futures in Education*, *6*(1), 87-96. Retrieved May 11, 2010, from http://dx.doi.org/10.2304/pfie.2008.6.1.87

Cox, J. (2004). E-books: Challenges and opportunities. *D-Lib Magazine*, *10*(10). Retrieved September 4, 2007, from http://www.dlib.org/dlib/october04/cox/10cox.html

Crane, G. (2006). What do you do with a million books? *D-Lib Magazine*, *12*(3). Retrieved May 11, 2010, from http://dx.doi.org/10.1045/march2006-crane

Digital Libraries Initiative – Phase 2. (1998). *Sponsored by the National Science Foundation, Defense Advanced Research Projects Agency, National Library of Medicine, Library of Congress, National Aeronautics and Space Administration and National Endowment for the Humanities*. Retrieved September 4, 2007, from http://www.nsf.gov/pubs/1998/nsf9863/nsf9863.htm

Dunlap, I. H. (2008). Going digital: The transformation of scholarly communication and academic libraries. *Policy Futures in Education*, *6*(1), 132–141. Retrieved May 11, 2010, from http://dx.doi.org/10.2304/pfie.2008.6.1.132

Frenkel, K. (1990). Women and computing. *Communications of the ACM*, *33*(11), 34-46. Retrieved May 11, 2010, from http://dx.doi.org/10.1145/92755.92756

GATT Digital Library: 1947–1994. (n.d.). Retrieved September 4, 2007, from http://gatt.stanford.edu/page/home

Glasgow Emblem Digital Project. (n.d.). Retrieved January 2007, from http://www.ces.arts.gla.ac.uk/html/AHRBProject.htm

Gunter, B. (2005). Electronic books: A survey of users in the UK. *ASLIB Proceedings*, *57*(6), 513–522. Retrieved May 11, 2010, from http://dx.doi.org/10.1108/00012530510634244

Helm, B. (2006, May 22). Life on the Web's factory floor. *BusinessWeek Online*. Retrieved September 4, 2007, from http://www.businessweek.com/magazine/content/06_21/b3985092.htm

Hughes, L. (2004). *Digitizing collections: Strategic issues for the information manager*. London: Facet Publishing (Part of Digital Futures Series).

JISC Digitisation Programme Blog. (n.d.). Retrieved September 4, 2007, from http://jiscdigitisation.typepad.com/

Jones, R., Andrew, T., & MacColl, J. (2006). *The institutional repository*. Oxford: Chandos.

Kalay, Y. (2008). Impacts of new media on scholarly publishing. *Policy Futures in Education, 6*(1), 122–131. Retrieved May 11, 2010, from http://dx.doi.org/10.2304/pfie.2008.6.1.122

Lagoze, C., Krafft, D., Payette, S., & Jesuroga, S. (2005). What is a digital library anymore, anyway? *D-Lib Magazine, 11*(11). Retrieved May 11, 2010, from http://dx.doi.org/10.1045/november2005-lagoze

Lesk, M. (2005). *Understanding digital libraries*. San Francisco: Morgan Kaufman.

Lynch, C. (2005). Where do we go from here? The next decade for digital libraries. *D-Lib Magazine, 11*(7/8). Retrieved September 4, 2007, from http://www.dlib.org/dlib/july05/lynch/07lynch.html

Mackie-Mason, J., Riveros, J., Bonn, M., & Lougee, W. (1999). A report on the PEAK experiment: Usage and economic behaviour. *D-Lib Magazine, 5*(7/8). Retrieved September 4, 2007, from http://www.dlib.org/dlib/july99/mackie-mason/07mackie-mason.html

Macworld. (2004, June 7). *Ebook sales rocket*. Retrieved September 9, 2007, from www.macworld.co.uk/news/index/cfm?NewsID=8848&Page=1&pagePos

Margolis, J., & Fisher, A. (2002). *Unlocking the clubhouse: Women in computing*. Cambridge, MA: MIT Press.

Marx, K. [1887] (1954 – reproduced text of English edition of 1887). *Capital: A critique of political economy* (Vol. 1). London: Lawrence & Wishart.

Murray, J. (2000, March/April). Librarians evolving into cybrarians. *MultiMedia Schools*. Retrieved September 4, 2007, from http://www.emeraldinsight.com/.../published/emeraldfulltextarticle/pdf/2760570603_ref.html

Nikolova-Houston, T., & Houston, R. (2008). Building the virtual scriptorium. *Policy Futures in Education, 6*(1), 109–121. Retrieved May 11, 2010, from http://dx.doi.org/10.2304/pfie.2008.6.1.109

Oxford-Google Mass-Digitisation Programme. (2006). *University of Oxford Director of University Library Services and the Bodleian Library*. Contribution to the Opening Plenary Panel session of the CNI Spring 2005 Task Force Meeting, Washington, DC, 4 April 2005. Retrieved September 4, 2007, from http://www.bodley.ox.ac.uk/librarian/rpc/CNIGoogle/CNIGoogle.htm

Pandian, M. P. (2008). Digital knowledge resources. *Policy Futures in Education, 6*(1), 22–38. Retrieved May 11, 2010, from http://dx.doi.org/10.2304/pfie.2008.6.1.22

Pearson, D. (2001). Digitisation: Do we have a strategy? *Ariadne, 30*. Retrieved September 4, 2007, from http://wotan.liu.edu/dois/data/Articles/doidoiariy:2002:i:30:p:digilib.html

Peters, T. (2008). Meeting and serving users in their new work (and Play) spaces. *Policy Futures in Education, 6*(1), 43-48. Retrieved May 11, 2010, from http://dx.doi.org/10.2304/pfie.2008.6.1.43

Petrelli, D. (2006). Creating the global digital library. *CILIP Update, 5*(9), 22–23.

Reeves, T. C. (1998). *The impact of media and technology in schools: A research report prepared for the Bertelsmann Foundation*. Retrieved May 11, 2010, from http://it.coe.uga.edu/~treeves/edit6900/BertelsmannReeves98.pdf

Rikowksi, R. (2001a). GATS: Private affluence and public squalor? Implications for libraries and information. *Managing Information*, 8-10. Also available in *Library Juice, 4*, 46, 19 December 2001. Retrieved September 4, 2007, from http://www.libr.org/juice/issues/vol4/LJ_4.46.html#7

Rikowski, R. (2001b). The corporate takeover of libraries. *Information for Social Change, 14*, 25-60. Retrieved September 4, 2007, from http://libr.org/isc/articles/14-Ruth_Rikowski.html

Rikowski, R. (2002a). What does the future hold for our public libraries? *Information for Social Change, 15*, 56–60. Retrieved September 4, 2007, from http://libr.org/ISC.TOC.html

Rikowski, R. (2002b). The capitalisation of libraries. *The Commoner, 14*. Retrieved September 4, 2007, from http://www.commoner.org.uk/04rikowski.pdf

Rikowksi, R. (2002c). The WTO, the GATS and the Meaning of 'Services'. *Public Library Journal, 17*(2), 48-50. (Part 1 of a two-part article, which is based on my talk on *The WTO/GATS Agenda for Libraries*).

Rikowski, R. (2002d). Takeover by stealth? *Public Library Journal, 17*(3), 73–76. (Part 2 of a two-part article, which is based on my talk on *The WTO/GATS Agenda for Libraries*).

Rikowski, R. (2002e). Globalisation and libraries In *Globalisation*. Report by House of Lords, Select Committee on Economic Affairs, Session 2002-03, 1st Report. London: The Stationery Office. In 'Volume of Evidence', part 2, HL5-11 – on CD-ROM, pp. 360–371.

Rikowski, R. (2003a). Value – the life blood of capitalism: Knowledge is the current key. *Policy Futures in Education, 1*(1), 163–182. Retrieved May 11, 2010, from http://dx.doi.org/10.2304/pfie.2003.1.1.5

Rikowski, R. (2003b). Library privatisation: Fact or fiction? *Information for Social Change, 17*. Retrieved September 4, 2007, from http://libr.org/isc/articles/17-Rikowski-2.html

Rikowski, R. (2003c). Females, computers and libraries. *Managing Information, 10*(6), 6–10.

Rikowski, R. (2004a). On the impossibility of determining the length of the working-day for intellectual labour. *Information for Social Change, 19*. Retrieved September 4, 2007, from http://libr.org/isc/articles/19-R.Rikowski-2.html

Rikowski, R. (2004b). Creating value from knowledge in the knowledge revolution. *Information for Social Change, 20*. Retrieved September 4, 2007, from http://libr.org/isc/articles/20-R.Rikowski.html

Rikowski, R. (2005). *Globalisation, information and libraries: The implications of the World Trade Organisation's GATS and TRIPS agreements*. Oxford: Chandos.

Rikowski, R. (Ed.). (2007). *Knowledge management: Social, cultural and theoretical perspectives*. Oxford: Chandos.

Sanett, S. (2002). Toward developing a framework of cost elements for preserving authentic electronic records into perpetuity. *College and Research Libraries, 63*, 388-403. Retrieved September 4, 2007, from http://216.239.59.104/search?q=cache:EIOYY3oRiPcJ:www.ala.org/ala/acrl/acrlpubs/crljournal/backissues2002b/september02/sanett.pdf+toward+developing+a+framework+of+cost+elements+by+sanett&hl=en&ct=clnk&cd=1&gl=uk&ie=UTF-8

Shade, L. (1993, 17–19 August). *Gender issues in computer networking*. Talk given at Community Networking, the International Free-Net Conference, Carleton University, Ottawa, Canada. Retrieved September 4, 2007, from http://feminism.eserver.org/gender/cyberspace/gender-issues.txt

Simon, A. (2006). Women's perceptions of technological change in the information society. *Aslib Proceedings, 58*(6), 476–487. Retrieved May 11, 2010, from http://dx.doi.org/10.1108/00012530610713560

Sylge, C. (1995). Wired women. Information technology, the workplace and the gender debate (might women have chance to rewire the new working environment to their advantage). *Managing Information, 2*(10), 17–21.

Tedd, L., & Large, A. (2005). *Digital libraries: Principles and practice in a global environment*. Munich: K.G. Saur.

Unsworth, J. (2000). *Supporting digital scholarship*. Retrieved September 9, 2007, from http://www3.iath.virginia.edu/sds/mellon.anrep.2000.htm

Woodward, W. (2001, October 29). Girls still choose 'Women's Jobs'. *The Guardian*, p. 10. Retrieved September 4, 2007, from http://society.guardian.co.uk/news/story/0,,582696,00.html

Young, J. (2006, January 27). Scribes of the digital era. *Chronicle of Higher Education*. Retrieved from http://chronicle.com/infotech/

Zizek, S. (2006, December 30). Is this digital democracy, or a new tyranny of cyberspace? *The Guardian*, p. 30.

Ruth Rikowski
Chandos Publishing, Oxford

M. PAUL PANDIAN

3. DIGITAL KNOWLEDGE RESOURCES

INTRODUCTION

The term "Digital Knowledge Resources" is used in a wider perspective to include all sources where the information is available in electronic formats and accessible with a help of computers. These sources are variously termed as automated library, electronic library, virtual library, paperless library, networked library, library without walls, and multimedia library and all of them are used interchangeably and synonymously. The term digital library has however become the preferred term due to growing interest and marries the missions, techniques, and cultures of physical libraries with the capabilities and cultures of computing and telecommunications. The advantages of digital information are well established and understood - it can be delivered direct to the user; multiple simultaneous use is possible with no degradation from use and with minimal storage costs; sophisticated searching techniques are available and retrieval is fast.

The term "digital library" has come to refer to any aspect of *text*, *image* or *sound*, as it exists in digital form as opposed to a traditional format. Digital information presently exists in a variety of formats: *online public access catalogs, library networks, CD-ROMs, local databases, online commercial databases, gopher space, the World Wide Web, image libraries, audio libraries, digital video libraries* and so forth (Lynch and Garcia-Molina, 1995).

One of the important characteristics of digital information resources is that by its very nature of being electronic it makes the information accessible and sharable regardless of time and space. While there are considerable efforts in creating comprehensive digital libraries across the globe, it can be safely said that there is not a digital library without a print library. What we have today is more like a "hybrid library". Corcoran, M (2003) in his overview of the hybrid library, defines it as the library that contains a mix of print and electronic resources, offered in a variety of formats and delivered either locally or remotely. It is neither a traditional, print-based library nor is it fully digital as it exists on a continuum somewhere between the two. He believes that the hybrid library is a very real model in and of itself and will continue to exist as a very real working model for a number of reasons including:

- Libraries have made huge investments in print resources; these legacy resources are likely to remain outside the e-domain.
- Even where decisions are taken to digitize legacy materials, this is an expensive and labour intensive activity. Furthermore permissions to digitize are not readily granted.

R. Rikowski (ed.), Digitisation Perspectives, 43–63.

- Despite rapid technological developments, the technologies to truly deliver digital libraries are not yet available. We are still operating in a changing environment with transient and immature technologies.
- Until publishers/suppliers can guarantee access to archived electronic journals, libraries will continue to rely on a hybrid journal collection development policy.
- As a corollary to the last statement, even if there is a guaranteed access to archived electronic resources, print counterparts cannot be dumped away. So, the hybrid library is here to stay. Of course, the scope of the hybrid library will include more and more digital resources. And what we discuss below is the other half (or even more) of the hybrid library, i.e., digital library. It can be safely declared that there will not be a library without digital components in its information collections.

DEFINITION OF DIGITAL LIBRARIES

Defining the digital library is an interesting, but somewhat daunting, task. There is no shortage of proposed definitions. One would think that there would be some commonly accepted and fairly straightforward standard definition, but there does not appear to be. Rather, there are many. And one common thread among all these definitions is a heavy emphasis on resources and an apparent lack of emphasis on librarians and the services they provide.

A review of digital libraries literature, written by scholars from a wide array of fields including Library and Information Science and Computer Science, reveals that even in the professional environment a large number of definitions are in use. In literature, the digital library may also be called the library without walls, virtual library, electronic library, e-library, desktop library, online library, future library, library of the future, logical library, networked library, hybrid library, gateway library, extended library or internet library. Of these many terms, digital library, virtual library, electronic library and hybrid library are most common.

D. Kaye Gapen provides a very comprehensive definition of a virtual library:

> The virtual library has been defined as the concept of remote access to the contents and services of libraries and other information resources, combining an on-site collection of current and heavily used materials in both print and electronic form, with an electronic network which provides access to, and delivery from, external worldwide library and commercial information and knowledge sources. In essence the user is provided the effect of a library which is a synergy created by bringing together technologically the resources of many, many libraries and information resources. (Gapen, 1999, p. 1)

The electronic library, however, is somewhat a different notion:

> The electronic library will be realized as an aggregation of catalogs, lists, and indexes of documents of every imaginable type, organized according to myriad schemes of classification, and linked and cross-indexed for search, so that they come to behave as a single database in which the lines between individual collections and catalogs are blurred. (Nunberg, 1993, p. 30)

According to Mel Collier, the electronic library is a:

> ...managed environment of multimedia materials in digital form, designed for the benefit of its user population, structured to facilitate access to its contents and equipped with aids to navigation of the global network. (Collier, 1997, p. 2)

In more understandable terms, digital libraries would ideally be able to store data at multiple sites and allow a user to search for information across these multiple repositories in a single step.

Collier (1997) says that a library becomes digital when the majority of its resources are held in electronic form. Sun Microsystems (2002, p. 3) defines a digital library as the electronic extension of functions users typically perform and the resources they access in a traditional library. These information resources can be translated into digital form, stored in multimedia repositories, and made available through Web-based services. The emergence of the digital library mirrors the growth of e-learning (or distance learning) as the virtual alternative to traditional school attendance. As the student population increasingly turns to off-campus alternatives for lifelong learning, the library must evolve to fit this new educational paradigm or become obsolete as students search for other ways to conveniently locate information resources anywhere, any time.

The Association of Research Libraries has defined a digital library as follows:

> There are many definitions of a "digital library." Terms such as "electronic library" and "virtual library" are often used synonymously. The elements that have been identified as common to these definitions are: The digital library is *not a single entity*; the digital library *requires technology* to link the resources of many; the *linkages* between the many digital libraries and information services are *transparent to the end users*; *universal access* to digital libraries and information services is a goal; digital library collections are *not limited to document surrogates*: they extend to digital artifacts that cannot be represented or distributed. (Association of Research Libraries, 1995, p. 1)

ACM defined digital libraries as follows:

> The phrase "digital library" evokes a different impression in each reader. To *some*, it simply suggests computerization of traditional libraries. To others, who have studied *library science*, it calls for carrying out of the functions of libraries in a new way, encompassing new types of information resources; new approaches to acquisition (especially with more sharing and subscription services); new methods of storage and preservation; new approaches to classification and cataloging, new modes of interaction with and for patrons; more reliance on electronic systems and networks; and dramatic shifts in intellectual, organizational, and economic practices. To many *computer professionals*, a digital library is simply a distributed text-based information system, a collection of distributed information services, or a networked multimedia information system. It may have materials that are mostly from an outside organization, that are generally of high value, and that have had special electronic services

> added to its quality during creation, collection, organization, and use. To *modern day users of the WWW* it suggests more of the same, with sure-to-come improvements in performance, organization, functionality, and usability...Those studying *collaboration technologies* see digital libraries as the space in which people communicate, share and produce new knowledge and knowledge products. Those working on *education technology* see digital libraries as support for learning, whether formal or informal. (ACM in Fox et al, 1995, pp. 24–25)

The Digital Library Federation defines digital libraries in the following way:

> Digital libraries are organizations that provide the resources, including the specialized staff, to select, structure, offer intellectual access to, interpret, distribute, preserve the integrity of, and ensure the persistence over time of collections of digital works so that they are readily and economically available for use by a defined community or set of communities. (Digital Library Federation in Walters, 1998, p. 1)

This definition involves three key components, which constitute the theoretical framework underlying digital libraries, namely:

- People
- Information resources
- Technology.

Cleveland (1998. p. 2) provides a working definition. Digital libraries are libraries with the same purposes, functions, and goals as traditional libraries -collection development and management, subject analysis, index creation, provision of access, reference work, and preservation.

HISTORY, TRENDS AND GROWTH

Libraries have gone through several generations of technology as they have evolved from print to electronic resources. Libraries are responding to the challenges of new technologies by taking the opportunity to redefine their fundamental role in the creation, distribution and provision of access to information.

Digital libraries have a short yet turbulent and explosive history. A number of early visionaries, such as Licklider (1965), had a notion of libraries in the future being highly innovative and different in structure, processing, and access through heavy applications of technology. But, besides visionary and futuristic discussions and highly scattered research and developmental experimentation, nothing much happened in the next two decades. By the end of the 1980s, digital libraries (under various names) were barely a part of the landscape of librarianship, information science, or computer science. But just a decade later, by the end of the 1990s, research, practical developments, and general interest in digital libraries exploded globally. The 1990s brought a revolution that made possible the extension of the automated library to a more enhanced electronic library or digital library. The accelerated growth of numerous and highly varied efforts related to digital libraries continues unabated in the 2000s.

Global Trends in Electronic Information

Libraries of all types and in all settings are developing a global vision of international networked collections and services. This model views libraries as both providers of worldwide knowledge resources and gateways for users to knowledge, which is increasingly electronic in form. This transformation requires recognition of important revolutionary changes, which are transforming collections, information services and the working relationships among libraries. An excellent summary of the multiple revolutions that this development brought about was outlined by James G. Neal, in his paper entitled "Electronic publishing and the future of library resource sharing" (Neal, 1998). Neal summarizes these multiple revolutions as follows:

- the personal computing revolution is at the core of individualized technology and the expanding power to access, analyze and control information
- the electronic revolution is producing vast amounts of digital information in all media and intelligent software that enables effective search and retrieval
- the network revolution is creating a vast telecommunications web and robust platforms for distributing an expanding volume of electronic resources
- the push revolution is shifting radically the nature of network searching by narrow casting automatically to users through customized packaging and delivery of information
- the self-service revolution is encouraging fundamental rethinking of user services in an environment where user initiated and controlled activities are becoming commonplace
- the partnership revolution is promoting higher levels of cooperation and collaboration among organizations as a fundamental requirement for success and as a basis for consortia co-investment in electronic information
- the authorship revolution is defining the facility and the creativity potential of the network where anyone with a minimal investment can post information to millions of potential readers on a global scale
- the intellectual property revolution is threatening fair use rights for digital information and creating extraordinary conflict between the interests of information providers and information consumers
- the digital preservation revolution is energizing concern about the integrity and archiving for future use of the vast amount of electronic information being produced and lost
- the information as commodity revolution is increasingly viewing data and its synthesized products, knowledge, as articles of commerce and sources of profit rather than property held in common for societal good
- the knowledge management revolution is spawning a new relationship among researcher, librarian and information technologist which maximizes the usefulness of data gathering and information generation

These trends illustrate dramatic new directions in the nature and role of library collections and services. In the early 1970s, libraries began to adopt software applications to allow them to perform specific functions more efficiently. The next phase of library automation combined several library activities into one integrated system, allowing librarians to perform almost all their functions online. Data entered once could be used in multiple ways, which increased efficiency and accuracy. The transition from large scale computing technologies to microcomputers was well under way by the mid-1980s. This trend required re-education of the library and systems IT staff, which added significant cost to libraries. Three changes followed: different library application providers, more powerful technologies, and software applications and networking configurations that were no longer developed in-house. Libraries of all types began utilizing new application systems to automate resource sharing. Union Catalogs and Inter-Library Loan modules were developed by library software vendors to allow cooperating institutions to combine their catalogs and allow patrons of one library to request and borrow materials from linked institutions (Sun Microsystems, 2002).

As the 1980s ended, libraries and computing centers were tackling communications, relational databases, and information distribution challenges. The 1990s saw greater use of campus communication infrastructures and commercial communication systems to create and store information and then to deliver it from libraries to end-users.

Large databases from periodical, magazine, and journal publishers became increasingly available in digital format — at first on CD-ROM; later via online services. Library services are transitioning from local traditional collections to global resources provided on demand via the most advanced networking technologies. Today, library collections are used by people on campus as well as by individuals who are not even located on the library's physical facilities. Thus, individuals associated with a given institution and accessing resources from afar need new electronic interface tools. As a result, professional librarians must be computer literate and knowledgeable about Internet technologies to fully participate in the planning, design, and implementation of future library services (Sun Microsystems, 2002).

Growth of Electronic Knowledge Resources

Although information in electronic format was created with the advent of the computer in the 1950s, it was not until the early 1960s that the first database suitable for searching was developed. MEDLARS was the first on-demand computer-based information retrieval service, and it was developed primarily for the medical profession. In 1971, MEDLINE, the online version of MEDLARS, was the first major online dial-up database search service. In the following year, DIALOG offered the first public online commercial database. With these first databases, there were no real acquisition decisions, as they were offered as access services to which libraries could subscribe. Actual searching of these databases produced charges that many libraries passed along to users. While the information revolution was clearly underway, it was not until after the introduction of the CD-ROM in the mid-1980s that electronic resources began to have a major impact on selection practices in libraries (Meadow, 1988).

Many of the first CD-ROM products offered to libraries were versions of larger online databases and were supplied on a subscription basis with ownership of the data remaining with the publisher/producer. Initially, the price of the product included licensing of the content and possibly the purchase of a computer and CD-ROM player as well. Products were guaranteed to work only with specified CD-ROM players, as standards were not yet established. The purchase of this equipment as part of the cost of the information product was not always easy. Often equipment was not considered an appropriate use of the library's materials budget. However, equipment budgets were not always large enough or flexible enough, initially, to accommodate this new demand. As with audiovisual materials, the unit price of these products was high and use was often limited to one individual at a time.

Although very expensive at first, CD-ROM products gradually became more affordable. As personal computers became widely available in most libraries, these products also became very popular. Initially, only one person could use these CD-ROM databases at a time, a major drawback, especially considering their high cost.

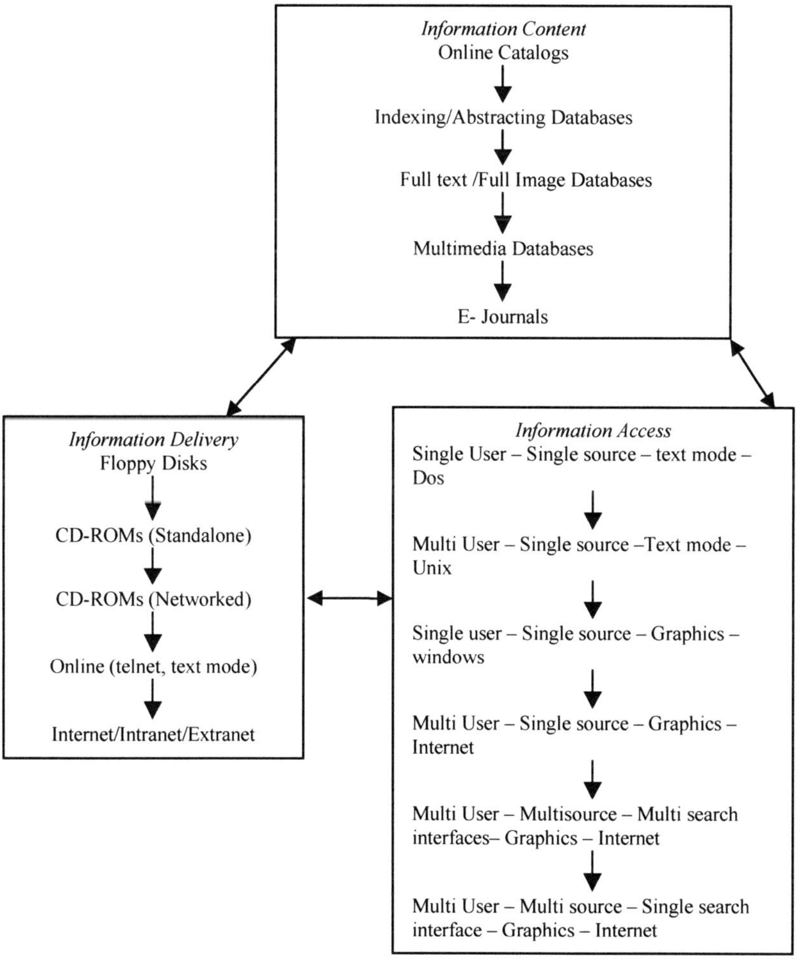

Figure 1. Growth of electronic information (Pandian & Karisiddappa, 2004).

The alternative was to purchase the needed database on magnetic tape and mount it on the local computer system, which could provide simultaneous access to many users. This, however, was a very expensive solution and one that most libraries could not afford. Gradually, hardware and software solutions were found that allowed several users to access the same CD-ROM database simultaneously. Some libraries even found ways to provide access to CD-ROM products to sites outside of the library (Thornton, 2000).

The World Wide Web permeates almost all aspects of computing. An ever-increasing array of information producers now relies on this media to distribute their products and services.

The developments in electronic information, development of networked access and delivery of new library services has seen a radical transformation in the information chain (Figure 1):

CHARACTERISTICS OF THE DIGITAL LIBRARY

One of the early authors on the electronic library was Kenneth Dowlin who wrote a book entitled "The Electronic Library" in 1984. He defined the characteristics of the electronic library as follows (Dowlin, 1984):

- Management of resources with a computer
- The ability to link the information provider with the information seeker via electronic channels
- The ability for staff to intervene in the electronic transaction when requested by the information seeker
- The ability to store, organize, and transmit information to the information seeker via electronic channels

While there is considerable uncertainty about what the digital library means, it can be contrasted with conventional libraries in important respects. Differing from the traditional library, the digital library has its own characteristics and functions can be generalized into the following aspects (Baohua et al, 2002, p. 529–530):

- The digitalization of the information resources
- The electronic transfer of information via Internet
- The sharing of the information
- The knowledge of information supply
- The fictitious information object

Digital libraries are a distributed network system environment since many different types of information resources will be interlinked together to provide the user with value added services. In this context, digital library is not a single entity (Ram et al, 1999).

Chowdhury and Chowdhury (2003, p. 8–9) have identified the following characteristics of digital libraries:

- Variety of digital information resources
- Digital libraries reduce the need for physical space
- Users at remote sites
- Users may build their own personal collections by using the digital library

- Provides access to distributed information resources
- Many users at the same time can share same information
- Paradigm shift both in use and ownership
- Collection development be posed on potential usefulness and appropriate filtering mechanisms be followed to negotiate the problem of plenty
- Ability to handle multilingual content
- Presupposes the absence of human intermediaries
- Should provide better searching and retrieval facilities
- Digital information can be used and viewed differently by different people
- Digital library breaks the time, space and language barriers

Mel Collier (Collier, 1997, p. 3) provides the following characteristics of digital libraries:

- Access to the digital library is not bounded in space or time. It can be accessed from anywhere at any time
- Content in electronic form will steadily increase and content in printed form will decrease
- Content is in textual, image, and sound form
- Usage of electronic information as a proportion of total usage will steadily increase, and usage of printed material as a proportion of total usage will decrease
- Expenditure on electronic material will steadily increase and, relatively, expenditure on printed material will decrease
- Expenditure on information will shift from ownership to subscription and licensing
- Expenditure on equipment and infrastructure will increase
- Usage of buildings will shift from stockholding to places for study, animation and citizenship
- Jobs, training and recruitment will be re-profiled

DIGITAL LIBRARY DEVELOPMENT

Building a digital library is expensive and resource-intensive. Before embarking on such a venture, it is important to consider some basic principles (McCray and Gallagher, 2001, p. 50) underlying the design, implementation, and maintenance of any digital library:

- Expect change
- Know your content
- Involve the right people
- Design usable systems
- Ensure open access
- Be(a)ware of data rights
- Automate whenever possible
- Adopt and adhere to standards
- Ensure quality
- Be concerned about persistence

A digital library, however, should be more than a digitized one. It should be built according to principles that are not necessarily the same as those employed for paper collections, and it should be evaluated according to different measures, which are not yet totally clear.

A digital library collection may include two types of information resource. One type comprises the "digital original" resources, which are sometimes referred to as resources, which are "born digitally". The other type comprises "digital surrogates", which are created from traditional information resources through format conversion.

There are essentially three methods of building digital collections:

- digitization, converting paper and other media in existing collections to digital form
- acquisition of original digital works created by publishers and scholars. Example items would be electronic books, journals, and datasets
- access to external materials not held in-house by providing pointers to Web sites, other library collections, or publishers' servers.

DIGITAL LIBRARY AND TECHNOLOGY

The development of the digital library (DL) requires the following technologies (Mukaiyama, 1997, p. 1):

- Contents processing technology

  Technology that provides effective creation, storage, and retrieval of primary information and secondary information: including digital conversion from conventional, non-digital media.
- Information access technology

  Technology that enables efficient accesses to myriad types of information without time or location limitations.
- Human-friendly, intelligent interface

  User interface that brings, to diverse users, increased intellectual productivity and an improvement to the active cultural environment.
- Interoperability

  Technology to make interoperable works possible in heterogeneous environments.
- Scalability

  Technology that enables DL systems to handle increases in information and users.
- Open system development

  Development using international and de facto standards, without loss of performance.
- Highly flexible system development

  Technology that can adjust quickly to new information and related changes to social systems.

DIGITAL LIBRARY ENVIRONMENT

The Association of Research Libraries through major studies identified a series of different activities considered essential to the formation of digital libraries. These included:

- Use of, or development of electronic document delivery services;

- Policies, services, or reallocations that emphasize access [to information] over ownership;
- Participation in cooperative development or purchase of electronic files;
- Participation in the development of a campus-wide information system;
- A written plan that states its goal as access to information from a single workstation;
- Enhancement of the online public access catalogue (OPAC) to include the holdings of other libraries besides those held locally;
- Providing a gateway from the OPAC to other databases or networks, such as the Internet;
- End-user access to online files from on or off campus;
- Connection with the Internet;
- Training faculty and students:
  - in the use of Internet sources; and,
  - in end-user searching;
- Subscribing to electronic journals;
- Digitization of text for electronic storage, retrieval and/or dissemination;
- An e-mail front-end that allows users to initiate interlibrary loan and document delivery requests, suggest purchases, or ask reference questions from within the OPAC; and
- Access to electronic full-text (Schauder, 1994, p. 20).

Amanda Magnussen (2003, p. 4) has grouped these activities into the following categories (table 1):

Table 1. Digital library environment

Category	*Activities*
The Internet and Intranets	Development of library internet and/or intranet sites Internet Connection
Integrated access to resources	Single workstation access to resources Use of OPAC as a gateway Inclusion of external holdings on local OPAC
Digitisation of materials	Digitisation projects
Electronic publications	Electronic Journals Electronic Full-text
Electronic document delivery	Commercial and library-to-library electronic document delivery
Resource Sharing	Access to resources over ownership
Cooperative activities	Cooperative purchasing or development of resources
End-User services	End-user access to online resources Internet training for clients Searching training for clients End-user electronic requesting

The above activities may provide a conceptual framework for "functional and operational" digital libraries. In order to have more "functional" and "operational" digital libraries, we need to do much more by integrating technology, content and users. The Report of the DELOS-NSF Working Group on Digital Imagery for Significant Cultural and Historical Materials provided a conceptual framework for digital libraries as follows (Chen, and Kiernan, 2002, p. 3):

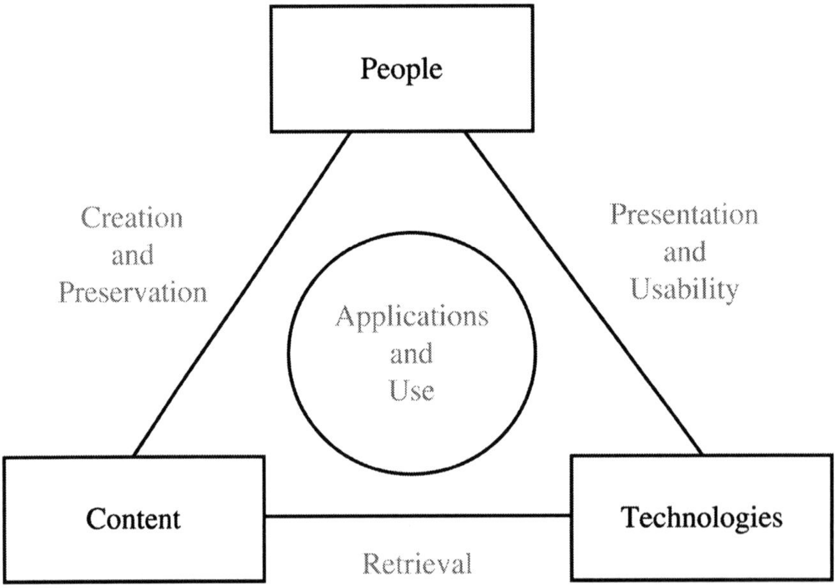

Figure 2. Conceptual framework for digital libraries (Adapted from Chen and Kiernan, 2002, p. 3).

This conceptual model attempts to illustrate the relationships among people, content, and technologies in developing research agenda.

DIGITAL LIBRARY COMPONENTS

As shown in the following figure (fig. 3), a fully developed digital library environment involves the following elements (Sun Microsystems, 2002, p. 5):

- Initial conversion of content from physical to digital form.
- The extraction or creation of metadata or indexing information describing the content to facilitate searching and discovery, as well as administrative and structural metadata to assist in object viewing, management, and preservation.
- Storage of digital content and metadata in an appropriate multimedia repository. The repository will include rights management capabilities to enforce intellectual property rights, if required. E-commerce functionality may also be present if needed to handle accounting and billing.

- Client services for the browser, including repository querying and workflow.
- Content delivery via file transfer or streaming media.
- Patron access through a browser or dedicated client.
- A private or public network.

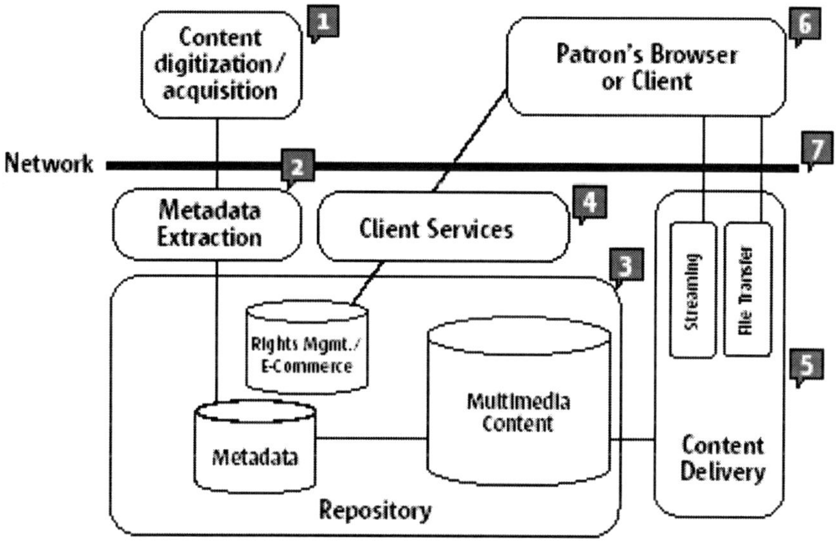

Figure 3. Functional components of a digital library (Adapted from Sun microsystems, 2002, p. 5).

A digital library includes five component parts (Dennis, p. 1):
- the host computer system - or server - where data is stored;
- system and application software that facilitates the organization, searching, display and maintenance of the digital objects;
- end-user desk top workstation where the digital collections are displayed and manipulated;
- the network that delivers digital objects from the host server to the end-user; and
- the creation and conversion of data.

It is the interactions of these component parts which determine the success of a digital library implementation.

DIGITAL LIBRARY ACCESS SYSTEM

A digital library access system is defined as "anything which gets digital content to the user or the user to the content." The digital library framework permits many different computer systems to coexist. The key components are shown in the figure below. They run on a variety of computer systems connected by a computer network, such as the Internet (Arms, 1997).

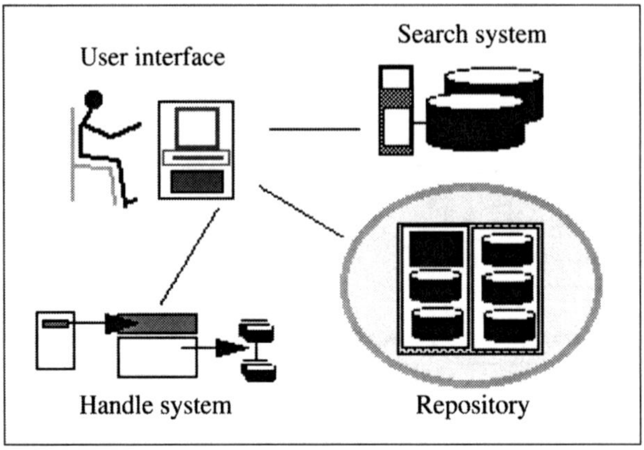

Figure 4. Major system components of digital library (Adapted from Arms, William Y, 1997, p. 9).

The Digital Library (DL) system should satisfy the access, browsing, search storage, rights management, and publishing needs of a broad range of users. Each group will have different needs and use the system in different ways. The DL system should be flexible enough to accommodate the different knowledge bases of each group of users as they seek to use the system. In addition, the system must provide sufficient management tools for library staff to maintain the quality and integrity of the information resources and administer the system on a daily basis. It should seamlessly integrate all library information resources.

DIGITAL LIBRARY AND PEOPLE

While a good deal of the literature on digital libraries emphasizes technology and resources at the expense of the service perspective, a number of authors and researchers have considered human interaction in the digital library environment. A number of studies at Lancaster University (Twidale, 1995, 1996; Twidale & Paice, 1996; Twidale, and Paice, 1997) have considered the importance of human interaction in the digital library. These studies focus on the social interactions of library users with librarians, librarians with librarians, and users with other users. By studying these collaborations in physical library settings, the authors have drawn some general conclusions that might be applied to digital library design:

- Collaboration between users, and between users and system personnel, is a significant element of searching in current information systems.
- The development of electronic libraries threatens existing forms of collaboration but also offers opportunities for new forms of collaboration.
- The sharing of both the search product and the search process are important for collaborative activities (including the education of searchers).
- There exists great potential for improving search effectiveness through the re-use of previous searches; this is one mechanism for adding value to existing databases.

- Browsing is not restricted to browsing for inanimate objects; browsing for people is also possible and could be a valuable source of information.
- Searchers of databases need externalized help to reduce their cognitive load during the search process. This can be provided both by traditional paper-based technology and through computerized systems (Twidale et al., 1996).

In a paper presented at the Digital Libraries '94 Conference, Ackerman (1994, p. 1) stresses that, while the concept of the digital library "includes solving many of the technical and logistical issues in current libraries and information seeking," it would be a mistake to consider solely the mechanical aspects of the library while ignoring the "useful social interactions in information seeking".

In a paper for the Digital Libraries '96 Conference, Brewer et al (1996) argue that intermediary services should play a crucial and essential role in the ongoing development of digital libraries so as not to limit the digital library to the role of "passive warehousing". The authors identify three major purposes for intermediation in the digital library environment:

- Interaction with potential information beneficiaries.
- Interaction with information resources.
- Mediation between information resources and users to add value during the information transfer process. (Value added services could include "searching, categorization, filtering, translation, publishing, or some combinations of these activities.")

Matson and Bonski (1997) discuss the development of the National Drug Intelligence Center within the U.S. Department of Justice. Based on these experiences, they outline three roles that have been proposed for the librarian in the digital age:

- the librarian as enhanced service provider in a proactive manner;
- the librarian as guru of copyright, licensing, and electronic redistribution– i.e., the understanding of what users and organizations actually want to do with information; and
- the librarian as system interface designer, making use of experience with how library users request, use, and process information.

Abbas (1997, p. 6–7) summarizes a number of roles that others have identified for future librarians:

- librarians as gateways to the future and to the past;
- librarians as teachers;
- librarians as knowledge managers/workers;
- librarians as organizers of networked resources;
- librarians as advocates for information policy development;
- librarians as community partners;
- librarians as "sifters" of information resources;
- librarians as collaborators with technology resource providers;
- librarians as technicians; and
- librarians as individual information consultants.

DIGITAL LIBRARY AND COLLABORATION

It is critical that digital libraries provide access to valuable, interesting content and assist users in selecting, evaluating, and utilizing resources, no matter what their format. Collections and expertise are the two invaluable additions we offer to the networked world. We must collaborate to optimize the technological opportunities before us. Creating true digital libraries, not just digital collections, will require librarians to work closely together.

Digital library contributors will need to collaborate in their efforts to digitize resources if they are to be successful and distinguish themselves from digitization projects, which have stood alone inside individual institutions or organizations. Several collaborative planning efforts are underway. These efforts are allowing participants to become more familiar with the formidable technical challenges facing them. They also prompt them to work together across lines, institutions, and professions to (Kranich, 1999, p. 3):

- create a mutual vision for a common future;
- share expertise and rich collections;
- build upon earlier models of cooperative activities such as preservation, interlibrary loan, and collection development;
- reduce redundancy and the waste of acquiring or converting materials more than once;
- leverage scarce financial resources;
- allow the development of selection criteria which focus on coordinated digital collection building;
- encourage coordinated preservation strategies;
- ensure equitable access to information from anyplace/anytime;
- reduce barriers of distance and time;
- permit users to leap to actual information;
- develop value-added components to the information contained in the digital library;
- assist libraries and other institutions in digitizing materials and managing library projects;
- build the library of the future; and
- create a new service paradigm for the 21st century.

As a result, collaboration to create digital libraries will need (Kranich, 1999, p. 4):

- new organizational frameworks;
- serious commitments by library leaders and their organizations;
- equal risk taking across all organizations;
- continuous evaluation and assessment of progress;
- brokering of relationships and entrepreneurial activities; and
- a flexible, creative, responsive learning environment.

DIGITAL LIBRARY AND ECONOMICS

The availability and management of information in digital formats has opened up varied means of fast and portable 24/7 access, encouraged new research routes, refreshed the information consumer-base and redefined the public domain, among other obvious benefits. The economic properties of digital libraries are (Hayes, n.d. p. 3–4):

- Cheaply Shareable
- Value Increases with Accumulation
- Self-Generating
- Costs Independent of Scale of Application

The short and long term effects of digital libraries will affect the users either indirectly, directly, or both. The potential economic value of digital libraries will be quantitative and qualitative. The qualitative value refers to the additions or subtractions to the users' quality of life due to the addition of a new product. While this may be difficult to measure before digital libraries are implemented on a large scale, quantitative costs are easier to estimate before the fact. Certain elements will be incorporated into the cost of digital libraries such as the costs of publishing, acquisition of materials, hardware, software, and a trained staff at the physical library. Library budgets can account for some of the monetary costs, but especially for the initial investments required for such a venture, they cannot cover all the expenses (Friend, 1995).

The publishing costs are a source of major controversy. Under the current publishing system each copy has a monetary value attached to it, but in the electronic environment multiple copies can be made with little effort and no paper trail. The ease in making multiple copies, whether electronic or printed, of electronic works complicates the issue of fair use. The disagreement lies mainly among publishers, librarians, and database vendors. Another source of disagreement is how to charge for the use of information and who gets charged. Libraries and schools prefer a flat rate because it is budgetable, while publishers and database vendors want a variable rate (like long distance calling or pay-per-view) to be in force so they can make money similar to how they do now.

To investigate the issue of value in depth, it is useful to re-evaluate the purpose of a library. Ranganathan (1931) provides the basis for library purpose as:

- Books are for use
- Every reader her/his book
- Every book its reader
- Save the time of the reader
- The library is a growing organization.

Reflecting on this fundamental statement of library theory in an electronic environment, Crawford & Gorman (1995) suggest that it is a valid basis for the assessment of digital libraries. To take this further, the concept of value can be seen from the perspective of the 'reader', or user, in the ability to locate and use that material which is relevant to their information need. This suggests that the streams of digital library research into usability, performance of virtual communities, new scholarly communication models and information seeking behaviour are a part of establishing an assessment of value. If the new uses of information provided an insight into value, perhaps the more fundamental issue arises of not just how information is found, but also the level of availability of relevant digital collections for the reader (Missingham, 2003).

Collections comprise many types of material, such as journals, monographs, conference papers, theses, original materials (such as manuscripts, pictures) and maps. For research and scholarly communication, the major resource documents have traditionally been journals in the scientific disciplines and a more even mix of journals, monographs and conference papers in the humanities. All of these resources are now in digital and print forms, to varying degrees.

To apply Ranganathan's principles to this situation, the reader would be optimally served by the library which enabled access to the required or relevant resources. Ranganathan's third principle would be met when the library enabled the relevant resources to be available, whether known to users or not. To put this in the perspective of value, the digital library creates value when the collections, needs of users and information production are in synchronization or harmony. A lack of value would occur where the overlap between these three aspects is minimized.

In examining the cost effectiveness of an electronic resources, White and Crawford (1998) confirm that expenses are not always reduced when new services are offered; they may just be shifted elsewhere in the budget. New services may increase customer expectations, and nontangible benefits should be considered, such as the immediacy of full text versus the time lapse for Inter Library Loan. These trade-offs–increased costs versus increased access–must be addressed by each library, time and again.

DIGITAL LIBRARY SERVICES

Just as the literature identifies a number of activities that together make up digital libraries, so too does it show that the development of digital libraries is heavily dependent on a number of inter-related enabling (or hindering) factors.

Harter (1997, p. 7) has identified the following problems and issues related to information resources (IRs) in the digital library:

- How can we establish and control the currency, accuracy, and integrity of information sources (quality problem)?
- What can be done to provide intellectual access to IRs? (Organizational problem)
- How can we maintain the data and intellectual integrity of IRs? (authority control problem)
- How can we recognize different versions of the same IR? (fluidity problem)
- How can we establish object surrogates, metadata, and corresponding fine-grained search tools so that we can find those objects that we are seeking?
- How can we address the issue of transient IRs? (preservation problem)
- How can we preserve the concept of authorship?
- How can copyright laws for IRs be observed? (legal problem)
- Will access to some IRs be limited to some classes of users? (political problem)
- What services, if any, should be offered by the digital library?
- Should digital libraries be integrated into traditional libraries? If so, how can this be accomplished?

- Does a digital library have librarians? If so, what do they do?
- Does a digital library have well-defined classes of users?
- Who will have access to which services, and at what price? Will our digital libraries of the future only be for the use of the "haves?"

Amanda Magnussen (Magnussen, 2003, p. 5) has grouped the above into the following categories of issues in the digital library environment:

- Legal issues
- Financial issues
- Client issues
- Personnel issues
- Organizational issues
- Management issues
- Technological issues
- Collaboration issues
- Subject discipline issues

CONCLUSION

A digital library is less about its collection than it is about its ability to be opportunistic. In a time when information is much cheaper to produce and transport, every effort will be made to take advantage of increased access to information. Similarly, the increased computing power that can be brought to bear on information stores such as data mining will be employed for a variety of purposes, subject to the needs of a digital library and an information community. Given the model of the role of digital libraries in information communities presented in this document, a digital library may achieve what Ranganathan called a growing organism. But through its activities, a digital library may also become a "learning organism." This ability to learn comes from the technological advancements of the last 40 years, particularly from the coupling of computing and telecommunications technology. Digital libraries are a natural extension of the evolution in which libraries have been involved for centuries. They represent a fundamental leap forward in the provision of services for, and the partnership with, information communities.

REFERENCES

Abbas, J. (1997). The library profession and the Internet: Implications and scenarios for change. *Katharine Sharp Review, 5.* Retrieved May 10, 2010, from http://mirrored.ukoln.ac.uk/lis-journals/review/review/5/abbas.pdf

Ackerman, M. S. (1994). Providing social interaction in the digital library. *Digital Libraries '94 (Proceedings).* Retrieved May 10, 2010, from http://www.csdl.tamu.edu/DL94/position/ackerman.html

Arms, W. Y. (1997, February). An architecture for information in digital libraries. *D-Lib Magazine.* Retrieved October 2002 from the web http://www.dlib.org/dlib/february97/cnri/02arms2.html

ARL. Association of Research Libraries. (1995). *Definition and purposes of a digital library.* Retrieved July 2002 from the Web http://sunsite.berkeley.edu/ARL/definition.html

Baohua, W., Xiaoyan, M., & Fei, G. (2002). *On the characteristics of the digital library and the influence to the work of reader service*. Retrieved August 2004 from the web http://www.jsai.or.jp/afita/afita-conf/2002/part7/p529.pdf.

Brewer, A., et al. (1996). The role of intermediary services in emerging virtual libraries. In *Proceedings of the International Conference on Distal Libraries*. New York: Association for Computing Machinery.

Chen, C.-C., & Kiernan, K. (2002). *Report of the DELOS-NSF Working Group on Digital imagery for significant cultural and historical materials*. Retrieved July 22, 2004, from the world wide web http://dli2.nsf.gov/internationalprojects/working_group_reports/digital_imagery.html

Chowdhury, C. G., & Chowdhury, S. (2003). *Introduction to digital libraries*. London: Facet Publishing.

Cleveland, G. (1998). *Digital libraries: Definitions, issues and challenges*. The Hague: Universal Dataflow and Telecommunications Core Programme, International Federation of Library Associations and Institutions. UDT Occasional Papers #8.

Collier, M. (1997). Towards a general theory of the digital library. In *Proc. of the International Symposium on Research, Development and Practice in Digital Libraries: ISDL'97, Japan*. Retrieved August 2002 from the web http://www.dl.ulis.ac.jp/ISDL97/proceedings/

Corcoran, M. (2003). *The hybrid library: Revolution or evolution. Overview of the hybrid library*. Retrieved December 2003, from the web http://lirgroup.heanet.ie/events/Lirseminar140203_files/TextOnly/document.html

Crawford, W., & Gorman, M. (1995). *Future libraries: Dreams, madness and reality*. Chicago: American Library Association.

Dennis, N. (n.d.). *Technology infrastructure supporting digital library developments*. Retrieved May 10, 2010, from http://www.unm.edu/~jreenen/dlbook/chapter6.html

Dowlin, K. (1984). *The electronic library: The promise and the process*. New York & London: Neal-Schuman Publishers.

Fox, E., Akscyn, R., Furuta, R., & Leggett, J. (1995). Digital libraries: Introduction. *Communications of the ACM, 38*(4), 22–28.

Friend, F. (1995). Economic models for electronic libraries. In A. Helal & J. Weiss (Eds.), *Electronic documents and information: From preservation to access* (Vol. 18). Essen, Germany: Publications of Essen University Library.

Gapen, G. (1993). The virtual library: Knowledge, society and the librarian. In L. Saunders (Ed.), *The virtual library: Visions and realities*. Westport, CT: Meckler.

Harter, S. (1997). Scholarly communication and the digital library: Problems and issues. *Journal of Digital Information, 1*(1). Retrieved August 2003, from http://jodi.ecs.soton.ac.uk/Articles/v01/i01/Harter/

Hayes, R. (n.d.). *The economics of digital libraries*. Los Angeles: University of California. Retrieved August 2007, from the web http://www.sibi.usp.br/sibi/crescer/economics_2.html

Kranich, N. (1999). *Digital libraries: Building a bridge to the 21st century*. Retrieved August 2003, from the web http://www.txla.org/pubs/tlj_3/diglibs.html

Licklider, J. C. R. (1965). *Libraries of the future*. Cambridge, MA: M.I.T. Press.

Lynch, C., & Garcia-Molina, H. (1995). *Interoperability, scaling, and the digital libraries research Agenda: A report on the May 18–19*. 1995 IITA Digital Libraries Workshop. Retrieved August 2002, from http://www-diglib.stanford.edu/diglib/pub/reports/iita-dlw/main.html

Magnussen, A. (2003). *Creating digital libraries: A model for digital library development*. Retrieved December 2003, from the web conferences.alia.org.au/shllc2003/papers/008.pdf

Matson, L., & Bonski, D. J. (1997, November). Do digital libraries need librarians? An experiential dialogue. *Online Magazine, 21*(6). Retrieved August 2002, from the World Wide web: http://www.onlineinc.com/onlinemag/NovOL97/matsonl1.html

McCray, A., & Gallagher, M. (2001). Principles for digital library development. *Communications of the ACM, 44*(5), 48–54.

Meadow, C. (1988, October). Back to the future: Rethinking the database industry timeline. *Database, 11*(14–16).

Missingham, R. (2003). *What makes libraries relevant in the 21st century? Measuring digital collections from three perspectives*. Retrieved September 2004, from the world wide web http://conferences.alia.org.au/online2003/papers/missingham.html

Mukaiyama, H. (1997). *Technical aspect of next generation digital library project.* Retrieved August 2002, from the web http://www.dl.ulis.ac.jp/ISDL97/proceedings/hiro/hiro.html

Neal, J. (1998, October 25–28). Electronic publishing and the future of library resource sharing. In *Proceedings of the international conference on new missions of academic libraries in the 21st century, Peking University* (pp. 35–60). Beijing, China: Peking University Press.

Nunberg, G. (1993). The places of books in the age of electronic reproduction. *Representations, 42*, 13–37.

Ram, S., Park, J., & Lee, D. (1999). Digital libraries for the next millennium: Challenges and research directions. *Information Systems Frontiers, 1*(1), 75–94.

Ranganathan, S. R. (1931). *The five laws of library science.* Madras: The Madras Library Association.

Schauder, D. (1994). Development of the e-library concept, with special reference to Australian libraries'. *Australian Library Review, 11*(1), 5–30.

Sun Microsystems. (2002). *Digital library technology trends.* Retrieved August 2003, from the web http://www.sun.com/products-n-solutions/ edu/whitepapers/pdf/digital_library_trends.pdf

Thornton, G. A. (2000). Impact of electronic resources on collection development, the roles of librarians, and library consortia. *Library Trends, 48*(4), 842–856.

Twidale, M. (1995). *How to study and design for collaborative browsing in the digital library.* A paper presented at the 37th Allerton Park Institute of the Graduate School of Library and Information Science. Retrieved August 2002, from the World Wide Web http://edfu.lis.uiuc.edu/allerton/95/twidale.html

Twidale, M. (1996). *Supporting the users of the digital library.* A paper presented at the Allerton Park Institute of the Graduate School of Library and Information Science. Retrieved August 2002, from the World Wide Web: http://edfu.lis.uiuc.edu/allerton/96/s2

Twidale, M., Nichols, D., & Paice, C. (1996). *Browsing is a collaborative process.* Technical Report – CSEG/1/96. Computing Department, Lancaster University. Retrieved July 1998, from the World Wide Web: http://www. comp.lancs.ac.uk/computing/research/cseg/projects/ariadne/docs/bcp.html

Twidale, M., Nichols, D., & Paice, C. (1997). *Recommendation and usage in the digital library.* Technical Report - CSEG/2/97 (1997), Computing Department, Lancaster University. Retrieved December 2007 from http://www.comp.lancs.ac.uk/computing/research/cseg/projects/ariadne/docs/recommend.html

Walters, D. (1998). What are digital libraries? *CLIR Issues, 4* (July/Aug). Retrieved July, 2002, from the world wide web http://www.clir.org/pubs/issues/issues04.html

White, G. W., & Crawford, G. A. (1998). Cost-benefit analysis of electronic information. A case study. *College & Research Libraries, 59*(6), 503–510.

M. Paul Pandian
Institute of Mathematical Sciences, India

RUTH RIKOWSKI

4. DIGITISATION

Research, Sophisticated Search Engines, Evaluation – All that and More

INTRODUCTION

This chapter leads on from my other chapter in this book, 'Digital Libraries and Digitisation: an overview and critique' (Chapter 2), which explored topics such as traditional, digital, hybrid and virtual libraries and different digital library projects on a global basis.

In the last decade there has been substantial research and development in the digitisation field, including projects such as Google, the Handle System, the Dublin Core and the Open Archives Initiative Protocol for Metadata Harvesting. Google, through its Google Print programme, for example, is involved in digitising research library collections.

All types of material are now being digitised, including books, journals, manuscripts, theses and images. In regard to the commercial sector, publishers are increasingly digitising their own material; there are also initiatives such as Eighteenth Century Collections Online and Early English Books Online. As Lagoze et al say we are in the 'adolescence of digital libraries'; also that within this there is both optimism and concern. Whilst this has all been very exciting and offers a wealth of new possibilities there have also been concerns. Pearson (2001) argues that people worry about the pace of change and the problems of digital preservation, for example, and whether the e-texts of today will be readable in 10 years time. The costs involved in having to constantly change and update technology are considerable.

Yet, whilst digital libraries are a relatively new phenomenon on the landscape, their make-up is already undergoing change. Crane (2006) considers how digital libraries have changed the overall map. First of all, Crane refers to the changing *scale* and the fact that so many more volumes and vast quantities of content can be contained in digital libraries. The largest academic digital libraries, such as *The Making of America*, for example, include tens of thousands of books, whereas *Google Library* is on a completely different scale, and has over 10 million items. Secondly, as digital collections have developed and expanded, organising principles have been established, resulting in fairly coherent, if not homogeneous, content. There is likely to be a continued need for improvement in organising principles and standards in the future, as digitisation broadens and deepens. Pearson makes the point that there is the problem of the absence of any agreed national strategy for decision making for digitisation, whilst Lazoge et al say that:

> ...with increasing amounts of rich information born in digital form and stored in institutional repositories, we still lack standard, scalable techniques for fully preserving that information. (Lazoge, 2005, pp. 1–2)

R. Rikowski (ed.), Digitisation Perspectives, 65–86.

Yet at the same time some important digital library standards have been developed through publishers, bibliographic utilities etc. Thirdly, Crane points out that over the last few years, there has been a move away from single catalogue entries with a few hundred words, to thousands of tagged objects, which he refers to as the 'granularity of objects'.

Subscription versus open access is another issue. Some digital collections support open access, but most depend on at least some subscriptions. Google, Yahoo and Microsoft use both models. They have an open access distribution model with advertising, whilst premium services are available by subscription. E-journals differ in their subscription policies. The refereed ejournal *Policy Futures in Education* (http://www.*wwwords*.co.uk/pfie/) charges a small subscription, for example, (although all articles become freely available after 18 months) whilst the ejournal *Information for Social Change* (http://www.libr.org/isc/) is free.

This chapter will focus on a number of areas in regard to digitisation, such as some of the research that has been undertaken; the use of sophisticated search engines within digital libraries; the development of digital libraries for the scientific communities in China and valuing and evaluating digitisation projects.

DIGITAL LIBRARY RESEARCH AND DEVELOPMENT

Research and development is continually being undertaken on digital libraries and digitisation. Choudhury and Choudhury (2003) look at some of these trends, and pinpoint some areas that need further attention.

A lot of funding has been given to digital libraries in the last decade. Choudhury and Choudhury argue that we are now in a position where the ordinary person, as well as the academic and researcher, can benefit from digitisation. They are of the opinion that digital libraries can overcome the barriers of language and geographical distance and that:

> Digital libraries will also have a tremendous impact on the information industry, affecting the information generators, publishers and distributors, and information service providers. (Choudhury and Choudhury, 2003, p. 294)

However, there have not been so many studies on the use and impact of digital libraries on specific sections of society. One exception here has been the research that has been undertaken on the impact of Alexandria Digital Library on undergraduate students.

Various people and organisations though have undertaken research on the topic of the digital divide specifically. This is a serious problem for those in the developing world, who struggle to obtain electricity, never mind using technology for sophisticated projects. There is also optimism though, and Shimmon (2000) is of the opinion that, despite the problems, digital libraries can help to bridge the digital divide. He says:

> ...information, knowledge and works of imagination are increasingly available throughout the world. Electronic transmission and delivery is faster than we could have imagined even a few years ago. It can also be significantly

> cheaper than traditional methods. The signs of hope are discernible. Just as governments in the West have begun to realise the need for public access, as well as private and corporate access, in order to bridge the digital divide in their own countries, so the G8 leaders have realised there needs to be similar initiatives to tackle the digital divide between the North and the South. And remarkably, just as some governments have, belatedly, realised that libraries can play an important role in this area in their own countries, so libraries may help in the rest of the world. (Shimmon, 2000, p. 5)

As Choudhury and Choudhury say, the success of digital libraries will depend on how well we can meet the information needs and search behaviour of users. However, they think that in the future, there might be a greater need for a personalised information service.

Meanwhile, as they say, the second generation of digital libraries will raise new issues. This will involve providing training and documentation, including best practice for digital library use; testing query templates and knowledge and information-based approaches in digital libraries and tracing and investigating techniques of expert information problem-solving processes.

Choudhury and Choudhury say that there is little evidence that digital libraries save money over printed libraries. Instead, it could even be more expensive. Researchers have proposed various models for calculating the costs for digitisation. Hopefully, though, providing a good information service can and will override cost considerations.

They also highlight the fact that digital libraries can play a key role in knowledge management in an organisation. And digitised reference services can and are being set up (see for example, Jia Liu's chapter in this book, 'Digital Library and Digital Reference Service'). However, digital libraries are not properly integrated yet and one might still have to use a number of different digital libraries to obtain the necessary information on a given topic.

As Choudhury and Choudhury conclude, digital library research is progressing well overall and there has been a lot of involvement from large organisations, universities, research institutions and businesses. Furthermore, that:

> ...at this fast rate of research and development the creation of a global digital library system no longer seems to be merely a lofty but unachievable goal. (Choudhury and Choudhury, 2003, p. 307)

RESEARCH ON DIGITISATION AT LOUGHBOROUGH UNIVERSITY, 2005

Many bodies in the UK are involved with, undertake research on and take a particular view on, digitisation; these include organisations such as the British Library, the Research Councils UK, the Museum and Archives Council and JISC - UK Joint Information Systems Committee which is a committee of UK Higher and Further Education Funding Councils (I examined JISC in my other chapter in this book).

Higher Education Funding Councils have been set up by joint subcommittees to deal with certain issues. This includes JISC, which provides a world-class infrastructure that develops programmes for the community and provides and encourages innovation. Then there is the Information Environment, which provides a platform for access to digital content for learning, teaching and research. There are also various government-funded activities, such as the Core e-Science Programme, which encourages e-science.

In 2005 JISC and the Consortium of University Research Libraries (CURL) commissioned Loughborough University to undertake a study into the current state of digitisation in the UK, (Loughborough University Study, 2006). The report charted where we have come from historically and argued that there is a need for strengthened coordination between different interested parties. A UK e-Content Strategy was to be formulated with a Digitisation Framework being a part of this. This would then become part of the EU framework, contributing to the EU e-Content programmes on Digital Libraries 2010 proposal.

The Loughborough University research found that although there was now considerable digitised material in the UK there was no UK register to map and chart individual digitisation projects. Furthermore, outsourcing was often chosen because of the apparent lack of expertise, equipment, resources and staffing on site. This meant that it could be somewhat difficult to keep accurate and up-to-date records of digitisation projects and digitised material in the UK.

A single access point to the range of services offering guidance on standards was recommended. It was thought that this would encourage interoperability and sustainability and that funders would benefit.

This important study drew attention to the fact that there was a lack of co-ordination among all the different parts of the digitisation process; which can be seen to be another clear failing arising from capitalism. A need for more coordination, cooperation, standardisation and clear procedures and strategies is clearly needed to ensure that digitisation progresses in a favourable way in the future, and so that ordinary people, as well as academics and researchers etc, can benefit from the programmes.

RESEARCH ON DIGITISATION IN HIGHER EDUCATION: THE ELIB INITIATIVE

Much important and worthwhile research has been undertaken on digitisation in higher education. This section reports on some of the main findings, as outlined by Whitelaw, Joy and Burke (2000) and Whitelaw and Joy (2000) of Phase 1 and 2 of the ELib Initiative, which was completed in 1998 by the JISC/JCEI (JISC Committee for Electronic Information) Evaluation Group, with funding provided by JISC. The research followed on and developed out of the Follett Report, which was published in December 1993 (see Follett Report, 1993; and Ratcliffe, 1996). The aim was to implement the IT recommendations from the Follett Report, within the context of the changing nature of libraries within higher education. The Follett Report attempted to:

> ...identify and address some of the problems faced by university libraries, particularly given the new universities created in 1992. (Graham, und., p. 1)

Leading on from this, there was also a Phase 3 of the eLib initiative in 1998, and that will also be considered briefly.

As Whitelaw and Joy (2000) report there were a number of objectives in the first 2 phases of the study. Firstly, to produce a high level survey of digitized material, both already available and in process of being created, that is held in UK research collections and then to identify the gaps in provision. Secondly to identify and prioritise future digitisation projects. Thirdly, to explore and review the existing and potential funding structures. Fourthly, to make some recommendations for standards and formats for digitisation projects in the future. Fifthly, to provide an outline action for a national digitisation strategy for the UK research community.

Whitelaw and Joy (2000) report on the findings of the primary research of this study. A web-survey was conducted, focusing on past, current and future digitisation projects, reasons for and against digitisation and experience of in-house and outsourced digitization and collaborative efforts. 47 institutions responded, including major research libraries and archives in the UK. 36 in-depth interviews were also conducted with representatives of different research disciplines and stakeholder groups. This included members of JISC and CURL; representatives of institutions with digitisation experience; three UK National Libraries and the National Archives of UK and Scotland, publishers; support services and scholarly societies.

Respondents were asked about their current and past digitisation activities. Two thirds had engaged in some type of digitisation activities. Many enjoyed the improved access that was made available through digitisation and reduced handling was also seen to be very beneficial. Whilst building 'virtual' collections were seen to be less important. Still images and manuscripts was the material that was most frequently digitised.

However, some of the institutions had not been involved in digitisation. The main reason for not digitising was a general lack of resources, mainly funding, but also equipment and expertise. Copyright restrictions and low priority were other reasons given.

All those researched approached digitisation in different ways. Some organisations formulated and responded to strategies and criteria when deciding what to digitise, whilst others digitised according to market need. For some organisations it was linked with funding opportunities and availability, cost, resources requirements and type of resources required. It is easier to apply for funding for some material, such as for fragile, rare and unique material.

In regard to the selection criteria for digitisation, relevance to the aims and objectives of the institution was considered to be very important and got a high response rate. Uniqueness or rarity was also a frequent response, as was demand and existence of coherent collections.

Commercial companies usually charge for access to their digitised material. Three main publisher charging models were identified in the study. Firstly, payment of a lump sum for general access (subscription). Secondly: payment on a usage basis, either by payment per view, or by payment per download. Thirdly, paying to own content (outright purchase). 21 provided free-access, whilst 11 provided fee-based access.

There are also different charging models. The National Archives of Scotland, for example, allows free viewing of their digitized wills, but charge for downloads.

Interviewees in general thought that collection management was the responsibility of the institution that hosted the digitised material. Good project management was seen to be vital for any digitization project and the need to add value to digitised resources was also considered to be important.

In regard to preservation, the Association of Research Libraries endorsed the production of digital surrogates as a method of preserving non-digital material. Digital preservation requires technical strategies and a sound supporting infrastructure. Technical strategies include migration and emulation. Having standards can help with preservation.

> The aim of emulation is to retain the look, feel and functionality of digital information through the use of software that allows new technological platforms to mimic the behaviour of older technology platforms. (Whitelaw and Joy, 2000)

Respondents were asked about their future digitisation plans. A large majority of institutions (41) had material that they thought ought to be digitised. This was for a variety of reasons, such as value for teaching and research; uniqueness/rarity; cultural heritage and access.

Studies on the costing of digitisation projects have looked at areas such as documentation and preparation; human resources; equipment and ongoing maintenance. 38 respondents outlined their funding sources and just under half combined external and internal funding.

> Many stressed that without significant external funding, digitization and the management of those digitized resources would not be possible. (Whitelaw and Joy, 2000, p. 117)

There has been some collaboration between higher education institutions, libraries, museums, archives, learned societies and trusts. There has been a lot of cooperative activity in Scotland, such as the Glasgow Digital Library, which is a co-operative hub for a number of Scottish libraries. There is also the Scottish Cultural Resources Access Network, which is a charity that is mainly financed by the Scottish Executive. It is a service for libraries and schools in Scotland and provides educational access to digital materials on Scottish material culture and history.

Most interviewees thought that there would be more digitisation in the future. Some are already preparing for this, such as by creating suitable posts, ring-fencing funding and having policies and strategies to deal with future digitisation. Interviewees were concerned about the lack of an overall strategy for digitisation in the UK. As one interviewee remarked:

> …you're actually saying that we want to shape what people are doing whereas I'm saying that at the moment we don't even know what they're doing…

Most thought digitisation activities should be more coordinated, but did not agree on how this should be done. It was thought that a UK-wide strategy could be beneficial and help to fill gaps in provision, reduce cross-overs between support services and assist with the use of open-access resources. It was also suggested that organisations such as the Research Information Network and JISC could lead a national strategy.

Priorities for future digitisation included looking further at rare, vulnerable and valuable material and that these collections should be investigated by organisations such as CURL, JISC and the Research Information Network. Metadata was considered to be a very necessary but expensive part of the digitisation process. Whitelaw and Joy (2000) noted that digitisers need guidance on long-term management and preservation and it was thought that the Digital Curation Centre could help in this regard.

Not surprisingly, the study found that a lack of funding was a major deterrent to digitisation. Whilst the Google initiative:

> ... has the potential not only to facilitate the digitization of library materials for libraries, but for the existence of the digitized material to become easily discoverable through Google services. (Whitelaw and Joy, 2000, p. 121)

However, as interviewees said, this will only be effective if material is digitised to an acceptable standard and if appropriate metadata is created.

Whitelaw and Joy (2001) also produced a final report summary of Phase 3 of the eLib Initiative project, which took place in 1998. They said that Phase 3:

> ...has had an important impact on HE libraries by accelerating the uptake of new technologies in a practical, user service oriented way. It has broadened horizons by exploring a range of approaches. By supporting the continuation of work in on-demand publishing and e-journal production, Phase 3 has also impacted broader communities. (Whitelaw and Joy, 2001, p. 14)

Meanwhile, Elizabeth Graham remarked that, taken as a whole the Phase 3 project:

> ...can be seen as an attempt to assimilate the knowledge gained from earlier phases of eLib and the wider community to build exemplar digital libraries for the future. (Graham, 1999, p. 1)

Four strands were identified in Phase 3: support for early projects aiming to become services; hybrid libraries; large scale resource discovery or 'clumps' and digital preservation.

In conclusion, with this eLibrary Initiative a valuable study was undertaken on digitisation in higher education and some important findings emerged. In particular, the importance of collaborative work and standardisation was recognised. Furthermore, there was an appreciation of the value to be gained from improved access with digitisation in higher education and reduced handling requirements resulting from digitisation. Other areas explored included strategies for digital preservation, the costing of digital projects and priorities for digitisation. Leading on from the eLibrary Initiative, the eLib Programme Office continued to work with JCEI (JISC Committee for Electronic Information) in order to develop a long-term strategy for dealing with digital material.

ELECTRONIC THESES

In my other chapter (Ch. 2) in this book I look at ebooks. In this chapter I will look briefly at e-theses (this obviously being a crucial part of the digitisation of higher education), as an example of the digitisation of certain type of material, drawing on the work of Copeland, Milner and Penman (2005).

Over the last 10 years many dissertations and theses in the UK have been transformed into electronic formats. The University Theses Online Group in the 1990s said that further developmental work was needed to encourage universities to focus more on electronic PhDs and this is now happening.

In 2002, Joint Information Systems Committee (JISC) provided funding for developmental work on digitisation as part of the 'Focus on Access to Institutional Resources' (FAIR) program. 3 of these 14 projects looked at electronic theses specifically. These were the 'Electronic Theses' project led by The Robert Gordon University, 'Theses Alive' at the University of Edinburgh and the 'Daedalus' project at the University of Glasgow.

Initially, the electronic theses project was funded for a 2-year period (from July 2002) with the aim of:

> Evaluating a wide range of existing practices of e-theses production, management and use against a set of criteria in order to produce models for use within the UK information environment (Copeland, Milner and Penman, 2005).

Then, further funding became available in 2003–4 to develop e-theses in a service environment. This included catering for the needs of an independent repository as well as a broader Virtual Research Environment.

The project set out:

> To evaluate a comprehensive selection of methods which are used to create, store, organise, manage and access e-theses (Copeland, Milner and Penman, 2005).

A number of organisations were investigated and different emerging technologies were examined.

As Copeland, Milner and Penman point out, in order to create electronic theses many established methods within higher education had to be challenged and changed. A cultural change had to be achieved, which involved some advocacy work and training, and the undertaking of necessary change management procedures. People had to be prepared to accept the theses in this new and different format – and recognise that the works were just as scholarly and academic as bound, hard-copy theses were.

It was recommended that advocacy work should be targeted at sections of the academic community including academics, researchers, students, administrators and librarians and that their different interests should be considered. As Copeland, Milner and Penman point out students might, for example, be pleased with the flexibility offered by the e-thesis and the opportunity to present their findings in a different way. Researchers, on the other hand, are likely to consider access as being very important; particularly immediate access with full content and rich information. In contrast, senior administrators might value the increased publicity, whilst librarians want to be able to provide a good service.

All three of the JISC projects have been involved with legal and organisational matters, thesis submission procedures and copyright issues and these are all available and updated on the project websites.

In conclusion, a lot of work has been undertaken on the development of e-theses over the last few years. For more detail on this, see Susan Copeland's chapter in this book, entitled 'Electronic Theses and Dissertations: promoting 'hidden' research'.

'GOOGLISATION', DIGITAL LIBRARIES AND INFORMATION

Moving on then, how can we effectively search for information in these complex digital libraries? 'Googlisation' is a very fashionable term today. Those of us in the IT world are 'googlised'; indeed, 'over-googlised' it seems. With 'googlisation' there is often an assumption that Google has solved, or will solve, everything information search-wise. Mostafa refers to the importance of Google, saying that:

> In less than a decade, Internet search engines have completely changed how people gather information. No longer must we run to a library to look up something, rather we can pull up documents with just a few clicks on a keyboard. Now… "Googling" has become synonymous with doing research. (Mostafa, 2005)

However, whilst Google provides good search and access facilities, digital libraries are clearly a lot more than just that. They can also respond more effectively to the communities they serve; not being hampered by the constraints imposed by a physical library, and users can have their own input. Material can be organised in specific ways and more sophisticated searches can also be undertaken.

Yet, others talk with alarm about the ever-increasing power of Google and the issues and problems around the 'Google Generation'. Tara Brabazon is one author who is quite critical in this regard. She says that Google encourages laziness, poor scholarship and 'compliant thinking' (Brabazon, 2007, p. 15). Furthermore, the Google mentality can have damaging effects on students:

> There is an ideology that learning mediated through computers improves social access to education because of the resultant flexibility. Actually, disconnecting students from the university, assuming that technological applications will intrinsically provide the platform for learning, discredits libraries and librarians. (Brabazon, 2007, p. 100)

Bell (2004) interestingly uses the term 'infobesity' to describe the way students now search for information, rather like consumption of fast food; a 'junk information' diet. Bell argues that students tend to want information quickly, but that they are not often concerned with quality.

Of course, Google is also involved with large digitisation programmes itself (for example, the important work being done on the Google Library Book Project – see http://books.google.com/googlebooks/library.html and Google Print Programme – see http://www.aaupnet.org/aboutup/issues/gprint.html.)

One wonders where the future of Google will lie, especially as recently it has a new (and potentially powerful rival) to contend with at www.bing.com, developed and powered by Microsoft. At present though, Google is still a leader in the search engine field. Thus, for now, I think we would do well to use and build on Google for effective digitisation projects.

SEARCH ENGINE TECHNOLOGY, DIGITISATION AND MOVING BEYOND SIMPLE 'SEARCH AND ACCESS'

As already stated, Google provides simple search and access facilities, but we also now need more sophisticated search and access search engines. This becomes ever more necessary as digitisation advances and becomes more complex. There have been a number of different initiatives here. Some of these initiatives are outlined in this section, along with some comparisons with Google.

Summann and Lossau describe the creation of a modern search-engined-based search environment. From the successful project 'Digital Library NRW' (1998–2000) which was conducted with Bielefeld University Library, Summann and Lossau designed a system model for an Internet-based library portal with an improved academic search environment. Various academic search engines were considered along with the suitable software products. Convera was the preferred search engine. By June 2004, approximately 600,000 documents had been captured and distributed in 15 collections.

Meanwhile, Brophy and Bawden (2005) conducted a study which compared Google with appropriate library database systems and assessed the strengths and weaknesses of the two systems. A case study approach was used and there were four studies in all. It was limited to the type of queries that are likely to be used by university students.

It was found that Google was better for coverage and accessibility, whilst the library systems were better for the quality of the results. Precision was similar for both the systems. So, it seems that ideally both systems are needed. The findings provided guidance for those giving support and training for the use of these systems.

Meanwhile, Xie (2004) compared online database systems Dialog and Factiva with three different types of web search tools - a search engine, a directory and a meta-search engine. The students were asked to search the same two topics on each system and give relevance scores to a total of 20 relevant documents. The study involved 4 test queries, which were analysed in detail by a single expert searcher. A case study method was used and both quantitative and qualitative data were collected. There were open-ended 'research based' questions, on four general subject areas – environmental science, music, education and law. No restrictions were placed on the number of searches for each session. Four issues were addressed in analysing the results: quality, relevance, accessibility of documents retrieved and coverage of these documents in the systems tested.

Altogether 723 documents were retrieved over all searches for the 4 test queries. Of these, 237 were from Google and 163 from library systems were considered relevant. The results indicated that neither system consistently provided a more precise set of results. 52% of Google results were found to be good quality, whilst library systems were 84%. Google provided immediate access to over 90% of its relevant results.

It was found that search engines and library databases complement each other. Google was found to be better for both coverage and accessibility, whilst library databases were better for the quality of results and precision was similar for both systems. Improving the skills of the searcher is likely to give better results from the library system, but not from Google.

The main conclusions from Xis's survey are that with Google a high proportion of relevant and precise documents can be retrieved; there are a high proportion of good quality results and unique documents and there are no major problems with accessibility. In regard to library databases, a moderate proportion of relevant documents can be retrieved; there is the ability to retrieve a fairly precise set of documents; there are a high proportion of good quality results and unique documents, but some problems with accessibility.

In conclusion, library systems were seen to be better for quality but Google was better for accessibility and coverage. Furthermore, it was discovered that accessibility was largely favoured over quality by students. The overall conclusion was that ideally the systems should merge, taking the best features of both.

In addition, Lagoze, Krafft, Payette and Jesuroga (2005) outline an 'information model for digital libraries' that moves 'beyond search and access'. The model includes 'search and access' but also the creation of collaborative and contextual knowledge and information environments. They say that the dynamic interplay of information within the context of digital libraries can then be more fully appreciated.

For this to take effect there needs to be an 'information network overlay', argue Lagoze et al. They say that the digital library in this context can be viewed as a

> ...graph of typed nodes, corresponding to information units (documents, data, services, agents) within the library and semantic edges representing contextual relationships among those units. (Lagoze et al, 2005, p. 3)

Furthermore, this information model brings together local and distributed information with web services, and rich documents such as learning objects can then be created. The model:

> ...expresses the complex relationships among information objects, agents, services and meta-information (such as ontologies) and thereby represents information resources in context, rather than as the result of stand-alone web access. (Lagoze et al, 2005, p. 3)

However, the resources in a digital library are not always easy to characterise; is an e-book a book or a piece of software, for example? Is information always either metadata or data? Thus, the early digital library work formulated the idea of 'digital objects', which are

> ...packages of information with multiple disseminations available through service requests. (Lagoze et al, 2005, p. 9)

Digital library systems usually implement these digital objects by using standards such as complex object containers that encapsulates the metadata and data streams associated with a digital object.

Lagoze et al say that their work at the National Science Digital Library (NSDL):

> ...has demonstrated that the familiar metadata-based model is not sufficient for this type of functionality. We have designed and implemented an information network overlay within Fedora, which includes the full functionality of the existing metadata repository, but models relationships, services, and multiple information types within a web-service based application. This rich information store will provide the basis for the next stage of work, implementing an expanding suite of user-visible library services that fulfil the "laboratory for sharing and building knowledge" envisioned in the original NSDL report. (Lagoze et al, 2005, p. 16)

So, the 'information network overlay' provides an additional layer of functionality and a far richer digital library environment for the National Science Digital Library. Such models can usefully be applied to some other digital libraries.

To conclude, as Lagoze et al note, digital libraries are more than just web search engines. They add value to web resources and this:

> ...consists of establishing context around those resources, enriching them with new information and relationships that express the usage patterns and knowledge of the library community. The digital library then becomes a context for information collaboration and accumulation – much more than just a place to find information and access it. (Lagoze, Krafft and Payette, 2005, p. 16)

DATA MINING LARGE DIGITAL COLLECTIONS AND APPLICATIONS PROGRAMMING INTERFACES

Extracting relevant information from large digital collections is also challenging. Cohen (2006) considers the data mining of large digital collections, and the use of effective search engines. This can be undertaken by computational methods, enabling patterns to be found and documents to be categorised.

Cohen explored how to provide such end-user tools. Application Programming Interfaces (APIs) were examined, which are the leading search engines enabling programmers to query their databases directly.

Cohen experimented with how one might build a specialized search engine for finding course materials on the web. Cohen chose to use 'keyword-in-context indexing' (KWIC) to develop this, leading to the Syllabus Finder (for document classification). The Syllabus Finder, which Cohen built himself, can also be useful for open-access reference material in the future. Cohen says that:

> These resources can be leveraged to better scan, sort, and mine other digital collections that are unwieldy because of their scale or lack of metadata. (Cohen, 2006, p. 4)

Furthermore, that:

> Beyond suggesting the power of using search APIs to retrieve relevant documents and subject them to further automated analysis or combine them with sources retrieved from other locations simultaneously, the Syllabus Finder also suggests an important role in the future for open-access reference materials and corpora. (Cohen, 2006, p. 4)

Cohen used an experimental tool called 'H-Bot', which is an automated historical fact finder. H-Bot accepts natural language queries about historical events etc., and uses a series of data-mining techniques to try to answer them. Thus:

> The Syllabus Finder and H-Bot, like the Web from which they extract information, may be imperfect, but they show what can be done by stitching together and processing digital collections using server-to-server communications and programming algorithms. (Cohen, 2006, p. 8)

Cohen's early experience of building these digital tools enabled him to learn three important lessons. First, that whilst computer scientists have been using these APIs since the 1960s, these APIs can now be usefully applied to more digital collections in general. As Cohen says:

> ...APIs hold great promise as a method for combining and manipulating various digital resources and tools in a free-form and patent way. (Cohen, 2006, p. 8)

APIs are still much more common in the commercial world, such as the APIs provided by Google and Yahoo. Users of APIs often take digital resources or tools in directions quite unthought of by their owners and Cohen says that:

> New resources based on APIs appear weekly, some of them hinting at new methods for digital research, data visualization techniques, and novel ways to data-mine texts and synthesize knowledge. (Cohen, 2006, p. 8)

Secondly, resources that are free to use, even if they are imperfect, are more valuable than those that are user-restricted. Thirdly, quantity may make up for a lack of quality. Cohen says that:

> ...high-quality digitization and thorough text markup may be attractive for those creating digital collections, but a familiarity with information theory and data-mining techniques makes one realize that it may be more worthwhile to digitize a greater number of books or documents at a lower standard for the same cost. (Cohen, 2006, p. 9)

Thus, in essence, these important tools can help us to extract relevant information from large digital collections.

MASSIVE DIGITAL LIBRARY PROJECTS AND THE 'EVOLVING RECORD OF HUMANITY'

How is it best to handle large and expensive digital libraries specifically? Crane and Jones (2006) have written a complex but interesting article, entitled

'Text, Information, Knowledge and the Evolving Record of Humanity'. Their focus is on massive and expensive digital libraries and they make a number of useful recommendations.

Firstly, they say that massive and expensive digital libraries should allocate some of their budgets to analyses of printed reference materials. Secondly, that we need more publications designed for machine as well as human readers. Within this, we need, for example, traditional specialists such as in palaeography, the study of earlier forms of handwriting in manuscripts. Crane and Jones say these specialists need to produce knowledge whereby document recognition systems can understand more about the content, text, graphics and layout of the collections. Thirdly, domain specialists are needed that can understand relevant areas of computer science and can critically assess and evaluate emerging technologies. Within this, it is necessary to consider whether it is best to augment the new technologies with the existing tools or develop new tools. Fourthly, various bodies and people such as computer scientists and internet powers such as Google, Yahoo and MSN, academics, researchers and librarians should develop relationships with broader communities. In this way, structured knowledge and information can be created and developed in order to manage and expand these vast collections. Crane and Jones conclude by saying that:

> Massive digital libraries, embodying much of the published record of humanity, can provide the structured data that we need to build increasingly sophisticated services, that grow more able to provide us with the information that we need not only to increase our productivity but to learn and to grow intellectually. (Crane and Jones, 2006, p. 11)

These then are all worthwhile aims for massive digital library projects in the future.

THE DEVELOPMENT OF DIGITAL LIBRARIES FOR THE SCIENTIFIC COMMUNITIES IN CHINA

It is important to be mindful of the fact that digitisation develops at varying paces with varying emphases on issues in different countries and within different communities. Leburn Rose and Dieu Hack-Polay consider digitisation in Africa in their chapters in this book. In this section, I will consider digitisation in China, focusing specifically on the Chinese scientific community, drawing on the work of Zhang Xiaolin in this area.

Xiaolin (2006) considers sustainable digital library development for scientific communities in China. Xiaolin explores the challenges toward sustainable digital libraries and presents a development strategy for digital libraries using the Chinese Academy of Sciences as an example.

Xiaolin says that digital library development in China can be grouped into two main groups – local digital library projects and national specialised digital library systems and programs. Local digital projects have produced rich digital cultural materials, whilst national programmes have made digital information resources more readily available, especially for scientific research and educational institutions.

Since the late 1990s several national digital library initiatives have been undergone. These include the Chinese Science Digital Library, started in 2001 by the Chinese Academy of Sciences as a digital information service serving its 91 research institutions across the country. CSdigital library provides full text scientific, technical and medical journals, conference proceedings, theses and dissertations, patents, reference books and e-books. Meanwhile, the CSdigital library has 4,000 core western journals and 10,000 Chinese journals. The Chinese Academic Library and Information System was first funded in 1998 by the Ministry of Education to organise a digital library consortium amongst academic libraries.

There is also the National Science and Technology Library. This was established in 2000 by the Ministry of Science and Technology. It is a virtual, national reserve library and consists of 7 special libraries from the basic sciences, agricultural sciences, medical sciences, and engineering. It is also a supply centre for scientific information. Furthermore, its whole collection of foreign and Chinese materials serves as a back-up system for all libraries in China.

Xiaolin points out that resources and information in digital form are the main information resource for many scientific users today. Furthermore, the preferred way of accessing information for scientific users is often through networks and collaborative work. Many physical libraries are now being integrated into virtual digital information systems and are now the first entry point for many scientific users. As Xiaolin says:

> While this trend has created a far more effective information space for scientific users and has provided libraries with great accessibility power, it also presents a revolutionary transformation of the information environment and of the ways in which libraries define themselves and operate their services. (Xiaolin, 2006, p. 141)

Xiaolin argues that there are two main challenges to sustaining and developing library services in China. Firstly, there is the need to try to ensure that the digital library also serves traditional information needs. Secondly, there is the need to move beyond the traditional library approach, and to support new user needs in new e-science environments. Digital preservation also requires new system infrastructures and financial support.

Xiaolin argues that in order to sustain the change, there needs to be new models of digital libraries. He notes that:

> E-science or cyber-infrastructure creates a networked infrastructure rich in data grids, computing grids, digital libraries, and collaboratories. (Xialin, 2006, p. 142)

Furthermore, that science is based increasingly on interactive virtual knowledge-networked communities. The scholarly community in general is changing in various ways with Google Scholar/Print, the open access movement, institutional repositories etc. Xiaolin says that they are all creating a new information supply chain.

However, Xiaolin says that the digital library is still modelled on the traditional library in many ways, but that this is rather limiting. Rather:

> Digital libraries need to be re-designed as integral parts of users' knowledge work environments instead of as stand-alones or add-on extras. (Xiaolin, 2006, p. 142)

Challenging and exciting times, indeed then, for the scientific community in China!

THE VALUE OF DIGITAL PRESERVATION

The decision-makers in regard to digitisation projects need to be convinced of the value and worthiness of these projects if meaningful progress is to be made. Within this context, Currall (2006) examines valuing intangibles within the context of digital preservation. This section considers his work in this area.

Currall focuses on 'information as thing' (Buckland's term, 1991) and information objects. Information objects convey some sort of information or representation of knowledge, used in everyday situations. Currall thinks this provides a valid description of what we think information-rich organisations deal with.

He argues that organisations need to retain assets in the long term and that we need to convince:

> ...senior managers and decision makers of the value of their digital objects in order that the objects' retention is not only embedded in their strategic management rhetoric, but is also acted upon and given consistent and long-term resources. (Currall, 2006, p. 2)

Currall asks how we can communicate the value of information objects to decision-makers and says that decision-makers often do not understand what assets they have.

Meanwhile, Lavoie (2004) says that preservation should be seen to be an investment and that decision-makers need to realise this. Tangible benefits for such an investment include profits whilst intangible benefits include aspects such as more kudos and the reduction of risk.

A project 'Espida' was undertaken at the University of Glasgow in 2006, with funding from JISC. It explored how intangible assets might be valued so that a sound business case can be made to try to ensure the longevity of information objects for sustainable digital preservation in the long-term. Three aspects were seen as being particularly important: the value of assets; the technological fragility of digital assets and the need for sustained support to ensure that the asset can be preserved.

Espida acts as an intermediary between information creators and managers. Methodology and tools created through Espida can also be applied to other higher and further education institutions and information-rich organisations.

Placing a value on information is very complex and the value of assets is often hidden, Currall says. He argues that:

> We wish to express the value of these assets in clear business terms whilst not reducing everything to a purely financial expression. (Currall, 2006, p. 4)

Currall proposes using a model to assess the value to an organisation of its information objects. This model is in four principle dimensions and these dimensions have some similarity to the Balanced Scorecard of Kaplan and Norton (2001).

> The four dimensions force a detailed analysis of what value information objects bring to the customers and external stakeholders, how the objects benefit the advancement of employees (including their well-being and personal development), what value the object brings to the workings of an organisation (in particular efficiency and effectiveness) and finally, the financial value through cost savings or income that the object can bring. (Currall, 2006, p. 4)

The four dimensions are Customer and External Stakeholders, Internal Business Process, Innovation and Development and Financial. Each dimension has many different elements, and in order to understand value as a whole, there is a need to identify all these elements, argues Currall. Furthermore, it is suggested that object creators and information professionals can help in this regard.

The methodology allows for the expression of value of many forms of objects, not just those in digital form. Hence, this adaptation of the balance score card can be of assistance to a lot of organisations that need to understand the value of their assets, in Currall's view. Currall indicates that:

> Problematically, value is a concept that is not absolute and therefore demands flexibility. How exactly do you measure the value that a digital asset brings to the Intellectual Capital within the University? (Number of academic papers? Research rating? Financial value of grants and contracts? (Currall, 2006, p. 6)

There is also the need to consider value-over-time and to remember that value is not static:

> Value is not constant. It does not remain static, nor indeed does it keep the same dimensions and elements. (Currall, 2006, p. 6)

Hence, the model needs to explore what happens to the value of different asset types over time.

Currall concludes by saying that digital preservation is an investment decision, and that benefits need to be weighed against costs. Also that Espida looked at the nature of the benefits and that returns can be other than financial. The role of risk is also important. The process of valuing information in general is complex:

> The task that espida is undertaking will be of relevance to people who need to be able to understand or communicate the value of information objects. This ability to communicate unlocks a number of doors: information creators will be able to rationalise expenditure on representations of intangible assets far more readily, and the methodology can be used to make lucid and strong business cases to decision makers about intangible objects and values. (Currall, 2006, p. 8)

Currall says that the model can be used to argue the case for sustainable resources and in this way to ensure the longevity of digital assets. Furthermore, that how this is taken forward can led to either the destruction of objects, or ensure their longevity. All these are interesting ideas, I think, but obviously need to be explored and examined in a lot more depth. Nevertheless, they help us to focus on the importance of endeavouring to convince others of the value of digitisation and digital preservation projects.

EVALUATION OF DIGITISATION PROJECTS

Leading on from this analysis of valuing information objects for the purpose of digital preservation, this section briefly considers evaluating the worth of digital material in general. Two initiatives are referred to here. Firstly, the 'Digital Libraries Initiative, Phase 2' which involved the evaluation of digital material by the National Science Foundation, the National Library of Medicine and the Library of Congress. This digital libraries research:

> …is faced with the challenge of applying increasing computational capacity and network bandwidth to manage and bring coherence, usability, and accessibility to very large amounts of distributed complex data and transform it into information and knowledge. (Digital Libraries Initiative, 1999, pp. 16–17)

Secondly, Bollen, Luce, Vemulapalli and Xu (2003) looked at how a methodology was applied to derive weighted journal relationship networks from reader logs at Los Alamos National Laboratory's Research Library from 1998–2001. This information can help digital library managers to assess and evaluate which parts of their digital collections are most highly valued by the local community. Research trends in user communities as they evolve over time can also be established. Bollen et al conclude by saying that:

> We have demonstrated a methodology to detect and interpret the nature of localized research trends as they occur in an institution by analyzing usage patterns derived from the institution's DL usage logs and comparing these to the ISI IF. (Bollen, Luce, Vemulapalli and Xu, 2003) (ISI IF = Institute for Scientific Indexing Impact Factors)

Continued evaluation of digitisation projects, including consultation with users, is clearly very important for the overall and long-term success of digitisation.

A 'VIEWPOINT ANALYSIS' OF THE DIGITAL LIBRARY

In this final section, I consider Arms (2005) 'viewpoint analysis' of the digital library. Arms asks whether digital libraries should be encouraged to develop independently or together. He suggests that in order to answer this question a 'viewpoint analysis' can be adopted, which is a technique which was developed in software development. The idea is to identify various stakeholders in a system and view the system from each of their viewpoints.

Arms looks at digital libraries from three different viewpoints – the organisational view, the technical view and the view of the user. From an organisational viewpoint the world consists of many separate digital libraries; but from the user's viewpoint the distinction is less clear, Arms says.

Before computers, the focus was mainly on the organisational viewpoint, argues Arms. Whereas with the technical viewpoint, the term *interoperability* describes the technical methods needed to combine services from discrete libraries. Arms makes the point that:

> Interoperability research assumes that there are many digital libraries: the challenge is how to encourage collaboration among independent digital libraries with differing missions and resources. (Arms, 2005, p. 3)

There has been impressive progress in the technical areas, such as with mark-up languages, metadata standards, harvesting protocols, and identifiers.

However, there has been less progress in turning digital libraries into a single digital library from the user's viewpoint. From the user's viewpoint, the technology is irrelevant and organisations are of secondary importance.

> A user who wishes to do serious work using online information will find that superficially similar services have deep semantic differences. Web search engines emphasize precision of the highly ranked hits, while scientific information services emphasize recall. Library gateways attempt to give coherence to the collections and services offered, but the underlying systems are so different that the gateway is only a veneer. (Arms, 2005, p. 4)

Arms argues that there is a need to rethink evaluation. The standard way to evaluate a digital library is to give a group of users a set of tasks to carry out within the library. This is evaluation from a system or organisational viewpoint. User testing does not usually take a holistic viewpoint, starting with the user. In evaluating the National Science Digital Library for science education, for example, a holistic evaluation would centre on a user (such as a science teacher preparing a course) and observe all the tools a person uses. But the requirements that are developed from the technical or organisational viewpoint, might not recognise the user's viewpoint.

> The Internet is truly disruptive technology, yet requirements developed from an organizational viewpoint tend to assume continuity of existing organisations, not disruption. (Arms, 2005, p. 4)

Arms concludes by saying that:

> Perhaps now is the time for digital libraries to strive for…. a single Digital Library. (Arms, 2005, p. 4)

Such an aim, the 'single Digital Library' is clearly bringing the user's viewpoint much more to the forefront. Thus, the basic point is that more attention should be given to the user's viewpoint. But how realistic is that in reality? The whole point of digitisation is surely to benefit the user. Or is it? On the surface it seems to be, but at a deeper level it is being driven forward by profits and the need to sustain and develop capitalism itself, rather than the wants and needs of users. This is why the organisational and technical viewpoints seem to be more powerful, but this is something that the user can obviously challenge.

CONCLUSION

In conclusion, this chapter has considered a number of different areas of digitisation, including digital library research and development; research on digitisation in higher education; e-theses; googlisation; sophisticated search engines; digital library development for scientific communities in China; the value of digital preservation; the evaluation of digitisation projects; policies and searching facilities within massive and expensive digital libraries and a viewpoint analysis of the digital library.

A number of threads have emerged. This has included the need for more and better standardisation procedures; the need for more cooperation and coordination; the importance of valuing digital preservation; the benefits to be gained from using sophisticated search engines; the pace of change and the increasing reliance on digitisation in the Chinese scientific communities and how to effectively handle and search large and expensive digital libraries.

Clearly, digitisation is here to stay and is developing and progressing at quite a pace. It is all very exciting. Within this, though, there are various concerns and issues. One such concern is whether the e-texts of today will be readable in a few years time (given the pace of change in the technologies); another is how to convince some decision-makers of the value to be gained from digital preservation. Yet another is the digital divide, particularly in regard to the developing world which consistently lags behind the developed world in regard to I.T. in general, as well as the difficulties they experience with moving forward digitisation projects, in particular.

The chapter closes with a focus on Arms 'viewpoint analysis', as I wanted to end on a note where the user was placed centre-stage (the 'user's viewpoint'). This is probably romantic (given the powerful and all-pervading nature of capitalism), but still – why should we just accept this? Within this frame of mind, I am also reminded of the beauty of art, music and literature which, if approached in a certain way, can take us somewhat beyond the narrow confines of the political scene. And of course, digital preservation plays an invaluable role here, enabling many more to enjoy great works of art (see for example, Nikolova-Houston and Houston's chapter in this book on 'Building the Virtual Scriptorium'). Let us aim then to focus on and enjoy the benefits and wonder that digitisation can bring us, in all of its many aspects and complexities.

REFERENCES

Arms, W. Y. (2005). A viewpoint analysis of the digital library. *D-Lib Magazine, 11*(7/8). Retrieved May 3, 2009, from http://www.dlib.org/dlib/july05/arms/07arms.html

Bell, S. (2004). The infodiet: How libraries can offer an appetizing alternative to Google. *The Chronicle of Higher Education, 50*(24), 815. Retrieved May 3, 2009, from http://chronicle.com/weekly/v50/i24/24b01501.htm

Bollen, J., Luce, R., Vemulapalli, S. S., & Xu, W. (2003, May). Usage analysis for the identification of research trends in digital libraries. *D-Lib Magazine, 9*(5). Retrieved May 3, 2009, from http://www.dlib.org/dlib/may03/bollen/05bollen.html

Brabazon, T. (2007). *The University of Google: Education in the [post] information age*. Hampshire: Ashgate Publishing.

Brophy, J., & Dawden, D. (2005). Is Google enough? Comparison of an internet search engine with academic library resources. *Aslib Proceedings, 57*(6), 498–512. Retrieved May 3, 2009, from http://www.emeraldinsight.com/Insight/viewContentItem.do;jsessionid=945A04D42B2654FC6F27BAE89581FE14?contentType=Article&hdAction=lnkhtml&contentId=1529375

Buckland, M. (1991). Information as thing. *Journal of the American Society for Information Science, 42*(5), 351–360. Retrieved May 3, 2009, from http://people.ischool.berkeley.edu/~buckland/digdoc.html

Choudhury, G. G., & Choudbury, S. (2003). *Introduction to digital libraries.* London: Facet.

Cohen, D. (2006, March). From babel to knowledge. *D-Lib Magazine, 12*(3). Retrieved May 3, 2009, from http://www.dlib.org/dlib/march06/cohen/03cohen.html

Copeland, S., Milne, R., & Penman, A. (2005, April). Electronic theses: A JISC 'FAIR' project. *Relay: The Journal of the University College and Research Group of CILIP, 57,* 13–19.

Crane, G. (2006). What do you do with a million books? *D-Lib Magazine, 12*(3). Retrieved May 3, 2009, from http://www.dlib.org/dlib/march06/crane/03crane.html

Crane, G., & Jones, A. (2006, March). Text, information, knowledge and the evolving record of humanity. *D-Lib Magazine, 12*(3). Retrieved May 3, 2009, from http://www.dlib.org/dlib/march06/jones/03jones.html

Currall, J. (2006, April). Investing in value: A perspective on digital preservation. *D-Lib Magazine, 12*(4). Retrieved May 3, 2009, from http://www.dlib.org/dlib/april06/mckinney/04mckinney.html

Digital Libraries Initiative, Phase 2. (1999). Retrieved May 3, 2009, from http://www.nsf.gov/pubs/1998/nsf9863/nsf9863.htm

Follett Report. (1993). Chapter 1: Summary of conclusions. *The Follet Report.* Retrieved May 3, 2009, from http://www.ukoln.ac.uk/services/papers/follett/report/ch1.html

Graham, E. (1999). *eLib: The UK Electronic Libraries Programme.* Retrieved May 3, 2009, from http://www.exploit-lib.org/issue3/elib/index.html

Kaplan, R., & Norton, D. (2001). *The strategy-focused organization. How balanced scorecard companies thrive in the new business environment.* Boston: Harvard Business School.

Lagoze, C., Krafft, D., Payette, S., & Jesuroga, S. (2005, November). What is a digital library anymore, anyway? *D-Lib Magazine, 11*(11). Retrieved May 3, 2009, from http://www.dlib.org/dlib/November05/lagoze/11lagoze.html

Lavoie, B. (2004). Of mice and memory: economically sustainable preservation for the twenty-first century. In *Access in the future tense.* Washingto, DC: Council on Library and Information Resources.

Loughborough University Study. (2006). *Digitisation in the UK – the case for a UK framework.* A report based on the Loughborough University study on Digitised Content in the UK Research Libraries and Archives Sector commissioned by JISC. Full study can be found at: www.jisc.ac.uk/digitisation (accessed 2007)

Mostafa, J. (2005). Seeking better web searches. *Scientific Amazon, 290*(2), 51–7.

Pearson, D. (2001). Digitisation: Do we have a strategy? *Ariadne, 30.* Retrieved May 3, 2009, from http://www.ariadne.ac.uk/issue30/digilib/

Ratcliffe, F. (1996, July). The Follett report: A blueprint for library/information provision in British universities. *The Reference Librarian, 25*(54). http://www.informaworld.com/smpp/content~content=a904835773~db=all~order=page

Shimmon, R. (2000). *From digital divide to digital opportunity.* UNESCO. Retrieved May 3, 2009, from http://209.85.129.132/search?q=cache:lirwBWkVh4YJ:www.unesco.org/webworld/points_of_views/shimmon.shtml+ross+shimmon+and+digital+divide&cd=2&hl=en&ct=clnk&gl=uk&ie=UTF-8

Summann, F., & Lossau, N. (2004, September). Search engine technology and digital libraries: Moving from theory to practice. *D-Lib Magazine, 10*(9). Retrieved May 3, 2009, from http://www. dlib.org/dlib/september04/lossau/09lossau.html

Whitelaw, A., & Joy, G. (2000). *Summative evaluation of phase 1 and 2 of the eLib Initiative: Final report,* details. Retrieved May 3, 2009, from http://www.emeraldinsight.com/Insight/manulDocumentRequest.do?hdAction=ref_document_request&r_contentId=0&r_atitle=&r_jtitle=Summative%20Evaluation%20of%20Phases%20One%20and%20Two%20of%20the%20eLib%20Initiative:%20Final

%20Report&r_issn=&r_year=2000&r_volume=&r_issue=&r_startpage=&r_endpage=&r_publisher=ESYS%20plc&r_authors=Whitelaw,%20A.,%20Joy,%20G

Whitelaw, A., Joy, G., & Burke, N. (2000). *Summative evaluation of phases 1 and 2 of the eLib initiative: Overview*. Prepared for the JISC/JCEI Evaluation Group. Retrieved May 3, 2009, from http://209.85.129.132/search?q=cache:80rmozOH4ywJ:www.ukoln.ac.uk/services/elib/info-projects/phase-1-and-2-evaluation/overview.pdf+JISC/JCEI+Evaluation+Group+summative+evaluation+of+phases+1+and+2+of+the+elib+initiative+overview&cd=2&hl=en&ct=clnk&gl=uk&ie=UTF-8

Whitelaw, A., & Joy, G. (2001). *Summative evaluation of Phase 3 of the eLib initiative: final report and summary*. Retrieved May 3, 2009, from http://209.85.129.132/search?q=cache:LVVkyuY9ot8J:www.ukoln.ac.uk/services/elib/papers/other/summative-phase-3/elib-eval-summary.pdf+summative+evalution+of+phase+3+of+eLib+Initiative:+final+report+summary+2001&cd=1&hl=en&ct=clnk&gl=uk&ie=UTF-8

Xiaolin, Z. (2006). Sustainable digital library development for scientific communities in China. *IFLA Journal, 32*(2), 140–146. Retrieved May 3, 2009, from http://ifl.sagepub.com/cgi/content/abstract/32/2/140

Xie, H. (Iris). (2004). Online IR system evaluation: Online databases versus web search engines. *Online Information Review, 28*(3). Retrieved May 3, 2009, from http://www.emeraldinsight.com/Insight/viewContentItem.do?contentType=Article&hdAction=lnkpdf&contentId=862254

Ruth Rikowski
Chandos Publishing, Oxford

PART II:
DIGITISATION AND HIGHER EDUCATION

ALAN ROSLING AND KATHRYN LITTLEMORE

5. IMPROVING STUDENT MENTAL MODELS IN A NEW UNIVERSITY INFORMATION SETTING

INTRODUCTION

Changes within the structure, culture and emphasis of Higher Education within the UK have had a direct impact upon the roles of librarians and information specialists. We are no longer 'just' librarians. We are seen as another source of information, support and guidance in relation to assessment and research. We are now teachers, with teaching qualifications and busy teaching schedules. This status begs certain questions though in the digital age: How well are our students able to make use of the digital resources we provide, and how, as teachers, do we in fact teach information literacy skills in the digital setting? This chapter will outline the culture and ethos at the University of Northampton and the nature of the students that we encounter directly and indirectly. We will also seek to link together issues surrounding information literacy, how librarians teach and the mental models that students have in relation to digital libraries and online research. A greater understanding of mental models by librarians will further inform our teaching and ultimately improve the learning of students, and hence, their experiences within the digital library.

The University of Northampton was awarded the title 'University' in 2005 and with it the powers to award research degrees. Although it is a 'new university' the institution was founded in 1924 and has a rich history of serving diverse students from technical, education and arts backgrounds. This is reflected today with a large and successful School of Education and excellent arts-based courses. The university is also a world leader in areas such as Waste Management and Leather Technology (The University of Northampton, 2008). The School of Health is also a large school bringing in much needed funding via contracts to train professionals in Nursing, Midwifery, Podiatry, Occupational Therapy, Paramedic Science and Social Work. The School provides courses for undergraduate and postgraduate students. Within the realm of health this means students pre and post registration, which the university trains to become registered nurses. The University trains registered nurses within particular professional areas such as cancer care, palliative care and nurse prescribing. It educates health professionals who have been absent from the profession and trains overseas professionals so that they can practice in the UK. Therefore, every type of student is catered for: young and older, pre and post registration, home and overseas students, from all ethnic backgrounds, with a variety of expectations and skills sets. In essence, we could be at any 'new' university in the UK dealing with all these different variables, and the issues we deal with on a daily basis are typical of the sector.

R. Rikowski (ed.), Digitisation Perspectives, 89–101.

The University of Northampton is the only higher education provider within Northamptonshire and in 2006/07 36.7% of all 1st year students were mature students (HESA, 2008). These figures reflect the type of student that is attracted to courses provided by the School of Health. There is no stereotypical student, the age range, background, ethnic group and experience of each student is very different. Many of our students live locally, have families of their own and have had other careers before embarking upon their course within healthcare. At first glance, it could be said that mental models of digital libraries could be very different for a student who is 18 years old and grew up with the Internet, mobile phones and uses social networking sites regularly, compared to a mature student who may not use PCs or the Internet very much, or very confidently. In fact some students we encounter have never even sent an email. These differences in our students present the first and most difficult challenge we have when teaching information literacy. How can you teach a class of 20 students how to utilise digital libraries when they all have different mental models, levels of IT skills and expectations? A good understanding of mental models would be a beneficial place to start and would help to supplement and inform more standard teaching activity in the information literacy context.

The final issue that needs to be outlined is the type of teaching we undertake. We often only see students a couple of times for formal teaching per academic year and typically they will receive the following instruction from a librarian during their time as a student: induction, referencing, lecture and workshop, literature search (how to access online and hard copy resources), dissertation session (preparation in terms of information sources for their dissertation) and one-to-one (tutorial) sessions. This is usually the average amount of contact time but does not include the student seeking help within the library from other staff. It can be seen that the authors have limited time to assess the student's awareness of digital libraries, how they perceive them, what their expectations are and their skills in utilising such sources. The range of experience that the authors have though places them in a good position to explore the use of mental models by these students. The other issue to highlight in terms of formal information literacy teaching is that we are not usually briefed on the students that are about to enter our lecture theatre or seminar room. We often have to think on our feet, assess the nature and skills of the students in front of us and tailor the teaching sessions to suit changing situations.

The profile of the type of students encountered by the authors does seem to contradict the apparent notion of the 'Google Generation' student that is so currently popular in academia, and indeed, the media as a whole. In order to understand the mental models of students, it is initially helpful to understand ideas around the 'Google Generation' mythology. A clearer understanding of students digital literacy will help us make sense of the mental model theories around the use of (and our teaching of the use of) digital resources.

THE GOOGLE GENERATION

The term 'Google Generation' is something that has become very fashionable within academia; it has been discussed in detail within research projects such as CIBER (2007).

The concept is also something that has been popular within the media, and also commented on by Dr Tara Brabazon in her comments about Google as a whole. Brabazon's views of how current students utilise Google and information on the Internet have attracted much comment. She refers to Google as 'white bread for the mind' (Frean, 2008, p. 8). Brabazon also discusses the influence of Wikipedia and how students cannot differentiate between good quality information and more suspect sources. Finally, Brabazon champions the role of the librarian, she states that librarians have a crucial role in ensuring that students of today and tomorrow can access digital libraries and evaluate the information they find there. To become scholars, they need libraries and librarians (The Times Higher Education Supplement, 2008). However, for the concept to add weight to our observations and experiences of health students what do we actually mean by the Google Generation? Is there an agreed consensus on what the terms means and if so, can it help us mould and inform our teaching?

Anyone born after 1993 could be described as being a member of the Google Generation (CIBER, 2007); but the influence of changing technology has also impacted on Generation X, and, more so, on Generation Y. The younger students going to university now, though strictly not of that post-1993 generation, show a lot of the characteristics of the Google Generation. So what is so special about them and the 'Google Generation'? What makes them different from students who have gone before? Well, ultimately they have grown up with widespread access to technology; the personal computer was invented before they were born; SMS messaging is the norm and an email account is an accepted way of life. From this description you would expect these students to be digital savvy, in fact they are often referred to as 'Digital Natives'. The label 'Google Generation' implies that these individuals have a natural affinity with anything online or digital, that they are completely comfortable with existing and new technologies, and hence, their mental models of digital resources are well developed – and easily translated into digital libraries. Is this a fair and realistic assessment of students? Some students we encounter have a degree of 'digital savvy-ness' about them. They are confident in using computers and accessing databases, but this could be on a very superficial level. The question is do they actually find what they are looking for? Surely, this measurement is the way to assess whether they are indeed digital natives and that they have well developed mental models.

The CIBER (2007) report discusses the assumption that young people are 'technologically savvy' but more importantly it goes on to say that there is no hard evidence that they are experts at accessing and searching the databases or digital libraries. The CIBER team state there is no indication that search skills have improved over time as technology has developed and people have become more used to accessing digital resources. These findings are supported from some research undertaken within the Department of Information Services at the University of Northampton. The Social Networking Survey is conducted once a year, during the induction period at the start of the academic year. This project started in 2007 and the hope is that the survey will, over time, build up a picture of the changing nature of students entering Higher Education in the UK in terms of social networking.

In 2008, 262 first year students took part in the survey and they were asked questions about their understanding, use of and views on SMS text messaging, email, blogs, podcasts; Wikis; social networking sites such as Facebook and MySpace; Second Life, online games and online forums.

The results, Table 1, show that SMS text messaging and email are the most popular forms of communication with 91.2% using SMS text messaging and 98.08% using email. However, other forms of social networking were known about but not utilised quite so readily. For example, only 21.46% read blogs and only 9.3% read and contributed to a blog. 81.23% of the students surveyed used Facebook. It seems that these young people do utilise digital technology but for socialising and communicating with others. It can be seen that these skills are not translated into their academic research. It could be asserted that those who use these resources regularly would have well developed mental models of digital resources. On the other hand, the authors feel that the 'Google effect' can have negative connotations: these students expect instant gratification. If the information they need is not located within one search then they are not content and do not want to make further searches. The authors have asked several students whether they know how search results within Google are ranked and we have not come across one student that knew the correct answer. Secondly, they make significant use of Google Scholar, without sometimes exploring the digital (and expensive) resources available to them from the University via their Athens authenticated accounts. This involves too much effort; they have been spoilt by this 'now' culture where one click is all they can manage. These students still in fact do need the teaching offered by librarians across the sector.

Table 1. Results of social networking survey of 1st Year undergraduates at the University of Northampton 2007 & 2008

Online Tools/Usage	*2007 Usage (%)*	*2008 Usage (%)*
SMA Text Messaging	87%	92.1%
Online 'real time'	98.4%	98.08%
Online Forums	36.7%	32%
Blogs	Read: 16.2% Read/Write: 7.9%	Read: 21.6% Read/Write: 3.92%
Podcasts	8.4%	13.14%
Wikis	Read: 54.5% Read/Write: 7.9%	Read: 66.27% Read/Write: 3.92%
Facebook	59.7%	81.23%
MySpace	50.3%	46.2%
Second Life	1.1%	2.48%
Online Games	18%	18%

Source: Department of Information Services, the University of Northampton, 2008.

INFORMATION LITERACY

Information literacy is one of the key skills that students are expected to acquire through a University experience (Virkus, 2003). Particularly in the digital age when information is so ubiquitous and accessible yet so very often lacking any academic credibility or usability. Over recent years definitions of information literacy have been useful for librarians in helping them think about how to teach information literacy and how to create lesson plans with relevant and meaningful learning objectives. Models of information literacy have also been helpful (SCONUL Advisory Committee on Information Literacy, 1999) in establishing 'levels' or steps in the acquisition of information literacy skills and thereby helping to break down learning into objectives to address these levels. For many librarians the overall span and challenge of this activity can prove daunting as actual student teaching and contact time can be short and the acquisition of more expert skills sometimes a lengthy process. The commitment of academic librarians to the teaching of these skills has meant that a range of local online skills packages have been created or sector products utilised which supplement the classroom teaching or can be used on their own (Intute, 2007). These digital packages can be the tutor 'proxy' but can sometimes be seen as unattractive tools to busy students who want to complete course work to strict deadlines.

It would appear, though, that any further insight into the student's understanding of digital information use might further facilitate better tutor understanding and practice of the use of information. Many students actually seem unable (or unwilling) to progress up the information literacy ladder and instead appear to languish on the bottom rungs with little or no change in information literacy skills. The reasons for this could be myriad but may centre on their lack of information technology literacy, inexperience with browser software and poorly developed cognitive skills. One of the other key reasons may be that students have poor mental models of the digital information world (how the internet works, how databases work, how searching works), which the 'normal' teaching they receive fails to change or improve. Mental models are tantalising, they appear to offer something extra for the tutor. They allow the tutor to feel that if they can change mental models, they can improve learning. It would also initially appear that mental models somehow link with the notion of deeper learning and of the engaged student. If with better mental models and information literacy skills the student can find better information more quickly and evaluate it more precisely, then synthesis and knowledge creation will be the inevitable result.

MENTAL MODELS AND THE USER

A further explanation of mental models would be helpful at this stage. Mental model theories are well established and used in many educational contexts, often in an attempt to improve learning. Craik (1943) was the first to describe them suggesting that they were 'small scale models' of reality. Later, Norman (1983) developed ideas around understanding the difference, as he saw it, between mental models and conceptual models. For him a 'mental model is what the user has in his or her mind and is not observable; a conceptual model is what is given to the user by a designer, trainer, or experimenter as an explanation for the system' (Borgman, 1999:436). Such distinctions are helpful in beginning to understand 'gaps' in understanding and to formulate questions about how we address those gaps. A definition by Doyle and Ford (1998) helps further explain the nature of mental models; 'a mental model of a dynamic system is relatively enduring and accessible, but limited, internal conceptual representation of an external system whose structure maintains the perceived structure of that system' (p. 17). Mental models are, importantly, dynamic with the potential to be changed, but also limited. They may only function at a 'minimal level' and may not even be accurate but can still be useful (Westbrook, 2006:565). Users will often not be aware of the efficacy, or the lack of efficacy, of their mental models, but rely on them nevertheless by necessity. Much of current research into mental models is also performed by industrial designers and psychologists. Human-Computer Interaction (HCI) is also an area where mental model research can help designers produce more useful computer interfaces. The importance of mental models in the learning context is suggested by Barker et al. (1998) who believe there are three basic roles that mental models perform: 'First, they control conventional dialogue processes (both with self and others). Second, they facilitate the use of technology-mediated communication ... third, they stimulate and guide teaching/learning processes ... towards the successful acquisition of skill and knowledge' (p. 312). All three functions can be seen as key in the librarians interaction with students as they attempt to acquire the skills and understanding associated with the use of digital technologies in an information-seeking context.

It is a truism, but nevertheless still worth stating, that the study and understanding of mental models in relation to information systems specifically is not easy. A review of the literature in this area reveals some ideas that need to be kept in mind if issues of digital information literacy are to be fully addressed. Initially it becomes obvious that as an unconscious process that affects behaviour, mental models are difficult to measure. Many studies use the methodology of asking subjects to draw diagrams of their mental models (Thatcher and Greyling, 1998; Westbrook, 2006; Papastergiou, 2005) and then add to this qualitative data. Subsequent results show 'classification' of mental models into hierarchies or schema that show differing positions or levels of mental model formation. Application of these results into the learning and teaching settings are not immediately apparent.

An obvious question would seem to be that if mental models are the users' internal representation of external information systems and processes then will not increased experience of using those systems naturally improve mental models? Thatcher and Greyling's (1998) research into mental models of the internet shows this to be a finding that is consistent with earlier research that shows experienced users have 'more detailed and complete mental models than inexperienced users' (p. 304). Yet they also find that some very experienced users still retained simple mental models of the Internet. Experience alone is not the magic key that will open the Internet treasure trove. It is also interesting to note that Westbrook (2006) confirms that there needs to be considerably more research into the formation of mental models by users. Westbrook (2006) cites a study by Von Hecher (2004), which showed that subjects with poor memories had difficulty in being able to form mental models, and had to fall back on strategies to use memory more successfully.

Another factor that makes mental models difficult to address in an information literacy context is that they can be difficult to change. Mental models can be 'comfortable' and if overly challenged in an unsupported environment students can easily be pushed into giving up and blaming the system for over-complication or themselves for lacking ability (the 'I'm no good with computers' response heard so often by tutors is simply reinforced). In challenging poor mental models as tutors we may be challenging deeper feelings or beliefs that the learner holds about them selves which simply cannot be addressed within the normal range of tutor-student learning interactions. The quality of teaching and ongoing support should, for some, mitigate against what may have become a learning pattern.

It is reassuring to know that in the one-stop-shop world of Google information searching that users' mental models of the library still include the librarian (Westbrook, 2006). Despite online access to a world of information, students still use the reference librarian for questions relating to their course information needs (whether it be using the library catalogue, online databases or the internet). It is perhaps more worrying that some librarians still hold onto the idea that we should be trying to turn users into replica librarians who can mimic the expert searching they use because they think it is the only way that works. Librarians have long lamented the poor search skills of students yet have often failed to find simple ways of assisting them. Library-centric training is one of the librarian's sins (Michell and Dewdney, 1998) but it may also be true that differences in tutor-student mental models are responsible for the ongoing gap between teacher and learner. We can audit our classes for experiences of which search engine they use but we cannot audit their mental models. What the librarian understands and is talking about can assume a shared mental model, which in fact does not exist. It may be the case that librarians have a model of the information (print and online) that is more conceptual (Michell and Dewdney, 1998) and are subsequently more able to navigate their way through more complex processes successfully. Teaching this conceptual approach is a real challenge.

It is also the case that inexperienced users of computers, Internet browsing software and bibliographic databases do in fact form utilitarian and simplistic mental models rather than 'structural mental models' (Papastergiou, 2005:356). Despite this study being performed with High School students the findings agree with other research on adults. This again goes counter to the idea that the Google generation have naturally more sophisticated skills and expertise in the digital world than mature learners. Younger students and mature adult learners harbour misconceptions about the Internet and how it works which will further limit their success in searching for information.

SEARCHING, THE INTERNET AND THE USER

So our user comes to their 'user education/information skills/information literacy' class bringing with them their past experiences and prior knowledge of computers and online searching and software. As they sit at the terminal they also bring with them their, often very incomplete, mental models of the information landscape, the Internet, how computers work and how they might search successfully. They will also have a belief about themselves as learners and differing degrees of motivation (an essay deadline will often help with this). They do not want to be turned into mini-librarians; they want information and they want it quickly (Amazon works quickly, online banking works quickly – why shouldn't the library systems?). They will also have feelings about what they are doing and the process as it unfolds. The affective domain is often an unremarked part of the information seeker's experience. Repeated failure to find what is being searched for can lead to frustration and eventual disengagement with the processes and services on offer.

For the mature university student with limited information technology (IT) skills the engagement with the world of IT and information can be an anxious experience. Many mature students that lack digital competence are often women and have significant gaps in their IT skills (Sutton, 2006). The Internet and its component parts can be disorientating. Hyperlinking by its nature disrupts the more linear processes of print resources and challenges cognition into making or understanding connections, which may not always be obvious. As Davies (2005) suggests 'searching is messy' and though librarians can teach searching by breaking down a search into its component parts (define the topic, brainstorm keywords, select information sources, search/refine and evaluate) the searchers actual experience of a search can often be more complex than this as the human-PC interaction evolves (back-tracking, re-searching, re-forming and the accompanying emotional reactions). In addition to this, things can go wrong with the computer, the software or the connection. Information 'blind-alleys' can be retraced to a previous page, or at worst the user's home page, but error messages, failing passwords, power problems and program crashes can leave users in a state of confusion. It is the equivalent of getting in the car to go shopping and not knowing if you are actually going to arrive at the shops.

For some users the internet is not seen as the vehicle for accessing rich sources of information but rather as an 'end in itself … consisting almost entirely of web sites' (Westbrook, 2006:571) the quality of which remain questionable. The user may 'envision' themselves in the searching process as 'active and decisive' but still 'shackled at times by internalised biases, assumptions, and knowledge limitations' (Westbrook, 2006:571). So the search environment is challenging and the process seen as one of 'deliberate focusing' (p. 572) that demands a degree of user flexibility and fluidity. Westbrook also found that though the librarian's friend, the bibliographic database, is core to academic information seeking, they were more 'part of the internet' and seen as a problematic part of the library experience (requiring user ID). How ironic that one of the key resources, in terms of financial outlay and promotion, supplied by academic libraries should be seen as problematic.

MENTAL MODELS AND INFORMATION LITERACY TEACHING

It would be too pessimistic to suggest that these problems with the digital information landscape and students mental models of that landscape mean searching is more often doomed to failure than success. Everyday students are completing challenging pieces of academic work based on good and timely research. Usage figures show full text journal articles do get downloaded in large numbers, that bibliographic databases are still popular and that often higher education libraries do get good value for money from the print and digital information sources they purchase. Having said that, it is equally true that we are living in the middle of a digital revolution and for many citizens of that revolution their involvement is fragmentary and stuttering. Students in higher education have a privileged foot on the digital information ladder, having as they do access to the hardware, software and knowledge sources of the age(s). Even the privileged few have differing levels of success in exploiting resources depending upon the complexity of their mental models and a range of other factors. The librarian too is learning the new skills required to work in the digital age, a time when the learner comes to them with pre-existing knowledge and skills associated with digital information provision. Librarians have in many instances grasped the nettle of online learning. Despite an initial lack of skills and an ongoing struggle with resource provision they have developed and produced a range of high quality online resources and reaffirmed their commitment to student learning and teaching in the digital age. What does mental model theory offer them though? In what ways can teaching be refined so that students use more resources, more quickly and find better information?

The first thing to do is to address the gaps in IT literacy (Brandt, 2001), particularly for older returners to higher education. Tutors can be faced with learners who do not have the skills to learn effectively in the digital environment. Yet the idea of testing for these skills on enrolment and addressing the gap seems a step too far for busy course managers who control curriculum time. Students are often left to find courses for themselves (on or off campus) or fall back on peer learning. The skills gap seems to remain hidden like a guilty secret no one wants to admit to or address.

Does the traditional librarian's approach of constructing a search strategy still work? Librarians do like to search whilst our students just want to find the information they need. There does remain at times a gap between what users need from librarians and what they are taught. Avoiding library-centric teaching methods and finding out more about how students search will help tutors make realistic changes to their teaching. Nadkarni (2003) looked at teaching methods related to mental models formation and found that students exposed to hybrid learning (a mix of experiential self-learning and lecture-discussion method) had more complex mental models post-teaching. Students were able to better identify issues and made 'comprehensive connections between key issues' (p. 347). The hybrid teaching method emphasises both the theoretical and practical aspects of learning, which is not something that library instruction can always do in the time allowed. Theory is often seen as distracting from the urgent process of hands-on practice.

Furuta (2000) also found that 'spontaneous descriptions' could impact on mental model development. If, in the classroom setting, students are encouraged to 'characterise what they see ... (it) may help them to gain deeper understanding' (p. 255). This involves what is called New Vocabulary (Furutua, 2000), but in educational terms may mean prompting students to characterise and interpret what they see in the information environment and thereby make links to their prior knowledge. This activity might be described as 'self feedback' and this points us again to a further way that the librarian can assist digital users. For many users a source of frustration when using computers programs is a lack of feedback. As Davies (2005:115) declares 'nobody tells you if you're doing it right'. Help pages may be useful but at many moments in a search process there is no feedback about doing things right or wrong. One of the key functions of any teacher is to appraise performance and to give feedback (Squires, 1994). Librarians can offer better ways of searching to novices by giving better and clearer guidance through varied feedback mechanisms.

Many commentators suggest that we do not have to understand how something works to make good use of it. You do not have to know how a car works to use it (though knowing that a flat tyre affects movement might suggest that you are not going anywhere). Twining (1995), Brandt (2003) and Papastergiou (2005) all suggest, for differing reasons, that some understanding of the underlying structure of the internet, how search engines index and understanding computer systems do relate to the development of mental models. Students without an understanding of the structure of the Internet will never fully understand an error message or slow connection speeds. Misconceptions about how search engines work will mean students fail to understand how results are ranked, that search algorithms are not 'neutral' or that other search engines might also be useful. This might be an area in teaching where librarians could work on online tutorials, which will serve as an addition to class-based teaching. Importantly an understanding of the physical structure of networking and connectivity of the Internet can be important in relation to information literacy. Many students with poorly formed mental models have the idea that the Internet is 'controlled' through a large central computer (Papastergiou, 2005). Such an idea reinforces unsound ideas about the origins and quality of information (it has some authority regardless of its origin). It helps information literacy if students realise that information has multiple points of origin and an associated quality (or lack of quality) related to those origins.

Librarians should wake up to the importance of emotional intelligence in the classroom (Mortiboys, 2005). Nahl and Tenepir (1996) found that when users questioned tutors in an information setting, 46% of the questions had an emotional content. Students are uncertain, nervous and need reassurance (Davies, 2005). Emotional intelligence is still in its infancy in library teaching terms but it is particularly pertinent in the digital searching environment. Davies (2005) also suggests strategies for students that go beyond the search strategy paradigm. To develop good mental models students should: 1) Play around with systems 2) Be more aware of unexpected results 3) Reflect more on practice and experience, and 4) Recycle, reduce, reuse and renew i.e. make use of experience in relationship to future tasks and so build more usable models of the digital environment (p. 143). The notion of play may seem strange to the busy tutor-librarian but a more relaxed and enjoyable set of learner activities (where mistakes are seen as less important) may indeed help mental model construction.

Makri et al's (2007:441) case study results show users as having 'impoverished…mental models' despite the subjects being MSc students on Library and

Information Science and Human-Computer Interaction courses with advanced training skills in search-related tasks. The research calls for better digital library design to facilitate richer mental models. On the teaching side they suggest providing search tips to help understand search engines. They suggest that users need support around formulating search queries, understanding results, making sense of document relevance, access rights and comparing systems. Failure to explore resources and an inability to interpret the outcome of exploration will result in limited development of more sophisticated mental models and search techniques.

CONCLUSIONS

It would appear that the authors' experience of working with students at the University of Northampton is very helpful in the current context of ideas around the Google Generation and how mental model research can aid information literacy skills. These ideas call for a holistic response, which will acknowledge the tripartite components of student success: IT literacy and information literacy under-pinned by contemporary teaching strategies based on mental model research. It is clear that the Google Generation's familiarity with digital technology gives them a degree of digital literacy but this does not translate into information literacy skills through a form of osmosis. It is also reassuring for librarians, who have felt under some threat from the apparent 'easy' internet search environment, that they are still needed to teach information literacy skills, and, just as importantly, seen as part of the student's mental models of the library.

The digital landscape requires more from the librarian than it did in the days of the print landscape. Teaching 'search strategy' skills is no longer adequate for the complex environment of the Internet and web-based search tools. Mental model research can help librarians to use more focused teaching strategies like encouraging students to explore (or even play), to target more sophisticated feedback towards specific digital problems (why searches fail, access rights, comparing systems). They may want to start finding simple ways of explaining how the Internet actually works (connectivity, networks) so that students can understand search engine results and the technical failings of the systems they use. Ensuring increasingly high levels of IT literacy will go a long way to underpinning all of this activity. None of this is easy though. To progress these ideas and further enhance classroom learning we must understand even more about user search behaviour in the digital environment, why and how they search, and how they feel about searching. If we can continue to use current mental model research to make even more sense of the student searching experience then we might establish even clearer learning strategies that will move learners further up the information literacy skills ladder.

REFERENCES

Barker, P., van Schaik, P., & Spencer, H. (1998). Mental models and lifelong learning. *IETI*, *35*(4), 310–318.

Borgman, C. L. (1999). The User's mental model of an information retrieval system: An experiment on a prototype online catalog. *International Journal of Human-Computer Studies*, *51*, 435–452.

Brandt, D. S. (2001). Information technology literacy: Task knowledge and mental models. *Library Trends, 50*(1), 73–86.

Brandt, D. S., & Uden, L. (2003). Insight into mental models of novice internet searchers. *Communications of the ATM, 46*(7), 133–136.

Centre for Information Behaviour and the Evaluation of Research (CIBER). (2007). *Information behaviour of the researcher of the future ('Google Generation' Project). [Online].* London: Centre for Information. Retrieved November 2008, 1, from http://www.ucl.ac.uk/slais/research/ciber/downloads/

Craik, K. (1943). *The nature of explanation.* Cambridge: Cambridge University Press.

Davies, C. (2005). *Finding and knowing: Psychology, information and computers.* London: Routledge.

Doyle, J., & Ford, D. (1998). Mental models concepts for system dynamics research. *System Dynamics Review, 14*(7).

Frean, A. (2008, January 14). White bread for young minds, says University Professor. *The Times (London)*, p. 8.

Furuta, T. (2000). The impact of generating spontaneous descriptions on mental model development. *Journal of Science Education and Technology, 9*(3), 247–256.

Higher Education Statistics Authority. (2008). *PIs 2006/07: Widening participation of under-represented groups (tables T1, T2.)* [Online]. Cheltenham: Higher Education Statistics Authority. Retrieved November 1, 2008, from http://www.hesa.ac.uk/index.php/content/view/1174/141/

Intute. (2007). *Intute Virtual Training Suite.* [Online]. Bristol: Intute. Retrieved November from http://www.vts.intute.ac.uk/

Makri, S., Blandford, A., Gow, J., Rimmer, J., Warwick, C., & Buchanan, G. (2007). A library or just another information source? A case study of users' mental models of traditional and digital libraries. *Journal of the American Society for Information Science and Technology, 58*(3), 433–445.

Michell, G., & Dewdney, P. (1998). Mental models theory. *Journal of Education for Library and Information Science, 39*(4), 275–281.

Mortiboys, A. (2005). *Teaching with emotional intelligence.* Abingdon: Routledge.

Nadkarni, S. (2003). Instructional methods and mental models of students: An empirical investigation. *Academy of Management Learning and Education, 2*(4), 335–351.

Nahl, D., & Tenopir, C. (1996). Affective and cognitive searching of novice end-users of a full-text database. *Journal of the American Society for Information Science, 47*(4), 276–286.

Norman, D. (1983). Some observations on mental models. In D. Gentner & A. Stevens (Eds.), *Mental models.* Hillsdale, MI: Lawrence Erlbaum Associates.

Papastergiou, M. (2005). Students' mental models of the internet and their didactical exploitation in informatics education. *Education and Information Technologies, 10*(4), 341–360.

SCONUL Advisory Committee on Information Literacy. (1999). *Briefing paper: Information skills in higher education.* [Online]. London: The Society of College, National and University Libraries. Retrieved November 4, 2008, from http://www.sconul.ac.uk/groups/information_literacy/papers/Seven_pillars2.pdf

Squires, G. (1994). *A new model of teaching and training.* Hull: Geoffrey Squires.

Sutton, C. (2006). Literacy, E-literacy and multiliteracies: Meeting the challenges of teaching online. In A. Martin & D. Madigan (Eds.), *Digital literacies for learning.* London: Facet Publishing.

Thatcher, A., & Greyling, M. (1998). Mental models of the internet. *International Journal of Industrial Ergonomics, 22*, 299–305.

The Times Higher Education Supplement. (2008, June 5). A google-eyed view of the world. *The Times Higher Education Supplement*, p. 25.

The University of Northampton. (2008). *History.* [Online]. Northampton: The University of Northampton. Retrieved November 1, 2008, from http://www.northampton.ac.uk/about/history/

Twining, P. (1995). Towards an understanding of the links between conceptual understanding of computer systems and information technology competence. *Journal of Information Technology for Teacher Education, 4*(3), 377–391.

Virkus, S. (2003). Information literacy in Europe: A literature review. *Information Research: An International Electronic Journal, 8*(4).

Von Hecker, U. (2004). Disambiguating a mental model: Influence of social context. *The Psychological Record*, *54*(1), 27. Cited in: Westbrook, L. (2006). Mental models: A theoretical overview and preliminary study. *Journal of Information Science*, *32*, 563–579.

Westbrook, L. (2006). Mental models: A theoretical overview and preliminary study. *Journal of Information Science*, *32*, 563–579.

Alan Rosling and Kathryn Littlemore
Department of Information Services
University of Northampton, UK

SUSAN COPELAND

6. ELECTRONIC THESES AND DISSERTATIONS

Promoting 'Hidden' Research

INTRODUCTION

Over the past ten years an increasing number of Higher Education Institutions (HEIs) and research-related organisations have been encouraging the submission of theses and dissertations in electronic format (Suleman et al., 2004). The creation of digital versions of such material began even earlier, as postgraduate students were quick to realise the advantages offered by word-processing packages and associated software. A survey of over 2000 PhD students, 1740 supervisors and 125 librarians undertaken in Great Britain by the 'UK Theses Online Group' (UTOG) in 1996 revealed that, even at this time, the majority of theses were produced using standard word-processing packages (Roberts, 1997). Responses to this questionnaire based survey indicated that most British students were positive about the idea of their thesis being made available on the Web although a significant proportion of supervisors expressed concerns. The results also indicated that most researchers found it useful to consult theses, yet librarians reported that many titles were seldom or never used. Within the United Kingdom, this report proved to be the basis of a turning point: it provided evidence that suggested that it would be worthwhile developing a service that enabled researchers to access electronic theses and dissertations (ETDs) quickly and easily on the Web (Copeland et al., 2005).

Where access to ETDs was already available in the late 1990s, via the Internet, and where usage figures were recorded (for example on the Virginia Tech Web site http://scholar.lib.vt.edu/theses/data/somefacts.html), it is evident that they were a much consulted resource. Given the context within which the early ETD discussions and developments were taking place, it is, at first sight, surprising that more universities did not encourage and adopt electronic submission procedures as soon as the technology made this feasible. At this time HEIs were purchasing an increasing number of journals in electronic format. Similarly, electronic abstracts and indexing publications were replacing printed versions and electronic books were making an appearance. The slow transition from print theses and dissertations to ETDs was due partly to a lack of investment in relevant research and development. Many individuals and institutions were working in isolation or in an unfunded capacity and facing technical, legal, administrative and political challenges which required a considerable amount of staff time to resolve.

CONCERNS AND DIFFICULTIES

A key concern voiced by some faculty members and supervisors centred on the potential extra work that would be required of students. As a minimum, electronic

R. Rikowski (ed.), Digitisation Perspectives, 103–113.

submission would necessitate the conversion of a 'Word' document into PDF (the 'portable document format' created by Adobe Systems). In many cases, however, the theses would include images, diagrams or photographs that would have to be scanned. There could even be multimedia items (such as video clips) that would most appropriately be integrated into the body of the work rather than just attached as an appendix (Kirschenbaum, 2004). As advocates of ETDs enthusiastically encouraged the adoption of embellishments that would enhance access to specific information within theses, such as links from contents pages and tables of illustrations to the main text, and links from reference numbers in the text to the relevant entry in the bibliography, concern began to grow about the additional skills needed to achieve these features. Some supervisors who were already worried about completion rates questioned whether the opportunities offered by the production of electronic theses outweighed the potential problems associated with placing extra demands on the students.

Some supervisors also expressed concern about how electronic theses would be examined. Where a print copy could be supplied for use during the viva, this was seen as acceptable. However, where the format would not allow for a hard copy equivalent to be produced it could cause difficulties: examiners could find it awkward to read a whole thesis online, they may lack the skills to access all the parts of the work, or they may omit sections in an ETD that was not produced in a traditional linear style. Even if readers at the time could access the full content easily, inadequate means of preservation or migration might lead to a situation where the material could not be read in future (Gladney, 2004).

The concerns of some of the supervisors matched those expressed by some librarians, I.T. staff and university administrators. If electronic submission becomes a requirement, universities have to ensure that adequate training is provided for students and their supervisors and that sufficient equipment, such as scanners, is made available. Policies and procedures need to be amended and approved by the appropriate committees if theses and dissertations are to be submitted (and made available on the Web) in electronic format on either a voluntary or a mandatory basis. Decisions have to be made regarding whether e-submission is to be compulsory or not and whether it will be introduced for everyone on a set date or whether its introduction will be staged so that only those enrolling from the date that the regulations are changed will be compelled to supply their thesis in electronic format. Decisions have to be made about which departments will undertake particular elements of the work, and overall workflows have to be changed to accommodate the new arrangements (White, 2007). Much time can be saved when members of library staff do not have to obtain hard copy theses from distant store rooms, or acquire and provide theses on inter-library loan. However, new, time-consuming, tasks (such as uploading theses and assigning metadata etc.) arise when an electronic submission and storage system is adopted. New routines might require the introduction of a programme of staff training and they might lead to changes to the distribution of the workload.

Over time, many of these initial concerns have subsided to some extent. The expansion of the 'open access' movement, the growth of institutional repositories in

HEIs, and the increasing number of prestigious organisations now accepting electronic theses is encouraging more institutions to consider replacing paper theses with ETDs. As more universities begin to make their theses available on the Web, however, one key topic remains an area of concern: copyright. Most students are happy to allow their thesis to be uploaded onto their university's Website, particularly since institutions generally employ a 'non-exclusive' deposit licence (which allows students to publish their work elsewhere) and most allow for an embargo period where there is a valid reason for delaying public access to it (e.g. where a patent is pending or where the student is intending to publish some of the material in a book or journal). The main area of concern relating to copyright is not the completed thesis; it is the inclusion of third party material. Where students have already sought permission to reproduce work by other authors or illustrators in their thesis, permission may have been granted on the assumption that the end product would be a traditional paper thesis which would only be viewed by a limited number of readers. Where the electronic thesis is to be made available on the Web, permission to reproduce the work of others should be obtained on this basis. Universities or national libraries which choose to digitise theses retrospectively and make them available on the Web need to take into account that there is a risk factor if the appropriate permissions have not been obtained.

All of these concerns and potential difficulties have contributed to the delay in the growth of a body of ETDs. However, in recent years an increasing number of institutions have realised that the benefits associated with making their PhD students' research output easily accessible on the Web outweigh the problems that need to be overcome.

ADVANTAGES AND BENEFITS

The key benefit of making PhD theses available on the Web is that more of them are read and some of them are read by many more people than was the case when they were held in paper format by university or national libraries. Given that each thesis represents years of research, that not all authors currently publish even the key findings of their endeavours in journals or monographs, and that some of the research is funded from sources of public finance, it seems obvious that action that publicises the results more effectively should be encouraged. For students embarking upon an academic career, in particular, it is advantageous to enable researchers to have easy access to their work: their names and their research will then quickly become known to a wide international readership. Institutions also benefit from the increased publicity associated with greater visibility of the work that is being undertaken by their students.

A growth in the body of theses available on open access on the Web is resulting in improved services to researchers. Where faculty members can obtain access to the full text of theses quickly and easily, they are more likely to make regular use of this type of resource. Making theses available in electronic format within institutional or national repositories allows researchers immediate access from any location, 24 hours a day, regardless of the number of other users. This contrasts significantly with the alternative: requiring readers to visit the library of the institution where the thesis was created, obtaining the work in hard copy on inter-library loan (for use in the requesting library only), or obtaining a microform version for use in a cumbersome reader-printer machine.

Students benefit from the opportunity to create their theses in electronic format when they have research results which can be expressed better through multi-media than in text. Digital format allows for a degree of flexibility and creativity which was not possible when print versions of the work were required. In subject areas such as music, design, art and the performing arts, students can address topics which would have been difficult to deal with previously. In subjects such as maths and engineering students can include elements, such as interactive formulae and graphs, which allow examiners and other researchers to test and appreciate their research findings more easily.

The inclusion of multimedia requires students to acquire an understanding of how to create such material and how to incorporate it into the body of the thesis. This not only improves the quality of the end product, it also enhances the students' skills base and should prove helpful in their future work. Many of those involved in graduate education endorse this viewpoint and use the same argument in response to concerns about the potential additional workload for students who have to learn more about I.T. and copyright when producing electronic theses for publication on the Web. It is a strong argument. At the lowest level, the I.T. skills involved in producing an ETD are only those which most employers would expect from recent graduates nowadays. Similarly, with an increasing emphasis on 'research methods' most universities would consider that they have equipped their graduates well for future academic and research careers if they have provided them with a basic understanding of copyright, intellectual property rights and publishing requirements.

Another reason to favour ETDs, and one which requires no justification, is the cost benefit associated with them. In places, such as some of the former Eastern European countries, which required students to submit a large number of copies of their bound paper theses, significant savings can be made when electronic versions are accepted as an alternative. Moreover, researchers, university departments and libraries can save money when theses do not have to be obtained on inter-library loan. There are also savings to be made on some of the 'hidden' costs associated with hard copy theses, notably with regard to storage space and staff time retrieving and re-shelving items.

SOURCES OF ADVICE

For individuals and institutions considering allowing, or mandating, the submission of theses in electronic format, an increasing amount of information and advice is being made available through Web pages, journal articles, and conference papers. Those involved in advocacy work and in producing training packages, dealing with queries, recording usage statistics, and establishing institutional and national repositories, etc., are encouraged to share their expertise and to make their material freely available on the Web.

At international level, the Networked Digital Library of Theses and Dissertations (NDLTD) is influential in encouraging the acceptance of ETDs and in offering advice and guidance on related matters. Its Web site (http://www.ndltd.org) provides a wealth of useful information on matters ranging from how to set up ETD programmes and how to create and locate ETDs to details of relevant current research, conferences and award-winning theses. Its membership list includes many of the institutions which have been involved in the creation of ETDs for a number of years and many of which have Web sites which are well worth viewing. Its 'Board of Directors' lists individuals who are committed to promoting the concept of electronic theses and dissertations and who can provide advice to those engaged in advocacy campaigns within their own institutions.

The NDLTD has its origins in the USA (Fox et al., 1996). It was established in 1996 as a result of a project led by Virginia Tech, and many of the current institutional members are based in North America. However, there is an increasing amount of involvement from institutions across the world. This international emphasis is perhaps demonstrated best by the success and development of the programme of annual ETD symposia promoted by the NDLTD. The first of these events was held in Memphis in 1998; this was followed by events at Virginia Tech in 1999 and the University of South Florida in 2000. In 2003 the symposium was held in Europe for the first time (at Humboldt University in Berlin) and the success of this conference led to an appreciation of the benefits of varying the location to attract new delegates (while also encouraging the growth of a strong network of experts with long term involvement in this subject area). After a return to the USA in 2004 (http://www.uky.edu/ETD/ETD2004/), the conference was held in Sydney in 2005 (http://adt.caul.edu.au/etd2005/etd2005.html), then in Canada, in Quebec, in 2006 (http://www6.bibl.ulaval.ca:8080/etd2006/pages/index.jsf), in Uppsala in Sweden in 2007 (http://epc.ub.uu.se/ETD2007/) and in Aberdeen in Scotland in 2008 (http://www.rgu.ac.uk/etd/home/). The venue for the 2009 symposium was once again in the USA, (http://www.library.pitt.edu/etd2009/), at the University of Pittsburgh.

The annual international conferences provide a good opportunity for delegates to network and to keep abreast of the latest developments relating to ETDs. Where possible, PowerPoint presentations and conference papers are made available on the Web to ensure as many people as possible can access the information. Nevertheless, there has been growing recognition of the advantages to be gained by forming regional groups and holding regional conferences for those who are unable to attend the international symposia. ETD focused conferences and seminars have been held at national level in countries across the world in recent years and the first NDLTD 'US regional conference' took place in St. Louis in October 2006 (www.wvu.edu/~thesis/News/ETD_2006_US_Regional_Conference_Web.pdf).

Within Europe, there have been efforts recently to share good practice and to identify gaps and areas of overlap. In January 2006 representatives from eleven European countries were represented at an invitational workshop on e-theses which was held in Amsterdam and organised by the Dutch SURFfoundation and the UK Joint Information Systems Committee (JISC). The group investigated interoperability and accessibility issues as well as business models, legal constraints, preservation concerns, and the ways in which participants might work together in future (Jacobs, 2006). The meeting revealed the variations between the countries (for example, with regard to the percentage of ETDs available relative to the total number of theses produced), areas of mutual concern (for example, legal issues), areas of overlap (for example, the existence of UK, French and German metadata sets), and areas where future co-operation would be of significant benefit (for example, multimedia developments and preservation requirements). A number of topics were identified as likely to benefit from future European-wide attention and, following further discussions, an advocacy and support group, 'GUIDE' (Guiding Universities In Doctoral E-theses), was formed. GUIDE later merged with the expanding 'DART-Europe' group: a partnership of research libraries and library consortia which are working together to improve global access to European research theses (http://www.dart-europe.eu/About/).

DART-Europe is endorsed by the Association of European Research Libraries (Ligue des Bibliothèques Européennes de Recherche), LIBER (http://www.libereurope.eu/), and works closely with the NDLTD. The DART-Europe partners have developed a single European Portal (http://www.dart-europe.eu/basic-search.php) to enable researchers to access European ETDs more easily. They participate in advocacy work to influence future European e-theses developments and the organisation provides partners with a useful networking forum on ETD issues.

'Digitala Vetenskapliga Arkivet' (DiVA), the 'Academic Archive Online' developed at Uppsala University in Sweden (http://www.diva-portal.org/), NARCIS, the gateway to scholarly information in the Netherlands, (http://www.narcis.info/) and the Australasian Digital Theses (ADT) Program (http://adt.caul. edu.au/) all provide good examples of what can be achieved at national level to make ETDs more easily accessible. In addition, many individual institutions have produced Web pages containing useful advice about ETD policies, procedures and programmes. Amongst the good examples from the USA are those at Virginia Tech (http://scholar.lib.vt.edu/theses/), West Virginia University (http://www.libraries.wvu.edu/theses/) and Brigham Young University (http://etd.byu.edu/start.html).

The NDLTD annual awards highlight how theses and dissertations can be enhanced through the inclusion of multimedia and presentation in electronic format. The NDLTD Web site contains links to recent award winning ETDs on subjects ranging from architecture to the performing arts. Awards in previous years have been given to the authors of theses dealing with topics as diverse as medicine and piano playing. (http://www.ndltd.org/events_and_awards).

OBTAINING SUPPORT FOR THE ESTABLISHMENT OF AN ETD COLLECTION

As the above summary of 'advantages' reveals, the creation and provision of theses and dissertations in electronic format benefits separate stakeholder groups to differing degrees. When establishing an ETD collection it is essential to obtain support from each of these groups. Senior managers may have to be approached to secure resources and to endorse changes to university policies. Senior administrators may have to approve changes to procedures and workflows and, if an institutional repository is to be created, IT managers may need to ensure that this development is incorporated satisfactorily within the university's IT infrastructure. Library staff will need to decide whether to buy-in to a commercial service, participate in a national scheme or establish their own ETD collection. Depending upon which route they choose to follow, they will have to decide which company to approach to maintain their theses holdings or which software to use as the basis of an in-house e-theses repository. They will also have to decide on the metadata set to be used. It is likely that a project team or working group will have to be established to ensure that there is adequate communication between the staff from many different sectors.

The support of academic staff and supervisors is essential if a cultural change is to be achieved. Students may need their support and encouragement to experiment with the use of multimedia and the presentation of their research results in electronic forms. They may need advice about copyright restrictions and intellectual property rights. At the very least, students wishing to produce their thesis in electronic media should not be dissuaded from doing so by faculty members who are resistant to change.

The students themselves are key to the success of attempts to move from print theses and dissertations to ETDs. In some HEIs it has proved necessary to introduce a voluntary system of e-theses deposit initially, with a view to mandatory e-submission later. This is likely to be the case where the university authorities feel it would be unfair to change the requirements placed upon students who are part-way through their studies and who enrolled in accordance with a set of regulations which made no mention of producing a thesis in electronic format. Where the submission of e-theses is on a voluntary basis, there has to be an emphasis upon advocacy work, the provision of training and a system in place to respond to enquiries etc. Decisions have to be made about how much support and guidance is offered and the way in which it is provided.

TRAINING

Training has to be provided for research students, to assist them to create their theses or dissertations in electronic format. The training requirements of library, administrative and IT staff also need to be taken into account, and academic staff need to be briefed about how ETD developments will affect their role as supervisors. The training may take a number of different forms.

Senior staff may wish to receive occasional updates on significant developments, achievements and problems. This could take the form of presentations, or the submission of briefing papers, to relevant committees. Where individuals need to be persuaded about the benefits of ETDs, or encouraged to become involved in work that requires new skills etc., it may prove worthwhile investing time in one-to-one meetings. The needs of the majority of the students may be catered for by the provision of periodic workshops. These may be relatively informal sessions, either bookable in advance or available on a drop-in basis. To ensure a high level of attendance at training sessions, and to ensure that students attend such events at an early stage in their studies, it may be preferable to organise formal timetabled training sessions. Such events may lack the flexibility of informal sessions, and may not include enough time to follow up on individual enquiries in depth, but they do allow for systematic coverage of the key issues.

Amongst these key issues, a number of themes can be identified. There is a need for the students to comply with institutional policies and procedures and to comply with legal requirements. There is also a desire for students to create ETDs that are easy to read and easy to navigate. Technical skills are needed to produce documents for use in an online environment and students need to be aware of aspects such as file size and structure. Students should be made aware of the benefits of making their work available on the Web but they should also be advised about the type of situation that would merit an application for an embargo period.

Much information, such as details relating to the rules and regulations for the presentation of ETDs, is best made available through Web pages. Where there is little to debate and no benefit to attending a practical workshop, Web pages may be the preferred option: they are accessible to distance learners and available to be consulted at any time. A good example of guidelines for the preparation of electronic theses and dissertations may be seen on the Web pages of the University of Pittsburgh http://www.pitt.edu/~graduate/etd/formatguidelineshtml.html#x1-3000

CONTENT

The University of Pittsburgh ETD guidelines make a distinction between the requirements for a Master's thesis and a doctoral dissertation. In keeping with this approach, most universities view the research output of masters' level students as being of a significantly different standard to that of doctoral students. The question of whether to include masters' theses and dissertations in an ETD collection on open access on the Web is a decision that has to be taken by individual institutions. Some organisations wish to make as many of their students' ETDs as possible available to a wide readership, others wish only to publicise the higher level of research that is represented in PhD theses. Between these extremes, there are many variations: some universities include MPhil, MLitt, or MBA ETDs but not MA theses and some select the best of the masters' ETDs for inclusion. The decision about which material to include depends upon the policy of the institution and the purpose of the collection: whether it is to encourage all postgraduate students to publish their work on the Web and to demonstrate the full breadth of the postgraduate work being undertaken, or whether it is to showcase high level student research (usually alongside the research output of faculty members).

Some HEIs may wish to digitise theses and dissertations retrospectively to improve ease of access to this valuable resource. If the number of paper theses is high, or the budget to undertake the work is limited, it will be necessary to agree a policy which takes into account the factors which influence the selection of titles. If a large collection is to be converted systematically into digital format, it may be most appropriate to select material by date: starting with those produced most recently and working backwards in case the resources to complete the project prove inadequate. If the available budget is known to be limited, it may be most beneficial to select those titles which are known to be used. The latter selection criteria maximises the likelihood of helping a significant number of researchers in their efforts to access the works they need quickly and easily, it ensures that as much staff time is saved as possible by eliminating the need to retrieve and re-shelve the most heavily used material, and it enhances the likelihood of generating statistics of use that demonstrate that the digitisation project was cost-effective and is worthy of additional support.

The choice of which theses and dissertations to digitise retrospectively may be made on a subject basis. If a university aims to promote the research it undertakes in particular subjects it may be worth selecting material in these areas to ensure that the ETD collection reflects the priorities of the institution. If there is significant variation between schools and departments in terms of their support for ETDs, it may be useful to focus on those which view the development positively. Prioritising the work of particular departments may provoke a reaction from staff in other areas; but any approach that raises the profile of the ETD collection at an early stage should prove beneficial in the long run.

POLICIES AND PROCEDURES

Once support has been gained for the establishment of an ETD collection, and decisions made about the material to be included, it is necessary to ensure that university regulations are amended appropriately to reflect the new policies and procedures. Where committees have to consider the proposals, it will be essential to allow adequate time for the process of approval to be completed.

Amongst the changes to be made will be the wording of regulations relating to the presentation of theses and dissertations and those relating to the submission procedure. Students will need to be made aware, at an early stage, of regulations on matters such as the inclusion of multimedia and the conditions associated with providing a copy of their work which will be made available on the Web. In order to avoid the need for university committees to have to periodically revise the regulations about multimedia, it may be best to concentrate on the mechanism for seeking approval rather than creating a list of acceptable software; for example, the regulations could state that students should restrict themselves to using mainstream software where possible and that approval for the formats used should be obtained from their supervisors and those maintaining the ETD collection.

University committees will have to decide whether the submission of theses and dissertations in electronic format is to be optional or mandatory. There are advantages and disadvantages to each approach and, therefore, the decision will have to be based on local circumstances. Requiring electronic submission results in a high volume of content, which may be made available for inclusion in an institutional repository, but it may be difficult to persuade a committee to approve such a proposal. It may also be difficult to enforce this regulation if a paper version of a thesis put forward for use at a viva has led to a decision to award the degree but the ETD is not subsequently provided. Optional submission of electronic copies may be an approach that is more acceptable to committee members, but this may lead to the need to devote more staff time to advocacy work to persuade faculty members and students to take advantage of this opportunity. A strategy which may be acceptable to both faculty and those trying to promote ETDs is to introduce mandatory e-submission in a staged way: making the compulsory aspect effective only for those students who enrol after the regulations have been changed but encouraging existing students to provide electronic versions on a voluntary basis.

In addition to obtaining committee approval, it may be necessary for those seeking to establish an institutional ETD repository to hold discussions with individuals in administrative and legal departments. The paperwork and the workflow will change as a result of a change in the submission system and the records that are kept may need to be changed. Advice may need to be sought from university lawyers regarding the wording of 'disclaimers' e.g. statements that the repository and the institution are not responsible for any mistakes, omissions or infringements in the deposited work. Legal advice may also be sought regarding the wording of both the 'deposit licence' (signed by the authors of the ETDs) and the end-user licence (to which those who access the ETDs are subject). In order to be able to respond quickly to legitimate complaints, it is also worth determining protocols for the removal of material from repositories (i.e. a 'take-down' policy).

ESTABLISHING AN ETD COLLECTION

Since a significant number of institutions internationally are now making their research students' theses and dissertations available in electronic format, much information exists about different ways of achieving this. In terms of which of the various options to follow, a key consideration is whether to encourage students to provide copies of their ETDs to a commercial organisation such as 'ProQuest' (for the 'ProQuest Dissertations and Theses Database') or whether to establish a repository. If the latter route is chosen, it is necessary to decide whether to 'buy-in' to services that manage digital assets, (such as 'Digital Commons', 'DigiTool', 'Open Repository' or 'EPrints Services' amongst others) or whether to create an in-house repository using internal resources and open-source software. The *Open*DOAR Web site (http://www.opendoar.org/index.html) reveals the range of academic open access repositories now in existence and the variety of ways in which these have been created. The range of repository software that has been used by HEIs for the ETD repositories reveals that different organisations have selected different approaches to meet different criteria. The choice for an in-house institutional repository may depend upon the level of technical expertise available. Popular choices include 'DSpace', 'EPrints', and 'Fedora' software. (Information about these products as well as much other useful detail associated with the establishment of institutional repositories is provided in a publication by Jones et al., 2006).

The choice of metadata used may be influenced by a number of factors, for example the need to comply with the requirements of national arrangements for ETD collections or the amount of staff time available to add detail beyond a basic level. The Electronic Theses Online Service (EThOS) that is being developed in the UK has agreed a metadata set (UKETD_DC), based on the widely used 'Dublin Core' metadata standard (http://dublincore.org/), that is generic enough to be applied to doctoral theses produced in a wide variety of UK institutions but specific enough to enable the central service to harvest all relevant material (http://ethostoolkit.cranfield.ac.uk/tiki-index.php?page_ref_id=25). Both the NDLTD and DART-Europe are currently engaged in discussions about metadata and the ways in which improvements could be made at international level to standardise some aspects in order to enhance access to ETDs.

Differences in terminology, procedures and requirements associated with how theses and dissertations are presented in different countries make it difficult to reach agreement in some areas. However, as liaison improves and those involved in development work gain a better understanding of why particular decisions have been taken in certain circumstances, it is becoming easier to work towards achieving enhancements to the current arrangements which will enable researchers to undertake federated searches to obtain relevant material from institutions across the globe. The NDLTD Web site offers researchers the opportunity to browse or search through ETD collections across multiple institutions at once (http://www.ndltd.org/find). It provides a link to the 'VTLS Visualizer' (ETD search and discovery system powered by VTLS) and the 'Scirus ETD Search' (an ETD search and discovery system powered by Scirus). The 'NDLTD Union Catalog' now contains over a million records of ETDs.

REFERENCES

Copeland, S., Penman, A., & Milne, R. (2005). Electronic theses: The turning point. *Program, 39*(3), 185–197.

Fox, E., Eaton, J., McMillan, G., Kipp, N., Weiss, L., Arce, E. et al. (1996, September). National digital library of theses and dissertations. A scalable and sustainable approach to unlock University resources. *D-Lib Magazine*.

Gladney, H. (2004). Digital document durability. In E. Fox, S. Feizabadi, J. Moxley, & C. Weisser (Eds.), *Electronic theses and dissertations*. New York: Marcel Dekker.

Jacobs, N. (2006). International workshop on e-theses: A report on a JISC-SURF-CURL-sponsored event at the Vrije Universiteit, Amsterdam, the Netherlands, over 19–20 January 2006. *Ariadne, 46*. Retrieved May 11, 2010, from http://www.ariadne.ac.uk/issue46/e-theses-rpt/

Jones, R., Andrew, T., & MacColl, J. (2006). *The institutional repository*. Oxford: Chandos.

Kirschenbaum, M. (2004). From monograph to multigraph: Next generation electronic theses and dissertations. In E. Fox, S. Feizabadi, J. Moxley, & C. Weisser (Eds.), *Electronic theses and dissertations*. New York: Marcel Dekker.

Roberts, A. (1997). *Survey on the use of doctoral theses in British universities*. (British Library Research and Innovation Report 57). Edinburgh: Edinburgh University Library.

Suleman, H., Atkins, A., Gonçalves, M., France, R., Fox, E., Chachra, V., et al. (2004). Networked digital library of theses and dissertations. In E. Fox, S. Feizabadi, J. Moxley, & C. Weisser (Eds.), *Electronic theses and dissertations*. New York: Marcel Dekker.

White, W. (2007, June 13–16). *Opening access and closing risk: Delivering the mandate for e-theses deposit*. Paper presented at ETD 2007: The 10th International Symposium on Electronic Theses and Dissertations, Uppsala. Retrieved May 11, 2010, from http://epc.ub.uu.se/etd2007/files/papers/paper-45.pdf

Susan Copeland
Robert Gordon University, Aberdeen, UK

PAUL CATHERALL

7. LEARNING SYSTEMS IN POST-STATUTORY EDUCATION

INTRODUCTION

According to the latest sector-wide research, some 95% of Higher Education institutions in the UK have some form of learning system, actively supporting and delivering educational programmes for tens of thousands of students (UCISA 2005). These systems are typically delivered via the medium of the World Wide Web, a socially interactive communications channel which has become ubiquitous in areas as diverse as commerce, entertainment and education, exacerbated by growing computer literacy, improved internet connectivity and ownership of computer devices:

> The widespread availability and popularity of the Internet has made it possible for people to communicate unlike any other time in history. Applications for instantaneous communication are as diverse as the global cultures utilizing the Internet. As more people join and participate in this global communication medium, these users are expecting more from their online experience. Consumers are increasingly asking questions such as, "why can't the Internet do", or "when will I be able to online"? (Chan and Welebir 2003).

Web-based learning systems provide a range of interactive functions, including communication channels, content-publishing and assessment tools. It can be seen that these systems have begun to permeate and impact many aspects of post-statutory education, with recent Web technologies allowing for closer systems integration across institutional systems, including library catalogue, student records and finance systems. In the UK, this institute-wide computing infrastructure is often considered an holistic learning environment:

> 'Managed Learning Environment' (MLE) refers to the whole range of information systems and processes of a college or university… that contribute directly, or indirectly, to learning and the management of that learning. (Erskine 2003).

Whilst terms such as the 'digital library' and 'e-university' have been used to describe the transformation of traditional library and information facilities toward increasing digitization and database-driven systems, it can be seen that the Web-enabled *MLE* represents a shift from campus-based systems to personalised and ubiquitous access for end-users.

The *MLE* typically includes a range of systems, such as library catalogues, learning systems, personalised student records, online journals, Web-based portals,

R. Rikowski (ed.), Digitisation Perspectives, 115–130.

directories, content repositories (e.g. containing self-directed learning resources) and 'social networking' facilities. It is perhaps important to consider the disparity between these systems before the emergence of the Web (e.g. relying on various computer applications or terminal systems) - resulting in the need for user training across several individual systems. In this sense, the term *Managed Learning Environment* describes a consistent or standardised interface to diverse systems (i.e. via the Web browser application); conversely, the *MLE* should not be considered as a single homogenous system - with educational organisations purchasing (or developing) a variety of Web systems; however, some homogeneity is usually possible, e.g. customisation of Web content to reflect an institutional design or integration of user login credentials (i.e. using a directory system such as *Microsoft Active Directory*).

Inevitably, the Web-based MLE relies fundamentally on ICT literacy and student-led approaches for information handling. In this context, we can consider the role of staff facilitating the educational experience themselves subject to change, from facilitators of education and related support services to facilitators (or intermediaries) of systems which themselves facilitate the educational experience.

Whilst in recent years, end-users could have been considered as members of the 'digital library', it may now be more pertinent to consider the educational experience in context to the 'digital native', i.e. an individual who moves seamlessly between Web-based resources for educational, vocational and leisure purposes, applying Web-browsing skills to interrogate information and discover resources within and beyond the institutional MLE.

To understand systemised approaches to learning it is perhaps necessary to identity some fundamental issues and perspectives in this field. Issues for discussion in the chapter will include:

- The technical background to learning systems.
- Defining systemised learning and its relationship with learning technology.
- Strengths, challenges and questions raised by systemised learning.
- The contemporary context for learning systems.
- Trends and likely future developments for learning systems.
- Critical, social and polemic perspectives on learning technology.

One of the key difficulties associated with contemporary learning systems is the disparity of terminology used to conceptually define learning systems. The following definitions may be helpful:

- Online Learning: Often used to refer to computer-assisted learning in an online, i.e. internet-based context where the student is able to access remote learning materials or communication tools via Internet software. Contemporary learning systems are almost entirely provided via a 'Web browser' client, such as *Internet Explorer* or *Netscape*, hence the association of 'Online Learning' with Web-based learning systems (ostensibly delivered via 'Web pages'). Other terms synonymous with 'online learning' include Computer-Mediated Communication (CMC) and Online Education.
- E-Learning: The prefix 'E' for 'electronic' has been applied to a variety of traditional labels, such as *E-marketing* and *E-library*. In this sense, *E-learning*

could be considered a label for any educational process involving an electronic device, however this term has more recently come to represent a Web-based learning experience.

- VLE: *Virtual Learning Environment* – this is the predominant form of learning systems since the late 1990s, involving a Web-based portal to a variety of communication, content publishing, assessment and related tools. The terms *VLE* and *E-learning* are now virtually synonymous in the UK. Other terms synonymous with *VLE* include:
  - LSS (Learning Support System).
  - CMS (Course Management System).
  - LP (Learning Platform).
  - LCMS (Learning Content Management System).
  - LMS (Learning Management System).
- MLE: *Managed Learning Environment* – often used to define the wider composition of Web-based systems within an educational institution, including – but not limited to the Library Management System (LMS), Student Records System (SRS), VLE, Finance system etc. Integration is perhaps a key aspect of the MLE concept, often involving 'single-sign-on' to access a diverse range of services and systems using uniform login credentials.
- CMS: *Content Management System* – this acronym describes a typically Web-based system for institutional documentation or information. VLE and CMS systems typically share the objective of providing an accessible interface for staff to upload or manage system features without considerable technical knowledge (e.g. to upload digital documents in a CMS or create an online assessment in a VLE); however, the CMS does not have an educational focus, but describes a system used to develop an organisational Web site or document repository system (e.g. for restricted access as a staff *intranet*).
- Portal: A term increasingly used to define a more fully integrated Web-based system, perhaps drawing together disparate systems but presenting them in a unified manner (i.e. using a standard layout and navigation structure to convey a sense of institutional identity). The Portal is sometimes a purely cosmetic concept but is increasingly used to describe a unified and integrated interface to systems.

This chapter will provide a broad overview of the present context for learning systems.

THE ORIGINS OF LEARNING SYSTEMS

At the time of writing, the VLE (Virtual Learning Environment) is the present model for computer-assisted learning, based on high-end server computers, with capabilities for integration with institutional authentication systems (i.e. user directory system for systems access) and delivered to any internet-connected computer via the Web client (such as *Internet Explorer, Mozilla* or *Opera*).

The Web-based VLE has evolved around several key principles, these include usability (i.e. of the system interface) for staff to manage and upload resources and for end-users to view and interact with resources - and secondly, the capability to deliver communication and collaboration facilities in a remote context, e.g. to the student's home or work computer.

We would be forgiven for thinking the rapid ubiquity of Web-based learning represents a fundamental shift in practice for post-statutory education, yet it can be seen that these systems represent only the most recent stage in the evolution of learning technologies, with origins as far back as the 1950s.

In 1956 the educationalist and computer technologist Gordon Pask developed his 'Self-Adaptive-Keyboard-Instructor' (SAKI) and in 1960, the University of Illinois developed the 'Programmed Logic for Automated Teaching Operations' system (PLATO), this system was run on one of the first computers (ILLIAC I), using a TV screen to display navigation menus. The PLATO system displayed several seminal concepts in systemised learning, including distinct 'system roles' such as 'instructors' and 'students', the use of programmable 'lessons' and a memo-based communication tool for student-tutor interaction. The PLATO system evolved throughout the 1970s and was 'ported' to a number of later computer operating systems, including the IBM PC. (Woolley 1993)

Later developments in learning systems can be seen in the emergence of the Internet during the 1960s as a military communication and defence system (the Advanced Research Projects Agency Network or ARPANET), which introduced basic internet technology such as email (1971) and File Transfer Protocol or FTP (1973).

Later developments saw the emergence of SERCNET (now the JANET network for UK academic and research organisations) in 1974 and CSNET (Computer Science Network) operating a similar academic network in the US.

The emergence of a networked university and scholarly community was initially dependent on early UNIX-like, mainframe-based computers, often requiring knowledge of command-line syntax (e.g. using a terminal client machine); however, the emergence of graphical operating systems in the early 1980s (such as Microsoft Windows) featuring *Windows, Icons, Menus and Pointers* (WIMP) quickly opened computing to a general user base and to more usable (graphical) Internet software, such as email, FTP (for file transfer), BBS (Bulletin Boards), USENET (Newsgroups) and early information networks, such as *Gopher* (providing access to text-based resources located on Gopher servers around the world).

WEB 1.0

By the mid 1990s, the *World Wide Web* had emerged as an attractive and usable alternative to earlier text-based Internet systems. Invented by Tim Berners-Lee in 1989 as a document retrieval system at CERN (European Organisation for Nuclear Research). Berners-Lee's *Web Browser* and *Hypertext* encoding system would become the basis of World Wide Web, eventually providing a graphical medium for the delivery of information across the existing Internet. This period was marked by increasingly usable interfaces to computing (mainly due to the arrival of IBM computers and early Windows Operating Systems) and the success of basic communication tools such as email.

The mid 1990s also saw an explosion in the use of Web editing software such as *Netscape Composer* to develop Web pages in HTML (Hyper-text Mark-up Language) - developed by Tim Berners-Lee as a means of encoding text (and eventually multimedia). The educational application of the Web became increasingly prolific, with 'static' HTML pages available for general viewing by any individual with access to a Web browser and internet connection.

The early Web, with its plethora of Web-based pages, still lacking interactive features for the better part, provided the foundation for the next stage of educational systems, establishing the viability and success of mass communication via the Internet.

The development of more sophisticated approaches to Web design such as *CGI* (Common Gateway Interface), *ASP* (Active Server Pages), *Java* and *JavaScript* (to name a few) soon provided the basis for the development of interactive Web systems, including Web-based bulletin and discussion boards, Web-based email, simultaneous chat and other interactive features delivered directly via the Web browser.

THE EMERGENCE OF TRAINING AND LEARNING SYSTEMS

The role of corporate and non-educational sectors in the development of early learning systems can be seen in the US military funding of ARPANET, the first Wide Area Network (ostensibly as a military communication system capable of withstanding nuclear attack, but facilitated by academic and research institutions), in the development of in-house corporate training systems by companies such as IBM and in the early implementation of electronic learning systems by the US military, for mass training purposes.

Early examples of learning systems developed or sponsored by non-educational interests also included the invention of the first mouse pointing device by Douglas Engelbart in 1963 and IBM's 'Coursewriter' system in 1966 – a system which included networked access for student access within campus.

The 1970s and early 80s saw a wide range of corporate experimentation in the development of learning systems, including the development by the PARC company (Palo Alto Research Center, Inc.) of the first graphical computer interface for teaching purposes (KiddiKomputer), whilst the CBT company (Computer Based Training) pioneered the use of CD-ROMs to provide training solutions for computer technology products (later becoming 'SmartForce The elearning company').

In *An informal history of eLearning*, a former CBT member, Jay Cross describes the focus of early learning systems in the corporate sector, emphasising the origins of e-learning as a form of systemised training, rather than an educational process in the traditional academic context. Cross' reference to 'eLearning' is perhaps the first use of this term in computing literature:

> In 1998, I wrote, "eLearning is learning on Internet Time, the convergence of learning and networks. eLearning is a vision of what corporate training can become." (Cross 2004).

By the mid 1990s, corporate providers had begun to use hypertext-based systems and the Web browser as the prevalent medium for delivering learning systems.

Some of the earliest Web-based learning systems included *Lotus Notes* (combining an in-built communication and email system with content publishing and course-work submission tools) and *Firstclass* (becoming a messaging and collaboration-focused system).

The corporate sector was never unchallenged however, with increasing interest in learning systems amongst the emerging Open Source community. Early not-for-profit and home-grown systems included the *Boddingtons* system developed by the University of Leeds in the late 1990s and the *COSE* system (Creation of Online Study Environments) developed by Staffordshire University.

It can therefore be seen that a range of perspectives have shaped the ongoing development of systemised learning, with perhaps two distinct influences with differing aims and philosophies - firstly educational approaches - reflecting the traditional structures and terminology of teaching, including a focus on longitudal and social interaction (e.g. communication and assessment aspects), and secondly instructional approaches to e-learning, characterised by early corporate and military systems, with emphasis on instructional design and sequential learning (i.e. breaking a defined objective into multiple smaller segments with the desired aim of imparting a routine-based task on the learner) rather than the development of subject expertise, critical analysis or learner insights:

> Learning objects and e-learning standardization bear the imprint of the ideology and culture of the American military-industrial complex–of ways of thinking that are related either marginally or antithetically to the interests and values of education generally and public education in particular. (Friesen 2004).

VLES

The growth of teaching and learning systems delivered via the Internet has accelerated in recent years with the emergence of the *Virtual Learning Environment* (VLE) as the general model for Web-based learning. These systems combine earlier developments in dynamic Web technologies such as *Java, ASP, PHP* etc. and recent developments in *modular systems architecture* - incorporating a range of network systems such as relational databases, directory systems, authentication systems and Web hosting services.

The VLE is typically Web-based, often running on a traditional Web server such as *Apache* or *Internet Information Server*, however, there are considerable differences between the VLE and traditional static Web pages (often termed Web 1.0).

Key characteristics of the VLE include individualised user access, often allowing for user profiles and portfolios within the system (e.g. within Moodle VLE). The VLE often relies on integrated systems, allowing for common login credentials (i.e. user-name and password) across a range of systems - avoiding the need for different credentials for email, VLE, library and other systems. *Single-Sign-on* is also a possibility, allowing a user to log into an institutional computer, then seamlessly access other systems without any further login challenge.

As a networked application, the VLE is typically optimised for a variety of user connection speeds, e.g. from a high speed broadband connection to an older and slower 56kbps modem. The interface itself typically offers a layout and behaviour familiar to existing Web users, including hyperlinks, navigation menus, frames (containing sub-pages) etc.

Whilst the VLE market has been dominated by commercial systems such as *Blackboard, WebCT* and *Learnwise*, there has been a growing interest across the post-statutory education sector in not-for-profit and Open Source solutions such as Moodle.

The most typical features of the VLE include the following:

- Content publishing and dissemination tools – to allow academic and other staff to upload document resources (such as Microsoft Office files) for access by students. Additionally, there are often features to organise or structure resources by category or using named folders.
- Assessment and 'quiz' tools – these often provide a means to create automated multiple-choice or similar style assessments (using tick boxes, text boxes and similar Web features). Online assessment tools such as *Questionmark* provide an automated approach for grading user responses. Other features include score weighting (for setting the value of particular questions or assessments within a wider assessment framework) and the use of question repositories to allow for the quick construction of assessments from an existing question archive.
- Collaboration and Communication features – these include *asynchronous* tools such as online discussion boards (resembling earlier *Bulletin Board Systems* for posting and replying to short topical messages), file exchange (e.g. for displaying group course-work and allowing other group members to develop and re-upload the file), versioning (to track changes to developed content), messaging (to provide a simple message system within the system for staff and users) and email (integrating the ability to send email to defined users who may then receive email via the VLE or their own email software). *Synchronous* tools include chat style features to allow rapid / real-time discussions and tutor-led debates, often including *whiteboard* tools for displaying images, Web sites, uploaded documents etc. in context to the discussion.
- Reusable Learning Objects and Learning Repositories – with origins in Instructional Design and military training research, *Reusable Learning Objects* have become a feature of VLEs and related Web-based software. The key aims of Learning Objects include portability (i.e. for the resource to function in any compatible learning system) and re-usability (i.e. to allow for easy retrieval from within a Learning Object Repository for sharing and re-use in another system). Learning Objects are typically considered self-contained learning units or resources, providing some level of user interaction (which could be provided in a wide range of digital formats, such as images, Flash movies or interactive applications such as Java etc.)

Applications of Learning Objects can include any of the following:

- An interactive Quiz or Assessment providing user feedback.
- A sequential presentation, seminar or lecture.

- A sequential task-based demonstration, split into slides or scenes.
- A movie or audio experience, with additional interactive features, such as a notes tool.

Another key aspect of Learning Objects are the formal specifications which determine how they are created (often using software or VLE-type systems) and uploaded into compatible systems; there are two principal Learning Object standards: *SCORM* (Sharable Content Object Reference Model) and *IMS* (company), both these standards share similar aims and approaches for 'wrapping' content using metadata (descriptive scripts) to define issues such as the resource title, description, subject-matter and educational level. More complex *metadata* may also allow for integration between the learning object and a host learning system (e.g. to store score values or user details). Whilst a key aim of Learning Objects has been to provide compatibility and ease of integration with VLEs, this has been hampered by lack of standardisation, resulting in a myriad of Learning Object specifications and differing levels of support for particular VLE systems.

CHALLENGES AND CONCERNS IN VLES

The deployment and delivery of the VLE is complicated by the vast range of commercial and open source systems available, by often prohibitive licensing models for commercial systems and by complex systems and integration requirements for software installation. Whilst it may be tempting to consider an Open Source or not-for-profit alternative VLE, it should be remembered that not-for-profit systems often lack a formal or accountable support service; however, Open Source systems often have a large network of voluntary developers and community enthusiasts able to offer help of some form to resolve system problems.

Other issues in choosing a VLE system include content portability – i.e. can course ware or published resources be easily extracted from a particular system and used within another system?

The issue of 'locked' content also has financial implications, i.e. it is possible the institution will become dependent on a particular system, preferring an ongoing license to maintain the historical system rather than risk the loss of content by migrating to another system (often involving a complex process of content conversion).

From an operational perspective, there are several key tasks faced for the deployment of learning systems, these include:

- Analysis of system requirements and the learning context, e.g. will the system simply support conventional teaching or distance learning, can the system deal with institutional capacity / user load.
- Assessment and selection of a system suitable for the institutional context (with several thousand systems on the market, this is no small endeavour).
- Liaison with (and potential recruitment of) institutional stakeholders in VLE procurement and eventual use, including managers, support staff, academic users etc.

- Deciding use of a commercial or non-commercial system and associated considerations, e.g. system support provision, licensing fee model and budget.
- Procurement of computer systems / servers to run the e-learning system according to VLE specifications.
- Installation and configuration of the VLE (often the initial configuration will be crucial in determining how the system will function).
- Integrating the VLE within the institutional infrastructure, from a technical perspective (e.g. to enable access to the VLE via an existing user login).
- Initial testing, training for high level system administrators etc.
- The initial pilot to test the VLE, obtaining feedback for user satisfaction.
- Gradual roll-out, possibly to selected academic schools/ faculties, providing suitable staff and student training and support materials, obtaining feedback and user satisfaction responses.
- Full roll-out of the system, with continued liaison with institutional stakeholders to report progress, obtain satisfaction feedback etc.
- Ongoing support provision, possibly including retraining of existing staff or procurement of new VLE-specific support staff.

There will be considerable social, political and educational issues for any staff engaged in the deployment of a new VLE or learning system. Workload and administrative support may be a factor (e.g. in managing online enrolments and supporting students in an online context via email etc.); other concerns can include fears of automation to replace teaching staff or skills challenges by staff expected to use the new system.

The resolution of challenges to deployment of learning systems is perhaps best considered as a process of consultation, negotiation and promotion of shared ownership for the system, achieved through dialogue with all 'stakeholders' from the earliest stages of system selection through to negotiation of student support mechanisms, balance of IT and academic support etc.

ACCESSIBILITY AND WEB STANDARDS

The early World Wide Web was characterised by considerable disparity across *Web browsers* (Internet Explorer, Netscape etc.). Each browser implemented standard forms of HTML but added additional proprietary functionality, special features and effects not found in other browsers. The development of proprietary HTML rules for individual Web browsers became less problematic with an improved awareness of HTML standards amongst both Web software developers and HTML coders; however, the problems of proprietary HTML remain due partly to the myriad range of Web browsers available and a continuing disparity in the way Web pages are produced (i.e. using various Web editing applications and manually coded HTML).

The open-ended nature of HTML and related standards (including *CSS* – Cascading Style Sheets) and HTML variants (such as *XHTML*), have resulted in considerable challenges for the provision of Web resources which are accessible and usable for the widest possible audience.

A variety of issues can impair the use of Web resources, particularly for individuals who rely on standards-based applications to enhance their Web browsing experience; Web accessibility issues include:

- Poorly generated or 'coded' HTML, which subsequently fails to display correctly in a standards-compliant Web browser.
- Difficulties enlarging fonts for visually impaired users.
- Difficulties 'reading' Web pages using a screen reader application.
- Issues converting a colour-based site to a high-contrast or other alternative style to suite a particular visual preference.

The main standards body for the Web is called the *World Wide Web Consortium* (or W3C), this body was founded by the originator of the World Wide Web, Tim Berners-Lee and has responsibility for the technical specifications of the Web and related guidelines for production of Web content. Several core standards are published to ensure content developers and Web editing system developers are able to work within common rules and guidelines, these include:

- Web Mark-Up standards (such as HTML – Hypertext Mark-up Language) and its variants, such as XHTML - Extensible Hypertext Mark-up Language (various versions).
- XML and derivatives (Extensible Mark-Up Language). XML is a basis for the encoding and exchange of data in a Web context.
- The Web Content Accessibility Guidelines (WCAG) - a set of fourteen guidelines for the production of accessible Web content. The WCAG are partly technical and partly stylistic, recommending developers consider a range of usability and accessibility issues from a unified perspective, i.e. developing material in a manner which is usable for all Web users. The specifications mentioned above are available at the W3C Web site (http://www.w3c.org).

In practice, the W3C guidelines and specifications endeavour to ensure all Web pages are built using the same technical rules, allowing Web browsers to display Web material in a consistent and compatible manner. Accessibility-focused specifications ensure a range of usability considerations such as:

- Use of standard headings to designate page titles (e.g. Heading 1, Heading 2 etc.)
- Use of titles, descriptions etc. for images, tables and other graphical features (to ensure alternative textual content is available for users with visual impairment).
- Use of key-based shortcuts to enable users with motor difficulties to access and navigate the Web page, including complex forms and menus.

These considerations are particularly important for the VLE, due to its increasing ubiquity in post-statutory educational life. Additionally, given the growth in student profile diversity (including diversity of age and disability) it is important to provide e-learning systems which offer considerable Web accessibility, e.g. for users with visual, motor or cognitive disabilities.

BLENDED AND DISTANCE E-LEARNING

Recent years have seen some agreement on terminology used to describe the use of learning systems in particular contexts.

The use of the VLE alongside conventional teaching has been termed 'distributed' or 'blended' learning, often supporting class-based teaching through emphasis on resource publication rather than communication or collaboration.

The VLE system may also be used as an exclusive platform to deliver a course of education, i.e. to support remote learners with minimal or no tutor contact. Issues which may arise from study delivered entirely remotely via the VLE can include student disassociation from the course or institution, isolation from peers and staff, poor coursework feedback or pastoral relationship with tutors and difficulties with the technology, including network connectivity, IT support etc.

WEB 2.0 AND E-LEARNING 2.0

More recently, we have also seen considerable growth in experimentation with models of e-learning, e.g. using a range of VLE systems within the same organisation to provide specific tools seen as strengths of particular systems or basic integration (often provided via hyperlinks) between the VLE and third party systems such as Microsoft Live (chat, email and discussion tools) and other 'Social Networking' services on the World Wide Web, such as *MySpace*. Additionally, the emergence of *Web 2.0* applications, such as *Social Networking* Web sites, *Wikis* (collaborative document systems), *Blogs* (collaborative Web logs) and other innovations have been seized upon by some educational institutions with the intention of promoting learning and teaching via technology and encouraging participation with peers and tutors.

The growth in mobile devices has similarly promoted adoption of mobile phones as a means for disseminating of information via *sms* messages, e.g. in order to notify students of a timetable change or other notable news.

The emergence of *Web 2.0* has seen the incorporation of these tools within VLE systems, purporting to improve interaction and collaborative aspects of Web content. However, negative issues arising from university-sanctioned use of Social Networking tools can involve uncensored and non-moderated comments amongst students and comments directed against the host institution.

M-LEARNING

With increasing dependence on e-learning systems and growing availability of mobile networked computing, students will increasingly access online study in a diverse range of contexts. Until recently, the majority of e-learning activities within educational institutions were restricted to use of static networked terminals (i.e. connected via cabling to a network socket). The advent of WiLANs (*Wireless Local Area Networks*) is allowing the use of portable computer devices such as laptops or PDAs at any location within the HE institution, e.g. allowing students to access institutional systems in the lecture theatre, refectory or any other location within the wireless transmission range. The rise of portable and hand-held networked devices may also widen access to institutional systems outside the academic institution; for example, a 'smart phone' could access institutional email, calendaring systems or even a WAP-enabled VLE.

Whilst current laptop computers are widely used for limited portable computing, the handheld device has the advantage of easy portability, with latest models combining phone and SMS functionality with PDA-style Internet access and personal computing functionality.

LEARNER TRENDS AND THE ROLE OF LEARNING SYSTEMS

Recent years have seen an emphasis by the UK Labour Government for widening access to post-statutory education and training and use of emerging technologies to achieve these aims. Reports such as the *Dearing Report* (1997), *The Learning Age* (1998) and *21st Century Skills Realising Our Potential* (2003) presented both industry and the education sectors with a number of goals focused on improving educational standards as a vehicle to strengthen the UK economy, the aims of this legislation can be summarised in the following extract from *21st Century Skills*:

There are four principles underlying our approach to improved publicly-funded training provision for adults. It should:

- Be led by the needs of employers and learners.
- Be shaped by the skill needs prioritised in each sector, region and locality.
- Make the best use of Information and Communications Technology (ICT) to deliver and assess learning.
- Give colleges and training providers maximum discretion to decide how best to respond to needs... (p. 87).

More recently, the government paper *Harnessing Technology, transforming learning and children's services* (2005) describes the Government's vision to develop the use of ICTs within all educational sectors.

These reports emphasise the importance of a demand-led approach within the education sectors and the development of links between education providers and industry - prompting a debate on the role of colleges and universities in the wider economy and implications for subject areas within a market-led approach to educational funding. Gibson, Newton and Dixon (1999) comment on this emerging agenda:

> ...sub-degree level courses and flexible structures of certification have become more common. Access to lifelong learning has increasingly been seen by policymakers at all levels as a social and economic priority.

Universities have been encouraged to adopt an inclusive approach to recruitment, i.e. for mature, disabled and ethnic minority entrants; recent statistics suggest an increase in the number of entrants matching these criteria, suggesting a growing trend in mature, part-time study:

> 1,236,300 (66%) of all enrolments are full-time, an increase in numbers of 3% since 2000/01. The number of part-time enrolments also grew by 3% over the same period. (Office of National Statistics, 2003).

Learning systems are often cited as a solution for the emerging trends of part-time study in educational provision. However we should consider the ICT literacy of this wider student context, many of whom may not have a prior knowledge of IT or the World Wide Web in their private or vocational lives.

Additionally, the VLE does rely on internet availability; many individuals such as the disabled or elderly may be unable to use Web based resources for accessibility reasons. Further, it should also not be assumed that all school-leavers may be satisfied studying via the Web, with class-based tuition remaining the prevalent medium of education. Cullen (2001) reflects this:

> A number of research and policy papers addressing the issue of the digital divide identify specific groups of people as being especially disadvantaged in their uptake of ICTs. These include: people on low incomes, people with few educational qualifications or with low literacy levels, the unemployed, elderly people, people in isolated or rural areas, people with disabilities, sole parents, women and girls. Because they are often already disadvantaged in terms of education, income and health status... (p. 312)

It can therefore be seen that reliance on ICT skills in an increasingly diverse student population raises a number of usability and accessibility concerns for the adoption of learning systems.

CORPORATE (AND GLOBAL) DEVELOPMENTS

We have already discussed the commercial background to the e-learning industry and its relationship with academic providers. There is arguably a new educational industry developing around the e-learning product which ostensibly facilitates education, solving many of the problems associated with low contact study;. However, it can be seen that in many ways, this emerging industry is facilitating a fundamental shift towards an entirely new medium of instructional design, based on the VLE model. Pailing (2002) comments:

> ...the industry has suffered from a lot of hype and suppliers and customers need to look at e-learning in perspective. It is hardly surprising that most of the predictions about the e-learning market come out of the USA.

In 'Digital Diploma Mills: The Automation of Higher Education' (1998), David Noble presents a theory of the 'commoditization' of learning, describing the emerging relationship between the education sectors, government and technology industries in the USA, reflecting similar developments in the UK and Europe:

> For the universities are not simply undergoing a technological transformation. Beneath that change, and camouflaged by it, lies another: the commercialization of higher education. For here as elsewhere technology is but a vehicle and a disarming disguise.

Noble links the growth of the e-learning industry with increasing commercialisation (commoditization) of post-statutory education, citing the growth of digital industries as a direct result of the collapse of older heavy industries in the 1980s:

> The foremost promoters of this transformation are rather the vendors of the network hardware, software, and "content" - Apple, IBM, Bell, the cable

> companies, Microsoft, and the edutainment and publishing companies Disney, Simon and Schuster, Prentice-Hall, et al - who view education as a market for their wares, a market estimated by the Lehman Brothers investment firm potentially to be worth several hundred billion dollars. (Noble 1998).

In this sense, we may be witnessing a transformation of education from the traditional taught approach to a commodity-based instructional model, where courses can be run through via systems without the imposition of experienced academic staff.

The widespread adoption of learning systems can therefore be seen to facilitate a new commercial market - part of the growing *information industry*. These developments reflect the concern of academic staff on the threat of automated systems. This systemification of learning is suggested as an inevitable outcome for education by Halket (2002):

> There is no need for the creation of courses by those who did not create them before. There is no need for any new institutions. There is every need for existing institutions and existing educators to rise to the new challenge and have the best possible tools put at their disposal.

The provision of training in an e-learning context, with minimal instructor input is already being deployed by some training companies such as Thompson NETg, with contracts for training in the business and public sectors in the USA and UK.

Nixon and Helms (2002) have indicated the spread of e-learning in some government and public bodies:

> Corporate universities are not new, but have experienced tremendous growth during the last ten years. Predictions are that corporate universities will outnumber traditional colleges and universities within the next ten years... ...Corporate universities exist in government settings and include the Internal Revenue Service, the City of Tempe's Learning Center and NASA's Marshall Space Flight Center.

Jay Cross describes the ethos of e-learning in its original corporate context, considering the imperative of systemised learning as a sequential training device, rather than encouraging the kind of developmental activity found in traditional models of education:

> Executives don't care about learning; they care about execution. I may talk about "learning" with you, but when I'm in the boardroom, I'll substitute "improving performance." (Cross 2004).

The role of learning systems, cited as a progressive solution to distance learning have therefore prompted concerns for the commoditization of post-statutory education. It remains to be seen if learning systems will diminish the role of academic practitioners, with the expansion of e-training in competition with traditional post-statutory education.

CONCLUSIONS

In conclusion, it can be seen that learning systems present both challenges and opportunities for academic staff and end-users. However, the prevalence and increasing reliance on these systems in post-statutory education should be approached with caution, especially with respect to motivational factors and support issues.

The emerging model of Further and Higher Education as a part-time occupation, undertaken by working students, with increasing numbers of mature and non-traditional entrants, presents a challenging context for staff with responsibility for teaching and supporting students via the medium of learning systems.

The barriers and operational questions for systemised learning are becoming more apparent as educational institutions become more dependent on systems for course delivery, blended learning and distance-learning models of study. What perhaps is less clear are the wider motives of educational providers and governments in encouraging the use of ICTs within the wider lifelong learning agenda, where systemised learning can clearly be seen as a facilitator in driving lifelong learning and the new 'knowledge economy'.

Furthermore, the increasing systemisation of learning and trend toward a market-led model of education represents both a digression from traditional focus on academic achievement and a serious challenge to underpinning values of critical and reflective educational practice.

Certainly, the diversity seen across VLE systems, with differing interfaces and emphasis on synchronous, asynchronous, collaborative, communication and content features makes any study or assessment of systemised learning all the more difficult.

Perhaps a concluding remark can be offered by Tim Berners-Lee, the developer of the first Web systems:

> As the Web passes through its first decade of widespread use, we still know surprisingly little about these complex technical and social mechanisms. We have only scratched the surface of what could be realized with deeper scientific investigation into its design, operation and impact on society. (Berners-Lee 2007)

REFERENCES

Berners-Lee, T. (2007). *Before the United States House of Representatives Committee on Energy and Commerce Subcommittee on Telecommunications and the Internet Hearing on the "Digital future of the United States: Part I – The future of the world wide web"*. Retrieved June 21, 2007, from http://dig.csail.mit.edu/2007/03/01-ushouse-future-of-the-web.html

Chan, P., & Welebir, B. (2003). Strategies for e-education. *Industrial and Commercial Training, 35*(5), 196–202.

Cross, J. (2004). An informal history of eLearning. *On the Horizon, 12*(3), 103–110.

Cullen, R. (2001). Addressing the digital divide. *Online Information Review, 25*(5), 311–320.

Department for Education and Employment. (2005). *Harnessing technology, transforming learning and children's services*. Retrieved June 21, 2007, from http://www.dfes.gov.uk/publications/e-strategy/

Department for Education and Employment. (1998). *The learning age*. Retrieved June 21, 2007, from http://www.lifelonglearning.co.uk/greenpaper

Erskine, J. (2003). *Learning and teaching support network. Resource guide in Virtual Learning Environments (VLEs)*. Retrieved December 6, 2005, from http://www.hlst.ltsn.ac.uk/projects/Specialists/erskine.pdf

Friesen, N. (2004). *Three objections to learning objects*. Retrieved June 21, 2007, from http://www.learningspaces.org/n/papers/objections.html

Great Britain, Home Office. (2003). *21st century skills: Realising our potential*. London: HMSO.

Gibson, A., Dixon, D., & Newton, R. (1999). Supporting open and distance learners: Practice and policy across further and higher education libraries. *Library Review*, *48*(5), 219–231.

Nixon, C., & Helms, M. (2002). Corporate universities vs. higher education institutions. *Industrial and Commercial Training*, *34*(4), 144–150.

Noble, D. (1998). Digital diploma mills: The automation of higher education. *First Monday*, (Online Journal), *3*(1). Retrieved June 21, 2007, from http://www.firstmonday.org/issues/issue3_1/index.html

Office of National Statistics. (2003). *Student enrolments on higher education courses at Publicly Funded Higher Education Institutions in the United Kingdom for the Academic Year 2001/2002*. Retrieved June 21, 2007, from http://www.hesa.ac.uk/Press/sfr56/sfr56.htm

Pailing, M. (2002). E-learning: is it really the best thing since sliced bread? *Industrial and Commercial Training*, *34*(4), 151–155.

UCISA - Universities and Colleges Information Systems Association. (2005). *VLE surveys – a longitudinal perspective between March 2001, March 2003 and March 2005 for higher education in the United Kingdom*. Retrieved June 21, 2007, from http://www.ucisa.ac.uk/groups/tlig/vle/index_html

Wooley, D. (1994). *PLATO: The emergence of online community*. Retrieved June 21, 2007, from http://thinkofit.com/plato/dwplato.htm

Paul Catherall
E-Learning Support Librarian
University of Liverpool, UK

ISAAC HUNTER DUNLAP

8. GOING DIGITAL

The Transformation of Scholarly Communication and Academic Libraries

Not since the age of Gutenberg has an information upheaval so thoroughly disrupted the processes of scholarly knowledge creation, management and preservation as the digital revolution currently under way. Academic libraries have traditionally been structured to facilitate the access, use and storage of mostly static, print-based research collections. In the midst of sweeping change university libraries are attempting to re-imagine services, embrace emerging technologies, reallocate resources and provide proactive leadership in a new digital knowledge society. This chapter provides both historical perspective and a forward-looking examination into how academic libraries are transforming themselves to both cope with, and help shape, unprecedented transitions in scholarly research and communication.

A DIGITAL REVOLUTION

Over the last 15 years academic libraries have found themselves in the throes of an information revolution probably without parallel since Johannes Gutenberg's invention of the movable type printing press in mid fifteenth-century Europe. The introduction of Gutenberg's technology meant that content formerly ensconced within handwritten manuscripts or handed down by oral tradition could now be rapidly formatted, organized and uniformly distributed to far-flung locales at an astonishing rate. The last 300 years of scholarly communication can scarcely be understood apart from this remarkable historical development (Collier, 2004; Giles, 1996; Holbert, 2002; Shuler, 2006).

While there are plentiful discontinuities between the print-based information revolution of the fifteenth century and the digital information revolution of the twenty-first, there are also strikingly similar thematic parallels. Unprecedented opportunities were created for remotely situated scientists and scholars to share discoveries; reproduce experiments; share, save and refer to mutual documents; conduct textual criticism; develop standards; challenge misconceptions and engage in high levels of relatively simultaneous dialogue. Indeed, in significant respects these chronologically disparate revolutions could be viewed as conceptually analogous.

Understandably, the monastic manuscript libraries of medieval times had been primarily tasked with securing and safeguarding rare, irreplaceable treasures. As knowledge came to be gathered, codified and transmitted in printed form, universities continued their steady rise in prestige and influence through the Renaissance and Reformation, Enlightenment, and early modern eras (Rüegg, 1992/1996). With academic libraries gradually holding books so common as to be entrusted

R. Rikowski (ed.), Digitisation Perspectives, 131–144.

to open shelves, new processes, functions and activities emerged as a matter of course. While maintaining continuity and solidarity with the long-standing monastic library tradition of knowledge preservation, university libraries also began to take on the complementary roles of systematic knowledge gathering, organization and access provision. Over time there also developed a need for basic finding aids, reference assistance and instruction in identifying relevant printed resources in existing collections (Battles, 2003).

To be sure, modern academic libraries hold innumerable advantages over their ancestral counterparts through their transition to a digital age. Today's libraries are built upon generations of achievements, contributions and sacrifices of countless individuals from both within and outside of academia. Even though long-established roles, structures and standards may sometimes hinder the way forward, they can also provide useful frames of reference and serve as conceptual bridges (or springboards) to new strategies, programs and schema during revolutionary eras filled with uncertainty and ambiguity. It is unclear how and to what degree academic libraries will meet the immense challenges that are being presented. Academic librarians have demonstrated significant leadership by quickly recognizing the fluidity of the times, and through galvanizing their profession to embrace emerging technologies for both traditional and innovative purposes (e.g., Boxen, 2008; Choi & Rasmussen, 2006; Mullins, Allen & Hufford, 2007; Regenstein & Dewey, 2003). At least in the near term this rapid and constructive response has placed academic libraries in a more favorable position to grapple with the issues created by a dynamic knowledge and information environment.

One means of better understanding how traditional academic libraries are evolving into digital libraries is to examine the internal changes occurring within library sub-units. Viewing the changing dynamics from within the framework of traditional library structures has two main advantages. The first is that the external environment can be more fully appreciated by studying it from different vantage points. The other is that viewing the overall dynamic from narrower concrete perspectives opens up possibilities for discerning the actual levels of transformation being realized throughout the entire system. Academic libraries are generally comprised of several departments or units responsible for performing a range of functions and services. Some of the more familiar academic library areas which require coordination include: collection development, reference, bibliographic instruction, and special collections. The following discussion explores some of the major themes and issues of the digital library revolution from these perspectives.

DIGITAL LIBRARY COLLECTION DEVELOPMENT

The notion of developing the so-called 'hybrid library' has received much attention in the professional library and information literature (e.g., Breaks, 2002; Casserly, 2002; Levrault, 2006; Lightman & Blosser, 2007; Pugh, 2005). Academic librarians find themselves in a complex, transitional phase as they attempt to bridge the gap between ongoing traditional information needs and a range of new expectations that the digital age has brought to university campuses. Because of massive investments in the printed word over generations, it is not a simple matter for libraries to simply 'go digital'. Though well-known digitization initiatives such as the Google Book Library Project have received much attention and have targeted high-profile university library collections, it remains unclear whether vast amounts of monographic content will ever be retrospectively digitized (Marcum, 2003; Walker, 2006). While libraries must continue the function of preserving and maintaining access to older resources, significant investments must also be made to acquire newer 'born digital' content and recently digitized traditional content (e.g. the *New York Times* historical backfile from 1851), which may already have been collected in permanent non-digital formats such as microfilm.

Within the scholarly realm, digital library development is not the sole domain of academic libraries. Publishers, vendors and scholarly associations continue to drive the scholarly content distribution process to a significant degree, though they have their own struggles in making the transition from a print-based market to a digital services culture (Bacher, 2004; Johnson & Luther, 2008; Seitter & Heideman, 2009; Shaver & Enright, 2002). Among other challenges, they must contend with collection development librarians who are asking tough questions, such as 'if we cancel our print subscription, what guarantee do we have that the digital content we supposedly "own" will be available if your company goes out of business or its servers fail?' Journal publications and other periodical content that was once collected and physically stored on climate-controlled library shelves has taken on an ephemeral quality in the digital age. Academic libraries are rightfully demanding 'archival rights' to the content they purchase. Not surprisingly, many university libraries have enthusiastically backed not-for-profit e-journal storage and perpetual archive initiatives such as JSTOR and Portico.[1]

For many years academic libraries have been struggling to cope with declining collection development budgets. Even libraries with budgets remaining relatively static have experienced a rapid deterioration in available spending power as inflation and spiking journal costs (particularly in the scientific fields) have taken their toll in both electronic and print formats (that is, when the print versions still exist) (Drake, 2007). While the scholarly publishing industry has been innovative in providing electronic access to scholarly journals, these initiatives have often come with high dollar values attached. Since the 1980s university libraries have become increasingly concerned with the prohibitive costs of collecting highly respected 'core' journal titles held by a handful of publishers who can demand almost any price.

In response to this predicament libraries have taken a significant leadership role in helping to form and shape the Open Access (OA) movement. Scholars are now actively encouraged to deposit their articles in freely accessible institutional or central repositories in addition to publishing their works in peer-reviewed commercial publications. The simultaneous development of peer-reviewed OA e-journals has also provided scholars with an alternate means for disseminating their research. OA assists authors by enabling the broad and rapid dissemination of their new research. There is also growing evidence that OA articles are cited more frequently and widely than non-OA articles published within the same journal, helping to further accelerate the value and impact of scholarly research.

The continuing development of the OA movement may assist libraries in potentially ameliorating the 'sky high' periodical pricing of publishing monopolies over the long term, and is an example of how libraries are working to develop new infrastructures as traditional scholarly communication models become untenable (Bergman, 2006; Hajjem & Gingras, 2005; Harnad et al., 2008; Norris, Oppenheim & Rowland, 2008; Van Orsdel, 2007).

Interestingly, it is not uncommon for libraries that are attempting to navigate these difficult periodical migration issues to face a determined backlash from scholars who remain wedded to traditional print collections, scholarly publishing and research practices. University libraries face other challenges, as they must commit resources and personnel toward developing infrastructures (e.g. computer classrooms, wireless networks, 'information commons' spaces, web gateways and portals) for supporting and providing access to rapidly expanding digital information resources that many faculty and students enthusiastically seek (Beard & Dale, 2008; Branin, 2007; Dallis & Walters, 2006).

In the area of collection development the last 20 years have seen the library and information science literature filled with accounts and investigations as to how the momentous advent of the digital age, along with innovations in scholarly publishing models, have altered the shape of scholarly communication and the research processes of most disciplines in fundamental respects. Academic collection development librarians will face considerable challenges in the coming years as they work to strengthen collections and maintain their viability in the face of rising price points and uncertainty regarding the long-term research and information needs of scholars and students alike (Greco, 2006; Head, 2008; Heath, 2007; Palmer, 2005; Walters, 2006).

DIGITAL LIBRARY ELECTRONIC RESOURCE DEVELOPMENT

Academic libraries depend upon their collection development processes to remain current, relevant and to fulfil their institutional missions. One of the dominant themes in the creation of scholarly digital libraries has been a focus upon the acquisition of digital collections. Obviously, collection building is a known and well-established function within university libraries. It is not surprising that many library directors have turned to their collection managers (or often, created new varieties of collection resource managers) in the pursuit of making their libraries more conversant in the digital age. In many cases, the more conventional collection development functions (e.g. monograph purchases) continue to be handled as they have been for decades, albeit academic book suppliers and their library clients have streamlined operations via the use of Electronic Data Interchange (EDI) invoicing, web-based portals and the gradual elimination of time-honored paper 'slips' ordering systems.

One popular means of blending traditional collection-building activities with digital collection development is by creating a new position with the title 'Electronic Resource Librarian'. A review of academic library job lists reveals a demand for librarians tasked with acquiring scholarly resources in digital formats. Their duties are many but often include: e-journal vendor/publisher negotiation, licensing/contract review (with a close eye on ensuring the retention of digital archival rights) and monitoring the contents of aggregated e-serial databases. Also included are managing link resolvers that create automatic 'on-the-fly' hypertext links between bibliographic citations in subject databases and their corresponding full-text articles residing in various multidisciplinary subscription databases, researching more advantageous subscription terms through consortium partnerships, and determining how to most effectively restructure or consolidate periodical subscription arrangements based on the research and information needs of the scholars and students at their institutions (Creech, 2006; Grogg, 2006; Fisher, 2003; Jacobs 2007).

While the digital collection development activities described above are a relatively new phenomenon for academic libraries, in some respects they remain closely aligned to traditional resource acquisition and collection management processes. What makes them particularly unique are their digital format, their networked access points (which electronic resource librarians frequently help configure by sharing their campus's IP (Internet Protocol) addresses with the online content provider), and the ongoing technical support that the librarian is often called upon to provide as end users experience difficulties with network connectivity, authentication, web browser configurations, and the missing full-text articles that were supposed to be available, but were not included in the printed journal's online version.

DIGITAL LIBRARIES VS. DIGITAL COLLECTIONS

In the popular mind, at least, there is a tendency to equate the building of digital library collections with building digital libraries. There are important distinctions to be made between libraries extending their collections to include digitally formatted materials and libraries performing the far more complex task of institutional transformation. Clifford Lynch (2003), Executive Director of the Coalition for Networked Information, has noted that:

> As we gain experience with the digitization of material, I think that we are starting to understand that digital collections and digital libraries are not co-terminus; they are not equivalent. Digital libraries are more than digital collections; they are software systems that are underpinned, in part, by digital collections, but, in fact, there is not a one-to-one relationship. We may have many digital libraries presenting material that is drawn from many digital collections in very complicated ways, over time. We understand digital collections, I would say, a whole lot better than we understand digital libraries. Digital libraries get us into a lot of *terra incognito*, and they invite us to go places where libraries have been very scared to go, where they have not gone historically. (pp. 287–288)

Quite appropriately, Lynch divides the frequently merged concepts of digital libraries and digital collections. With proper funding and a sound technical infrastructure in place, a competent electronic resources librarian can acquire an impressive collection of digital academic resources including: subject-specific bibliographic indexes, multidisciplinary full-text article databases, standalone e-journals, retrospectively digitized serial titles, reference and monographic e-books, image collections, streaming music collections, primary source materials, and many more. This kind of collection-building is extremely valuable – indeed, it is difficult to imagine how an academic digital library could begin to function or even have any meaning without providing access to these types of digital resources.

Perhaps one of the main reasons that digital libraries and digital collections are so often equated is due to the magnitude of the overwhelming scholarly tradition that has been handed down in printed form. With this amazing wealth of knowledge physically arranged in row upon orderly row of unending library book stacks, it may seem natural for some observers to view the digital library revolution as fundamentally an alteration in how scholarly content is packaged – a format change – much like the successful historical process of transferring deteriorating newspaper collections onto microfilm for improved access and safe-keeping. Certainly, a fundamental format shift has occurred and its effects continue to reverberate. Never before has scholarly content been made so accessible, transportable and malleable. Digital content is capable of being rapidly integrated into derivative forms, formulated into building blocks for research and study, and assimilated into more complex frameworks and online learning systems.

Digital libraries, however, are about far more than packaging. They also transcend Lynch's rather narrow labelling of being mere 'software'. Digital libraries have become a complex, interactive and interdependent network of resources, user services, social technology interactions, databases, virtual meetings, gateways, 'real time' online instruction opportunities and content management systems. While digital libraries actively develop and utilize software systems as tools, this is but one facet of a much larger, dynamic framework that academic libraries are building for the institutions they serve. Just as a 'brick and mortar' library is far more than an inventoried warehouse (e.g. traditional libraries provide access services, reference services, instructional services, interlibrary loan services, learning spaces, etc.), digital libraries in academic environments must necessarily provide an entire range of 'cutting edge' information services to support teaching, learning and research in both general education disciplines and highly specialized fields.

Lynch is right to note the historical tendency for libraries to let others take the lead (e.g. computer and information sciences) in developing electronic knowledge architectures, albeit many innovative library development initiatives have occurred over the last 30 years.[2] While the impetus for innovation is driving libraries to focus their attention on creating and leveraging exciting technologies, heavy shoulders burdened with print-based scholarly collections have also worked to bring academic libraries into a sort of equilibrium that has given birth to the 'hybrid' digital library model. As academic libraries strive to serve and respond to the curricular needs of their institutions, it is not surprising that many would adopt an intermediate approach which attempts to bridge the print and digital worlds.

DIGITAL LIBRARY REFERENCE SERVICES

So-called 'social networking technologies' have made major inroads into the academic library arena as reference librarians have quickly adopted blogs, wikis, discussion boards, chat programs, text messaging, Instant Messaging (IM), and related 'virtual reference' services over the last few years. More 'traditional' email reference services have continued to be a mainstay as students and faculty send their messages via a web-based form or via direct emails to a generic library reference desk email account. Since virtual services may reference and provide user assistance with both traditional and digital resources, it is the intentional and creative use of innovative technologies which give these library services their digital character. Library vending companies have developed software allowing reference librarians to 'push' content to the end user's web browser during the online reference interview process. The content that is forwarded may include full-text articles and online reference sources. On other occasions librarians may showcase 'live' demonstrations of navigating a website, finding books via a library catalog or effectively searching a bibliographic database to address a user's specific information needs (Bishop, 2006; Boxen, 2008; Chase, 2007; Cummings, Cummings & Frederiksen, 2007; Erdman, 2007).

Efforts at providing 'late night' and even 24 hour virtual reference services are well under way at many university libraries. Through consortium-based initiatives and other partnerships, librarians from many institutions take turns 'staffing' the virtual reference desks. Partnerships with institutions located in different time zones have also provided a convenient means of offering online reference services on a continuing basis. One of the difficulties that is sometimes experienced in these exchanges involves the lack of uniform digital collection access. For instance, a student at a small college in California may have access to a different set of subject databases than does a librarian at a large university in North Carolina or Australia (Devlin et al., 2006; Devoe, 2008; IFLA, 2008; Library of Congress, 2006).

New generations of students and scholars have never known life without the existence of the Internet. Along with the Web's ubiquity and the advent of cellular and wireless technologies which improve access, the information needs and expectations of users have radically changed. Librarians in public service positions are continuing to discuss and explore new and better ways to assist increasing populations of users who may never physically visit a library reference desk, and may not understand that some of the scholarly resources they need are not yet (and may never be) available online.

DIGITAL LIBRARY BIBLIOGRAPHIC INSTRUCTION

One of the greatest services that academic librarians can provide is helping users to better understand and navigate the rapidly changing information resource environment. Though this educational process has always been very important, it has taken on increased significance in the evolving digital world. What used to be called 'bibliographic instruction' is increasingly being redefined as a process to promote 'information literacy'. While bibliographic instruction harkens back to the scholarly print culture of educating people how to research, identify and acquire knowledge contained in static sources such as 'books' (*biblio*), the increased application of the phrase 'information literacy' denotes the recognition that the entire information-seeking process has fundamentally been changed by the digital revolution.

The format and nature of scholarly communication access has effectively been transformed.

Even the most basic vehicles of library access have evolved as users must be at least minimally fluent with computer hardware and software applications to have any chance of successfully acquiring information in the current knowledge environment. Instructors who not very many years ago were presenting library research methods with the use of chalk, transparencies and the physical demonstration of a printed index, are now routinely operating in electronic classrooms with interactive whiteboards, digital projection units, and computer workstations for every student in the class (Jackson, 2007; Kimura, 2007; Williams, 2007).

The indexing and abstracting tools which once filled library reference shelves have largely been reformatted, digitized and transferred to searchable databases. Along with this development, libraries have begun to embrace complex (and not always user-intuitive) federated search engines, created with an eye towards improving information access by simultaneously conducting keyword searches across multiple academic databases. This 'shot-gun' approach to database searching allows for broadly-distributed queries, but tends to overlook the value of using authority-level subject headings and descriptors that are often unique to each disciplinary database. End users looking for speed and general relevancy over precision continue to seek simple, 'Google-like', keyword queries over carefully crafted information retrieval strategies based on complex Boolean searches (Cervone, 2005; Linoski & Walczyk, 2008; Wrubel & Schmidt, 2007).

One of the scholarly research values which may have been lost in this unfolding process is the need for a moderate measure of perseverance and determination. The successful navigation and identification of the best and most appropriate information resources sometimes requires the application of some effort and skill. However, the information-seeking behavior of undergraduates (and even of graduate students and faculty) is in migration as information researchers seem to regard speed over relevancy and comprehensiveness (George, Bright, Hurlbert, et al., 2006; Head, 2008; Martin, 2008; Weiler, 2005). Researching how academic users search for content, Angela Weiler (2005) found that:

> Regarding criteria for information seeking, the concern for time spent locating information was brought up the most often across the board, among undergraduates, graduate students, and faculty. It was considered to be both of great importance and also in undersupply. Indeed, they rated most information-seeking experiences based on how much time they took, and often will accept inappropriate information or information of lower quality if finding it takes less time. They referred to information seeking as taking time away from other things that they viewed as more important. (p. 50)

Significantly, students are also having increased difficulty critically assessing the quality, reliability and validity of information resources. Given the torrents of digital information flooding the diverse channels of access, it is little wonder that students and others are becoming overwhelmed in the deluge. Reference and instructional librarians continue to serve as valuable educational agents within the research process. As they facilitate the growth and development of critical thinking and evaluation skills, academic librarians are helping students to become better informed and more responsible information researchers and consumers. Library user services such as these are likely to become even more important in the coming years as digital information creation and use continues to escalate (Dunlap, 2006; Griffiths & Brophy, 2005; Hutton, 2008).

DIGITAL LIBRARY SPECIAL COLLECTIONS

The digitization of special collections is one of the most exciting areas of academic librarianship. An astonishing renaissance is well under way in the attention and care directed towards rare manuscripts, books, photographs, art, papyri and other cultural treasures found in the archives of university libraries. Collections that were once cordoned off and assigned restricted use policies are now being revitalized as new technologies have improved preservation and enabled unprecedented levels of access (Dunlap, 2005; Hockey, 2006; Hutton, 2008; Mattison, 2006).

As aging primary sources deteriorate over time, the creation of digital collections is particularly important in the humanities. John Unsworth (2004, see also Salsich, 2006) has noted the importance of establishing collaborative relationships between scholars and librarians during the digitization process:

> With respect to the humanities, objects of study can be images, texts, sounds, maps, performances, concepts, three-dimensional objects. When we make a digital surrogate for any one of these, we always believe that our aim is to represent it as accurately, as faithfully as possible, with the least possible interference, or noise, in the process – but when, as scholars, we deal with these digital surrogates, or produce our own, we learn that there's no such thing as an innocent act of representation: every representation is an interpretation ... the real value of digitization for humanities scholarship is that it externalizes what we think we know about the materials we work with, and in so doing, it shows us where we have overlooked, or misunderstood, or misrepresented significant features of those materials.

Libraries need to support and enhance this dynamic interplay unfolding between scholars and librarians tasked with digitizing and preserving special forms of knowledge for future generations. The process of preserving and rejuvenating the study of these precious materials continues to evolve as new technologies and standards are introduced. While the long-term impact on the scholarly research process is unknown, critical digitization decisions are being made on a daily basis which will undoubtedly influence how future generations of researchers go about accessing and evaluating rare and unique materials.

There is often an expectation that researchers in the so-called 'hard sciences' are the most comfortable and adept at using computers and incorporating new technologies into their activities. Yet even in the humanities, where one might presume that scholars would happily ignore advanced technology altogether, they too are enthusiastically embracing the digital age. In his book *Digital Libraries and the Challenges of Digital Humanities*, classicist Jeffrey Rydberg-Cox (2006) notes:

> Digital technologies have had a profound impact on the way that many scholars in the humanities conduct and share their research. Once a text is digitized, even the simplest search facilities allow users to interact with and study texts in entirely new ways. Electronic media open new modes of dissemination and new ways of thinking about texts; scholars can use interactive music scores, dynamically generated maps, or other multimedia elements to communicate information in ways that are very different from prose printed on a page. (p. 1)

Libraries are actively using technology to bring 'dead' works back into the field of study as they are made more accessible, usable and known. In some respects the digital archivists of today are applying similar forms of wizardry and skill to valued materials as manuscript artists and curators of medieval times. However, a more esteemed connection may persist in their shared commitment to the preservation of knowledge for future generations.

CONCLUSION

Academic libraries are responding proactively to the challenges of a dynamic information environment that is thoroughly revamping long-standing research and scholarly communication processes. Concurrently, libraries themselves are being transformed at every institutional level in profound, systemic ways. Librarians are grappling to identify 'best practices' in the use of innovative technology to provide outstanding services to users who may need to interact with both traditional and digital collections. The digital libraries being created are frequently drawing from (or reacting against) established structures, roles and functions that academic libraries successfully employed in a print-based knowledge society.

While it remains to be seen, the creation of the 'hybrid' digital library model could be a short-term phenomenon based on a current, and undeniable, need for a continuum between traditional and emerging structures. As the digital information environment continues to evolve, academic libraries must be prepared to address a variety of pressing issues and challenges including: funding, staff training and development, digital archival rights management, scholarly publishing concerns, rising journal costs, budget prioritization, identification of innovative (and useful) technologies, preservation and maintenance of dynamic multimedia knowledge sets, digital content management, accessible web design, database development and public services enhancements, among others. Libraries must also respond to an almost unlimited assortment of new and changing user expectations as faculty and students go about their digital research and learning activities.

The commonalities observed between Gutenberg's print-based revolution and the digital revolution of today serve as a reminder that certain universals tend to endure. In whatever form or format scholarly content may need to inhabit, there will be an ongoing need for it to be gathered, organized, made accessible and preserved.

As the digital revolution is in its infancy, it is certainly possible that new institutions will emerge to perform these responsibilities. However, one is also struck by the incipient ability of academic libraries to rapidly adapt, make important contributions and energetically engage this new digital environment in significant ways. It can at least be fairly observed in this most primordial of stages that academic libraries are electing to seek innovation and adaptation rather than fatalistically turning themselves over to mumpsimus recalcitrance. This is a significant trend in the early history of academic digital libraries as researchers and students will undoubtedly seek information services that are relevant, user-friendly and viable in the years to come.

NOTES

1 See *JSTOR* (Journal Storage Archive) at http://www.jstor.org; and the *Portico* scholarly e-journal archive at http://www.portico.org. *Portico*'s stated mission is to 'preserve scholarly literature published in electronic form and to ensure these materials remain accessible to future scholars, researchers and students' (see also Fenton, 2006; Spinella, 2007).

2 There are countless examples including the introduction of the LCS (Library Computer System) at the University of Illinois at Urbana-Champaign in the late 1970s, which led to state-wide resource sharing (Sloan, 1986); the 'MyLibrary' user-customized library portal at North Carolina State University (Morgan, 2003); the development of numerous Open Source software applications (e.g., Albanes, 2008; Dunlap, 2005; Rhyno, 2003); and the early adoption of numerous "social networking" technologies to enhance reference services (Boxen, 2008; Erdman, 2007).

REFERENCES

Albanes, A. (2008). Duke open source ILS funded. *Library Journal, 133*(14), 22.

Bacher, T. (2004). When terrabytes meet terra firma: Scholarly information digitization and distribution. *Journal of Library Administration, 40*(1/2), 107–125.

Battles, M. (2003). *Library: an unquiet history*. New York: W.W. Norton.

Beard, J., & Dale, P. (2008). Redesigning services for the Net-Gen and beyond: A holistic review of pedagogy, resource, and learning space. *New Review of Academic Librarianship, 14*(1/2), 99–114.

Bergman, S. S. (2006). The scholarly communication movement: Highlights and recent developments. *Collection Building, 25*(4), 108–128. Retrieved May 10, 2010, from http://dx.doi.org/10.1108/01604950610705989

Bishop, B. W. (2006). Virtual reference services: Consortium versus stand-alone. *College & Undergraduate Libraries, 13*(4), 117–127.

Boxen, J. (2008). Library 2.0: A review of the literature. *The Reference Librarian, 49*(1), 21–34.

Branin, J. J. (2007). Shaping our space: Envisioning the new research library. *Journal of Library Administration, 46*(2), 27–53.

Breaks, M. (2002). Building the hybrid library: A review of UK activities. *Learned Publishing, 15*(2), 99–107. Retrieved May 10, 2010, from http://dx.doi.org/10.1087/09531510252848854

Casserly, M. F. (2002). Developing a concept of collection for the digital age. *Portal: Libraries and the Academy, 2*(4), 577–587. Retrieved May 10, 2010, from http://dx.doi.org/10.1353/pla.2002.0073

Cervone, F. (2005). What we've learned from doing usability testing on OpenURL resolvers and federated search engines. *Computers in Libraries, 25*(9), 10–14.

Chase, D. (2007). Transformative sharing with instant messaging, wikis, interactive maps, and Flickr. *Computers in Libraries, 27*(1), 7–56.

Choi, Y., & Rasmussen, E. (2006). What is needed to educate future digital librarians: A study of current practice and staffing patterns in academic and research libraries. *D-Lib Magazine, 12*(9). Retrieved May 10, 2010, from http://www.dlib.org/dlib/september06/choi/09choi.html

Collier, M. (2004). After the digital library decade: Where are the next frontiers for library innovation. In J. Andrews & D. Law (Eds.), *Digital libraries: Policy, planning and practice*. Aldershot: Ashgate.

Creech, A. L. (2006). Managing digital resources, or, how do you hold electrons in your hand? *Against the Grain, 18*(2), 30–34.

Cummings, J., Cummings, L., & Frederiksen, L. (2007). User preferences in references services: Virtual reference and academic libraries. *Portal: Libraries & the Academy, 7*(1), 81–96.

Dallis, D., & Walters, C. (2006). Reference services in the commons environment. *Reference Services Review, 34*(2), 248–260.

Devlin, F. A., Bunch, N. J., Stockham, M. G., Summey, T. P., & Turtle, E. C. (2006). Getting beyond institutional cultures: When rivals collaborate. *Journal of Library Administration, 45*(1/2), 149–168.

Devoe, K. (2008). Chat widgets: Placing your virtual reference services at your user's point(s) of need. *The Reference Librarian, 49*(1), 99–101.

Drake, M. A. (2007). Scholarly communication in turmoil. *Information Today, 24*(2).

Dunlap, I. H. (2006). *Open source database driven web development*. Oxford: Chandos.

Dunlap, I. H. (2005). Open source digital image management. *Computers in Libraries, 25*(4), 6–48 (6).

Erdman, J. (2007). Reference in a 3-D virtual world: Preliminary observations on library outreach in Second Life. *The Reference Librarian, 47*(98), 29–39.

Fenton, E. G. (2006). An overview of Portico: An electronic archiving service. *Serials Review, 32*(2), 81–86. Retrieved May 10, 2010, from http://dx.doi.org/10.1016/j.serrev.2006.03.004

Fisher, W. (2003). The electronic resources librarian position: A public services phenomenon? *Library Collections, Acquisitions, & Technical Services, 27*(1), 3–17.

George, C., Bright, A., & Hurlbert, T., et al. (2006). Scholarly use of information: graduate students' information seeking behaviour. *Information Research, 11*(4).

Giles, M. W. (1996). From Gutenberg to gigabytes: Scholarly communication in the age of cyberspace. *Journal of Politics, 58*(3), 613–626. Retrieved May 2010, from http://dx.doi.org/10.2307/2960435

Greco, A. N. (2006). Recent trends in scholarly communications: 2001–2005. *Journal of Scholarly Publishing, 37*(4), 287–306.

Griffiths, J. R., & Brophy, P. (2005). Student searching behavior and the Web: Use of academic resources and Google. *Library Trends, 53*(4), 539–554.

Grogg, J. E. (2006). Innovative uses of the OpenURL. *Library Technology Reports, 42*(1), 35–37.

Hajjem, C., Harnad, S., & Gingras, Y. (2005). Ten-year cross-disciplinary comparison of the growth of open access and how it increases research citation impact. *IEEE Data Engineering Bulletin, 28*(4), 39–47.

Harnad, S., Brody, T., Vallieres, F., Carr, L., Hitchcock, S., Gingras, Y., et al. (2008). The access/impact problem and the green and gold roads to Open Access: An update. *Serials Review, 34*(1), 3640.

Head, A. (2008). Information literacy from the trenches: How do humanities and social science majors conduct academic research? *College & Research Libraries, 69*(5), 427–445.

Heath, F. (2007). The impact of evolving information-seeking behaviors upon research libraries: A case study. *Journal of Library Administration, 46*(2), 3–16.

Hockey, S. (2006). The rendering of humanities information in a digital context. *ASLIB Proceedings, 58*(1/2), 89–101. Retrieved May 10, 2010, from http://dx.doi.org/10.1108/00012530610648699

Holbert, G. L. (2002). Technology, libraries and the Internet: A comparison of the impact of the printing press and World Wide Web. *Electronic Journal of Academic and Special Librarianship, 3*(1–2).

Hutton, J. (2008). Academic libraries as digital gateways: Linking students to the burgeoning wealth of open online collections. *Journal of Library Administration, 48*(3/4), 495–507.

International Federation of Library Associations (IFLA). (2008, March). *IFLA digital reference guidelines*. Retrieved March 25, 2009, from http://www.ifla.org/VII/s36/pubs/drg03.htm

Jackson, P. A. (2007). Integrating information literacy into Blackboard: Building campus partnerships for successful student learning. *Journal of Academic Librarianship, 33*(4), 454–461. Retrieved from http://dx.doi.org/10.1016/j.acalib.2007.03.010

Jacobs, M. (Ed.). (2007). *Electronic resources librarianship and management of digital information:Emerging professional roles*. Binghamton, NY: Haworth Information Press.

Johnson, R. K., & Luther, J. (2008). Are journal publishers trapped in the dual-media transition zone? *ARL: A Bimonthly Report on Research Library Issues & Actions, 257*, 1–6.

Kimura, S. (2007). Information literacy assessment: Standards-based tools and assignments. *Reference & User Services Quarterly, 46*(4), 96.

Levrault, B. R. (2006). Integration in academic reference departments: From print to digital resources. *Acquisitions Librarian, 18*(35/36), 21–36.

Library of Congress. (2006, April 24). *Global reference network*. Retrieved March 25, 2009, from http://www.loc.gov/rr/digiref/

Lightman, H., & Blosser, J. P. (Eds.). (2007). *Perspectives on serials in the hybrid environment*. Chicago: Association for Library Collections & Technical Services.

Linoski, A., & Walczyk, T. (2008). Federated search 101. *Library Journal, 133*, 2–5.

Lombardo, S. V., & Condic, K. S. (2001). Convenience of content: A study of undergraduate periodical Use. *Reference Services Review, 29*(4), 327–337.

Lynch, C. (2003). Digital library opportunities. *Journal of Academic Librarianship, 29*(5), 287–288.

Marcum, D. (2003). Requirements for the future digital library. *Journal of Academic Librarianship, 29*(5), 276–279. Retrieved May 10, 2010, from http://dx.doi.org/10.1016/S0099-1333(03)00065-X

Martin, J. (2008). The information seeking behavior of undergraduate education majors: Does library instruction play a role? *Evidence Based Library and Information Practice, 3*(4), 4–17.

Mattison, D. (2006). The digital humanities revolution. *Searcher, 14*(5), 25–34.

Morgan, E. L. (2003, Fall). Putting the 'My' in MyLibrary. *Net Connect*, 24–26.

Mullins, J. L., Allen, F. R., & Hufford, J. R. (2007). Top ten assumptions for the future of academic Libraries and librarians: A report from the ACRL research committee. *College and Research Libraries News, 68*(4), 240–246.

Norris, M., Oppenheim, C., & Rowland, F. (2008). The citation advantage of open-access articles. *Journal of the American Society for Information Science & Technology, 59*(12), 1963–1972.

Palmer, C. L. (2005). Scholarly work and the shaping of digital access. *Journal of the American Society for Information Science and Technology, 56*(11), 1140–1153.

Pugh, L. (2005). The management of hybrid libraries. *Library & Information Research, 29*(92), 13–31.

Regenstein, C. E., & Dewey, B. I. (2003). *Leadership, higher education, and the Information Age: A new era for information technology and libraries*. New York: Neal-Schuman.

Rhyno, A. (2003). *Using open source systems for digital libraries*. Westport, CT: Libraries Unlimited.

Rüegg, W. (Ed.). (1992/1996). *A history of the university in Europe* (Vols. 1–2). Cambridge: Cambridge University Press.

Rydberg-Cox, J. A. (2006). *Digital libraries and the challenges of digital humanities*. Oxford: Chandos.

Salsich, A. C. (2006). Collaboration: Paradigm of the digital cultural content environment. *Journal of Archival Organization, 4*(3/4), 119–131.

Seitter, K. L., & Heideman, K. F. (2009). Whither print? Staying nimble in the face of uncertainty. *Learned Publishing, 22*(2), 113–116.

Shaver, L., & Enright, N. (2002). The day of the electronic library: The digital transformation. *Information Outlook, 6*(8), 26–32.

Shuler, J. (2006). The revolution will not be cataloged: Gutenberg's librarians and the 21st century. *Journal of Academic Librarianship, 32*(5), 540–542. Retrieved May 10, 2010, from http://dx.doi.org/10.1016/j.acalib.2006.07.002

Sloan, B. G. (1986). Resource sharing among academic libraries: The LCS (Library Computer System) experience. *Journal of Academic Librarianship, 12*(1), 26–29.

Spinella, M. P. (2007). JSTOR: Past, present, and future. *Journal of Library Administration, 46*(2), 55–78.

Stevens, C. R. (2007). Beyond preaching to the choir: Information literacy, faculty outreach, and disciplinary journals. *Journal of Academic Librarianship, 33*(2), 254–267. Retrieved from http://dx.doi.org/10.1016/j.acalib.2006.08.009

Unsworth, J. (2004, May 17). *The value of digitization for libraries and humanities scholarship.* A paper presented at the Newberry Library. Retrieved March 25, 2009, from http://www3.isrl.uiuc.edu/~unsworth/newberry.04.html

Van Orsdel, L. C. (2007). The state of scholarly communications: An environmental scan of emerging issues, pitfalls, and possibilities. *Serials Librarian, 52*(1/2), 191–209.

Walker, L. (2006, May 18). Google's goal: A worldwide web of books. *Washington Post*, p. D1.

Walters, T. O. (2006). Strategies and frameworks for institutional repositories and the new support infrastructure for scholarly communications. *D-Lib Magazine, 12*(10).

Weiler, A. (2005). Information-seeking behavior in Generation Y students: Motivation, critical thinking, and learning theory. *Journal of Academic Librarianship, 31*(1), 46–53. Retrieved from http://dx.doi.org/10.1016/j.acalib.2004.09.009

Williams, G. (2007). Unclear on the context: Refocusing on information literacy's evaluative component in the age of Google. *Library Philosophy & Practice, 9*(3), 1–10.

Wrubel, L., & Schmidt, K. (2007). Usability testing of a metasearch interface: A case study. *College & Research Libraries, 68*(4), 292–311.

Isaac Hunter Dunlap
University Libraries
Western Illinois University, USA

PART III: DIGITISATION AND INEQUALITIES

TONY WARD

9. HEGEMONY AND THE WEB

The Struggle for Hegemony in a Digital Age

BACKGROUND

For five years, from 2001 to 2006, I worked as Director of Programme Development at Te Whare Wananga o Awanuirangi – one of three Maori Tertiary Institutes in New Zealand. Prior to that I taught and practised Architecture in Britain, the US and New Zealand, and completed my PhD in Architecture/Critical Pedagogy in 1997.

My new job at the Wananga included writing degree and sub-degree programmes in a wide variety of subjects and gaining accreditation for them from the Government's Qualification Authority (NZQA). During that time I helped to develop a wide range of degree programmes – Art and Visual Culture, Media Studies, Nursing, Matauranga Maori (Maori Knowledge), Maori Language and Early Childhood Education. All of them were unique in that they were founded upon traditional Maori practices, understandings and codes of behaviour (tikanga). All these progammes also had a critical anti-colonial perspective. There are three recognised Wananga in New Zealand that were developed in response to Maori community pressure which led to the 1991 Education Amendment Act. This Act recognised the importance of structuring education to take account of cultural differences and identities and, in the case of Maori, their demand for *Tino Rangatiratanga* (Maori Sovereignty) which they saw as guaranteed under the 1840 Treaty of Waitangi. The programmes that we were developing therefore had a very heavy cultural, social and political undertone.

At the same time that I was developing programmes I was also teaching Critical Pedagogy and Contemporary Cultural Studies in a Teacher Education programme based on *BlendEd* principles – that is, a mixture of face-to-face and online learning. Our face-to-face contact took place over block one-week residential courses. The rest of the time I would work online with the students two evenings a week. In general, the process worked very well. Working in critical education with indigenous peoples is not hard work. They already have a critical perspective on the education system and see it as an instrument of colonisation and assimilation, and this was no less true of my Maori students. When difficulties occurred, it was usually around issues of access or technology. Some of the students did not have their own computers or access to reliable phone lines for dial-up connection. Very few had high-speed DSL connections. This made communication fragmented and difficult at times but we persevered and by and large did well. The experience did, however, bring to mind the issue of the so-called *Digital Divide*. This became even more apparent when later I was asked to participate in developing a range of programmes in Computing – from the earliest levels up to and beyond degree level.

R. Rikowski (ed.), Digitisation Perspectives, 147–166.

Then the Digital Divide became a sobering reality as I studied the statistics of digital penetrations and exclusions. What became clear was that in the modern (digital) world the realms of politics, economics, education and the media have never before been so closely interwoven. In this brief reflection I look at some of the interconnecting links and relationships between them.

INTRODUCTION

The term *Digital Divide* has been in use since the mid-1990s, when it was first used to describe the growing gap between those who have access to digital technologies and those who do not. It is often used to describe the serious issues of access to computer technologies between the West (OECD Countries), the "Developing" Countries (DCs) and "Least Developed Countries" (LDCs), but it has also been used to describe the differences in access that exist within nations and between communities. At the global scale the repercussions of a widening IT gap carry significant social, political and economic implications. As international commerce becomes increasingly digitised, and as time and space accordingly shrink, it is precisely the most digitally-capable economies and peoples that are best placed to exploit the flow of capital, and to access company information that can only be accessed through digital technology. Those (Least Developed) countries in what used to be called the Third World who lack access to the digital world stand to once again be the object of economic exploitation.

It has been suggested that the digital and Internet revolution of the last twenty years has created what amounts to a "virtual space" which transcends nation-state boundaries. It is this space that is now potentially the site of a new and extremely powerful wave of neo-colonialism. As with other spaces that have been subject to the forces of globalisation, the digital space and economy can be expected to exacerbate the growing economic disparities not only across the global community but within the communities of the developed world as well. The struggle for control of the digital environment promises to become a major battle-ground to determine the information available to citizens as well as the normative meanings of key concepts like "democracy", "representation" and so on.

The battle-lines to occupy and control the nature and form of that space and the information that constitutes it are already drawn. A 2007 report on Wikipedia editing[1] showed that the CIA and FBI had been involved in editing entries on Guantanamo, Iraq casualty figures and other relevant items. It is to be expected, of course, that the struggle for hegemony involves the control of information, and the Internet provides merely another extended field of struggle. The (electronic) struggle between the power status quo and the advocates of Open Access for control of cyberspace is ongoing, and in no small part sites like Wikipedia which describe the multiple cultural and historical realities of society are the prime targets of neo-colonial hegemony-creation. Faced with the issue of authenticity, Wikipedia has already begun to introduce its own criteria for "legitimate" editing.

As George Orwell once profoundly wrote:

> Who controls the past controls the future. Who controls the present controls the past.[2]

THE DIGITAL DIVIDE

The term *Digital Divide* has been used to mean several different things. It can be used to describe the differing levels of access to computer hardware, to Internet access, or (as mostly in the case of my Maori students) to differences in access to Broadband technologies. As education systems and global economies become increasingly digitised disparities of access to digital technology (whether it be hardware, software of transmission/reception systems) become increasingly critical, and many authors have voiced their concern about what we might call digital colonialism. As electoral systems increasingly embrace digital technology these same disparities raise questions about digital citizenship – the ability of every citizen to participate equally in the political process.

Politicians stake their futures on being able to "bridge" or "close" the digital divide, in general, by promising "universal Broadband" or, in education, by promising to provide computers to all school children. Accordingly, the political emphasis, particularly under the Bush administration in the USA, has now generally switched from focusing on disparities between social and economic groups and more on the *growth* of broadband access. Nevertheless, criteria associated with the Digital Divide are generally recognised as including socio-economic status, income, educational level, race, gender and age. One might also reinsert here that much neglected term *class*. The social variable of class has been elided from critical discourse since the advent of Poststructuralism and Postmodernism. It has been replaced by the discourses of cultural pluralism and identity. The benefit of reinscribing class in any analysis of economic or technological disparity is to reinstate the critical issue of *agency* together with an awareness of the moving principles of displacement, exploitation and subjugation of peoples in the name and interests of capital. While digital technology is increasingly promoted as a vehicle for reducing class inequality, in reality, it provides merely another vehicle for the creation of class divisions that are the necessary compost to "development", investment and the growth of capital.

For while there is a great deal of literature extant on attempts to "diminish", "reduce", "cross", "bridge" or "narrow" the Digital Divide the fact remains that at both the scale of the nation state or the global economy, the need to maintain an underclass of exploited workers in order to keep wages low has always been a basic requirement of the capitalist system, and for this to happen, there needs to be an unspoken ethic of systematic *exclusion* operating at all times. This process of exclusion is integral to the production and sale of all commodities – including knowledge.

If we view the Internet and ICT as another space in which knowledge is created, shaped, disseminated and controlled in the interests of maintaining the hegemony of and sustaining the power of the status quo, then there is much that we can learn from a brief reflection on how this process operates on the basis of inherent exclusions.

THE PROMISE OF THE INTERNET

Advocates of Open Access maintain that the transparency of communicative actions offered by the Internet offers the most robust safeguard for Democracy. The Internet is seen as a space where everybody can have a voice, can be heard and can express their own realities, in this way helping to moderate and balance the operations of power and capital that have shaped and constrained all prior media systems. But even a brief surf across the Internet shows that the vast majority of communications are about trivia. Whether this will continue to be the case as people find their public voice is a moot point.

In any case, we are increasingly overwhelmed by the cacophony of voices that the Internet has made available. This morass of inconsequentiality which has been released by the promise of being a public citizen has become itself an obstacle to democratic engagement. We are awash and overwhelmed with information, and sifting through it all to find relevance and pertinence has now become such an onerous task that the greatest capital gains are to be made by those who are able to sift it for us – the *Googles* of this world. Mining the Internet for the nuggets of significant information can be an arduous and time-consuming process, because like all valuable commodities, high-value knowledge is mostly characterised by its *scarcity*.[3]

A WORD ABOUT SCARCITY

We tend to think of scarcity as a natural consequence of the ebb and flow of "market forces". When something is "hot" – like iPods were a few years ago, demand exceeds supply and a state of scarcity exists until the manufacturer can lift production. Until then, the price of iPods remains high. As the market becomes "saturated", supply exceeds demand and the price of iPhones goes down. But things are a little more complicated than that. As Xenos points out (citing the OECD) - until the late nineteenth century, the concept of scarcity connoted a temporary dearth, as in the case just described. But:

> This remained the case until....neoclassical economics made the scarcity postulate its foundation and the term passed into general usage through its transformation into a concept signifying a general condition: not "a scarcity of", or "a time of scarcity" but simply "scarcity". This etymology suggests a history that is discontinuous; that scarcity in the general sense is a modern *invention*. (my emphasis)….. it was in London …. that the first systematic theory of scarcity was developed. Eighteenth-century London was a central location of the so-called Industrial Revolution then underway, but more importantly, it was also a central location - perhaps *the* central location - of a related transformation in consumption, a transformation one historian has termed the "Consumer Revolution". Alongside the evolution of high-volume, standardised production there emerged a pattern of high-volume, standardised consumption driven by the social imperatives of fashion.[4]

Critical to the development of an ethic of fashion was the invention of *scarcity*. It was an invention that developed alongside the growth of capitalism, and has become a major instrumental relation in the law of supply and demand - the *rarer* a commodity, the more valuable. Under the conditions of consumer-capitalism that have existed and grown for the last fifty years this is particularly true. Scarcity, besides being a condition, has itself become a commodity – manufactured to increase the value of important symbolic and cultural capital. Scarcity in these conditions is not an accidental event, but a much-desired and highly-crafted condition for maintaining profit margins of high-value commodities. It is also a key component in the creation and maintenance of systems that seek to reproduce the hegemony of the status quo power of the military-industrial complex. In our so-called knowledge society or knowledge economy we should not be surprised to discover that the same laws of scarcity-supply-demand hold sway. The conditions of manufactured scarcity are deeply implicated in any assessment of what constitutes "legitimate" communication or knowledge, and the manufacturing process of knowledge-scarcity is tightly controlled by the power status quo culture. At the apex of the system of control stands the system of education, particularly at the University level, which offers to the dominant culture an unchallengeable vehicle for the legitimation of specific forms of knowledge and the de-legitimation of others.

This point is developed by curriculum theorist Michael Apple who unpacks the education system's imperative for the reproduction of social stratification, by distinguishing between high status and low status knowledge. He notes that the former is distributed unevenly throughout the society and of course throughout the educational system. The higher up the system one moves the more scarce the pearls of wisdom and the greater their knowledge-status or cultural capital.

Apple points out how the possession of high-status knowledge - that is knowledge which is useful to the structure of corporate economies - is specifically framed by its scarcity. In other words, its high status value depends upon its non-possession by others, and "its scarcity is inextricably linked to its instrumentality."[5] Or, as Raymond Williams expressed it:

> It is not only that the way in which education is organised, can be seen to express, consciously and unconsciously, the wider organisations of a culture and a society, so that what has been thought of as simple distribution is in fact an active shaping to particular social ends. It is also the fact that the content of education, which is subject to great historical variation, again expresses, again both consciously and unconsciously, certain basic elements in the culture, what is thought of as 'an education' being in fact a particular selection, a particular set of emphases and omissions. Further, when this selection of content is examined more closely it will be seen to be one of the decisive factors affecting its distribution.[6]

In other words, the status-content of legitimate(d) knowledge is reciprocally constitutive of its social distinction. For example, making sure that blues, rap and popular music do not form part of a music curriculum automatically excludes those groups in society for whom they constitute a meaningful reality, a source of voice through which their oppression might be expressed and ultimately resisted. The late French sociologist Pierre Bourdieu, taking the field of Art as an example, described this relationship eloquently:

> The definition of cultural nobility is the stake in a struggle which has gone on unceasingly, from the seventeenth century to the present day, between groups differing in their ideas of culture and of the legitimate relation to

> culture and to works of art, and therefore differing in the conditions of acquisitions of which these dispositions are the product... The logic of what is sometimes called... the "reading" of a work of art, offers basis for this opposition. Consumption is, in this case, a stage in the process of communication, that is, an act of deciphering, decoding, which presupposes practical or explicit mastery of a cipher or code. In a sense one can say that the capacity to see *(voir)* is a function of the knowledge *(savoir)*, or concepts, that is, the words, that are available to name visible things, and which are, as it were, programmes for perception. A work of art has meaning and interest only for someone who possesses the cultural competence, that is, the code into which it is encoded. The conscious or unconscious of explicit or implicit schemes of perception and appreciation which constitutes pictorial or musical culture is the hidden condition for recognizing the styles characteristic of a period, a school or an author, and, more generally for the familiarity with the internal logic of works that aesthetic enjoyment presupposes... Thus the encounter with a work of art is not "love at first sight" as is generally supposed, and the act of empathy, *Einfühlung* which is the art-lover's pleasure, presupposes an act of cognition, a decoding operation, which implies the implementation of a cognitive acquirement, a cultural code.[7]

What is true of art is true of every specialised field of knowledge. The codes may be different, but the meaning is the same – the creation of an exclusive domain (and coded language systems) over which one can exercise gate-keeping in the management of scarcity-profit. Advocates of Open Access hold that through the freedom of expression offered by the Internet, the inequalities associated with such codifications will progressively disappear, leading to a more progressively democratic society. I believe that they underestimate the tenacity of a gate-keeping system built upon hierarchy and privilege over 600 years of capitalism as well as the socially constructed meaning of our notions of "progress" – of progressive liberty. Not only is there great profit to be made in the creation and control of knowledge and information systems, but they play a key role in preventing social and political change and unless the structural (i.e. economic) basis of knowledge production is addressed we can only expect the process of social and cultural exclusion and exploitation that it engenders to continue as it has in every other field.

DEMOCRACY, PROGRESS AND THE INTERNET

The predominant myth of Milton Friedman's free-market capitalism is that everybody wins and nobody pays – that the market will eventually balance out the economic inequalities in society as the profits from development eventually "trickle down" to those in greatest need. This mythology serves to reinforce not only the capitalist system as a whole, which is seen as the source of the generalised and continuing increase in prosperity, but of the science and technology which lies behind the productive capacity which drives the growth. The reality behind the myth is somewhat different.

Figure 1. American progress leading settlers across the Prairie.[8]

Like all social constructions it hides its own partiality. Progress, in the sense in which we understand it, ignores the histories of its own victims. In the painting above, she is seen sweeping away the savages and superstitions of the old era as she marches, Bible in hand across the Great Plains, stringing telegraph lines and leading civilisation towards the West. It is not, perhaps, a perspective shared by the Cherokee, Cheyenne, Lakota, Navajo or Apache. Nor is the relation between exploitation and "progress" confined to indigenous peoples.

While it is true that life circumstances have improved for millions in the Western democracies, for a very great number of others, who have provided the basis for this growth, life has become very much worse. The wealth of the European elites from the Fifteenth Century onwards was paid for by the indigenous peoples of the colonies, and just as the increased wealth of the landed gentry in the Seventeenth and Eighteenth centuries was acquired by the dispossession of the peasants through the Enclosure Acts, so in the Nineteenth Century the economic servitude of the workers (forced off the Enclosed land and into the cities to provide a huge pool of cheap labour) was the basis for the accumulated wealth of the land-owning proprietor-employers. The painting by Gainsborough of Mr. and Mrs Andrews (below) depicts an idyllic pastoral scene as they survey their estate. The only indication of the political and social turmoil of the time is perhaps the rifle nonchalantly held at the ready.

Figure 2. Mr. and Mrs, Andrews by Gainsborough.[9]

Figure 3. An advertisement for tourism to Indonesia.[11]

A powerful argument can also be made that in the Twentieth Century, with the apparent burgeoning of commodities and the rise of the middle class, *this latest* accumulation has been acquired at a cost to women, ethnic minorities and Third World populations.[10]

Are we really to believe that the smiling coolie in Jakarta (below) is only too happy to retrieve the golf balls that unthinking Western tourists clout into the probably disease-ridden water of the local pond? And is not the advertisement itself an inducement to do so? Yet the myth of guilt-free, universal progress persists in spite of the obvious evidence to the contrary, and together with the ideology of the free-market, coupled with materialist notions of freedom and harnessed to technical rationality, it succeeds in masking the actual costs of Western hegemony.

Yet the evidence of *regress* as opposed to progress is not hard to find, even in the capitalist democracies themselves. We may note the extensively-researched refutation of the results of Reaganomics by Pulitzer Prize-winning journalists Paul Bartlett and James Steele's *America What Went Wrong?*,[12] and, at the scale of international relations, Frances Moore Lappé and Joseph Collins along with Hayter, have written extensively to demystify the normative ideology of unproblematic and value-free resource distribution within the "global economy".[13] Indeed, the regime of exploitation-masquerading-as-progress which has been a factor of Western forms of progress since the sixteenth century has not ended with the introduction of the digital technology, but has merely been extended.[14]

BACK TO KNOWLEDGE: WWW.HEGEMONY

In a market place which has become truly global (until at least the very latest financial crisis when the universal collapse of the world economy seems to be ushering in a new era of national economic protections) it works just as well that these social groups of exploited wage-slaves are in Bangladesh, India, or Mexico. When we look at the Internet in the context of previous colonisations it becomes clear that the frequently used term "Postcolonialism" may be more than a trifle premature, or at least a term denoting an ongoing struggle rather than a social, cultural and political state. Looking at the cost of fixed Broadband services across different national economies, for instance, we find that:

> The Least Developed Country (LCD) users are asked to pay extortionate rates for relatively low-speed broadband access – over US$2,000 per 100kbits/ per month in Cape Verde, for instance, and over US$199 per 100kbits/ per month in at least 12 other LCDs where broadband is available, compared to below 10 US cents per 100kbits/ per month in Japan and the Republic of Korea.... A broadband connection in a high-income economy (like the OECD countries) costs, on average, about US$16 per 100kbits/ per month... The average price in low-income economies is more than US$186 per month – almost 12 times more. Furthermore, in terms of affordability (or price relative to monthly income), the gap between high-income and low-income economies is a staggering ratio of 432. Consumers in a high-income economy spend only 2% of their average monthly income on broadband connectivity, whereas in a low-income economy, even the cheapest broadband offering costs more than 900 times the average income....[15]

The reasons for such disparities cannot just be explained by the higher cost of installing infrastructure. Lack of direct competition for services contributes significantly. OECD countries have a wide variety of connection systems available in a highly competitive market. Also, the small markets in developing countries do not have access to economies of scale or to the bulk discounted purchases of international bandwidth enjoyed by the First World. Most significant, though, is the fact that compared to voice telephony systems (for which developing countries receive income from developed countries for terminating calls), for Internet connections, they must pay the full cost to the developed countries where most of the traffic originates.

Taking Africa as one example, this means that a sample of representative offers for broadband service (on the basis of 100 hours or 1 Gigabyte of data per month) costs on average $745 per month – more than three times the average for Asia (and nearly six times higher, expressed as a percentage of GNI per capita). These typical costs for poor countries stifle demand and discourage investment and development, meaning that their economies, already burdened with Third World debt fall further and further behind in their ability to grow and develop.[16] Furthermore, the average costs cited here mask a deeper problem. Within these countries, it is only the very small number of wealthy individuals and companies (often multinationals) who can afford the broadband connections that are on offer, deeply dividing the societies in which they live and exacerbating political instabilities that dissuade further investment. It is difficult to see, under these circumstances how some Western analysts might suggest that the Digital Gap is diminishing, or that it does not really exist except as a transient state.[17]

WHO MEASURES THE DIGITAL DIVIDE?

On the basis of such information you would think that it would be self-evident to analysts that the Digital Divide extends a system of exploitation that has historically kept vast populations of the undeveloped world in abject poverty. But such is not the case. There seems to be a great deal of ambiguity in the research about whether the Digital Divide is increasing or decreasing. This is because most of the available research seems to concentrate upon the differences between the top and middle-income groups in society and to exclude those at the very bottom of the economic ladder.[18] Much of the research is conducted by agencies such as the World Bank and the OECD or by companies attempting to determine rates of penetration in different social settings in support of their strategic planning and "development" priorities. The bottom line is profit. And there is little profit to be made in either researching or attempting to develop a market with people who cannot even afford food. Yet the poverty of Africa, Latin America, Asia and the rest of the "Underdeveloped" World is not unrelated to the affluence of the North and West. Four Centuries of plunder masquerading as trade, of colonisation, oppression, genocide, dispossession and enslavement in the cause of Western capitalist profit has had a disastrous effect upon the productive capacities of their peoples. To put it simply, they are poor because we brutalised them and robbed them of their ability to create or increase their own wealth. We stripped them of their natural resources and we enslaved their populations - continuously, for four hundred years - and now we wonder at their poverty!

Unwilling to make the causal association between their poverty and our own wealth, we in the West, or North, as the Brandt Report would have it, look upon their poverty as though it were always so.[19] Yet, with one or two minor exceptions the opposite was invariably the case. When European explorers like Marco Polo, Vasco Da Gama and Christopher Columbus set off on their explorations they discovered civilisations far more wealthy, egalitarian and sophisticated than those they left behind in Europe. As Marx so eloquently put it:

> ... (the) discovery of gold and silver in America, the extirpation, enslavement and entombment in mines of the aboriginal population, the beginning of the conquest and looting of the East Indies, the turning of Africa into a

warren for the commercial hunting of black skins, signalled the rosy dawn of the era of capitalist production.[20]

From those first encounters, the wealth of the European colonial powers increased in direct proportion to the impoverishment of the colonised. As Professor H. Merivale noted in a lecture at Oxford University in 1840 (the same year that the British Crown signed the Treaty of Waitangi with Maori in New Zealand!):

> What raised Liverpool and Manchester from provincial towns to gigantic cities? ... Their present opulence is as really owing to the toil and suffering of the Negro as if his hands had excavated their docks and fabricated their steam engines.[21]

Such realisations come slowly if at all to the uncritical perceptions of Western (or Northern) analysts, who fail to see how the foundations of North/Western power and wealth are built upon the bodies of its colonial victims. But the victims know. Commenting on Western notions of progress and noting that the endowments for Rhodes Scholarships were acquired through the persecution and exploitation of the black people of Zimbabwe, through the exploitation of its natural mineral resources - diamonds, gold etc., African American activist Stokeley Carmichael noted:

> ...progress will not be measured for us by white people. We (black people) will have to tell you when progress is being made. You cannot tell us when progress is being made, because progress for us means getting you off our backs, and that's the only progress that we can see.[22]

Not surprising, then, that nowadays discussions of the Digital Divide invariably fail to account for the exploitative arm of Western capitalism in the underdevelopment of Third World digital technologies, or in the instrumentality of their own technological superiority in the perhaps wilful maintenance of Third World poverty.

DIGITAL DIVIDE IN THE FIRST WORLD: BACK TO NEW ZEALAND

As I noted earlier, these global discrepancies are mirrored increasingly *within* the economies of the First World, where indigenous communities, minorities, people of colour, the elderly and women are reduced to poverty, dependency and hopelessness. This is evident to those, like myself, who work on the boundaries between cultural groups and who are involved in community engagement. As I worked online with my Maori students, it was noticeable that they seemed reluctant to engage fully with the literature of critical education theory – at least in the general sense. They were comfortable in their discussions of the education of *Maori* of which they all had direct personal experience, but they tended to avoid or to not extend their experiences to the wider concepts of education in general.

All were practicing teachers (their course was a one-year top-up to lift their credential from Diploma to Degree level) and they were all sincere in their belief that by trying harder in the classroom they would be able to ameliorate or eliminate the distressing failure and non-completion rates of the Maori students that they taught. They became angry as our studies embraced the history of Maori education in New Zealand, and as the realisation dawned that the failure of their students was not coincidental (as the politicians and media suggest in their oft-repeated promises to "Close the Gaps" between Maori and non-Maori students), but was rather a planned and 150 year-long strategy to consign Maori to employment in the service industries of white employers.[23] This is a truth rarely mentioned in the public discourse around education, and the New Zealand public (including these Maori teachers) remain unaware of the institutional racism that has been an essential historical part of the education system and that lies hidden behind the rhetoric of reform.

In addition to their difficulties in coming to terms with the inherent racism of the education system, the Maori students discovered other obstacles to their advancement. As we worked online through the difficulties that were experiencing in their course material the issue of language complexity was frequently raised. They found it difficult to understand the obtuse, convoluted and frequently impenetrable jargon of Critical Education theorists. The very authors who were offering to "liberate" minority students were doing so in a language that the students themselves could not understand, and here again, a critique of the influence of capitalism proves useful.

EDUCATION AS COMMODITY

Since the mid-1970s, education in the Western world has changed. Critical Education theorist Michael Young has suggested that the perceived role of education in society has not been stable. At different times, its purpose has been viewed differently. He roughly divides its perceived social role into three phases:

- From the early 1900s to 1945 - as a means of social pacification
- From 1945 to 1974 as a means of national economic productivity
- From 1974 to the present, as a national economic burden.[24]

The last thirty years have accordingly seen a significant shift in the employment conditions and work of academics. The introduction of "user pays" regimes for enrolments, the imposition of productivity ("publish or perish") criteria for staff, the increasing use of adjunct faculty and the substantial increase in paper workload to take account of accountability have all substantially reduced not only the emphasis on teaching-learning, but also on the quality of research, academic analysis and critical reflection. In the increasingly competitive space of academic scholarship, the need to have a marketable academic commodity has resulted in an escalation in the use of private codes and languages. These are seen as necessary to demarcate specific areas of research and knowledge, but also to imbue these defined areas with the requisite aura of scarcity to increase their cultural and symbolic capital. In critical studies, this tendency has been exacerbated by the need to mask politically unpalatable public truths behind unintelligible jargon. We are simply afraid of being understood lest we draw to ourselves the attention of an increasingly reactionary and punitive administration.[25] The result of these dual pressures has been to produce a discourse that purports to liberation while simultaneously creating the conditions for further exclusions. As Friedrich Wilhelm Nietzsche famously wrote:

> Those who know that they are profound strive for clarity. Those who would like to seem profound to the crowd strive for obscurity. (Nietzsche, 1974, Section 173, pp. 201–2)

The Maori students found themselves caught up in this nexus and unable to easily overcome this additional obstacle to their learning.

All of this went to underline the importance of the Wananga ideology of *Tino Rangatiratanga* and its insistence upon the need for a separate and culturally appropriate education for indigenous students (in this case involving instruction using Maori pedagogies in the Maori language and honouring traditional Maori cultural practices). One of the major reasons for this is that working within the mainstream educational system, "successful" Maori become assimilated into the dominant culture, forming a "brown" elite – a new emancipated middle class that shares the values and lifestyles of the dominant colonial culture and the ideals of capitalist development. In the process no change is made to the fundamental structure of those exclusions that are necessary for the continuance of the economic system. Rather, the myth is created that because a few are successful, the opportunity for emancipation must be universal, consigning those that "fail" to ever increasing reflections of inadequacy and ongoing dependence.[26] It remains to be seen whether improved broadband access will address these issues, except perhaps by making it easier for indigenous students worldwide to come together in cyberspace to tell their stories and to strategise their own liberation.

DIGITAL ACCESS AND EDUCATION IN THE FIRST WORLD

In 2006 the New Zealand Labour Government legislated to cut funding to Community Education programmes nationwide, largely in response to the unprecedented growth of the three Wananga. Community Education programmes were low-level educational courses, which were funded by the State to encourage people without qualifications to re-engage with the learning process. Students in the courses were not tested or examined and were allowed to progress at their own pace. For Maori students this was a godsend. All of the statistical evidence indicates that the High School environment is toxic to Maori youth.[27] They drop out and fail to complete in large numbers and in general exit the education system with a low self-esteem and a feeling of being stupid. The reasons for this have been isolated down to the incipient racism in classroom interactions, but whatever the cause, they exit school with a definite aversion to further education.

Getting them back into learning is not easy, and the Community Education programmes provided a very appropriate vehicle for the Wananga to reignite the curiosity and enthusiasm of disillusioned Maori youth. Programmes were offered in a range of Maori subjects (Maori language, knowledge, traditions etc.) and they proved remarkably successful. In the five years that I worked at the Wananga the roll increased from 400 EFTS (Equivalent Full–time Students) to more than 3000. One of the sister Wananga offering Community Education Courses had enrolments that rose to more than 35,000, making it the largest tertiary institution in New Zealand. All courses were offered free to students and the costs of running the courses were absorbed by canny strategic planning and programming. Surplus funds were used to build infrastructure and to develop higher-level programmes (Bachelors, Masters and PhDs) into which students would eventually staircase and often to provide free digital resources (mobile phones, free laptop computers) in an effort to improve communications and assist students from low-income families or remote locations to establish and maintain a digital connection.

Following considerable pressure from the Universities and other mainstream tertiary institutions (who were witnessing a fall in their own enrolments and related State subsidies), the media and a rising tide of racially motivated complaints by the general public about “Maori privilege”, the Government stepped in to shut down the Community Education Programmes, and all three Wananga which had until then been in accelerated growth mode posted immediate and large deficits resulting in massive redundancies and “restructurings”. Student enrolments dropped dramatically, academic programmes that had previously been well staffed and well attended were “shelved”, and the institutions themselves were barely able to continue. Four years later they continue to struggle to survive in an emaciated form, so much, perhaps, for political promises to “close the gaps” or to “reduce” the digital divide.

I left to devote myself to the task of creating my free, open-access educational resource website.[28] In the process of building my website I came to discover first hand, up close and personal, the meaning of the Digital Divide. One of the things that I discovered in building my website, and in writing this and similar articles is that the task of continuing to write and research is economically punitive. In 2008 my social security cheque amounted to about NZ$440 a month, of which my phone and broadband access plus my cell phone amounted to more than a third. Add to this the costs of setting up and maintaining a website and the costs approached 60% of my income. These costs were substantially increased by additional costs for access to quality information. While it is possible to manage somewhat through sites like *Google* and *Wikipedia*, amongst others, these sites offer relatively ‘low grade’ information of limited cultural capital and the ‘high-grade’ information to which they sometimes point is frequently held by online journal agencies and digital archives such as *JSTOR* or *High Beam*. These institutions are not open access.

JSTOR does not allow for individual membership or access. All access must be through an associated academic institution, which requires the payment of student fees or residence in an urban location with a good public research library. *High Beam* and numerous similar for-profit archives charge a fee for membership (approx. $10 per month) and/or a fee for individual articles (usually about $10 per article).[29] My local, provincial, town library has very limited resources, and books or articles not held in stock must be ordered through *Interloan* systems at a considerable cost.

OPEN ACCESS OR HEGEMONY?

It is to be hoped that the struggle to maintain and grow an open access Internet service will be successful, to the extent that, for instance, all public libraries might have the facility for free Internet. Such has been the case, in the New York Central Library. Carrie Bickner started her librarianship career there in the late 1990s and writes incisively of the struggles to maintain an open access system in the face of well-intended but counter-productive anti-porn censorship legislation and physical conflicts between game-playing youths and frustrated internet and email users.[30]

The work of people like Bickner represents an important ingredient in the struggle to maintain an open and free access to the web and ensure that the excluded and disaffected are encouraged into a space where their voice can make a difference. The Open Access enthusiasts are firm in their conviction that the "trivia" that is to be found in abundance on the web will slowly give way to a more politically aware participation in democratic dialogue – noting, of course, that one person's trivia is another person's wisdom, and that judgements such as those made here are themselves part of the repressive armoury of the establishment.

In the *Introduction* to their book *Literatures in the Digital Era: Theory and Praxis,* editors Amelia Sanz and Dolores Romero note that:

> What is happening is that the heritage from literary traditions based on authors, books and, for the most part, paper, is also playing a major role in *hyper*text, which is an actual referent and not just a metaphorical one. Scholars such as MacLuhan, Bolter or Chartier have demonstrated that books are first and foremost a kind of technological artefact—a machine to be used and a product to be bought and sold; this is the economic dimension of text-supporting materials....If books, on the one hand, are indeed teaching and communicating *machines* (see Landow), then the "electronification" of universities and research institutions does not imply technologizing them or applying further technology to them in some way alien to their essential spirit. The future will, in fact, be collaborative, because new media can support or facilitate the traditions of scholarship in the humanities, which are, namely, those of reflection and reflective reading...[31]

HISTORY, MEDIA AND CLASS STRUGGLE[32]

Connecting and tracing the relationship between electronic and print media in this way opens up some interesting comparisons, especially around issues of literacy, the Popular Press, open democracy and censorship. The latter was first introduced as early as the mid-1500s in an attempt to prevent heretical interpretations of the Bible. Following the Reformation and Counter-Reformation, censorship of books was legislated to distinguish orthodoxy from heresy. Widespread literacy did not emerge in Britain, for instance until about 1700 with the rise of the new Middle Class (merchants, traders, shopkeepers etc.) who began to constitute a substantial readership for broadsheets about financial and shipping news, the price of stocks and shares etc. Gradually these increased in number, size and content, and were immediately perceived as a potential political threat by the Establishment.

From almost the beginning the State attempted to control and censor the new medium, imposing stamp duties and advertising taxes as "the most effective way of suppressing the libels". But the pressure to advertise (think of *Google*!) overcame all of these restrictions and in 1730 the *Advertiser* was first printed, including only news items when advertising clients were scarce. The number of such publications also increased, and advertising became for the first time the predominant mode of finance for publication – a situation that has continued down to the present time. Throughout the 1700s, the Government oscillated between repression (increasing advertising taxes and stamp duties) and control (bribery and financing of selected publications to foster the "correct" views.

By the mid-Century, many of the publications had been floated and become public companies, and together were becoming a powerful political force. At this time also, the Methodist Church was in its ascendancy and helped to greatly accelerate general literacy (and the size of the reading public) through its Sunday School Movement. It is interesting to note that the Methodists also attempted to censor the kinds of readings that this public were exposed to. The British educationalist Hannah More, who established a series of Sunday Schools in the Mendips at that time was careful to make sure that her students only read the Bible, and at no time were encouraged to learn to write. Replying to critics of her reading programme who believed that it would encourage sedition among the lower classes, she said:

> I allow of no writing for the poor. My object is not to make them fanatics, but to train up the lower classes in habits of industry and piety.[33]

But "fanaticism" was not so easily suppressed! It was at this time also that serious political analyses were being published in book form. In 1776, Price's *On The Nature of Civil Liberty* came out and marked an emerging trend leading to Thomas Paine's *Rights of Man* in 1791. The Government attempted to suppress the reporting of Parliamentary debates, and it did not take long for "the freedom of the press" to become a familiar catch-cry beginning in 1762 when Wilkes, owner of the *North Briton* wrote:

> The liberty of the press is the birthright of a Briton, in 1762 and is justly esteemed the firmest bulwark of the liberties of this country.[34]

The French Revolution (1789–99) had a dramatic impact, increasing State-attempted censorship with further sharp rises in taxes and stamp duties as the Government and Establishment attempted to forestall a similar uprising in Britain. As the Tory *Anti-Jacobin* review put it:

> We have long considered the establishment of newspapers in this country as a misfortune to be regretted: but since their influence has become predominant by the universality of their circulation, we regard it as a calamity most deeply to be deplored.[35]

THE MODERN MEDIA

Since those times, the struggle between the owners of the print media and the public has been waged incessantly. Advertising, of course, has made its own significant impact, not only in the print media but in *all* media, and has been partly responsible for the creation of media empires like those of Kerry Packer, Robert Maxwell and Rupert Murdoch as well as for the establishment of huge conglomerates like Time-Warner-AOL. As Raymond Williams was able to conclude as long ago as the Sixties:

> Is it all to come to this, in the end, that the long history of the press in Britain should reach its consummation in a declining number of newspapers,

> in ownership by a few very large groups, and in the acceptance (varied between social groups but evident in all) of the worst kinds of journalism? The process is obviously something… that is happening to the whole society, and all the elements – not only the bad journalism but also the questions of ownership and the relation to advertising – have to be considered if the process is to be understood.[36]

All of which could be repeated with even greater accuracy almost fifty years later. And yet it should not surprise us. As Marx pointed out so precisely more than a century and a half ago, and during the struggle for a peoples' press:

> The ideas of the ruling class are in every epoch the ruling ideas; i.e., the class, which is the ruling material force of society, is at the same time its ruling intellectual force. The class which has the means of material production at its disposal, has control at the same time over the means of mental production...[37]

Ruminating on all of this, it becomes clear to me that the Digital Divide will never be "bridged" or "closed" as long as we have an economic system that operates on the basis of exclusions. Nor, despite the power of the media moguls, will the opportunity for freedom of expression ever be foreclosed. There have, indeed, been many instances of suppression since those far off days at the birth of the popular press. The modern digital media holds an enormous sway over the public mind and in the hands of powerful groups and individuals poses a formidable obstacle to the emergence of a popular democracy as indefatigable researchers like Noam Chomsky have illustrated. But there have also been many gains in that time. The struggle for hegemony will be ongoing and endless.

As long as capitalism continues to be the underlying structure of our economic lives, I can see little hope that those that it excludes or reduces to invisibility will be able to access the digital world in ways that matter. Their main hope lies in taking control of their own economies (as many of the countries like Venezuela, Bolivia and Peru – with their huge indigenous populations - seem to be doing) as well as the means of production that drive them.

Yet in the privileged world of the American cognoscenti there are also signs that the emergence of the Web 2.0 world is actually beginning to fragment the hold that the media networks have had over the public mind. It is clear, for instance, that in the final days of Senator Barak Obama's run to the White House, there was a sea change in the relationship between the networks and populist media such as *Facebook* and *YouTube*:

> The Republicans have made a habit of running against the media in elections past. This year, the mainstream media found itself at times running against both parties. Perhaps drawing on Mr. Obama's background as a community organizer, his campaign decided early on to build a social network that would flank, and in some cases outflank, traditional news media.
>
> With a Facebook group that had 2.3 million adherents and a huge push on YouTube — last week alone the campaign uploaded 70 videos, many of

> them tailored to battleground states — the campaign used peer-to-peer communication to build a juggernaut that did not depend on the whims and choices of the media's collective brain trust.
>
> The campaign mined its online community not just for money, but for content. A video titled "Four Days in Denver" about the Obama campaign had the kind of access that journalists would kill for, including the candidate working over his acceptance speech with a staff member and showing the family backstage making ready for their moment in the spotlight.
>
> It looked like a big-time network get, but it was produced by the campaign itself.[38]

The question remains whether such shifts in the use of technology will ever provide the access to public voice that the truly oppressed can use for their own emancipation or whether the example of Obama signifies the emergence of yet another media empire, this time more explicitly connected to the political environment. Only time will tell and during that time the movement for open access may be one of the most critical in our age.

NOTES

1 http://www.wired.com/politics/onlinerights/news/2007/08/wiki_tracker
2 Orwell, G. (1977). p. 199.
3 "Significant information" is here taken to mean either knowledge that is useful to corporate economies or (at a personal level) knowledge which might dramatically increase the economic well-being of the individual. Usually these two definitions coincide.
4 Xenos, N. (1989), pp. 3–8.
5 Apple, M. W. (1979). p. 36.
6 Williams, R. (1971). p. 125.
7 Bourdieu, P. (1984). pp. 2–3.
8 American Progress. From a 1872 painting by John Gast, Library of Congress, Washington, DC.
9 Mr. and Mrs. Andrews. From a 1748 painting by Thomas Gainsborough, National Gallery, London.
10 For a critical analysis of the reciprocal relationship between First World wealth and Third World poverty see: Hayter, T. (1982). For a detailed analysis on the economic invisibility of women and children in the world economy see: Waring, M. (1988).
11 Garuda Indonesia advertisement.
12 Barlett, D. L., and Steele, J. B. (1992) show that under the Reagan administration the salaries of those earning more than $1 million rose by a total of 2,184% and the total salaries of those earning between $200,000 and 1 million rose by 697%. By comparison, the total salaries of those earning $20,00–$50,000 rose by 44%. During the same period, tax concessions increased progressively with salaries so that while those earning between $10,000 and $20,000 saved 6% in taxes, those earning above $500,000 earned in excess of 34% extra in tax deductions.
13 Lappé, F. M. and Collins, C. (1988), esp. Chapter 7: "The Free Market Can End Hunger" and Chapter 8: "Free Trade is the Answer". See also: Hayter, T. (1971) and Horowitz, D. (1967).
14 This most recent "meltdown" of the global economy points not only to the inherent instability of "perpetual growth" models but also to the naked exploitation of the community by the captains of the "finance industry" (more properly termed the "corporate greed" industry), the Bernard Madoff Ponzi scheme, and the 2008 Wall Street (and AIG) executive bonuses being but all too typical if extreme examples.

15 *World Information Society Report* 2007, Chapter 2: Bridging the Digital Divide, pp. 25–7. (http://www.itu.int/osg/spu/publications/worldinformationsociety/2007/report.html) (Data valid at August 2006).

16 *ibid.* p. 27.

17 http://en.wikipedia.org/wiki/Digital_divide.

18 *ibid.*

19 Commission on International Development Issues, (1980).

20 Cited in: Wallerstein, I. (1974). p. xv.

21 Cited in Huberman, L. (1936).

22 Carmichael, S. (1968). p. 156.

23 Ward, A. (2005). See also: (http://www.tonywardedu.com/content/view/152/40/)

24 Young, M., Education (1987), p. 167. A great deal of the research into the relationship between education, power, economics, culture and class has evolved from the British experience over the last thirty years. The theories arising from this experience have had a profound effect upon theorising in other Western States, particularly in the USA.

25 Ward, A. (1996). See also: http://www.tonywardedu.com/content/view/158/123/

26 Hau'Ofa, E. (2008).

27 Ward, A. (2008),

28 www.TonyWardEdu.com

29 One notable exception is the recent Open Access Journal (http://openhumanitiespress.org/), a peer review Journal for scholarly articles. It provides "a grassroots response to the crisis in scholarly publishing in the humanities, (and) is an international open access publishing collective whose mission is to make leading works of contemporary critical thought freely available worldwide".

30 Carrie Bickner, C. (2001).

31 Sanz, A. and Romero, D. (eds.) (2007).

32 The historical detail in this section is largely derived from Raymond Williams two revealing essays, "The Growth of the Reading Public", and "The Growth of the Popular Press", both to be found in: Williams, R. (1961). pp. 156–213.

33 More, H., cited in: Lankshear, C. and Lawler, M. (1987). p. 45. and in: Simon, B. (1960). p. 133.

34 Cited in: Williams, R., *op. cit.* (1961). p. 184.

35 *ibid.* p. 185.

36 *ibid.* p. 213.

37 Marx, K. (1947). p. 39.

38 Carr, D. and Stelter, B. (2008).

REFERENCES

Abel, S. (1997). *Shaping the news*. Auckland, New Zealand: Auckland University Press.

Apple, M. W. (1979). *Ideology and curriculum*. New York: Routledge and Kegan Paul.

Atkinson, M. (1986). *Our masters voices*. London: Methuen.

Bagdikian, B. H. (1987). *The media monopoly*. Boston: Beacon Press.

Barlett, D. L., & Steele, J. B. (1992). *America: What went wrong*? Kansas City: Andrews & McMeel.

Bourdieu, P. (1984). *Distinction - A social critique of the judgement of taste*. Cambridge, MA: Harvard University Press.

Carmichael, S. (1968). Black power. In D. Cooper (Ed.), *The dialectics of liberation*. London: Pelican.

Carr, D., & Stelter, B. (2008, November 2). *New York Times*.

Chomsky, N. (1989). *Necessary illusions: Thought control in democratic societies*. Boston: South End Press.

Commission on International Development Issues. (1980). *North-South: The Brandt Report*. London: Pan Books.

Comrie, M., & Mcgregor, J. (1992). *Whose news?* Wellington, New Zealand: Dunmore Press.

Curran, J., & Seaton, J. (1988). *Power without responsibility*. London: Routledge.
Hau'Ofa, E. (2008). *We are the Ocean*. Honolulu, HI: University of Hawai'i Press.
Hayter, T. (1971). *Aid as imperialism*. Harmondsworth: Pelican.
Hayter, T. (1982). *The creation of world poverty*. London: Pluto Press.
Hebdige, D. (1988). *Hiding in the light*. London: Routledge.
Herman, E. S., & Chomsky, N. (1988). *Manufacturing consent. (The Political Economy of the Mass Media)*. New York: Pantheon Books.
Horowitz, D. (1967). *From Yalta to Vietnam*. Harmondsworth: Penguin.
Huberman, L. (1936). *Man's worldly goods: The story of the wealth of nations*. New York: Monthly Review Press.
Lankshear, C., & Lawler, M. (1987). *Literacy, schooling and revolution*. London: Falmer Press.
Lappé, F. M., & Collins, C. (1988). *World hunger: 12 myths*. London: Earthscan Publications.
McChesney, R. W., & Nichols, J. (2000). *Our media, not theirs: The democratic struggle against corporate media*. New York: Seven Stories Press.
Marx, K. (1947). *The German ideology*. New York: International Publishers.
Nietzsche, F. W. (1974). *The gay science* (W. Kaufmann, Trans.). New York: Random House.
Orwell, G. (1977). *Nineteen Eighty-Four*. New York: Penguin Books.
Parenti, M. (1992). *Make-Believe Media*. New York: St. Martin's Press.
Sanz, A., & Romero, D. (Eds.). (2007). *Literatures in the digital era: Theory and praxis*. Cambridge Scholars Publishing. Retrieved May 11, 2010, from http://www.reelc.net/index.php?q=node/574
Schiller, H. I. (1969). *Mass communications and American empire*. Boston: Beacon Press.
Simon, B. (1960). *Studies in the history of education, 1780–1870*. London: Lawrence & Wishart.
Wallerstein, I. (1974). *The modern world system, I: Capitalist agriculture and the origins of European world-economy in the sixteenth century*. New York: Academy Press.
Ward, A. (1996). Walking our Walk: The mystification of critical language. In M. Peters, W. Hope, J. Marshall, & S. Webster (Eds.), *Critical theory, poststructuralism and social context*. New Zealand: Dunmore Press. Retrieved May 11, 2010, from http://www.tonywardedu.com/content/view/158/123/
Ward, A. (2008). *High school confidential* Retrieved from http://www.tonywardedu.com/content/view/278/40/
Ward, A. (2005). *Hegemony and education in New Zealand*. Hamilton, NZ: Proceedings of the World International Peoples Conference in Education.
Waring, M. (1988). *Counting for nothing: What men value, what women are worth*. Port Nicholson: Allen and Unwin.
Weaver, P. H. (1994). *News and the culture of lying*. New York: The Free Press.
Williams, R. (1961). *The long revolution*. New York: Columbia University Press.
Xenos, N. (1989). *Scarcity & modernity*. New York: Routledge.
Young, M. (1987). Education. In P. Worsley (Ed.), *The new introducing sociology*. London: Penguin Books.

Tony Ward
Tony WardEdu Consultancy
2009–10 Wepking Distinguished Visiting Professor
Miami University, Oxford, Ohio

DIEU HACK-POLAY

10. DIGITAL LIBRARY

An Opportunity for African Education

INTRODUCTION

The scarcity of resources represents a difficult issue for African educational systems. Almost everywhere on the continent, most institutions would face the crucial issue of learning resources, which makes the learning and teaching process lag behind those of many other parts of the world. The reliance on traditional paper based libraries and learning resources has meant that publications long outdated remain core texts in African reference lists.

This chapter argues that the development of digital libraries presents incommensurable benefits for Africa. These stand at many critical levels. First the paper argues that digital libraries could provide a forum for inter-institution communication and updating on the currency in different subject areas; second, the chapter explains that digital libraries could facilitate teachers and students' access to valuable data that is easy to retrieve, which in traditional libraries, the learning community would rarely notice its existence. The chapter also argues that digital libraries present an opportunity for internal dissemination of valuable unpublished and published work within African teaching and research institutions, which rarely goes beyond the defence of a thesis or a local conference. In addition, the exploration and exploitation of digital libraries would 'coerce' the student and academic communities in broadening the much needed information technology skills which are now key requirements in learning and teaching contexts, as well as in one's positioning in the job market. Furthermore, in a land where financial resources are rare, being able to access digital learning and teaching resources could be a source of economies of scale both in terms of buildings, maintenance and travel costs for the individuals, the collectivities and national governments. Akst (2003:1) argues that 'the dawning of the digital age is bringing radical changes to the whole notion of the library, with vast implications for the price, availability and durability of knowledge'. The author further points out that this development presents tremendous challenges as well as possibilities but in this paper we will crystallise the analysis mostly on the opportunities.

The immense possibilities residing in the digital library could give African scholars and the learning community a well needed voice in an era of increasing globalisation. However more crucially, researchers from outside of the continent could finally come face to face with some hidden African research which could foster wider investigation in little known social phenomena, particularly in business and management practices. From the perspective of global interconnectedness, the digital library then becomes, for most African nations, an exciting novelty worth exploring.

R. Rikowski (ed.), Digitisation Perspectives, 167–177.

THE DIGITAL LIBRARY IN AFRICA TODAY

Some Recent Developments

There are several initiatives taking roots in Africa in the area of digital libraries. However, most could be said to be in their infancy and few have emerged as authorities in the field. For example, Rosenberg (2006) argues that some African higher education institutions have attempted to establish digital libraries but have not gone much beyond the conception stage fundamentally due to the lack of funding. The availability of e-resources according to the author, is not what causes problems but the facilities for access and dissemination as well as the shortage of qualified staff to ensure maintenance and further developments. The Fulbright Academy (2007) found that the implementation of digital library systems in parts of Africa faces the issues of content development, management infra-structures, as well as training for managers and users. These findings are echoed by Ngimwa (2006) who also point to the inadequacy of information technology infrastructure which is fundamental to positive exploitation of the possibilities offered by digital library systems. Ngimwa quotes the example of the African Virtual University (AVU), a World Bank pilot development of a pan-African educational network. Set up in 1997 to be available in Sub-Saharan African countries, the AVU has experienced only a relative degree of success, though still active in the designated region and beyond.

Another currently active digital library initiative is the pioneering of the African Online Digital Library (AODL) whose principal remit is the generation of multilingual and multimedia material for researchers and students investigating or teaching about aspects of life, history and cultures of the western and southern parts of the continents. Considering the technological constraints highlighted earlier, this initiative seems to be an invaluable resource for teaching and disseminating sources of knowledge about the African continent, i.e. making Africa accessible to both insiders and outsiders. In recent years, the UNESCO has been involved in promoting digital libraries in Africa as well as equipping professionals with the technical abilities to take on the challenges of developing this valuable tool. UNESCO (2005) estimates that its workshop organised in South Africa in November 2005 provided professionals with much relevant skill in that respect, e.g. hands-on experience in creating and customising digital libraries.

Growing Awareness of Potentials of Digital Libraries

From a review of current initiatives, it appears that the importance of digital libraries is being realised on the continent. There is being developed a profound awareness that the development and growth of digital library systems could harbour inextricable linkages with economic and intellectual capabilities. This realisation is engendering concrete actions despite funding issues and sharp IT connectivity difficulties. These efforts have struck deeper roots in the educational sector particularly in higher education. This explains to a large extent why Akst (2003) believes that 'one thing Third World library users have in their favour is rapid advances in digitising technology'. However, these remain limited and not commensurate with the potentialities that exist with digital libraries. The next sections outline the current level of presence and use of digital libraries in teaching and learning as well other opportunities not fully exploited within the higher education sector.

THE DIGITAL LIBRARY AND TEACHING AND LEARNING

Developments in the West

Around the world, many areas and institutions in the social sphere are increasingly reaping the benefits of technological advances (or revolutions) such as that involving the digital age. Specialists in education, publishing, local government and private libraries in the United Kingdom and other more advanced nations are exploiting the incommensurably immense opportunities and possibilities of digital media for the cataloguing, storage and wider dissemination of important published and unpublished materials traditionally hard to access. This has brought about a sort of revival of academic curiosity and intellectual thirst among communities of researchers, teachers and students who find vital materials easily assessable via the internet and more local library information systems within individual institutions.

Digital Libraries in African Educational Contexts

In the African context, such initiatives (though with a degree of vitality), remain in their infancy. Rosenberg (2006) rightly points out that university libraries in Africa are attempting to develop digital libraries but progress is not homogenous through the continent and remains uneven between neighbour countries. This raises the question of the viability of both the human and technological infrastructure to support these vital innovative works. The same author is unequivocal that the sustainability of a reliable digital library is inexorably connected with the implementation of a library management system which in turn is faced with issues at three critical levels: the lack of funding (particularly indigenous funding), the lack of training facilities and the inadequacy of retention packages offered to the few locally trained professionals. With political and economic conditions deteriorating in many parts of Africa, the continent continues to face the difficult issues of brain drain which threatens retention efforts in the many sectors of individual nations' economic systems. The situation has caused frustrations on the continent for decades, with countries being in a position to cope with the phenomenon.

Diversity of Learning Material

From a purely academic perspective, a great strength of a digital library lies undeniably in the variety of documents it offers. African educational systems have long been fed with information, research outputs and literatures from the West. This was predominantly as a result of colonial influences on these systems. However, since most African nations gained their independence in the 1960s, the academic community, writers, journalists, etc. have produced a large volume of materials which have barely been seen and read. In history, science, politics, language and literature, there is a lot more available than one might imagine. These constitute a rich intellectual domain and assets for academics, providing variety, diversity of perspectives and sometimes correcting some imperialist stereotypes. A recent UNESCO project, the Intergovernmental Information for All Programme (IFAP) set out to raise awareness in Africa about the availability of public information susceptible of use in their drive for socio-economic improvements and for teaching and learning. The project which generated CD-ROM anthologies containing educational and training documents in agriculture, history, science and technology and politics with a local content, is an example of the tremendous diversity of materials that digital libraries are able to bring to a target audience in African educational contexts.

Currency of Research and Educational Resources

There is little doubt that with technological advances, digital libraries will harness more current teaching and learning materials. The ease with which one can adapt, alter and update information is incredible. For example, resources available online can be changed instantly and learners and users receive the amended version immediately. The use of blackboard in teaching is an example of the cyber speed today. Teachers upload materials on their teaching site and learners can download at the same time and put comments for their professors. The use of LISA (library information system) provides other means for speedy updating of information and materials used by learners and teachers. However, one could argue that these technological developments in education can be sophisticated and highly complex for small and impoverished communities of learners in Africa. To a certain degree, this may be a valid assumption but it is important to acknowledge that there has been some steady progress in large cities and the opportunities highlighted above could be available subject to funding at both indigenous and external levels. However, for more traditionally excluded communities of learners and teachers, the availability of resources on CDs was earlier presented as an opportunity brought to them by digital libraries. More importantly, such resources can also be amended or replaced more easily and quickly than traditional printed documents that would require reprinting in large amounts. So, whatever form of digital resources are made available through digital libraries, it remains that there are tremendous advantages and benefits in such developments. In a knowledge world, accuracy, relevance, easy access and credible information is vital for different actors, be they nations or individuals, who are competing to shape their place in the global arena. In that respect, the digital library provides much needed opportunity for African actors.

I remember being an undergraduate student in Francophone Africa in the 1980s and 1990s. Much of the textbooks and reference manuals dated back to the 1940s to 1960s which provided interesting historical backgrounds in many subjects. But when it came to recent developments in those subjects, then the African students and indeed the teacher, was disadvantaged. My encounter with UK learning environments in the late 1990s and early 2000s illuminated such personal reflections. In fact, recommended materials and those available in the library were published mostly in the same decade or the same year.

Equal Opportunity in Teaching and Learning

An issue that is not often stressed sufficiently is the equality of opportunity that digital libraries can propagate. Education in most African counties is not evenly distributed (Hack-Polay, 2000). Perhaps this is one of the fundamental reasons for the UNESCO's (2008) call for more inclusiveness and equity. The organisation argues that 'in Africa where poverty, hunger, disease, illiteracy, rural isolation and conflict are commonplace, the need for education systems that are inclusive, is particularly acute'. The IFAD project referred to above aimed more crucially at the most disadvantaged communities. Paper format of educational materials are usually expensive in Africa. There is also the infrastructure issue to store volumes of books, etc. The digital library requires less space and removes to a certain extent the requirement to have a formal place termed 'the library'. If a computer is available in a local community, CD-ROMs can be placed in local community centres, village halls, and church halls for the benefit of a large number of people who traditionally may not have had access to the information. In fact, traditional libraries in most African countries, particularly in Sub-Saharan Africa, are located in larger cities with more modern infrastructures. The digital library could, therefore, potentially or at least to some extent, resolve the often cited issue of premises (Hack-Polay, 2000). Dwellers of small towns and villages were typically excluded from participation in intellectual life. Even in the larger cities, it is not uncommon to notice that documents harboured in traditional libraries are from old sources, outdated and sometimes no longer relevant. This status quo was maintained due to the lack of government funding but also the paucity of local neighbourhood resources. The availability of up to date information is often a privilege for the fortunate few. It is not argued that digital libraries are likely to remove all sense of inequity and disadvantage in the short term, but certainly more opportunities are being created for the traditional disadvantaged and excluded communities both in urban and rural Africa. In addition to being relatively cost-effective, Servaes (2003) believes that with the opening of information channels and their availability to all social strata, with a contextualised and culturally-sensitive content, an increasing number of people will be afforded the opportunity to participate in the global information age. Thus, there is a sense of urgency for the development of alternative delivery forms that are both adapted to socio-cultural realities and harbour the capacity to 'respond to the continuously changing needs of learners and society' (UNESCO, 2008).

Pan-African Education for Sustainability

When speaking about African social realities, many do not always acknowledge the wide variety of socio-cultural and economic diversity in terms of paradigms, orientations and practices. Africa is a vast continent with almost twice the population of Europe. There is a plurality of languages and dialects spoken on the continent and indeed in a single country. In a geographical sphere such as the Ivory Coast, there are over sixty different linguistic groups. Although it is often acknowledged that the stories of slavery and colonialism are inherent and a common theme for

African countries, there are several histories, values and complexities across the land. Africa is also often credited with important philosophical developments, which underpinned traditional life. To put this diversity in perspective, it could be argued that this is an important source of moral, social and scientific wealth which has not been shared because this was jealously kept to the micro-geographical or because the micro-cultural level or means of disseminating it was not available.

Digital libraries will offer an unprecedented vehicle of dissemination. Beyond the well-publicised stories of slavery and colonialism earlier mentioned, digital libraries could be a platform where the education system makes available notions about country or culture-specific histories, stories, good practice models in terms of educational, political, scientific and technological development. For instance the application of the well-revered notion of democracy has had varying degree of success and failure in different countries. Courses in political economics and wider social sciences will have access to models of implementations in other countries, which could then provide models and examples upon which individuals and states might be inspired to work towards change. For instance, it is more and more acknowledged that South Africa is emerging as a strong democracy in Africa. They have gone through a process of reconciliation after a century of Apartheid system which oppressed the Black majority. Such a move has enabled South African racial groups to overcome to a certain extent past bitterness and look in the same direction. Such peaceful movements and democratic applications could be transported via digital libraries and through the educational system. In South Africa itself the recently established DISA (Digital Imaging Project of South Africa) project aims to engage people with the country's fascinating social and political history and make accessible other interesting collections of a proud cultural heritage and support the relishing of a democratic future (Peters & Pickover, 2001).

It could be argued that the lack of cooperation between African countries could as well be explained by the lack of knowledge about other countries than our own. The ordinary citizen is far remote from other nationals in a way that a strong emphasis on the sense of otherness leads to the perception of people from a neighbouring country as dangerous, strangers and enemies. Information shared through digital libraries could enable a reconnection, a reshaping of alliance and discoveries, particularly in terms of awareness of cultural unity rendered blurred by imperialism and years of foreign domination. What it is all about here is the utilisation of digital library for community education for citizenship and peace.

DIGITAL LIBRARY AND RESEARCH COMMUNITIES IN AFRICA

There is a greater understanding of the role of digital libraries in research and development. This is why I deal with this in the last section of this paper. On the one hand because there is increasing realisation of the vital contribution of digital libraries, it was important to reassert and re-emphasise such criticality in the very competitive modern research environment. On the other hand, it is essential to ensure that the perceived greater awareness of the capabilities harboured by the digital library does not lead to complacency and a sense of 'taking for granted'. More specifically, in the African context, because digitisation is a new experience, there is some urgency in emphasising the interplay between digital library and research.

Digital Library and Internal Dissemination of Research

In the past decade there has been a dramatic increase in the number of academic journals dedicated to disseminating research done by African scholars and the learning and research community. This is in sharp contrast with earlier periods. Due to lack of funding and 'political punishment' of vocal intellectuals, many such dissemination media were banned, suppressed or under-funded. Despite the recent growth, African academic and scientific journals remain largely unknown and preceded with somehow pejorative reputation. As a result, some good research done in Africa by Africans does not reach much of the locality and the national arena. Even within the same institution, different departments find it hard to disseminate their research findings and share with departments of similar interests. Thus, it is generally the case that research sits in individual university or departmental libraries in paper copies and is not adequately disseminated. The body of knowledge generated through the hard work of intrepid researchers escapes scientific scrutiny, is not available to inform and guide others and leads to the risk of duplication. However, research is most viable when it is built upon and the findings critiqued and refined and, in the context of digitisation, Copeland (2008: 87) argues that "Where access to electronic theses and dissertations is available via the Internet, usage figures indicate that this is a much consulted resource". There has been increasing frustrations that extremely valuable Masters theses and doctoral research lie in the darkness. With fewer local journals available and young graduates unable to get into more internationally credible journals, the sense of frustration reaches epic proportions.

It is here that one could sense the viability of digital libraries. Research findings made available digitally will be easily transportable and scientific discoveries easily communicated and shared. It may not be too ambitious to advocate the establishment of small local e-research and learning communities with similar interests or the emergence of what could be termed communities of practice. As WSIS (2005) argues that digital libraries are a cost-effective method to share information in the public domain. The presence of more locally constructed library information system, could be a first step which gives confidence to the African research and academic community and excites and stirs their thirst to contemplate global aspirations.

Digital Library: Ambassador of African Research in an Era of Globalisation

The value of digital libraries cannot be emphasised enough within the context of globalization. Many in academia and in research as well as in the wider economic environment would agree that Africa, in most areas of social life, has long been isolated, marginalized and exploited. The causal factors to this do not lie with foreign agents only. In fact, while former colonizers and capitalist agents have not publicised or disseminated the real value of Africa for various selfish and imperialist endeavours, it should also be recognised that Africans themselves have contributed to maintaining the continent on the margins (Fanon, 1961) and at the outskirts of global movements. Researchers have often not done enough research to bring the plight of Africa to the international scene and the hard work of some tenacious and intrepid inventors has often been ignored or sold cheaply in the international markets. The reason often evoked has been the lack of funding. However, such an explanation may not necessarily hold ground. Negative political forces and the lack of cooperation between different researchers have also undermined the field.

However, now an opportunity exists in the form of the digital library. These new systems of disseminating information and knowledge in the wider sense have the ability to help bring African research output to the world stage. Through initiatives such as African Online Libraries the world could come face to face with some hidden research treasures waiting to be seized and developed. The work of African scholars and students, even those that have been subject to political censure could become easily accessible by outsiders. Such a move will aid not only scientific inquiry but also political mobilisation and awareness. In this perspective, researchers in the West and other parts of the world would pick up valuable research issues arising from hidden academic and scientific data generated by Africans. More critically, online library systems harbour the power to foster dialogue and cooperation between the continent and other areas of the developing world that share similar characteristics, e.g. South America, Middle East, South East Asia and the least advanced parts of Europe. The phenomenal rise of China and India to world powers, industrial and financial centres could well be good practice models that should be widely available on African digital library sites and other resources. Such models are crucial data for educational case studies and reflections.

Information available on digital library systems, beyond its academic and scientific usefulness, could represent a marketing tool for African economies to multinationals. Attracting investments requires a large degree of self-marketing. Via digital libraries, the vast potentialities of some areas could be prominently highlighted, for example the availability of local labour force in the form of the graduate and skilled population, communication media, cultures, etc. There is some consensus that one of the most critical difficulties multinational companies and international aid agencies face in the developing world is lack of information or access to information.

It may be appropriate to suggest that with the complexification of the world order, the development of reliable and well documented digital libraries enables Africa and its education institutions to be truly connected. This affords Africa a voice and a seat that it deserves within the global learning community. Digitisation becomes then the silent but mighty ambassador of scientific, social, economic, political and cultural research and educational efforts of those who toil unceasingly to generate knowledge fit for development. In fact, for Dunlop & Rikowski (2008: 2) "digital libraries have become simultaneously ubiquitous, deeply enmeshed, and indispensable knowledge and information resources".

CONSTRAINTS TO DIGITISATION IN AFRICAN EDUCATION

Despite the advantages outlined, there are constraints which should not be brushed aside. There are cost implications (Tanner, 2003), logistics implications and manpower implications which are critical issues commanding respect. In most of Africa the GNP is among some of the lowest in the world and countries are heavily indebted (New Internationalist, 2000). These constraints make it difficult for governments to shift funding to an area of which they may have a poor understanding at present, particularly in terms of the extraordinary benefits of digital libraries. However, governments have pledged that education remains their priority of priorities and claim willingness for education provision to reach most traditionally excluded communities. If this vision remains (or is to remain) a reality, then cost alone should not deter the nations from taking the path of digitisation. That is where ministers, senior officials and community leaders should demonstrate a spirit of enterprise and a strategic framework that enables them to bring valuable learning and tools for skills acquisition to their communities. The business-like approach of voluntary and community organisations in some western countries could enlighten. These organisations have grown a culture of doing more with less and are engaged in robust fundraising and development activities which Hack-Polay (2007b) refers to as "tireless beggars". They ought to involve local business, multinationals and African diasporas who are capable of making invaluable contributions provided there is evidence that corruption and the lack of financial probity is being combated and that resources reach the very people who most crucially need them.

In terms of manpower, academics and commentators largely agree that they are available but many tend to leave as part of the so called brain drain movement due to the lack of opportunities to utilise the skills some key professionals harbour or simply due to very high unemployment rate (ILO, 2007) The widening of the digital library would lead to certain retention among the few qualified professionals available in the land. Digitisation, like any other socio-economic engineering project, requires political will and commitment. However, as Fanon (1962) argued, this has often been an issue in Africa. For digitisation to be a reality, this needs to change.

CONCLUSION

Beyond the interest in the digital library which may be seen as a fad, in an African context, there are strategic imperatives that command respect for this new approach to managing and disseminating information as well as knowledge. There are economic imperatives which when closely considered make apparent the cash crisis that resonates throughout the continent and many different areas. There are also globalisation imperatives which exacerbate the need to position the nation-state in the interconnected network in order for it to extract its fair share of the world wealth and opportunities. And more specifically connected with the subject of this paper, there are educational imperatives; these in turn raise the issues of quality in education. Quality in education is infallibly linked with the availability of resources, which have long been the causal factors in the shortcomings in education in Africa. Another way of explaining these educational imperatives is to consider the dynamic nature of knowledge particularly in this century. Change is so rapid that what is significant today may not stand tomorrow. In this context, quality education and scientific inquiry would require continuous updating of the knowledge base of a community of learners and researchers. In this respect, it could be vehemently argued that the digital library constitutes a core vehicle.

In the perspective of quality in education, Hack-Polay (2007a) has argued that African educational systems require imminent re-engineering. This fundamental rethinking should touch all aspects of the systems in terms of how knowledge is generated, managed and cascaded down to future generations of development artisans. In this context, digitisation becomes a much welcome and powerful tool in the sense that it brings about an unprecedented way of producing, managing and disseminating knowledge. The imperatives for digitisation are real as digitisation will take Africa to the world and the world to Africa. The real benefits for students reside in more awareness and more skills and for researchers in the availability of more data, as well as more extensive exposure to scrutiny from their international counterparts. In addition, researchers are more able to disseminate their own research findings. The educational system as a whole benefits as its sheer realities are broadcast to a wider international audience to attract investment and expertise to be shared.

There has been an increased awareness of the centrality of digitisation in new learning environments but more should be done. The perceived initial cost of digitisation is only a fraction of the real cost of widening and investing only in traditional forms of libraries. With digitisation, knowledge is shared more evenly and quickly within a specific country and across African regions, providing new opportunities for those traditionally excluded from higher participation in learning. Digital libraries could ultimately, more than any other means before, aid literacy development in Africa and in higher education, foster more quality academic output and research. The digital library is an opportunity not to be missed in the information age. As the United Nation's Science, Education and Culture Organisation (2008) contends, the continent's nations' educational systems should develop mechanisms to adapt to deep changes born as a result of the emergence of 'the global knowledge society and information-driven economic growth'.

REFERENCES

Akst, D. (2003, Fall). The digital library: Its future has arrived. *Carnegie Reporter*, *2*(3).

Copeland, S. (2008). Electronic theses and dissertations: Promoting 'hidden' research. *Policy Futures in Education*, *6*(1), 87–96. Retrieved May 10, 2010, from http://www.wwwords.co.uk/pdf/freetoview.asp?j=pfie&vol=6&issue=1&year=2008&article=9_Copeland_PFIE_6_1_web

Dunlap, I. H., & Rikowski, R. (2008). A library revolution of digital proportions. *Policy Futures in Education*, *6*(1), 1–4. Retrieved May 10, 2010, from http://www.wwwords.co.uk/pfie/content/pdfs/6/issue6_1.asp#2

Fanon, F. (1962). *Les damnés de la terre*. Paris: Maspéro.

Fendin, M. L. (2003). *Digital libraries in the Nordic countries: With practical examples for the creation and development of 'libraries without walls' from the Nordic Africa Institute Library and other libraries within the Nordic countries*. Uppsala: Nordic Africa Institute.

Guthrie, K., & Nygre, T. (2007). *Aluka - Building a digital library of scholarly resources from Africa*, JSTOR.

Hack-Polay, D. D. (2007a). Re-engineering: A relevant concept for educational organisations. *Education Today*, *57*(1).

Hack-Polay, D. D. (2007b). *Compassionate leadership in voluntary service organisations and the integration of forced migrants*. A paper presented at 7ème Conference du Réseau Inter-Universitaire sur l'Economie Sociale et Solidaire (RIUESS), Université de Rennes, France.

Hack-Polay, D. D. (2000). *Re-engineering education in Cote d'Ivoire: Examination of a possible integration between secondary and higher education to increase quality in tertiary education*. Doctoral Thesis, Lincoln, NE: University of Lincoln.

ILO. (2007). *The decent work agenda in Africa 2007–2015*. Geneva: International Labour Organisation.

INASP. (2005). *Towards the digital library in Africa*, Info Brief 5, March. Oxford: International Network for the availability of Scientific Publication (INASP).

Kanyengo, C. (2006, September 6–8). *Managing digital information resources in Africa: Preserving the integrity of scholarship*. A paper presented at the Bridging the North-South divide in scholarly communication on Africa – Threats and opportunities in the digital era, Leiden, The Netherlands.

Kyama, R., & Waititu, J. (2008, May 28–30). *Digital project heralds new dawn for African libraries*. A paper presented at the 3rd Conference on ICT for development, education and training, Accra, E-learning Africa, www.elearningafrica.com

Marx, K. (1970). *Capital – Volume 1*. Harmondsworth: Penguin Publishing.

Ngimwa, P. (2006). An African experience in providing a digital library service: The African Virtual University example. *Africa Higher Education Online*. Retrieved May 10, 2010, from http://ahero.uwc.ac.za/index.php?module=cshe&action=downloadfile&fileid=81806115511712696569416

New Internationalist. (2000, August). Africa: The facts. *New Internationalist, 326*.

Peters, D., & Pickover, M. (2001). DISA – Insights of an African model for digital library development. *D-Lib Magazine*, *7*(11). Retrieved May 10, 2010, from http://www.dlib.org/dlib/november01/peters/11peters.html

Rosenberg, H. (2006). *Towards the digital library: Findings of an investigation to establish the current status of university libraries in Africa*. Oxford: International Network for the Availability of Scientific Publications (INASP).

Servaes, J. (2003). *Harnessing the UN system into a common approach for development*. Retrieved from http://portal.unesco.org/ci/en/files/24016/11712792011jan_servaes_paper_10th_round_table.pdf/jan_servaes_aper_10th_round_table.pdf

Tanner, S. (2003). Economic factors of managing digital content and establishing digital libraries. *Journal of Digital Information*, *4*(2), article 229.

UNCTAD. (2007). *Asian Foreign Direct investment in Africa: Towards a new era of cooperation among developing countries*. United Nations Conference on Trade & Development (UNCTAD).

UNESCO. (2008). *Education*. Retrieved May 22, 2008, from http://portal.unesco.org/education/en/ev.php-URL

UNESCO. (2005). *Unesco supports training for building digital libraries in Africa*. Retrieved from http://portal.unesco.org/ci/en/ev.php-URL_ID=20808&URL_DO=DO_TOPIC&URL_SECTION=201.html

West, P. (2001). *The African digital library: Concept and practice*. Retrieved from www.usq.edu.au/electpub/ejist/docs/old/vol4no1/2001docs/west.html

Dieu Donné Hack-Polay
Faculty of Business
London South Bank University, UK

LEBURN ROSE

11. CRITICAL PERSPECTIVES ON DIGITISING AFRICA

AUTHENTIC DIGITISATION: A DEVELOPMENTAL PERSPECTIVE

The issue of what constitutes authentic development among African nations be it driven by technological, social or economic change has long been the subject of debate among development ethicists. Amongst these, the contribution of Croker (2004) is relevant to the concerns of digitisation, particularly in relation to the African context. Croker's ideas not only offer an enlightened view of authentic development, but also provide an important means of reframing digitisation in ways that enable both its nature and scope to be more appropriately evaluated within a specific African context. In establishing a framework for guiding the praxis of authentic digitisation, the following ideas are relevant:

- Development practices such as digitisation export underlying ethics and values, which may need re-evaluation and re-orientation toward the proposed operating context;
- The multi-disciplinary nature of digitisation can yield many pathways toward positive social well-being and change. Authentic digitisation calls forth and promotes the most appropriate pathways for the specific developmental circumstance;
- Those who seek to sponsor authentic digitisation should focus on strategies that build upon and engender social well-being and are contextually sensitive to the relevant domains of practice;
- Just as those who sponsor authentic digitisation, those who experience it should understand the aims and objectives of the particular development project, how authentic digitisation is to be achieved, and whom the endeavour is likely to franchise, or disenfranchise. They should also be cognisant of the potential transnational ramifications of the development technology and share mutual expectations of its intended beneficence;
- Authentic digitisation projects must seek to occupy a middle-ground in achieving development objectives. On the one hand the economic benefits accruing to benefactors should not be maximised at the expense of gains in the social well-being of the beneficiaries. Yet, on the other hand, the liberties of one party should not be unduly usurped by the will of the other.

Croker's ideas on authentic development provide an additional dimension for authenticating digitisation projects within the context of the developing nation. It presents opportunities for both the benefactor and beneficiary of the digitisation project to engage in thinking that reconciles the instrumental-volitional duality noted

R. Rikowski (ed.), Digitisation Perspectives, 179–188.

earlier. Implicit within this framework are also the concepts of 'creating beneficence' and 'contextual sensitivity', which in combination engender the useful notion of 'contextual beneficence'. That is the notion that technology when deployed within the developing nation ought to empower individuals, be congruent with their ways of knowing and practice, and should enhance their social well-being.

DIGITISATION TECHNOLOGY: PERSPECTIVES ON INSTRUMENTALITY AND VOLITION

The philosopher Frederic Ferré defines technology as: "the practical implementations of intelligence" (Ferré, 2003, p. 26). This elegant and yet succinct definition speaks of technology as necessarily possessing both a purpose and end, and not merely a means to fulfilling others' ends. The use of the word 'practical' in this definition speaks of achieving ends, which should, for example result in a creative ensemble of objects, knowledge and actions that facilitate the saving of energies, the alleviation of poverty and hunger, and the bringing about of empowerment. Equally, the word 'implementations' evokes the need for caution, not only about technology's potential to cause harm, or to heal, but also of the need for foresight and judgement in its deployment. Lastly, the word 'intelligence' conveys the exclusive relationship that technology shares with humankind. This does not mean that other species are precluded from, or may not partake of the fruits of technology, but instead speaks of humankind's unique relationship with technology as its creator, evaluator, and decision-taker. Yet as eloquent as Ferré's definition of technology may be it still falls somewhat short of that important essence of technology, which Mitcham (1994) describes as the "protean character of volition" (1994, p. 247). It is this transmutable character of technology, as distinct from its nature as an ensemble of objects, knowledge and actions, that presents the greatest challenge to its effective deployment, especially when the implications are transnational, or even global. Technology embodies notions of instrumentality as well as notions of volition: the former speaks of humankind as designer, and the latter, as judge and jury. The endeavour of design or instrumentality is amoral since the underlying motivations stem purely from a natural urge to be creative. But this does not of itself constitute the practise of technology. Rather, to practise technology requires ones engagement with its dual nature as being at the same time instrumental and volitional: in effect two sides of the same coin. Thus volition; namely, the will to control, power, or to impose ones choices, decisions and agendas on another is a direct corollary of the creation of technology. The volitional perspective on technology is quintessentially Western, and presents a distorted view of technology as something that is being created for and imposed upon. It speaks of received wisdom and offers little on the consequential received experiences and contexts of this received wisdom. Clearly, an alternative Africanist perspective could be one that conceives of, and seeks also to fulfil Afro-centric potentialities which the received wisdom can deliver. So volition in this sense should be seen as having both Western and African potentialities.

On the African continent, the imported technologies of oil exploration or for that matter motor vehicles are powerful exemplars of the perspective of 'received wisdom', and the technology of digitisation should be no less significant. Digitisation is an imported set of techniques: ensembles, knowledge and activities, if you will, which are the product of Western ideas. Though few would disagree on the instrumental benefits that technologies can confer on African countries, it is technology's volitional perspective and the uncertain consequences these often impose that cause the most controversy. The much popularised 'digital divide' is one such concept that encapsulates these controversies: that is, the potential for information and communications technologies (ICTs) to create and exacerbate gaps between the rich and poor, the young and old, and to reinforce pre-existing maladies (Ono, 2005; Yue, 2006). Given that digitisation is a particular instance of an ICT, it too possesses both instrumental and volitional potentialities.

While the literature is replete on ICTs and the extent to which they can contribute to underdevelopment on the African continent, much of that reviewed on the topic of digitisation indicates a paucity of thinking and inquiry on the volitional perspectives of digitisation. Likewise, definitions of digitisation seem merely to reinforce its instrumental, and to understate its volitional potentialities. The following definitions of digitisation serve to illustrate this point:

> The process of converting information into a digital format. For example, taking a digital photograph of a painting, and scanning a literary manuscript, are both digitisation activities. Digital material produced by digitisation can be referred to as 'made digital', as distinct from 'born digital'. (Collections Council of Australia Ltd, 2006)

> The process of converting information (legacy documents including, text, images, audio and video) into a digital format, to make it easier to preserve, access, share and/or repurpose such information. (UK National Occupation Standards for Publishing, 2005)

> The process of converting information into a digital format. In this format, information is organized into discrete units of data (called bits) that can be separately addressed (usually in multiple-bit groups called bytes). This is the binary data processed by computers and devices like digital cameras. (IFLA, Guidelines for Digital Projects, 2002)

From these definitions flow a number of noteworthy observations. The first, points to underlying assumptions about the existence of and ease of access to the requisite know-how, skills and material means to make digitisation possible. The second concerns the taken-for-granted cultural and behavioural contexts within which technologies in general and digitisation in particular come to be practised. The third is the received wisdom in relation to the known limits and purposes that circumscribe the technology, which often acts as a barrier to its creative deployment in the proposed new context. Fourth, is the assumption of logical instrumentality in which successful implementation of the technology in one context is presumed to be directly transferable to another context. Lastly, and in all three definitions is the absence of any notion of the volitional impact which the technology is likely to impose within the proposed new operating context.

The instrumental perspective of digitisation requires, that as a given, the human and physical tools, techniques and know-how should be in place to make successful implementation possible. As a former student of engineering statics one of the key cornerstones in understanding this particular branch of science was to be able to conceptualise the idea of a 'free-body diagram'. In so doing, one was then able to isolate from its immediate surroundings that part of the technology which was being investigated so that it could be subjected to analysis. Once the analysis was complete the answers would be determined and thus presented as a 'generalised' solution to the problem in question. The notion that this 'generalised' solution applied only to the specific instance under which the part of the technology – the specific free-body conditions – was being investigated seemed always to be significantly under-stated, and more often than not, totally ignored. In reality, the 'free-body' state of any technology is no more than a textbook illusion – a way of conceptualising. So what is crucial in determining the relevant solutions of parts of the technology when isolated from the surroundings of which they were originally a part is an understanding of the way in which changes to conditions that define the surroundings affect the desired solutions or outcomes of the technology. The conclusion here is not surprising: that the problems which technology attempts to resolve and the outcomes sought are contingent upon the surroundings of which the technology may be a part. One cannot simply export a technology into an unfamiliar context and assume that it will yield similar results to those achieved in the original setting.

In thinking about 'digitising Africa', there are a number of important ways in which African contexts where technology is to be applied differ markedly from those of Western nations. First, whereas in Western nations access to skills and competences to establish, disseminate and sustain the technological project are more often than not a given, these critical skills and competences lie well beyond the reach of the vast majority of African nations. Allied to this is the Western notion of technological obsolescence where the practice is to discard a current mode of technology when a successive new variant becomes available. The effect of this way of thinking about and deploying technology is luxurious to say the least. Apart from exacerbating the prevailing chronic lack of technological skills and competences among African nations, it serves also to narrow the possibilities for securing the necessary in-situ skills and competences to deal with the emergent technology.

One trap that often ensnares African nations which import Western technologies is that the associated costs of commissioning, training and maintenance can be significantly understated by the benefactor as well as the beneficiary of the technological project. While the dependencies between these phases of the project and the available skills and competences is obvious, it is probably the issue of the differing objectives placed on the project itself by the actors involved that presents the greatest dangers to entrapment. Western benefactors may be overly driven by the urge to enact their technological will, of which profit-seeking plays a key role. By contrast, the African beneficiaries may seek to content themselves merely to the enactment of 'political will' through the symbolism of the technology within the particular African context and the immediate prospect it holds for enriching a limited cadre of Africans. In this battle of wills the principal objective that contextual beneficence should result from the deployment of the technology is seldom achieved. Instead, what one observes are landscapes within the African nations that manifest symbols (some may say monuments) of technology projects the majority of which appear to have failed, in part, due to chronic deficiencies in local skills and competences, and in part due to the prominence of myopic attitudes towards sustainable development.

Second, to a significant degree, African nations suffer from a lack of access to the practical implements that make possible the deployment of the particular technology. Note that the use of the term 'practical implements' refers directly to Ferré's definition highlighted earlier as 'the practical implementations of technology'. Accordingly, as with other technologies in general, digitisation should be interpreted as a collection of 'practical implements' centred on the key defining implement of digitising. The technology of digitisation could thus be construed as a proactive complement of 'practical implements' – of 'practical implementations' if you will – each of which play an important role in contributing to what we have earlier referred to as authentic digitisation. What then are the 'practical implementations' that should constitute authentic digitisation?

Recently, Puglia (2009) argued strongly for digitisation technology to shift its narrow focus away from the digital repository, toward a wider perspective encompassing what he describes as the 'entire digitisation process' (NARA, 2009, p. 6). A decision to embark on a digitisation project is followed by a number of logical consequences, which according to Puglia, involve:

- Project planning
- Pre-digitisation
- Digitisation
- Post-digitisation

Therefore, from Puglia's standpoint, the technology of digitisation obtains authenticity not just from the narrow focus of the implements of digitisation itself; namely scanners, associated software tools, meta-data structures, automation technologies, and so forth. Authentic digitisation, also, and perhaps more significantly, encompasses process thinking and implementation both upstream and downstream of the activity of establishing the digital repository. Authentic digitisation in the sense Puglia connotes is the project in its widest sense. Moreover, inherent to Puglia's four logical consequences of the decision to digitise is the notion that critical discourse concerning the contextual beneficence of the project should not just be entered into at its inception, but should pervade the entire project, not least of which is the post-digitisation phase.

DIGITISATION TECHNOLOGY: PERSPECTIVE ON CONTEXTUAL BENEFICENCE

The *contextual beneficence* of technology and particular the digitisation of indigenous knowledge (IK) is an issue about which a number of writers have recently commented. The story of *Hoodia Triebneri Hans Schuldt* (*Asclepiadaceae*), an indigenous plant discovered by a Western botanist nearly 250 years ago provides a salutary reminder of the importance of creating *contextual beneficence* in the digitisation of IK within a developing country. Augusto's (2008) eloquent exposé on this issue informs us that by merely documenting and describing a piece of IK – in this case medico-botanical – without also profiling the historical and socio-cultural narratives that enfold the particular piece of IK, could result in the loss of "unknown future options for resolving common needs such as medicine or food, and more balanced use of the environment, not to mention for the multiple complex ways of being human" (Augusto, 2008, p. 217). The important need to properly articulate digitisation within the indigenous context was also noted by Star and Strauss (1999). This notion of articulation speaks not only of the conjoining of digitisation's instrumental and volitional perspectives, but significantly of the ultimate responsibility of the benefactors of the technology to assure its *contextual beneficence*. Authentic digitisation as it ought to be applied to African nations calls forth a multi-dimensional approach: namely, one that demands conscious thought, action and praxis to be conducted not only instrumentally and volitionally, but also in ways that engender beneficence.

AUTHENTIC DIGITISATION IN AFRICA

A recent paper presented by Limb (2007), in which he heralds the 'Digitisation of Africa' presents a contrasting perspective on digitising Africa. The achievement of the ends of digitising Africa, however desirable those may be, should not solely be predicated on the basis that transplanting out of context a technology to a handful of African nations and their associated librarian professionals constitutes completion of the mission of digitising Africa. Africa is a collection of forty-seven countries on the continent itself with myriad cultures, dialects and ways of knowing and operating. With some, if not most countries on the African continent, the goal of digitisation may neither be desirable nor even possible in the longer term.

What are the potential pitfalls and benefits that lie ahead for the 'project' of 'digitising Africa'? Is there a case for broadening the meaning of digitisation in ways that cede its current Western-centred perspectives in favour of a middle-ground that reconciles digitisation's instrumental, volitional and beneficent purposes? If the prevailing technological notion of digitisation can be broadened, then would it not be possible to envision African contexts in which levels of social and intellectual well-being can be elevated? This is not to say that digitisation should cease to play a purposive role in advancing intellectual welfare in Africa, but that given the endemic nature of poverty and its associated maladies, informed and creative digitisation may well provide more immediate and effective approaches to dealing with social welfare. There is a compelling need to reframe what is presently a naïve notion of 'digitising Africa' away from one that is predicated on imposition to an alternative perspective. Such a perspective ought not just to decide whether Africa should or should not be digitised. It must inquire into the 'conditions within and among African nations that would make the deployment of digitisation maleficent, or beneficent?

The question about the wider legitimacy of digitisation for Africa raises two important issues. First, though the instrumental notion of digitisation is but one perspective of the instrumental-volitional duality of digitisation technology noted earlier, it is concerning that the existence of the means with which technologies can be successfully implemented on the African continent are at worst assumed to be given, and at best seriously understated. Digitisation is a complex, dynamic technology, which requires state-of-the-art expertise, integrated action among subject specialists, a supporting physical infrastructure, and investment especially for start-up costs and longer-term sustainability. A key question then is: 'to what extent do Western nations act responsibly by simply willing the technological *means* by which digitisation can be exported, without reasonably securing the *ends* by which successful deployment can be achieved and sustained within the particular African context?'. Second, the volitional perspective raises further noteworthy concerns about the process of digitisation in African nations. For it is at this conjunction between the digitisation process and the contexts in which digitisation becomes possible for the African nation that the greatest opportunities and threats exist to maximising beneficence to affected individuals. Creative digitisation that is interwoven with the socio-economic and cultural contexts of the specific domain of practice must not only educate, but crucially also contribute to the empowerment as well as the social well-being of Africans in rural and urban conurbations.

CONCLUSION: TOWARDS A NEW MINDSET OF AUTHENTIC DIGITISATION

Digitising Africa calls forth a new mindset: one in which digitisation projects come to be seen as contributing to the genuine needs of African nations, rather than just fulfilling the narrower volitional agenda of the Western exporter or satisfying the political motivations of the African elite. This new mindset is egalitarian and as such multi-dimensional. It speaks both of upholding a doctrine of equality of purpose with regard to development projects such as digitisation, and of construing digitisation projects as characterised by *complex* technical endeavours, with unique life-cycles, and underpinned by the goal of contextual beneficence. These are the three dimensions upon which the particular Western exporter and the potential African recipient of a digitisation project ought to deliberate, and which, in the author's view constitute the starting point of authentic digitisation. The dimension of *complexity* does touch upon issues such as project size, technical complexity, and even project duration. However, it also demands that those who devise digitisation projects of this nature should adopt a *systems approach* that accounts for the negative and positive consequences that flow from the interconnectedness of these projects with both the global community of which they will be a part, and the local communities which they are intended serve. There are many ways in which *systems thinking* can shed new light on the challenges presented by authentic digitisation, not least of which concerns the relationship between known international guidelines/standards (such as those of the U.S. National Archives and Records Administration (NARA)), and the capability of the potential African participant to deliver and sustain these internationally recognised guidelines over the life of the digitisation project. Sub-Saharan African nations remain extremely challenged by the rigours of assuring and controlling quality standards, especially with regard to the deployment of technology processes/implements which demand the use or manufacture of standardised, repeatable implements. In these circumstances, the *systems approach* will ensure that only those African nations capable of delivering the exacting standards imposed by international guidelines/standards ought to undertake the digitisation project. In other words, the *degree of complexity* of action which international standards demand should also reflect the prevailing capability of the proposed African participant to engage in commensurate *complex* action in assuring and controlling international standards. Critics of this capability notion of development would no doubt argue that such a course of action would lead inevitably to circumstances where a lack of capability on the part of the African nation would result in the denial of developmental opportunities, and thereby contradict the very case being made for authentic digitisation. However, as argued earlier, if the project idea stems from and is articulated by the African participant in such a way that the potential contextual benefit to the key stakeholders is self-evident, then the principle of authentic digitisation is not undermined.

The author's plea that authentic digitisation should also take account of the life-cycle of the digitisation project is equally relevant to the arguments presented earlier in the chapter on volition: namely, the will to impose ones choices, decisions and agendas on another. One interpretation of a project is that it is a purposeful series of controlled interventions aimed at creating an alternative state of affairs. Given that volition is both wilful and intrusive, it follows that the action of undertaking a project is itself tantamount to an act of volition. The point about the interrelationship between volition, the life-cycle of a digitisation project, and the goal of authentic digitisation is that the will to impose a project and its ideals on the recipient is often strongest at the early phases of the project life-cycle, particularly at origination and initiation; for it is during these early phases that key contractual and pecuniary commitments are likely to be consolidated. As contractual responsibilities are progressively discharged during the *planning*, *execution and control*, and *close-out* phases of the project life-cycle it is possible that real agendas relating to short-term pecuniary gains and political expediency emerge, resulting in the rapid, early diffusion of human energies and project resources during the later phases of the project. In general, whilst poor planning is often cited as a key reason for most project failures whether they are undertaken in Western or African contexts, it is the *execution and control* and *close-out* phases that pose the greatest challenges for African nations, and which often lead to the premature failure of digitisation projects. Unrealistic, naïve, and overly optimistic analysis and evaluation at the planning phase can often fail to identify the impacts of key constraining factors such as insufficient installed electricity capacity, weak information infrastructure, low levels of literacy and numeracy, and a lack of availability of crucial skills-sets throughout the phases of the life-cycle. Thus, it is the insidious weaknesses in the infrastructures of sub-Saharan African nations that cause significantly shortened project life-cycles, and that most significantly contributes to the failure of digitisation projects to deliver contextual beneficence. In addition, in many African nations, the scourge of corrupt practices serves to add substantially to the cost burden and thus the risk of project failure along the life-cycle. For these reasons the goal of authentic digitisation depends very much on the success with which digitisation projects survive their evolutionary sojourn through the stages of the life-cycle.

Finally, whilst this chapter strongly implores collaborators on digitisation to adopt a mindset that is multi-dimensional and accounts for the *complexity*, *life-cycle,* and *contextual beneficence* of the digitisation project, it is the emergence of relatively recent statistical trends on the adoption of mobile phone telephony, particularly in sub-Saharan Africa, that raises the most profound implications for the future direction and nature of digitisation projects in Africa. A recent paper by Avila (2009) contrasts the penetration rates of telephone landlines between Europe, The Americas, and sub-Saharan Africa. Avila observed that whilst telephone penetration rates in Europe and The Americas peaked at 39 percent and 35 percent, respectively in 2001, and to date continue to progressively fall. By contrast, that of the sub-Saharan African nations barely increased above 3 percent since 2002. Yet during the period 2001 to 2006, the rise in mobile cellular subscriptions in Africa in general had grown exponentially from 30 millions to nearly 200 millions. This dramatic shift in the telecommunications landscape of the African continent opens the way for the development of novel approaches to digitisation based around the widespread use of mobile devices which now contain condensed forms of the key technology implements to enable the conversion of images, textual content, and voice to digital objects. Such approaches would by their very nature engender authentic digitisation, since they tap into deeply embedded oral and auditory cultural traditions that are unique to the continent of Africa. Significantly, however, they offer immense opportunities for informing, educating, and enabling remote communities to begin to deal with current maladies such as AIDS, mal-nutrition, and malaria, which continue to threaten the survival of millions of men, women and children in sub-Saharan Africa.

REFERENCES

Augusto, G. (2008). Digitising IKS: Epistemic complexity, data diversity and cognitive justice. *The International Information and Library Review*, *40*, 211–218.

Avila, A. (2009). Underdeveloped ICT Areas in sub-Saharan Africa. *Information Economics*, *13*(4), 136–146.

Brown, I. (Compiled 2005). UK National Occupational Standards for Publishing. The publishing training centre. Glossary, p. 3.

Birtley, M. (Compiled 2008). Collections Council of Australia Ltd. Digital Heritage Collections, Glossary of terms, p. 2.

Croker, D. A. (2004). Development ethics: Sources, agreements and controversies. In M. Kransz & M. Chatterjee (Eds.), *Globalisation, development and democracy*. Lanham, MD: Rowan & Littlefield.

IFLA. (2002). *IFLA Guidelines*. International Federation of Library Associations & Institutions. Retrieved May 10, 2010, from http://www.ifla.org/

Ferre, F. (1995). *The philosophy of technology*. Athens, GA: The University of Georgia Press.

Limb, P. (2005). The digitisation of Africa. *Africa Today*, *52*(2), 3–19.

Mitcham, C. (1994). *Thinking through technology – the path between engineering & philosophy*. Chicoago: University of Chicago Press.

Puglia, S. (2009). *Digitisation – Support tools and technical approaches*. National Archives and Records Administration, United States of America. Retrieved from http://www.archives.gov/

Star, S. L., & Strauss, A. (1999). Layers of silence, arenas of voice: The ecology of visible and invisible work. *Computer Supported Cooperative Work, 8*, 9–30

Yue, C. S., & Ono, H. (2006). *Commentary: The Earth Institute Asian Economic Papers 4:3*. New York: Columbia University and the Massachusetts Institute of Technology.

Leburn Rose
Faculty of Business, London South Bank University, UK

PART IV: DIGITAL LIBRARIES, REFERENCE SERVICES AND CITATION INDEXING

JIA LIU

12. DIGITAL LIBRARY AND DIGITAL REFERENCE SERVICE

Integration and Mutual Complementarity

INTRODUCTION

Nowadays, neither the digital library nor the digital reference service is seen as exotic. Both of them are evolving at an amazingly rapid pace. Though they have mutual interests, it has been argued that there is a 'lack of interaction between the digital reference and digital library communities' (Lankes, 2004, p. 301). However, the fact is that, on the one hand, the purpose of establishing a digital library is certainly not only building up the digital collection but also providing services on the basis of the collection; on the other hand, the foundation for offering a successful digital reference service is a solid reference collection. Thus, it should not be a question that there might be a point where the digital library and digital reference service match. The digital reference service could be one type of service the digital library provides (seen as Figure 1) while the digital library collection might be a part of the reference collection contributing to the digital reference service (seen as Figure 2).

Nonetheless, the relationship between the digital library and digital reference service has seldom been discussed. Chowdhury actually looks at the current state of research in personalised information services in digital libraries (2002, p. 258) while Pomerantz focuses on integrating digital reference services into the digital library environment (2003, p. 23). Attempting to extend the former research, this chapter will deal with the symbiotic interest between the digital library and the digital reference service and mutual promotion and their three-dimensional integrations, i.e. parallel combination, the digital reference service affiliated with a digital library and the digital library integrated into the digital reference service collection.

The key research questions of this chapter are whether there is any relationship between the digital library and the digital reference service and how to integrate them into a systematic organism. The author assumes that there is a close relationship between the digital library and digital reference; based on their symbiotic interest, they could develop at the same time with mutual complementarity; and there are three ways to merge them on the basis of the mutual interest.

In this research, the digital library and its services will be discussed at first. This is followed by a section dealing with the digital reference service and its collection. Then, after the points where the digital library and the digital reference service match are outlined, how they are facilitated by each other through mergence in three dimensions will be described based on some case studies.

R. Rikowski (ed.), Digitisation Perspectives, 191–212.

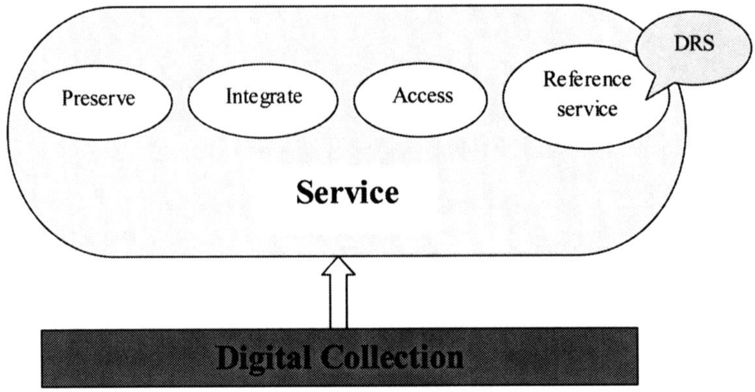

Figure 1. Model of the digital library.

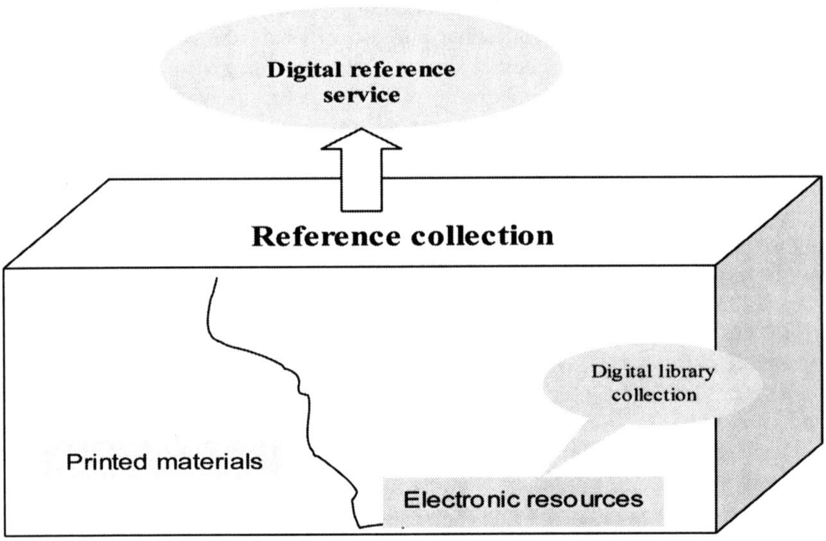

Figure 2. Model of the digital reference service.

THE DIGITAL LIBRARY AND ITS SERVICES

With the development of the computer network, the digital library has become a very common term. However, there is no uniform definition. From different perspectives and standpoints different communities define digital libraries in different ways. As Christine L. Borgman commented, 'research and practice in digital libraries (DL) has exploded worldwide in the 1990s'. Through exploring the reasons for the development of digital libraries and the influence of key players, Borgman outlines and analyzes a variety of definitions of digital libraries separately from the perspectives of researchers and librarians (Borgman, 1999, p. 227). According to

Borgman's summarization, digital libraries have been defined as content, collections and communities; institutions or services; and databases. She notes that the most general of the definitions of digital libraries, discussed during the 1995 National Science Foundation (NSF) sponsored Social Aspects of Digital Libraries workshop, is given by Lynch & Garcia-Molina. They define a digital library as a system that provides 'a community of users with coherent access to a large, organized repository of information and knowledge' (Lynch & Garcia-Molina, 1996, p. 85).

The working definition of digital libraries set forth by the Digital Library Federation represents the point of view defining digital libraries as institutions:

> Digital libraries are organizations that provide the resources, including the specialized staff, to select, structure, offer intellectual access to, interpret, distribute, preserve the integrity of, and ensure the persistence over time of collections of digital works so that they are readily and economically available for use by a defined community or set of communities. (Digital Library Federation, 2006)

One early informal definition was given by William Y. Arms, an authority in the field of the digital library, at the end of the twentieth century. According to his understanding, 'a digital library is a managed collection of information, with associated services, where the information is stored in digital formats and accessible over a network' (Arms, 2000a). Obviously, this definition fits the topic of this research very well.

Gary Marchionini comments that 'digital libraries marry the missions, techniques, and cultures of physical libraries with the capabilities and cultures of computing and telecommunications' (Marchionini, 2000, p. 304). In another paper, he also argues that 'Digital libraries (DLs) are extensions and augmentations of physical libraries' (Marchionini & Fox, 1999, p. 219).

No matter how the digital library is defined, its service – its main function – could never be neglected. One of the main reasons for the existence of the physical library is no doubt to serve the user. The digital library succeeds the intention of the physical library and extends its service to the remote user without spatial and temporal limitations.

In a biography of the digital library, Daniel Greenstein & Suzanne E. Thorin (2002) divide the development of the digital library into three periods:

- Aspiration and the 'skunk works': the young digital library;
- Rolling projects into programs: the maturing digital library;
- From integration to interdependency: the adult digital library.

In their opinion, one of the main characteristics of the maturing digital library is a 'focus on the user': 'The maturing digital library takes very seriously its users' needs and interests through its support for a suite of activities that have become known as "e-scholarship" (Greenstein & Thorin, 2002). In the recent development of the digital library, establishing the collection and providing service are of equivalent importance to the digital library community.

Generally, the digital library functions to preserve the cultural heritage, integrate a variety of digital materials (born-digital or digitized resources), and provide access to its digital collections. Providing 'browse' and 'search' are two basic service features of a digital library. For example, the Association for Computing Machinery (ACM) Digital Library is defined as 'a vast collection of citations and full text from ACM journal and newsletter articles and conference proceedings' (ACM, 2007a). Aside from basic and advanced search, it allows the user to browse its collection by type of ACM publication: journals, magazines, transactions, proceedings, newsletters, publications by affiliated organizations, special interest groups (SIGs) and ACM oral history interviews (ACM, 2007b).

One more example comes from the Networked Digital Library of Theses and Dissertations, which provides three functions as follows (Networked Digital Library of Theses and Dissertations, 2001):

- Browse the Networked Digital Library of Theses and Dissertations Union Catalog by theses and dissertation author, subject, title and library call number;
- Search for words or exact phrases anywhere in the theses and dissertation catalog record;
- The Expert search function allows the user to use Boolean operators in a command mode.

As the digital library evolves, its service has been extended through coordinating with other communities. The Metadata and Digital Library Services (MDLS) provides a wide array of services to assist members of the University of Oregon community with organizing collections of materials or making them more widely available. Their services include the following (Grenci, 2007):

- Designing a digital project;
- Creating digital or photographic reproductions of materials;
- Creating posters or exhibits;
- Choosing an appropriate metadata schema, subject list, or classification system;
- Evaluating software to help organize and provide access to materials;
- Caring for and preserving digital or print materials;
- Determining appropriate security and use policies for collections;
- Providing access to collections through the Libraries' catalogs, or;
- Developing grant proposals related to any of the above topics.

The MDLS also maintain the University of Oregon's Scholars' Bank. In addition to these direct public services, it provides intellectual, virtual and physical access to the libraries' collections. Many of the services offered by this digital library have gone far beyond the understanding of the early digital library community.

The domain the digital library contributes the most to might be education and research. The educational digital library is grounded and the digital library could act as a network and community center (Manduca et al, 2006). For instance, the Alexander Digital Earth Prototype (ADEPT) is an emerging digital library that provides instructors and students with the means to discover, manipulate, and display dynamic geographical processes (Borgman, et al, 2000). And the University of Michigan Digital Library eXtension Service (DLXS) provides the foundation and the framework for educational and non-profit institutions to fully develop their digital library collections. The DLXS's impressive and comprehensive suite of tools includes a powerful search engine and an array of class-based middleware (DLXS, n.d.).

Just as the situation in the metadata community, where registries of metadata application profiles are more and more important for the purpose of communicating and interoperating with the development of metadata, the registry related to the digital library service has also become an urgent demand. A digital library service registry was suggested during a one-day workshop on 23 March 2006 supported by supplemental funding from the National Science Foundation and cosponsored by the Digital Library Federation and JISC/UKOLN (Frumkin, 2006a, b). It was proposed that 'a digital library service registry allows a machine or human to discover available digital library services, locate those services, and obtain configuration information to services for the purpose of interfacing' (Frumkin, 2006c).

Sayeed Choudhury's description sounds reasonable as regards to a single digital library project. Normally, 'digital library projects began with collections [i.e. digitization]', followed by 'the subsequent development of associated services' and then 'development of digital library infrastructure [e.g. repositories]'. Furthermore, he suggests using 'open standards and build[ing] interfaces between service modules' so as to integrate the digital library services through repositories; in other words, to optimize the usage of digital library services through sharing their collections (Choudhury, 2004). The request for cooperation among digital libraries has come into being.

THE DIGITAL REFERENCE SERVICE AND ITS COLLECTION

The digital reference service is a response to the information need raised in the networked environment. The popularization of the computer network refers to the change in people's information-seeking habits. At present, the majority of people are turning to the Internet to meet their information needs, especially students. Libraries are service-oriented organizations. Most librarians find that it is not sufficient to simply offer their content on the Web. Rather, they feel they should complement that content with professional experts who can assist patrons in learning to use these resources and in finding the information they need (Breeding, 2001, p. 42). To serve the remote user, libraries are exploring ways of expanding their reference services via the Web. Marshall Breeding declared that 'in the last year [2000] or so, interest in providing digital reference service has grown enormously'. In addition, she argues that 'the web now allows us to offer remote support with more sophistication and immediacy, and maybe even do it with a more personal touch' (Breeding, 2001, p. 43).

Compared with the digital library, there are many more variations for the term 'digital reference service'. The following are only some of the most popular substitutes:

- Digital reference;
- Virtual reference service;
- Online reference service;
- Electronic reference service/e-reference;
- Ask a/the librarian service;
- Ask the library.

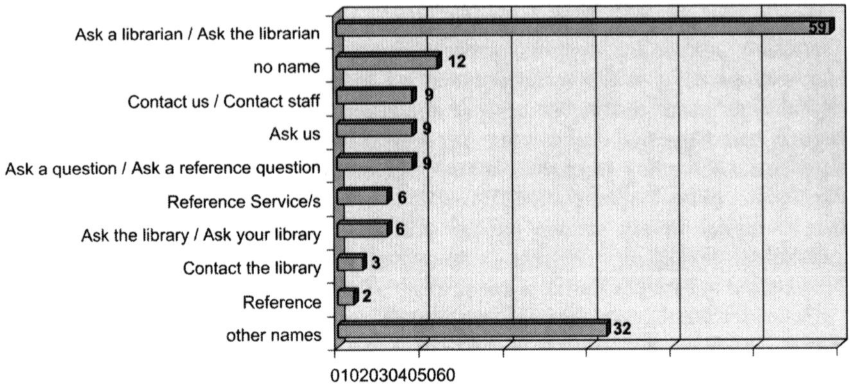

Figure 3. Names of the digital reference service.

Practically, in a research project[1] during which 147 digital reference services in worldwide libraries were evaluated by a German group, it was reported that the most commonly used name for such service is 'Ask a/the librarian'; 'Ask a (reference) question' and 'Ask us' follow with regard to the frequency of use (see Figure 3) (Liu, 2007, p. 79).

No matter what the service is called, whether 'digital', 'virtual', 'live', 'real time', 'interactive', 'web-based' or 'synchronous', its essence is to provide a reference service via the computer network with the professional's intermediation. The author thinks that the term 'digital reference service' is the clearest one for reflecting the connotation of this kind of service. Normally, she uses 'digital reference service' or 'digital reference' in this chapter while in some cases virtual or online reference service is also used instead to avoid too much repetition.

In terms of the definition of the digital reference service, again as the Chinese idiom 'the benevolent see benevolence and the wise see wisdom' says, different people or institutions have different ideas according to their own understanding, experiences and standpoints. The following lists some dominant definitions:

- 'Digital reference service (DRS) can be thought of as an online reference interview which can run to less than a minute to "as long as it takes" to reach a satisfactory response' (Katz, 2002/2003, p. 2);
- 'Digital reference service is, human-intermediated assistance offered to users through the Internet' (McClure & Lankes, n.d.);
- 'Virtual reference is reference service initiated electronically, often in real-time, where patrons employ computers or other Internet technology to communicate with reference staff, without being physically present. Communication channels used frequently in virtual reference include chat, videoconferencing, Voice over IP, co-browsing, e-mail, and instant messaging' (MARS Digital Reference Guidelines Ad Hoc Committee of the United States, 2006);
- 'Digital reference and AskA services are Internet-based question-and-answer services that connect users with experts in a variety of subject areas' (Wasik, n.d).

According to the definitions above, it can be summarized that DRS is a kind of reference service provided on the platform of the computer network and the human experts are involved in such a service.

What stays the same in all kinds of reference service is that the reference collection is fundamental and crucial to the success of the service. As William A. Katz comments, 'the only real purpose of the passable reference work is its content' (Katz, 2002, p. 27). Moreover, Saxon evaluates the reference service and provides a meta-analysis about its effectiveness that considers nine variables (expenditures, total collection size, reference collection size, collection size per patron, volumes added per year, volumes discarded, overall change in collection size, proportion of change to total size, and number of hours open) (Saxon, 1997, p. 267). Out of these nine variables, all except the last one are directly related to the reference collection.

In the light of the characteristics of the reference collection, Christopher W. Nolan notes the following (Nolan, 1999, p. 2):

- Reference departments and their collections are usually located in very prominent locations in libraries so that users can easily find them;
- Expenditures for reference materials make up a significant portion of most libraries' budgets;
- Reference librarians use the reference collection, along with the library's catalog, as the principal tool for aiding users who seek help;
- Users ascribe considerable authority to this collection;
- Because many users start their information searches with indexes, encyclopedias, and bibliographies, what they find cited in the reference collection influences what materials they will retrieve from the remainder of the collection (or what items they will request via interlibrary loan);
- With the growing numbers of full-text and numeric databases being made available in reference departments, these sources are frequently being used instead of the rest of the library's collections;
- Finally, the reference resources available to users have an impact on how the users perceive the entire library.

These points clarify the dominance of the reference collection in detail; the situation is the same in both the non-electronic and electronic environment. Jane M. Subramanian notices that there are two extremes in the attitude of patrons toward computerized and print resources (Subramanian, 1998, p. 127):

> In an academic setting, those patrons with very limited knowledge of computers may show a very strong preference toward print resources.

On the other hand:

> … those patrons who view computerized resources very positively may pose the opposite problems in terms of their present opinions and impact on reference assistance. In many cases, patrons have found computerized resources so much easier and faster to use that they may reject the use of print means of access altogether.

Furthermore, Subramanian states that the 'amount of expected use, importance of currency of the content, and most important types of searching access needed usually dictate the final choice' regarding 'what reference resources to provide in computerized form and what items to supply in print format, which at present is usually the less expensive option of the two'. These are the library's considerations. In the meantime, 'the user who has discovered remote access to online public access catalogs and other off-site computerized resources naturally is [also] attracted to the strong advantages of such access' (Subramanian, 1998, p. 127).

In comparison with the fax machine, which has already made it more practical for libraries to buy copies of single articles on demand, Michael Lesk points out that 'digital storage carries with it even more advantages of service, and now looks as if it is to offer cost benefits as well' (Lesk, 2001, p. 64). In the same chapter, he also declares that 'digital information can be more effective for the users and cheaper for the librarians. Access will become more important than possession, but this must be used to encourage sharing, not competition' (Lesk, 2001, p. 81). Faculty members at the Association of Research Libraries (ARL) institutions cite convenience, timeliness, and the ability to search text as the most important factors in choosing electronic journals over print (Lenares, 1999, p. 329). Besides, in the Netherlands, Tilburg University faculty members take timely availability, easy access, full text searching, and access from home as factors that promote the use of electronic journals (Roes, 1999, p. 118).

Commonly, the user group has recognized and benefited greatly from the characteristics of electronic information resources as follows:

- Convenience: theoretically, the user could use the reference material without any spatial and temporal limitation;
- Ability to search through the full text: searching the full text is the basic feature of every electronic information resource, which enables the patron to locate a certain term or phrase in a very short period;
- Ability to cross-search: the majority of the current library systems support the function of searching across multi-databases (Online Public Access Catalog [OPAC], local and remote databases, and a variety of digital collections);
- Access to rare materials: the digitized collection includes vast numbers of archives, manuscripts, rare books that are not available as originals to common users, let alone remote users. It provides access to these rare materials with no worry about damage or loss;
- Multimedia feature, etc.: the multimedia feature of the digital resource allows the user to take full advantage of her/his sense organs to get as comprehensive an understanding as possible about the resource. Additionally, the digital material might provide the user chances for viewing the image in different resolutions and from different angles and layers.

To the reference librarian, the electronic information resource, especially the networked information resource, is appreciated more and more because of its other virtues (such as saving physical storage space, sharing among institutions, etc.) Furthermore, only the networked information resource enables some functions of the online reference service to be implemented. For example, during a chat session, only the networked information resource could support the cobrowsing feature of the digital reference service enabling the reference staff to share the reference material with their patron at the same time. That is why more and more such resources have been included in the reference collection of the digital reference service. Marshall Breeding notices that, 'libraries, in general, are channelling more of their resources toward web-based information services. ... They work hard to construct new digital collections' (Breeding, 2001, p. 42).

THE MERGED DIGITAL LIBRARY AND DIGITAL REFERENCE SERVICE

Thomas A. Peters notes that 'in general, humans are becoming accustomed to pursuing their information needs in an online environment' (Peters, 2000, p. 221). Basically, both the digital library and the digital reference service are developed for meeting the user's information needs under the networked settings. The relationship between them is not mandatory. Nevertheless, their common interests and the benefits from their mutual promotion are evident. Their mergence is the optimal solution for severing the remote user in the most effective way.

Necessity of the Mergence

Although, literally, the digital library deals with collection and the digital reference service talks about service, they match on several points, as follows:

- Operation platform: the computer network. As has been clarified in the earlier parts of this chapter, both the digital library and the digital reference service operate on the computer network. They are established on the network and serve the user in the same environment;
- Content: electronic information resource. The digital library is composed of either born-digital or digitized resources, or both. Though there is no regulation prescribing that the content the digital reference service provides to its user must be the electronic information resource, the fact is that most of the information resource served during the online reference service session is digital because of ease of transmission of the digital material and the possibility of information delivery and sharing;
- Purpose: to serve the user. Providing service to the remote user is the purpose and motivation of constructing the digital library and the digital reference service. This is also the fundamental reason for their existence and development. They exist and develop because they serve the user in a non-replaceable effective manner;
- Personalized service: meeting special information needs. The digital reference's question–answer mode defines that it serves the user with personal information needs. The digital library, especially its extension – the hybrid library – also pays much attention to the user's personal information needs and manages to fulfil such needs. Based on his profound knowledge of the development of the digital library, Clifford Lynch mentions a handful of areas that he finds particularly compelling nowadays. The first area he points out is the personal

information environment (Lynch, 2005). One of the other areas that Lynch feels is particularly compelling is the role of digital libraries, digital collections and other information services in supporting teaching, learning, and human development. In his opinion, 'information resources and services can be partners over development and learning that spans an entire human lifetime, from early childhood to old age' (Lynch, 2005). This is doubtlessly also one of the goals of the digital reference service.

The intersections discussed above have provided solid foundation to the mergence of the digital library and the digital reference service. Their symbiotic interests are the best proofs justifying that they could improve themselves via joining forces and mutual promotion.

The digital library is far from just a digital collection of intellectual property. Its value could be realized only through serving the user. On the basis of former definitions of digital libraries, Borgman encompasses two complementary ideas (Borgman, 1999, p. 234):

- Digital libraries are a set of electronic resources and associated technical capabilities for creating, searching and using information;
- Digital libraries are constructed, collected and organized, by (and for) a community of users, and their functional capabilities support the information needs and uses of that community.

Obviously, both of these ideas notice one of the digital library's crucial roles, which is facilitating the use of information.

With the evolution of the digital library, William Y. Arms puts forward the concept 'automated digital libraries' to describe 'a digital library where all tasks are carried out automatically'. Nevertheless, he also admits that 'even with the most advanced parallel computers, nothing on the horizon approaches human judgment in understanding such subtleties'. 'Since few users ever mastered the complex rules for the main and supplementary headings, or the intricate filing conventions, serious users turned to reference librarians for help. ... She [the reference librarian] simply had more expertise in the idiosyncrasies of the information available and how to navigate through it. Automated libraries are a very long way from providing such insights' (Arms, 2000b). The digital reference service is absolutely essential for helping pull the user out of the puzzle in utilizing the digital library.

On the other hand, the digital reference service does need the digital library to enrich its reference collection in order to supply more effective service to the remote user. Robert R. Downs & Edward A. Friedman indicate that 'classic models of information seeking suggest that both form and content of information resources support the inquiry process' (Downs & Friedman, 1999, p. 281). While conducting an effective evaluation, Katz comments, 'aside from content the librarian must ask at least four basic questions about a reference work: What is its purpose? Its authority? Its scope? Its proposed audience? Finally, the format of the work must be considered for print and the navigational tools for electronic databases' (Katz, 2002, p. 27). These questions are raised in relation to the general reference work and are also applicable to the digital reference service. The digital library has accumulated the treasure of human beings' splendid cultural heritage and its collection is built up through authoritative selection. Now that the electronic information resource is more convenient for the user and more proper to the essence of the digital reference service, the digital reference staff should include as many digital materials as possible in their service. It is logical, reasonable and necessary for the digital reference service to take the digital library as a part of its reference collection.

An excellent model of the combination of the digital library and the digital reference service can be found in the American Memory, a pioneer digital library program implemented in the Library of Congress (LC) of the United States. On December 15, 1993, LC released a document reporting a user evaluation of the American Memory conducted between 1991 and 1993. One of the broad themes the American Memory developers were concerned with in the report was 'what collections are used' (Library of Congress, 1993, p. 7). Through the evaluation, it was proved that 'the concept of American Memory – the idea of providing electronic versions of selected Library of Congress archival collections to the nation's libraries – was validated in all types of libraries' (Library of Congress, 1993, p. 7). The latest definition is that 'American Memory is a multimedia web site of digitized historical documents, photographs, sound recordings, moving pictures, books, pamphlets, maps, and other resources from the Library of Congress's vast holdings' (The Library of Congress, n.d.) At the same time as expanding its collection in both type and number of the information resources, the American Memory facilitates the digital reference service (so-called 'Ask a Librarian' in LC). The fact that the linkage directing to the 'Ask a Librarian' appears in the home page of the American Memory (see Figure 4) has shown the closed relationship between the digital library and the digital reference service LC intends to build up and maintain.

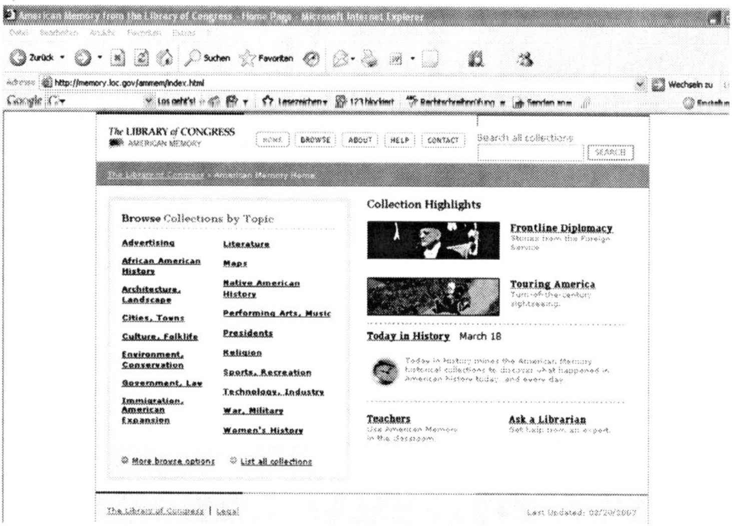

Figure 4. Home page of the American memory.

Moreover, in the home page of the 'Ask a Librarian' services of LC, it is declared that the services provide 'assistance using American Memory and Library of Congress online resources'. Though it is difficult to calculate the number of the reference questions directly related to LC's digital collections, Laura Gottesman, a member of staff of the Digital Reference Team of the 'Ask A Librarian' services in LC, states that 'anecdotally and unofficially speaking, it seems to us that the availability of digital materials does generate inquiries, from traditional as well as entirely new audiences (in the Library's case, the Library's online collections, combined with some targeted outreach programs have encouraged inquiries from teachers and primary and secondary school students (and their parents)' (Gottesman, 2007). In this case, the digital library and the digital reference service combines in an equal and flexible way. LC integrates them without any preference. This is one kind of model combining them together. The other two ways reflect privilege to the other to some extent. They refer to integration in opposite directions, i.e. the digital reference service affiliated with a digital library and a digital library integrated into a digital reference service.

Digital Reference Service Affiliated with a Digital Library

As Marchionini summarizes, digital library success is aided by (Marchionini, 2000, p. 329):
- Clear missions;
- Strong leadership and a strong talent pool;
- Good technical vision and decisions;
- Quality content and data management;
- Giving users multiple access alternatives; and
- Ongoing evaluation effort.

Essentially, the user's satisfaction with her/his information need is the most convincing way to prove the success of the digital library.

One fundamental constant during the development of the digital library is the mission to maximize access to its collection. The aim of constructing the digital collection is to make it widely available in spite of the geographical and temporal obstacles. At the first meeting of the DLib Working Group on Digital Library Metrics (held January 7–8, 1998 at Stanford University), a definition of digital library was proposed (Leiner, 1998):

The Digital Library is:
- The collection of services
- And the collection of information objects
- That support users in dealing with information objects
- And the organization and presentation of those objects
- Available directly or indirectly
- Via electronic/digital means.

As regards to the first point of the definition, it was interpreted that 'a digital library is much more than just the collection of material in its repositories. It provides a variety of services to all of its users (both humans and machines, and producers, managers, and consumers of information)' (Leiner, 1998). Beyond question, there is a symbiotic relationship between digital collections and digital library services.

It is obvious that the digital reference service is helpful to optimize the utilization of the digital library collection and increase the level of user satisfaction.

As Downs and Friedman point out, 'facilitating remote research from private and public locations offers learners opportunities that are unconstrained either by the limited resources found in particular physical libraries or by their schedules of operation' (Downs and Friedman, 1999, p. 281). Ideally, the user of the digital library could conduct the behaviour of browse or search by herself/himself for her/his research. However, the situation dealing with the digital library is more or less the same as that appearing in the traditional library. In the traditional library, as much guidance as possible has been available; but the personal reference service is still indispensable there. It is the same in respect of the digital library. The remote user might need help from the system intermediaries and domain experts while using the collection of the digital library. The personalized service is one kind of service the digital library intends to provide.

Even 'some patrons who are extremely comfortable using computers do not fully understand their searching methods and/or results and sometimes may not even realize that their search has not been as successful as it could be if a better search strategy and technique were used' (Subramanian, 1998, p. 127). In some cases, 'the patron is frequently unaware of how much they have missed' (Subramanian, 1998, p. 127). During an unobtrusive data analysis of digital reference questions and service at the Internet public library, David S. Carter and Joseph Janes claimed that 'users seem to have difficulty in assigning subject categories to their questions, and to determine whether they are factual or require sources for assistance, and these decisions were often overridden by questions administrators' (Carter and Janes, 2000, p. 257). Furthermore, a lot of questions require deep intellectual understanding which the machine could not deal with. All of these facts prove the necessity of the digital reference service which provides human intermediaries to give the patron personalized help.

The specialities of the digital reference service help to improve the digital library. In comparison with the traditional reference service with the reference desk and telephone reference service, the current online reference service is text-based. It means that there are documents created during the digital reference transaction. Such documents not only satisfy the immediate information inquiry but also serve other purposes for enriching the reference collection through establishing the special subject collection, summarizing the current user's information need and forecasting the tendency of the user's information need, and so on. While suggesting integration of the digital reference service into the digital library environment, Jeffrey Pomerantz explores two issues that are unique to the intersection between digital libraries and digital reference: collection development of previously-answered questions, and presentation of specialized subsets of the materials in the digital library's collection (Pomerantz, 2003, p. 23).

Based on the consideration and recognition discussed in the above texts, more and more digital libraries have started to provide a digital reference service, ranging from a simple service to a more complex one. Aside from traditional reference services, most of such services are email based and some of them have been both email and chat based. Bernie Sloan proposes a model of the electronic reference service in the digital library which is 'an attempt to develop a service that combines video-based reference services with e-mail-based reference services in a manner that makes effective use of the advantages of both media' (Sloan, 1997).

The University of California libraries have stood in a pioneering position in providing a remote reference service. In an early effort 'the Science Library librarians at the University of California, Irvine implemented a pilot "telereference" project in January 1997 designed to generate needed information about the use of real-time, face-to-face, desktop videoconferencing to conduct reference interviews with student users at a remote location' (Lessick et al, 1997). Presently, in addition to being involved in the 'Ask A Librarian' service provided by librarians at various University of California (UC) campuses, the California Digital Library (CDL), set up as a UC library in 1997, also provides a rough email reference service independently. CDL is an advanced digital library system which offers a variety of in-depth services to its users based on its marvellous digital collections. At the left bottom corner of the home page of CDL, there is a linkage entitled 'Question? Comments' which leads to the web page of 'Feedback' (see Figure 5).

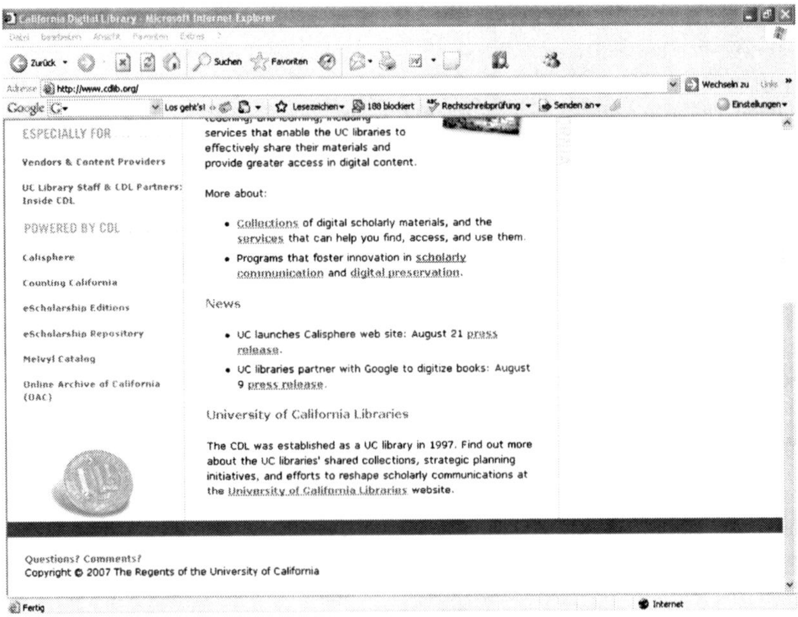

Figure 5. Home page of the California digital library.

On this web page, the user of CDL gets an opportunity to send her/his inquiry or comment and might get a response via an email. Although, strictly to say, it is not in the form of an online reference service, it does have the function of an email reference service. Consequently, it is logical to take this model as a preliminary prototype of the digital reference service affiliated with a digital library. Inspired by the CDL model, the author thinks that one thing might be noticeable: it seems that if a digital library is not completely independent (i.e. belonging to a larger institution), it might be unnecessary to establish a separate digital reference service just for the digital library.

However, the focus of this section is actually the digital reference service involved in a digital library standing comparatively alone. For instance, the Public Health Digital Library is 'Public Health – Seattle & King County's gateway to online public health resources, including free and feebased full text articles, links to authoritative public health websites and searchable databases, and access to document delivery and reference assistance' (Public Health Digital Library, 2006). When the patron of this digital library needs information, journal articles, online resources, and search assistance or training, she/he could ask for help from its 'Ask the Librarian' service, which is basically an email reference service.

Another model of the digital reference service affiliated with a digital library is the Internet Public Library (IPL). Though IPL is not a digital library literally, its characteristics (well-organized digital collections with service) have shown that basically it is indeed a digital library. According to its home page, initiated in 1995:

> ...the IPL was founded by a class at the University of Michigan's School of Information, and Michigan SI students almost exclusively generated its content and managed the Ask a Question reference service. Now, 14 other schools are actively taking part in the development and maintenance of the IPL. And, as of January 1, 2007, the IPL has moved to Drexel University's College of Information Science and Technology. (School of Information, n.d.)

The IPL has provided the digital library functions as well as digital reference service from its beginning. Its 'Ask a Question' service is an email reference service with considerate instruction to almost each field in the IPL Ask A Question Form. Furthermore, aside from a variety of digital collections, IPL continuously establishes and maintains a collection of ready reference. A similar approach could be found in Germany. Starting on January 1, 2002, the German Internet Library (Deutsche Internet Bibliothek, DIB) provides linkage to 6488 networked information resources as of September 12, 2007 (Deutscheinternet Bibliothek, 2007a). In the meantime, it offers an email reference service to the user through coordination among 73 academic and public libraries as well as 20 private libraries that focus on specific subjects (Deutscheinternet Bibliothek, 2007b).

In fact, it is not very easy to find an example for this type of service. In a sense, this phenomenon reflects the necessity of such an application once again.

The Digital Library Integrated into the Digital Reference Service

In his exploration of coping with information overload, Richard L. Hopkins indicates that a combination of both types and formats will be needed and comments that 'published guides, research handbooks and state-of-the-art review publications, for example, will undoubtedly continue to be important' (Hopkins, 1995, p. 305). He goes on to point out that those wanting in-depth understanding of a subject area will probably choose to use these sources in print format, while those who wish to 'focus quickly on the key sources of information in an area of knowledge' will select these same materials in computerized format (Hopkins, 1995, p. 309). Hopkins's research indicates that both printed and electronic materials would be necessary in the digital reference service.

Nonetheless, no one could neglect the tendency that the electronic information resource is more and more dominant in the reference service, especially the digital reference service. William A. Katz declares that:

> ...there is no question about the future of digitized information. In 2000 approximately 80 percent of American libraries, regardless of type or size, have some type of electronic reference work, usually an encyclopedia and/or an index. The larger and richer the library, the more evidence there is of electronic forms of information. (Katz, 2002, p. 12)

In an overview and analysis of recent research studies about use and users of electronic library resources, Carol Teopir also notes that 'users perceive electronic resources – in particular electronic journals and, for students, the Internet – to hold many advantages' (Tenopir, 2003). Lesk argues that 'in the digital world, it matters much less what libraries own and hold on their own shelves. It matters much more what they can access for their patrons'. Furthermore, he comments that:

> ...although the instantaneous availability of online information accounts for some of its interest, one of the most important advantages of digital libraries is the ease with which they can be searched. ... it makes several kinds of tasks faster and more accurate for library users. In addition, digital storage means that items are never off-shelf; it means that a copy is as good as an original, so there is no need to worry about deteriorating physical media; and it means that a copy can be electronically delivered across campus as easily as within the library. (Lesk, 2001, p. 63)

Additionally, one outstanding reason is that one of the special features of the digital reference service, co-browsing, requires the resource used during a chat session to be online. Only the electronic information resource could serve the function. As Carol Tenopir & Lisa Ennis conclude through four surveys from 1991 until 2001 in academic library reference services in the United States, 'there is no doubt that digital information sources have had profound effects on university reference departments over the last decade and have changed libraries forever' (Tenopir & Ennis, 2002, p. 264).

Libraries are continuously constructing digital collections ranging from full-text to image databases and so forth to support their services, within which the reference service is of major importance. While preparing digital materials for the reference service, some questions might be asked, such as, 'is the full-text version predominantly a reference source, designed for quick consultation, or is it a collection of articles from which some are selected and then read continuously? Obviously, this type of source serves both purposes' (Nolan, 1999, p. 7). Michael Lesk comments that the digital information and digital libraries have great value in the future. He summarizes the development of the digital library as follows (Lesk, 2001, p. 80):

- Digital libraries are now economically efficient, and the area is booming;
- Digital technology offers great advantages for libraries;
- The adoption of digital information will mean changes in the role of libraries, and in how we manage them.

The digital library is much more than a collection of electronic information resources. In a case study of the Alexandria Digital Earth Prototype (ADEPT), a digital library of geo-referenced information resources, Borgman et al assert that 'digital libraries are more than storehouses of information; they should be aids to the question-asking, information-gathering, information-organizing, information-analyzing, and question-answering process of users' (Borgman, 2000, p. 228). Predominantly, the digital library plays a significant role in supporting scholarly research. It enables scholars to access the archives, manuscripts, and rare book texts which are difficult or even impossible to reach under other circumstances:

> Digital libraries containing representations of original works provide opportunities for students and scholars to conduct research from personal computers and workstations located in their homes, offices and laboratories. Facilitating remote research from private and public locations offers learners opportunities that are unconstrained either by the limited resources found in particular physical libraries or by their schedules of operation. (Downs & Friedman, 1999, p. 282)

With its great advantage, the digital library collection has been included into the reference collection to enable the digital reference staff to provide a more efficient service to the patron. Meanwhile, the service of the digital library could also help the user and the digital reference librarian to have better access to the information they want to approach.

Opposite to the situation outlined in the section on 'digital reference service affiliated with a digital library', there are numerous examples of digital libraries integrated into the digital reference service.

Diane Granfield introduced a McConnell funding project about a digital reference service for a digital library. The chat technology in a remote reference service employed in the Ryerson University Library, which initiated one of the first collaborative virtual reference service networks in Canada, was described in her report (Granfield, 2002). Nevertheless, what the 'Ask A Librarian Live' of this library assists its patrons to use is actually its 'inside licensed databases'. So this is still an example of digital collections (but not digital libraries in an exact sense) integrated into the reference materials of a digital reference service.

It is well known that librarianship in the Nordic countries is quite advanced. In the light of the digital reference service, the Nordic countries stand in the frontier. In the research project which the author was involved in and which was mentioned earlier in this chapter, among the 147 email reference services in the worldwide libraries evaluated, Australian and Swedish libraries rank top in many aspects (Liu, 2007, p. 78). In the Goeteborg University Library, one of the major research libraries of Europe, 'the use of the Digital Library makes as much as about half of the total use of the material available at Goeteborg University Library' (Goeteborg University Library, 2006a). The 'Ask the Library' service of this library, an email-based reference service, assists the user in locating subject-specific information and advises him or her on details of information and literature searching (Goeteborg University Library, 2006b). Though there are no concrete statistics about the usage of the digital library, it is very much possible that this online reference service takes full advantage of the digital library collection.

One thing that presents a challenge for including the digital library in the digital reference service is searching across a variety of repositories. The latest effort on this point is the CrossRef project, in which the ACM Digital Library is involved. 'In order to open published scholarly content for the first time to free, full-text interpublisher searchability, a group of 45 leading journal publishers are participating in a CrossRef Search Pilot' (CrossRef, n.d.a). It is:

> ...a not-for-profit network founded on publisher collaboration, with a mandate to make reference linking throughout online scholarly literature efficient and reliable. As such, it is an infrastructure for linking citations across publishers, and the only full-scale implementation of the Digital Object Identifier (or DOI) System to date. (CrossRef, n.d.b)

The CrossRef pilot progresses in a big step in searching across the repositories of electronic information resources and lays one more foundation for the integration of the digital library with the digital reference service.

CONCLUSION

The reference questions could be roughly divided into fact questions and research questions according to the complexity and depth of the answer requested. It is reasonable that normally the librarian prefers to reply to the fact questions, though they should treat the two kinds of questions equally. Nonetheless, with the development of the digital reference service, more and more research questions might be answered better and better. On the one hand, it is because the reference librarian might accumulate more and more knowledge and experience and the knowledge base of the digital reference enlarges step by step; on the other hand, the digital reference service could benefit more from the reference collections, especially the digital collections, developed simultaneously. Nowadays, almost every library has more or less established its own digital collection, which might be called electronic resources, digital library, virtual library, or whatever. Normally, the subject of the digital library of a library is closely related to the library's special collection.

For example, the Wuerzburg University Library, Germany has amassed a great number of rare books, ancient manuscripts, maps and other valuable documents about the area of Lower Franconia. On the basis of these materials, the library creates a digital library through digitization. When the patron has an inquiry dealing with this special collection, the digital reference librarian would be able to provide her/him with a reply in depth. With the powerful support from the digital collection, the reference library would not rest at the superficial and shallow level but extend to the deep one while replying to the patron's inquiries.

Both the digital library and the digital reference service are outcomes under the networked environment and evolve with the development of information and communication technology (ICT). The trend is that as they evolve, the digital library develops more services and the digital reference service enriches its reference collection. The key point of all their activities is to serve the patron better. Without any doubt, the digital library and the digital reference service have a close relationship and need each other; in another words, one is a necessity to the other. Based on this symbiotic interest, though not obligatory, their combination is not only reasonable but also feasible. Nevertheless, the combination does not mean simply putting the two together but establishing a systematic and dynamic organism within which they could reach a new stage through mutual promotion. This study mainly deals with the necessity of their integration. Further research on how to integrate them is under way.

ACKNOWLEDGEMENT

The author would like to express her gratitude to the digital reference librarians of the Library of Congress who never disappointed her when she asked for help. Her study, research and teaching have benefited a lot from both the on-site reference service in the library and through the digital reference service. She believes that numerous people have the same feeling as her.

NOTES

1 In the summer semester of 2005, a student research project took place in cooperation with the Faculty of Information and Communication, Stuttgart Media University, Germany and the Department of Information Management, Peking University, China. The subject of the project was evaluating the worldwide digital reference services in the libraries. During this project, 14 German students and 21 Chinese students separately evaluated nearly 200 email reference services all over the world.

REFERENCES

Arms, W. Y. (2000a, July/August). Automated digital libraries: How effectively can computers be used for the skilled tasks of professional librarianship? *D-Lib Magazine*. Retrieved December 19, 2006, from http://www.dlib.org/dlib/july00/arms/07arms.html

Arms, W. Y. (2000b). *Digital libraries*. Online edition. Cambridge, MA: MIT Press. Retrieved March 11, 2007, from http://www.cs.cornell.edu/wya/DigLib/MS1999/Chapter1.html; http://www.dlib.org/dlib/july00/arms/07arms.html.

Association for Computing Machinery. (2007a). *Using the ACM Digital Library (DL): FAQs – frequently asked questions*. Retrieved March 12, 2007, from http://portal.acm.org/dl.cfm?dl=ACM

Association for Computing Machinery. (2007b). *The ACM portal*. Retrieved March 12, 2007, from http://portal.acm.org/dl.cfm?dl=ACM

Borgman, C. L. (1999). What are digital libraries? Competing visions. *Information Processing & Management, 35*(3), 227–243. Retrieved December 20, 2006, from http://scholarsportal.info/pdflinks/06112115004329259.pdf

Borgman, C. L., Gilliland-Swetland, A. J., & Leazer, G. H. (2000). Evaluating digital libraries for teaching and learning in undergraduate education: A case study of the Alexander digital earth prototype. *Library Trends*, Special Issue on Assessing and Evaluating Digital Library Services, *49*(2), 228–250. Retrieved March 10, 2007, http://polaris.gseis.ucla.edu/cborgman/pubs/BorgmanetalLibTrends ADEPT2000.pdf.

Breeding, M. (2001). Providing virtual reference service. *Information Today, 18*(4), 42–43.

Carter, D. S., & Janes, J. (2000). Unobstrusive analysis of digital reference questions and service at the internet public library: An exploratory study. *Library Trends, 49*(2), 251–265.

Choudhury, S. (2004, January 14). *Integration of digital library services through repositories*. A paper presented at the Educause Mid-Atlantic Regional Conference. Retrieved March 10, 2007, from http://www.educause.edu/ir/library/powerpoint/MAC0434.pps

Chowdhury, G. G. (2002). Digital libraries and reference services: Present and future. *Journal of Documentation, 58*(3), 258–283. Retrieved from http://dx.doi.org/10.1108/00220410210425809

CrossRef. (n.d. a). *Crossref.org: DOIs for research content*. Retrieved March 26, 2007, from http://www.crossref.org/crossrefsearch.html

CrossRef. (n.d. b). *FastFacts*. Retrieved March 26, 2007, from http://www.crossref.org/05researchers/16fastfacts.html

Deutsche Internet Bibliothek. (2007a). Retrieved September 6, 2007, from http://www.deutscheinternet bibliothek.de/index_user.jsp

Deutsche Internet Bibliothek. (2007b). *Re: Ihre Anfrage an die Deutsche Internetbibliothek*. Email to Jia Liu. 21 June.

Digital Library Federation. (2006, August 2). *A working definition of digital library* [1998]. Retrieved February 22, 2007, from http://www.diglib.org/about/dldefinition.htm

DLXS. (n.d.). *Overview*. Retrieved March 12, 2007, from http://www.dlxs.org/about/aboutdlxs.html

Downs, R. R., & Friedman, E. A. (1999). Digital library support for scholarly research. *Information Processing & Management, 35*(3), 281–291. Retrieved from http://dx.doi.org/10.1016/S0306-4573(98)00062-4

Frumkin, J. (2006a). The need for a digital library service registry. *OCLC Systems & Services, 22*(1), 23–25. Retrieved May 10, 2010, from http://dx.doi.org/10.1108/10650750610640766

Frumkin, J. (2006b, March 23). *Service registries in a digital library world*. Digital Library Service Registry Workshop. Retrieved March 10, 2007, from http://wiki.library.oregonstate.edu/confluence/download/attachments/6727/Workshop+-+Overview.ppt?version=1

Frumkin, J. (2006c). *Draft definition: Digital library service registry*. Retrieved March 10, 2007, from http://wiki.library.oregonstate.edu/confluence/display/DLSRW/WorkshopResources

Goeteborg University Library. (2006a, September 1). *Collections*. Retrieved from http://www.ub.gu.se/info/samlingar/

Goeteborg University Library. (2006b, September 8). *Ask the library*. Retrieved March 26, 2007, from http://www.ub.gu.se/kontakta/fraga/

Gottesman, L. (2007). *Library Question – Answer* [Question #2132170]. Email to Jia Liu. 23 February.

Granfield, D. (2002, May 15). *A digital reference service for a digital library: Chat technology in a remote reference service*. Retrieved May 16, 2006, from http://www.ryerson.ca/library/ask/McConnell.pdf

Greenstein, D., & Thorin, S. E. (2002). *The digital library: A biography*. Retrieved March 11, 2007, from http://www.clir.org/PUBS/reports/pub109/pub109.pdf

Grenci, M. (2007). *Metadata services and digital projects: Formerly called metadata and digital library services*. Retrieved March 12, 2007, from http://libweb.uoregon.edu/catdept/home/index.html

Hopkins, R. L. (1995). Countering information overload: The role of the librarian. *Reference Librarian, 49*(50), 305–333.

Katz, B. (2002/2003). Digital reference: An overview. In B. Katz (Ed.), *Digital reference services* (Vol. 1–17). Binghamton: Haworth Press.

Katz, W. A. (2002). *Introduction to reference work* (8th ed.). New York: McGraw-Hill.

Lankes, R. D. (2004). The digital reference research Agenda. *Journal of the American Society for InformationScience and Technology, 55*(4), 301–311. Retrieved from http://dx.doi.org/10.1002/asi.10374

Leiner, B. M. (1998). *The scope of the digital library*. Drafted on January 16, 1998 and revised on October 15, 1998. Retrieved December 7, 2007, from http://www.dlib.org/metrics/public/papers/dig-lib-scope.html

Lenares, D. (1999). Faculty use of electronic journals at research institutions: Racing towards tomorrow. In H. A. Thompson (Ed.), *Proceedings of the 9th National Conference of the Association of College and Research Libraries*. Chicago: ACRL (Association of College and Research Libraries).

Lesk, M. (2001). The future of digital information and digital libraries. In D. B. Marcum (Ed.), *Development of digital libraries: An American perspective*. Westport, MD: Greenwood Press.

Lessick, S., Kjaer, K., & Clancy, S. (1997). *Interactive Reference Service (IRS) at UC Irvine: Expanding reference service beyond the reference desk*. Retrieved March 24, 2007, from http://www.ala.org/ala/acrlbucket/nashville1997pap/lessickkjaer.htm

Library of Congress. (1993, December 15). The American memory user evaluation team. *American Memory User Evaluation 1991–1993*.

Library of Congress. (n.d.). *Frequently asked questions*. Retrieved March 18, 2007, from http://memory.loc.gov/ammem/help/faq.html

Liu, J. (2007). *The evaluation of world-wide digital reference services in libraries*. Oxford: Chandos.

Lynch, C. (2005). Where do we go from here? The next decade for digital libraries. *D-Lib Magazine, 11*(7/8). Retrieved January 18, 2007, from http://www.dlib.org/dlib/july05/lynch/07lynch.html

Lynch, C., & Garcia-Molina, H. (1996). Interoperability, scaling, and the digital libraries research Agenda. *Microcomputers for Information Management, 13*(2), 85–132.

Manduca, C. A., Fox, S., & Iverson, E. R. (2006). Digital library as network and community center: A successful model for contribution and use. *D-Lib Magazine, 12*(12). Retrieved March 10, 2007, from http://www.dlib.org/dlib/december06/manduca/12manduca.html

Marchionini, G. (2000). Evaluating digital libraries: A longitudinal and multifaceted view. *Library Trends, 49*(2), 304–333.

Marchionini, G., & Fox, E. (1999). Progress toward digital libraries: Augmentation through integration. *Information Processing and Management, 35*(8), 219–225.

MARS Digital Reference Guidelines Ad Hoc Committee, Reference and User Services Association prepared. (2006). *Guidelines for implementing and maintaining virtual reference services*. Retrieved March 13, 2006, from http://www.ala.org/ala/rusa/rusaprotools/referenceguide/virtrefguidelines.htm

McClure, C. R., & Lankes, R. D. (n.d.). *Assessing quality in digital reference services: A research prospectus*. Retrieved February 23, 2006, from http://iis.syr.edu/tiki-index.php?page=Digital+Reference+Quality+Standards

Networked Digital Library of Theses and Dissertations. (2001). *Scan search*. Retrieved March 12, 2007, from http://zippo.vtls.com/cgibin/ndltd/chameleon?sessionid=2007031221365524582&skin=ndltd&lng=en

Nolan, C. W. (1999). *Managing the reference collections*. Chicago: American Librarian Association.

Peters, T. A. (2000). Introduction. *Library Trends, 49*(2), 221–227.

Pomerantz, J. (2003). Integrating digital reference service into the digital library environment. In R. David, S. Nicholson, & A. Goodrum (Eds.), *The digital reference research Agenda*. Chicago: Association of College and Research Libraries.

Public Health's Digital Library. (2006). Retrieved March 24, 2007, from http://www.metrokc.gov/health/library/

Roes, H. (1999). *Promotion of electronic journals to users by libraries: A case study of Tilburg University Library*. Retrieved September 12, 2007, from http://drcwww.uvt.nl/~roes/articles/london99.htm

Saxon, M. (1997). Reference service evaluation and meta-analysis: Findings and methodological issues. *LibraryQuarterly*, *63*(3), 267–289.

School of Information, University of Michigan. (n.d.). *IPL: Internet Public Library*. Retrieved March 25, 2007, from http://www.ipl.org/

Sloan, B. (1997, December 16). *Service perspectives for the digital library remote reference services*. Retrieved from March 10, 2007, http://people.lis.uiuc.edu/~b-sloan/e-ref.html

Subramanian, J. M. (1998). Patron attitudes toward computerized and print resources: Discussion and considerations fro reference service. *Reference Librarian*, *60*, 127–138.

Tenopir, C. (2003, August). *Use and users of electronic library resources: An overview and analysis of recent research studies*. Retrieved January 9, 2007, from http://www.clir.org/pubs/reports/pub120/pub120.pdf

Tenopir, C., & Ennis, L. (2002). A decade of digital reference: 1991–2001. *Reference & User Services Quarterly*, *41*(3), 264–273.

Wasik, J. M. (n.d.). *Building and maintaining digital reference services*. Retrieved March 31, 2006, from http://www.michaellorenzen.com/eric/reference-services.html

Jia Liu
Visiting Scholar
Faculty of Information Studies
University of Toronto
Canada

MENGXIONG LIU AND PEGGY CABRERA

13. THE NEW GENERATION OF CITATION INDEXING IN THE AGE OF DIGITAL LIBRARIES

INTRODUCTION

Fifty-two years ago, Eugene Garfield envisioned the potential powerful function of citation indexing in science, and developed the theory and application of citation analysis with the evaluative index of impact factor. With the creation of *Science Citation Index*, *Social Science Citation Index,* and *Arts and Humanities Citation Index,* citation analysis has become a widely used tool for retrospective and up-to-date literature research, identification of visible scholars in a specific subject and mapping of intellectual structures of a discipline, and measurement of impact for justifying tenure and funding decisions in the academic and scientific community. With the development of information technology, all three citation indexes were incorporated into the Web-based citation database *Web of Science (WoS).* Prior to the Internet age, *WoS* has been the sole research tool for citation tracking.

With the advancement of Internet technologies, changes have taken place in scholarly communication. New means of sharing digital research information has emerged, which include preprint and postprint servers, unpublished papers or technical reports via the Internet, and open access e-journals (Bauer and Bakkalbasi, 2005). However, it was not until late 2004 that Elsevier introduced *Scopus* and Google produced *Google Scholar* in Beta version, both offering citation indexing. Gradually, other databases began to offer loosely designed cited reference searching. According to Roth (2005), services currently offering cited reference searching include: *SciFinder Scholar*, *NASA*, *Amazon*, *Scitation, PROLA*, *Citation Bridge*, *USPTO*, *Optics InfoBase*, *CiteSeer*, *Science Direct*, *PsycINFO*, *IEEE Xplore*, *Spires HEP*, *IOP*, and *CrossRef.* However, the cited reference search function in these databases is very limited and varies from one database to another. In addition, Ballard and Henry (2006) observed that: "a host of citation tracking resources are now available, all of which can contribute to a thorough search for citing references. There are those freely available on the Internet (*Google Scholar*, *Google Book Search, Window Live Academic*, *PMC*, *CiteSeer*); full-text subscription databases (*ScienceDirect*, *JSTOR*); and a host of subject-specific subscription databases such as *PI* and *CINAHL.* All subject-specific databases and Web sites, free or by subscription, are important complements to ISI's citation indexes" (p. 30). In a more recent review, Golderman and Connolly (2007) cited other citation-enhanced sources in addition to *WoS, Scopus* and *Google Scholar*. They include *Cambridge Scientific Abstracts (CSA),* American Chemical Society's *Chemical Abstract Service (CAS),* several *EBSCO* databases, *IEEE Xplore,* American Mathematical Society's *MathSciNet,* National Library of Medicine's *PubMed Central (PMC)*, *Sage Publications,*

R. Rikowski (ed.), Digitisation Perspectives, 213–226.

and Elsevier's *ScienceDirect*. It is obvious that citation indexing has found new applications in the environment of digital libraries.

Literature Review

A literature review has found that many researchers began to notice the emergence of the new generation of citation indexes, and a number of them conducted studies to examine and compare the classic *WoS* with its new competitors, namely *Scopus* and *Google Scholar*. As early as 2004, Jacso first picked the two newest versions of *Web of Science* and the new *Scopus* database for library use, because they "represent the state of the art in indexing/abstracting databases" and "are endowed with cited references, make superb use of citation indexing and facilitate citation searching" (p. 51). LaGuardia (2005) presented an introduction to a review of two major citation databases, *WoS* and *Scopus*, for use in libraries. Her brief review suggested that both systems are effective in allowing researchers to follow the development of research through cited searching. In addition to reviews given to the *WoS*, *Scopus* and *Google Scholar* separately, Jacso (2005) continued an extensive comparison of major features of these three citation-based and citation-enhanced databases in terms of their subject scope, database size and dimensions, and search results.

Bauer and Bakkalbasi (2005) presented a case study comparing the citation counts provided by *WoS, Scopus* and *Google Scholar* for articles published in a scholarly journal to determine statistical significance. The study found that *WoS* provided the largest citation counts for the older articles, whereas, *Google Scholar* provided significantly higher citation counts for newer publications than either *WoS* or *Scopus*. However, the authors warned "it is important for all researchers to note that until *Google Scholar* gives a full account of what material it is indexing and how often that index is updated, it cannot be considered a true scholarly resource in the sense that *Web of Science* and *Scopus* are. An understanding of the material being covered is central to the validity of any search of scholarly material" (p. 7).

In a newer study, Bakkalbasi & et al (2006) used citation analysis to examine these three databases, comparing citation counts for articles from physics and medical publications to test the hypothesis that the different scholarly publication coverage provided by the three search tools will lead to different citation counts from each. This study did not identify any one of these three databases as the answer to all citation tracking needs. While *Scopus* showed strength in providing citing literature for more current medical articles, *WoS* produced more in physics. All three tools retrieved some unique materials. The data indicated that "the question of which tool provides the most complete set of citing literature may depend on the subject and publication year of a given article" (p. 8).

Noruzi's (2005) study focused on *Google Scholar* while making comparison with *WoS*. This study began with an overview of how to use *Google Scholar* for citation analysis, and identified advanced search techniques not well documented by *Google Scholar*. It compared the citation counts generated from *Google Scholar* and *WoS*, and documented the advantages and disadvantages of *Google Scholar*.

The study concluded that *Google Scholar* provides a free alternative or complement to other citation indexes.

As a former student of Michael O. Rabin, the mathematician and computer scientist, Bar-Ilan (2006) did an ego-centric citation analysis of the works of Rabin in *Web of Science* and the two citation-enhanced search engines: *Google Scholar* and *CiteSeer*. The study identified the most cited works, citation identity, citation image makers and co-authors, and found significant differences among citation image makers generated from the three search tools. Two major issues were raised from this study, namely, "the multiple manifestations of the same work have a crucial influence on citation analysis" and "the different collection and indexing policies of the different databases lead to considerably different results" (p. 1565).

Currently, the three major sophisticated citation indexing databases represent different approaches to citation tracking. *WoS* and *Scopus* are fee-based commercial databases while *Google Scholar* is an open access search engine. The subject coverage of *WoS* and *Google Scholar* is multidisciplinary whereas that of *Scopus* is more science-focused. *Scopus* offers a search of Internet resources in its *Scirus* component, but web results are separated and are not included in citation tracking.

In order to further evaluate the effectiveness and the differences of the citation tracking functions of the emerging citation indexing databases/search engines, this study aims at applying citation analyses in the comparable search tools to examine whether the design and structure of the different citation tracking search tools will lead to different search results in spite of the fact that the searches are performed on the equal parameters. Based on the literature review and the pre-tests, the authors chose to focus on three major citation indexing databases *WoS*, *Scopus* and *Google Scholar* while testing the citation indexing functions of *ScienceDirect*, *Scirus*, *EBSCO* and *CiteSeer* which tend to enhance citation indexing.

METHODOLOGY

As the founding father of the original citation tracking tools, Eugene Garfield and his most frequently cited articles on citation indexing were chosen as the test samples for this study. Garfield's homepage chronologically listed roughly 464 publications, which include books, journal articles, letters, editorials, interviews, reprints, and presentations during 1952–2007. This study conducted a series of searches in the selected citation databases to compare the differences in the search results, evaluate the search effectiveness and analyze the reasons for the discrepancies. This is a case study in which a generalized conclusion cannot be assumed. The limitation of this study also lies in its inability to search the entire *Web of Science*. The authors' institutional subscription to *WoS* only covers the citation sources of 1975-present while the entire *WoS* covers the sources back to 1900. However, this limitation, otherwise, makes the comparisons more equal with *Scopus* which covers the sources back to 1970.

As a first step, an author/keyword search was performed in each selected database. Table 1 shows the drastic differences of citation counts of Garfield's publications on citation indexing in different databases.

Table 1. Search results of Eugene Garfield's works

Search Query	*WoS*	*Scopus*	*Google Scholar*	*Science Direct*	*Scirus*	*CiteSeer IST*	*EBSCO*
Eugene Garfield's citation indexing articles ("Garfield, E" and "Citation")	219	36	361	2	34	13*	12
"Garfield, E" and "citation index*"	69	20	298	1	25	7*	6
Author search only	1,138	52	507	7	19	88	22

* CiteSeer.IST's search interface is limited so the search terms were modified to fit the search engine.

The major reason for these discrepancies is due to the different coverage and indexing policies of the selected databases and search engines. *Web of Science* provides access to 8,700 prestigious research journals. As Eugene Garfield created the original citation indexes that are part of the *WoS* database, most of his work is included in this database. Included are the citations for the "*Current Comments*" column Garfield wrote for *Current Contents* published by ISI and his writings in *The Scientist,* the online scientific magazine of which he is the President and Founding Editor. About 91% of the citations retrieved from an author search on Garfield are linked to these two publications. Excluding citations for these two titles resulted in 78 citations out of 1,138 citations found in *WoS*.

An author search for Eugene Garfield in the *Scopus* database retrieved much fewer results. *Scopus* includes materials that date back to 1970, covering over 15,000 peer-reviewed titles from more than 4,000 international publishers, including journals, open access journals, conference proceedings, books and book series, patents, institutional repositories, and digital databases. As a relatively new citation database, half of its 30 million records date from 1996 to the present; the remaining 15 million records date from 1970–1995. Starting in 2006 *Scopus* began loading retrospective content and expects to load millions of older records. As a result, total coverage for older titles is incomplete. Examining the results from the "author search only," *Scopus* indexed citations for Eugene Garfield from 1979–2006 with 45 out of 52 citations published from 1992–2006. The authors anticipate more citations to Garfield's work as more content is added to the *Scopus* database.

In contrast, *Google Scholar* retrieved a greater number of Garfield's work including citations to journal articles in different databases, books, web pages, cited references, conference presentations, and his "Current Comments" column among all his many and varied writings. The *Google Scholar* search engine is unique as it provides access to multiple forms of the same work as it searches the Internet for academic materials. Because of its focus on retrieving academic sources, *Google Scholar* searches the Web including educational, e-repositories, and publishing sites.

Only 7 abstracts of Garfield's publications were included in the *ScienceDirect* database. *ScienceDirect* states that it provides access to about a quarter of available literature in science, medical and technical information including 128 full text computer science journal titles with some abstracts dating back to the 1960's. The date range offered on the search interface starts with 1997, although it is possible to search older dates. ScienceDirect only provides abstracts for a few of Garfield's work from 1977–1992 and several of these were minor writings such as letters to the editor. There were a few citations to his work by other authors. Like *ScienceDirect*, the citations for Eugene Garfield's publications in the *EBSCO* databases were limited to a few journals and books about using citations in the field of chemistry and the sciences and the majority of citations were limited to a few of his older publications.

Scirus is a relatively new search engine launched in 2001 that is programmed to search the deep internet for scientific information in databases, websites and e-depositories. Retrieved journal articles for "Eugene Garfield" are limited to the *PubMed* and *PubMed Central* databases. Another search on "Garfield E" and "citation index" includes citations from the *ScienceDirect* database. *Scirus* like *ScienceDirect* and *Scopus* are all published by Elsevier and are designed to work as a suite providing information on science, medicine and technology. The *PubMed, Science Direct, Biomed Central* databases and the U.S. patent offices are formal partners with the *Scirus* search engine. Included in the journal articles for Garfield are citations to his patent applications.

The *CiteSeer.IST: Scientific Literature Digital Library* retrieves publications in the Computer and Information Science fields. Because of this focus, there were more citations available on Eugene Garfield than in the *Scirus* search engine or the other databases tested. The majority of citations that *CiteSeer.IST* did retrieve came from Eugene Garfield's website at the University of Pennsylvania and most of them – 80 out of 88 citations – were links to the essays Garfield wrote for his *Current Comments* column. Unlike *Google Scholar* or *Web of Science*, *CiteSeer.IST* did not have as many citations to his journal articles. Since this case study was conducted, the name of this Digital Library has changed to CiteSeer^{x}, although originally, the authors referred to it as CiteSeer or by its former formal name, CiteSeer.IST.

After analyzing these results, the authors decided to eliminate the *ScienceDirect* and *EBSCO* databases, and the *Scirus* and *CiteSeer.IST* search engines from their case study. In spite of its focus as a science database, *ScienceDirect* had too few citations to truly analyze and compare with the other citation tools. The *EBSCO* databases likewise had too few citations to compare. The *Scirus* and *CiteSeer* search engines were eliminated in favor of *Google Scholar* that retrieved more citations, and has a greater use in the academic scientific community. As a search engine, *Scirus* is a relatively new product and it is expected to have potential for future growth. The *CiteSeer.IST* search engine is more focused on computer and information science materials, so although it retrieved a good number of citations for Garfield, the researchers decided to select *Google Scholar* given the range of its materials.

Due to the limitations of the *ScienceDirect* and *EBSCO* databases, and the *Scirus* and *CiteSeer* search engines, the authors decided to focus on the *WoS* and *Scopus* databases and the *Google Scholar* search engine for further research comparisons.

Powerful Citation Tracking Tools in WoS and Scopus

There are two unique citation tracking tools in *WoS* and *Scopus* which are not available elsewhere. They are the "Citation Report" in *WoS* and "Citation Tracker" in *Scopus*. The "Citation Report" in *WoS* provides a single report showing all of the citation activities within a user-defined set of records. The report includes the sums of citations, averages of citations, citation counts by year, graphs displaying paper publication, citation trends, and a quality/quantity indicator (the *h*-index). With an author and keyword search, the Citation Report in *WoS* provided aggregate citation statistics for Garfield's 219 articles. The statistics showed that these 219 articles have been cited 1,079 times and each article has been cited an average of 4.93 times during the period of 1975–2007, with the *h*-index of 15.

Similarly, the "Citation Tracker" in Scopus provides an overview of citation data for a user-specified set of articles over a selected time period. It displays the most highly cited authors in a field, finds and tracks hot topics in specific subject areas, checks the most up to date citation data on specific authors and articles, and tracks and evaluates research trends. However, an author search in *Scopus* with Citation Tracker generated different results. Only 52 articles of Garfield's were found in *Scopus*. These 52 articles have been cited 663 times by 477 documents during the period of 1996–2007 with the *h*-index of 10.

In order to find out the most frequently cited papers of Eugene Garfield for this study, the authors used these two powerful tools in *WoS* and *Scopus*. By using the equal search parameters, the top ten most frequently cited articles were identified in each database (see Table 2). It is notable that, among the ten frequently cited articles, there are only four common titles. The table also shows the different rankings of the most frequently cited articles by Eugene Garfield, except for the top ranking article "How can impact factors be improved?". This article was cited 145 times in *WoS* while the citations in *Scopus* keep changing as new references are added.

Table 2. Top ten most frequently cited articles by Eugene Garfield

Articles in WoS	*Times Cited*	*Articles in Scopus*	*Times Cited*
*How can impact factors be improved? *British Medical Journal*, 1996	145	*How can impact factors be improved? *British Medical Journal*, 1996	149
Is information-retrieval in the arts and humanities... *Library Quarterly*, 1980	43	*From citation indexes to informetrics: Is the tail now wagging the dog? *Libri*, 1998	22

Table 2. (*Continued*)

Of Nobel class – a citation perspective on high-impact research authors *Theoretical Medicine*, 1992	30	100 citation classics from the Journal of the American Medical Association. *Journal of the American Medical Association*, 1987	17
The most-cited physical sciences publications in… *Current Comments*, 1990	29	Random thoughts on citationology. Its theory and practice *Scientometrics*, 1998	16
*From citation indexes to informetrics: Is the tail now wagging the dog? *Libri*, 1998	25	The impact of fraudulent research on the scientific literature. The Stephen E. Breuning case *Journal of the American Medical Association*, 1990	13
History of citation indexes for chemistry – a brief review *Journal of Chemical Information and Computer Sciences*, 1985	20	The diverse roles of citation indexes in scientific research *Revista de Investigacion Clinica* 1998	11
Random thoughts on citationology. Its theory and practice… *Scientometrics*, 1998	16	*The growth of the cell death field: An analysis from the ISI-Science citation index *Cell Death and Differentiation*, 1997	10
*The growth of the cell death field: An analysis from the ISI-Science citation index *Cell Death and Differentiation*, 1997	14	*Historiographic mapping of knowledge domains literature *Journal of Information Science*, 2004	8
The diverse roles of citation indexes in scientific research *Revista de Investigacion Clinica*, 1998	9	Mapping the Output of Topical Searches in the Web of Knowledge and the Case of Watson-Crick *Information Technology and Libraries*, 2003	4
*Historiographic mapping of knowledge domains literature *Journal of Information Science*, 2004	6	The microbiology literature: Languages of publication and their relative citation impact *FEMS Microbiology Letters*, 1992	3

* The four commonly cited Garfield articles.

Google Scholar

Different from the fee-based commercial databases of *WoS* and *Scopus*, *Google Scholar* is a free and powerful Web search engine for scholarly research. It allows researchers to locate a wide range of scholarly literature on the Web, including books, journal articles, theses/dissertations, preprints, PowerPoint presentations, open access journals, technical reports, etc. According to Noruzi, "What makes *Google Scholar* most useful is its citation index feature." (2005). The search results are returned in a relevance-ranked format with easily accessible citation tracking information in the left-hand column. In order to compare *Google Scholar*'s citation tracking function and search results with *WoS* and *Scopus*, the authors performed a search for the four common articles in *Google Scholar*. The search generated very different results (see Table 3).

Table 3. Times references cited for the four common articles

Cited Work	*Times Cited in WoS*	*Times Cited in Scopus*	*Times Cited in Google Scholar*
How can impact factors be improved? *British Medical Journal*, 1996	145	149	140
From citation indexes to informetrics: Is the tail now wagging the dog? *Libri*, 1998	24	22	28
The growth of the cell death field: An analysis from the ISI-Science citation index, *Cell Death and Differentiation*, 1997	14	10	8
Historiographic mapping of knowledge domains literature, *Journal of Information Science*, 2004	6	8	8

ANALYSIS OF CITING REFERENCES

In order to find out why the search results are so different, the authors further analyzed the citing references to the selected articles (see Table 4). This analysis identified the total unique citing references to three of Garfield's frequently cited articles in *Web of Science*, *Scopus* and *Google Scholar*. Although each database/search engine retrieved a number of overlapping citing references, each database included unique citations not found in the others.

Tracking the citations in the *WoS* database had some limitations. It is a journal-based database with selected sets of academic journals, and indexes only the first author of the publication. Hence, citation information for books, book chapters, conference papers, technical reports, patents and many other formats are not to be found in this database. As a result, the citations retrieved were mainly journal articles. Of the three databases/search engines tested, *WoS* was the only one that included an erratum and subsequent release of a corrected journal article reprint.

Table 4. Times references cited for the three most frequently cited articles

Cited Work	*Number of Citing References in WoS*	*Number of Citing References in Scopus*	*Number of Citing References in Google Scholar*	*Total Number of Unique Citing References*
From citation indexes to informetrics: Is the tail now wagging the dog? *Libri*, 1998	24 (22 in common with Scopus; 2 monographs; missed 12 articles)	22 (21 in common with WoS, 1 unique journal; missed 14 articles)	28 (12 in common with WoS; 10 in common with Scopus; 6 unique articles; missed 8 articles)	36
The growth of the cell death field: An analysis from the ISI-Science citation index, *Cell Death and Differentiation*, 1997	14 (10 in common with Scopus; 2 books; 2 articles in med/bio journals; missed 1 letter to the editor)	10 (10 in common with WoS; missed 2 books, 2 articles in med/bio journals, and 1 letter to the editor)	8 (7 in common, 1 unique letter to the editor; missed 2 books and 5 journal articles)	15
*Historiographic mapping of knowledge domains literature, *Journal of Information Science*, 2004	6 (missed 3 foreign language journals and 3 conference papers)	8 (6 in common with WoS; 2 unique foreign language journals; missed 1 Chinese journal and 3 conference papers)	8 (4 in common with WoS & Scopus; 3 unique conference papers; missed 3 foreign language journals, and 2 English journals.)	12

* An example of the total number of unique citing references for Historiographic Mapping of Knowledge Domains Literature is listed in Appendix.

Another limitation of *WoS* includes the problem of distinguishing between similar citations. Two of the citations retrieved had the same brief bibliographic information. Only by selecting and opening the complete bibliographic record for each citation, was it apparent that the citation was for the same journal article, one listing its source as a *Web of Knowledge* festschrift honoring Eugene Garfield in the *ASIST* Monograph series, and the other referencing the original monograph series. Another problem with bibliographic formatting in *WoS* is when a citation has been included that is misspelled. This type of error can lead to confusion in identifying duplicate citations from unique ones. These examples point to the need to standardize citation formats across all citation indexing tools.

The major advantages of *Scopus* are that it includes citations to newer materials, and it retrieves many of the same journal articles as the *WoS* database. *Scopus* is adding more retrospective materials but it did not provide as much access to older materials as the *WoS*. *Scopus* does include citations to research written in other languages.

Google Scholar returned the greatest number of citations and unique citations to Garfield's work. One advantage to using *Google Scholar* is that researchers have access to many materials not included in the other databases, such as monographs, e-print articles, conference proceedings, book chapters, interview transcripts, theses and patents, although *Scopus* cites patents as well. In addition, it provides access to many foreign language materials in Spanish, Italian, German, etc., and even non-roman languages, such as Chinese and Japanese. Another advantage is that researchers can track the development of a theory through an article's different versions and subsequent articles. For instance, *Google Scholar* located all versions of a journal article including the original and reprinted versions. Like *Scopus*, *Google Scholar* includes access to citation references in other languages, and of the three citation tools, *Google Scholar* had more unique citations to articles in other languages.

A mixed benefit and limitation of *Google Scholar* is that it tracks citations to research found on websites–some with broken links– although it is possible to do a web search for different versions of a missing article. One major limitation of using *Google Scholar* is that the bibliographic formatting differs from the formatting found in *WoS* and *Scopus*, so a researcher will need to do more work to compare the data found across all three search engine/database. *Google Scholar* retrieved one unique citation in the form of a "letter to the editor" of a journal. However, the researchers have been unable to track the citation from the "letter to the editor" to Garfield's work. This example is not typical, but it does highlight the need to clearly trace the path to the cited work.

Citation Tracking of Garfield's Classical Works

Among all the available citation tracking databases, only *Google Scholar* covers the citation tracking information for books. Garfield's classic book *Citation Indexing: its Theory and Application in Science, Technology and Humanities* (1979) was found cited 460 times in *Google Scholar*. It is interesting that Garfield's classic article "Citation analysis as a tool in journal evaluation" in *Science* (1972) could not be found in either *WoS* (due to the limited subscription to *WoS* at the test site) or *Scopus*, whereas in *Google Scholar*, this article was cited 370 times. Another early and important work "Citation indexes for science…" in Science (1955) which was reprinted in *Int'l Journal of Epidemiology* in 2006 could only be found in *Google Scholar* with 157 citing times (see Table 5).

When referring to his 1955 paper in *Science*, Garfield (2006) commented "As a confirmed citationist, I must point out that it is not my most cited work.

Table 5. Citation data of Garfield's classical works

Cited Work	*Times Cited in WoS*	*Times Cited in Scopus*	*Times Cited in Google Scholar*
Citation indexing: its theory and application in science, technology and humanities (book) 1979	N/A	N/A	460
Citation analysis as a tool in journal evaluation *Science*, 1972	N/A	N/A	370
Citation indexes for science... *Int'l Journal of Epidemiology*, 2006 (Reprinted from Science, 1955)	1	2	157
100 citation classics from the Journal of the American Medical Association. *Journal of the American Medical Association*, 1987	31	17	N/A

It is my 1972 paper in *Science*, on using citation analysis to evaluate journals, which has attracted much more attention... In that sense, I am like many other authors who feel that their most-cited work is not necessarily their best. My most-cited work is in fact my 1979 book *Citation Indexing*" (p. 1127).

CONCLUSION

This paper is a case study analyzing the numbers of citing references to Eugene Garfield's most frequently cited works in three major citation tracking tools, *WoS*, *Scopus* and *Google Scholar*. The limitations of this study included a short time frame to conduct the case study, March 2007 – July 2007, and the changes that occurred in the databases during the study either through new added content or changes to the databases themselves. As a result, the authors have concluded that none of the three tools can satisfy all of a researcher's citation tracking needs. *Web of Science* showed strength in providing citing references to traditional academic journals while *Scopus* performed better in providing citing literature for more current articles. *Google Scholar* returned a significant number of non-traditional citing references. With its advantage of free availability via the Internet, *Google Scholar* is an important compliment to *WoS* and *Scopus*.

This study agrees with the previous studies in that a researcher has no single solution to a comprehensive literature search. None of the citation tracking tools tested covered the complete set of citing references. However, the authors question whether there should be a universal citation database that covers every single academic work ever published no matter what format it is carried? In fact, Robert D. Cameron (1997) proposed a model of universal citation database which would link every scholarly work ever written. He proposed that "...we consider a model for a universal citation database organized as a distributed database over the Internet and maintained primarily by the academic institutions and other organizations that originate scholarly work. Each site would contribute, in a standardized format, the bibliographic and citation data for papers written by its scholars. Two devices would be necessary to make it possible for the database to be developed in this way: an institutional requirement on authors to submit bibliographic and citation data and a bibliographic software system to help prepare it."

This universal citation database requires that all the contributed publications follow the standardized entry format to facilitate scholarly research freely via Internet. This model would transfer the effort in the labor-intensive data preparation from the citation indexer to the author. While arguing its feasibility, there are also technical and institutional issues to explore. Song & Liu (2003) attempted to address the technical issues associated with this universal citation database by proposing a XML citation digital library using XQuery as search language. It requires that all scholarly publications with their reference citations be published to XML documents based on a universally-defined document schema. An XML Schema should be designed and the rules be defined for all published papers. Then a searching mechanism based on the XQuery language can intelligently search through these XML documents. The proposed model will create a free data sharing environment, simplify the process of document processing and greatly improve the search accuracy.

However, the issues associated with the universal citation database are beyond the discussion of this paper. The authors believe that, only when a Universal Citation Digital Library is established, will there be a solution to revolutionally increase the effectiveness of scientific research and scholarly communication.

Note: Since this piece was originally written, a number of changes have occurred in the databases tested. Web of Science has a new feature of citation map in beta mode, which gives a visual representation of a cited article, the articles it cites (backward citing) and the articles that cite it (forward citing). Scopus now has a new feature for tracking citations, in which researchers can now create author citation alerts or document citation alerts so they can be notified when an author or document has been cited by another article. More new features can be expected when the databases and search engines make further improvements in their search mechanism. Therefore, the findings and conclusion of this study were only valid when the study was conducted. However, its methodology can be utilized for future studies.

REFERENCES

Bakkalbasi, N., Bauer, K., Glover, J., & Wang, L. (2006). Three options for citation tracking: Google Scholar, Scopus and Web of Science. *Biomedical Digital Libraries*, *3*(7). Retrieved April 15, 2010, from http://www.pubmedcentral.nih.gov/picrender.fcgi?artid=1533854&blobtype=pdf

Ballard, S., & Henry, M. (2006). Citation searching: New players, new tools. *Searcher*, *14*(9), 24–33.

Bar-Ilan, J. (2006). An ego-centric citation analysis of the works of Michael O. Rabin based on multiple citation indexes. *Information Processing & Management*, *42*(6), 1553–1566.

Bauer, K., & Bakkalbasi, N. (2005). An examination of citation counts in a new scholarly communication environment. *D-Lib Magazine*, *11*(9). Retrieved April 15, 2010, from http://dlib.org/dlib/september05/bauer/09bauer.html

Cameron, R. D. (1997). A universal citation database as a catalyst for reform in scholarly Communication. *First Monday: Peer-Reviewed Journal on the Internet*. Retrieved April 15, 2010, from http://www.firstmonday.org/issues/issue2_4/cameron/index.html

Deis, L., & Goodman, D. (2005). Web of Science (2004 version) and Scopus. *Charleston Advisor* [online], *6*(3). Retrieved April 15, 2010, from http://www.charlestonco.com/

Garfield, E. (2006). Commentary: Fifty years of citation indexing. *International Journal of Epidemiology*, *35*, 1127–1128.

Golderman, G., & Connolly, B. (2007). Who cited this? *Library Journal*, *132*, 18–26.

Jacso, P. (2004). ISI Web of Science, Scopus, and SPORTDiscus. *Online*, *48*(6), 51–54.

Jacso, P. (2005). As we may search – Comparison of major features of the *Web of Science, Scopus*, and *Google Scholar* citation-based and citation enhanced databases. *Current Science*, *89*(9), 1537–1547. Retrieved April 15, 2010, from http://www.ias.ac.in/currsci/nov102005/1537.pdf

LaGuardia, C. (2005). Scopus vs. Web of Science. *Library Journal*, *130*(1), 40–42.

Myhill, M. (2005). Google scholar review. *Charleston advisor* [online], *6*(4). Retrieved April 15, 2010, from http://www.charlestonco.com/

Noruzi, A. (2005). Google scholar: The new generation of citation indexes. Libri: *International Journal of Libraries & Information Services*, 55(4), 170–180.

Persson, O. (2005). 'Citation Indexes for Science' – A 50 year citation history. *Current Science*, *89*(9), 1503–1504. Retrieved April 15, 2010, from http://www.ias.ac.in/currsci/nov102005/1503.pdf

Pomerantz, J. (2006). Google scholar and 100 percent availability of information. *Information Technology & Libraries*, *25*(2), 52–56.

Roth, D. (2005). The emergence of competitors to the *Science Citation Index* and the *Web of Science*. *Current Science*, *89*(9), 1531–1536. Retrieved April 15, 2010, from http://www.ias.ac.in/currsci/nov102005/1531.pdf

Song, D., & Liu, M. (2003). A new model of XML citation database using XQuery as search language. In *Libraries and associations in the transient word: New technologies and new forms of cooperation*, 10th Anniversary International Conference <<Crimea 2003>> (pp. 301–308). Moscow: Russian National Public Library for Science and Technology.

Whitley, K. (2002). Analysis of *SciFinder Scholar* and *Web of Science* Citation Searches. *Journal of the American Society for Information Science & Technology*, *53*(14), 1210–1215.

Mengxiong Liu and Peggy Cabrera
San José State University, USA

APPENDIX

The total 12 unique citing references of Garfield's article "Historiographic mapping of knowledge domains literature" *Journal of Information Science*, 2004, retrieved from three different citation databases.

Data-bases	Retrieved citing references
Google Scholar Web of Science Scopus	Janssen, M., Schoon, M., Ke, W., et al. (2006) Scholarly networks on resilience, vulnerability and adaptation within the human dimensions of global environmental change, *Global Environmental Change – Human and Policy Dimensions*, 16 (3), 240–252. Byrne, F. & Chapman, S. (2005) The most cited authors and papers in tobacco control, *British Medical Journal,* 14 (3), 155–160. Small, H. Tracking and predicting growth areas in science, Scientometrics, (3), 595–610. Ackermann, E. Indicators of failed information epidemics in the scientific journal literature: A publication analysis of Polywater and Cold Nuclear Fusion, Scientometrics, 66 (3), 451–466.
Web of Science Scopus	Shneiderman, B. & Aris, A. (2006) Network visualization by semantic substrates, *IEEE Transactions on Visualization and Computer Graphics,* 12 (5), 733–740. Persson, O. (2005) 'Citation indexes for science' - A 50 year citation history, *Current Science,* 89 (9), 1503–1504.
Scopus	*Kizek, R. & Adam, V. (2007) Scientometrics and their relevance, *Listy Cukrovarnicke a Reparshe*, 123 (1), 25–26. *Garfield, E. Paris, S. & Stock, W. (2006) HistCite: a software tool for informetric analysis of citation linkage, *Information – Wissenschaft und Praxis,* 57 (8), 391–400.
Google Scholar	*Zhou, J. & Sun, T. (2005) The Application of Information Visualization in the Digital Libraries, Modern Library and Information Technology. **Mann, G., Mimno, D. & McCallum, A. (2006) Bibliometric impact measures leveraging topic analysis, *Proceedings of the 6th ACM/IEEE*-CS. **Chen, T. & Hsieh, L. (2006) Uncovering the Latent Underlying Domains of a Research Field: Knowledge Visualization Revealed, *Proceedings of the conference on Information Visualization.* **Jin, B. & Rousseau, R. (2005) China's quantitative expansion phase: exponential growth but low impact, *Proceedings of ISSI.*

* Foreign language journals.
** Conference proceedings.

PART V: DIGITISATION OF RARE, VALUED AND SCHOLARLY WORKS

TATIANA NIKOLOVA-HOUSTON AND RON HOUSTON

14. BUILDING THE VIRTUAL SCRIPTORIUM

INTRODUCTION

Manuscripts, archives, and early printed books contain a documentary record of the foundations of human knowledge. Many elements restrict access to this corpus, from preservation concerns to censorship. On the assumption that the widespread availability of knowledge benefits the human condition more than the restriction of knowledge, elements restrictive to the dissemination of manuscripts, archives, and early printed books should be overcome, and the intellectual content of such items should be available to as wide an audience as possible through the digital library equivalent of the medieval scriptorium, termed here the "virtual scriptorium."

This chapter presents the many restrictive elements that have worked against the creation of the virtual scriptorium, specifically, the obstacles to digitizing and publishing medieval manuscripts on the Web and through optical media such as CDs and DVDs. Examples of restrictive elements include preservation concerns, misunderstanding of research needs, overestimation of digitization costs, reliance on authority figures, misapplication of digitization standards, the problem of selection, fear of equipment obsolescence, lack of subject expertise, lack of permission, historical prejudice, and fear of changing research needs. This chapter presents methods by which the authors overcame these restrictive elements and presents recommendations for further action.

BUILDING THE VIRTUAL SCRIPTORIUM

Ancient manuscripts document much of human knowledge prior to the widespread use of the printing press. Once lost, they cannot be replaced, and manuscript repositories justifiably restrict access to their collections (cf. ALA & SAA, 1994). This restricting, however, obscures the vital foundation of our cultural heritage represented by manuscripts. How can we preserve the knowledge contained in manuscripts and simultaneously provide access to it?

An answer has emerged through the development of technology that captures and stores images digitally: "digitize" (create digital photographs of) the manuscripts and publish these digital images on the Web and through optical media such as CDs and DVDs. In other words, create a "virtual scriptorium" on the Web, with duplicate electronic copies stored on durable and long-lasting optical media (cf. CLIR, 2005). Yet, those who undertake such a project will find that objections arise at every step of the way. This paper discusses typical objections and the responses that the digital librarian might make.

And what is a "digital librarian?" In the past, the activities of creating manuscripts, publishing books, and caring for them through the activities of librarianship

R. Rikowski (ed.), Digitisation Perspectives, 229–244.

Figure 1. Illumination from "Gospel, Slepchevo monastery, 16th century," HACI collection.

and archival enterprise remained largely discrete: individuals would train and practice in one or another of the fields, but seldom more than one. With the advent of digital technology, however, one person can perform all of these activities. Therefore, this chapter addresses such a person and uses the term "digital librarian" to refer to a person who might create, publish, and disseminate digital images of manuscripts, acting as both a scribe and a clerk in a Web-based virtual scriptorium.

TO DIGITIZE OR NOT TO DIGITIZE?

One of the most common obstacles to arise in the path of the digital librarian comes from curators of traditional manuscript collections: "Is digitization a method of preservation, or not?" (ECPA, 1997) This question has merit in the world of traditional curation with its primary mission: to preserve physical objects in spite of limited money, personnel, and time. Why spend money on digitization, when those resources could be used, for example, for archival re-housing of manuscripts? Similarly, curators ask: "What do we achieve by digitizing? How will digitizing further our secondary mission: to support the scholar?" Again, the question has merit. Why not devote resources to improved finding aids, for example?

These otherwise valid objections rest on an improper conflation of the research needs of the scholar. In other words, the people who raise these objections do not discriminate between the intellectual content of a manuscript and its evidentiary and forensic values. Obviously, a digital photograph of a manuscript page will not allow the researcher to test the age of the manuscript's ink and paper.

Figure 2. Prof. Dr. Hristo Temelski, director of the HACI (left), and a visiting scholar, examining images.

However, a digital photo *will* convey the intellectual content of a manuscript. To determine the research needs of scholars, the digital librarian might query the scholars directly. For example, such a survey at the Historical and Archival Church Institute (HACI) in Sofia, Bulgaria in 2001 found that *all* researchers agreed that the manuscripts needed to be digitized, while 45% would *prefer* digital copies. Thirty-six percent stated that a digital copy would not serve as a substitute for the original (Nikolova-Houston, 2002).

As the second largest manuscript repository in Bulgaria, containing 1,509 manuscripts and early printed books, HACI attracts scholars comprising a representative sample of all manuscript scholars (see Figure 2 below). Many of the HACI researchers had journeyed to HACI from other countries and continents. How many *more* would have accepted digital images on the Web to avoid the hardships and expense of travel? Among the HACI researchers who did visit the facility, digital images could have reduced the handling of the original manuscripts by more than one-half. When we consider the reduced handling of an original manuscript that results from access to its digital copy, digitization would appear to be a useful means of providing access to those researchers who require access only to intellectual content, and the provision of digital access would reduce wear and tear to the original documents. Manuscript curators who separate the research needs of scholars into the need for intellectual content of a document versus the need for physical access to a document realize that digitization furthers both of the missions of the curator: to preserve and to provide access.

"DIGITIZATION COSTS TOO MUCH"

Yet, this digital furthering of the curator's dual mission of preservation and access comes at a price, and the question becomes "at what price?" Many of those reading this book will remember the days when a modest computer cost over $2,000–eight weeks of the 1980 American National Average Wage (SSA, 2005). Affordable digital scanners did not exist until the late 1980s. Affordable digital cameras did not exist until the late 1990s. In the early days of digitization technology, the equipment necessary to "capture" (to photograph) and store digital images cost so much that only institutions could afford to acquire it.

In the late 1990s, the situation changed. Technology advanced, increasing the quality of digital images and lowering the prices of the equipment. The amount of possible detail in a digital image increased from hundreds of dots per inch (dpi) to thousands. Prices decreased (see Figure 3 below) to the point that a computer, scanner, camera, and digital storage suitable for large-scale digitization projects now cost $800–about one week of the projected American National Average Wage (SSA, 2005).

The difficulty of learning digital capture and storage techniques decreased as much as the price of the equipment. The spread of digital cameras to the "snapshot" consumer market required the development of easy-to-use digital cameras, "invisible" or "seamless" camera-to-computer interfaces, and self-explanatory software for the manipulation and sharing of digital images. In other words, the digital librarian's job

Figure 3. Typical computer ad, October 6, 2006.

became easier as we began to e-mail summer vacation photos to Uncle Bob. Digitization project budgets no longer must include the expense of a high-priced computer technician or programmer. One person, the digital librarian, with minimal training, now can capture, format, organize, and publish digital images for access by researchers the world over. Lower equipment costs and lower labor costs have made digitization feasible for almost any project.

Let us be clear about one thing, however. The previous paragraph discusses digitization at an *acceptable* level of quality. Beyond this level, more money and more expertise will result in images with more information content. For example, the acceptable image will present legible text, where the extremely high quality image will allow the scholar to count individual brush strokes. Further, the addition to a project of more money and more expertise will permit the capture of documents more efficiently (less wasted time and money) and more effectively (more images captured). However, the choice facing the digital librarian today is NOT "acceptable images versus high quality images." The choice today is "acceptable images versus NO images!" Therefore, this paper discusses digitization at an *acceptable* level, rather than at higher levels. The digital librarian who uses more expensive equipment and who studies digitization theory and technology will be able to preserve more knowledge. Schools and special seminars teach the technology and practice of digitization, and a significant and growing body of specialized literature exists, such as reports from the Council on Library and Information Resources (CLIR, 2005). Digitization no longer "costs too much," and the digital librarian no longer has that excuse not to act.

"LET THE GOVERNMENT/CHURCH/UNESCO DO IT"

Still, money intrudes into most conversations about digitization. "We just applied for a grant . . ." or, "Who is funding this type of project?" Many dreams about digitization projects include dreams about large grants of money and, in truth, many governments, religious organizations, and non-governmental organizations do fund digitization projects.

The digital librarian (and any other librarian) has an ethical mandate to uphold the principle of intellectual freedom (ALA, 1995). Yet, financial dependence on funding institutions has the potential to compromise intellectual freedom. After all, why would a grantor fund a digitization project that would not further the interests of the grantor? The digital librarian must balance the utility of grant funding against the concurrent loss of independence in, for example, the selection of manuscripts for digitization and in the choice of venues in which to publish the digital images. Selection bias and venue bias can represent a subtle form of censorship, antithetical to the librarian's mandate. Therefore, the ethical digital librarian will digitize, publish, and administer collections of digital images as best possible, with or without grants. Yet, the clever digital librarian will apply for preservation and conservation grants, emphasizing conventional archival techniques such as re-housing and cataloging, while understating the digital aspects of the project.

Taken to extreme, dependence on funding from an entity leads to the thought that the funding entity itself should administer and conduct the digitization project. For example, a digital librarian could apply to the Digital Humanities Initiative of the U.S. National Endowment for the Humanities (an "agency" of the U.S. federal government) for a grant to digitize a manuscript collection, or the digital librarian could wait for the Smithsonian Institution (a "body" of the U.S. federal government) to digitize that collection. In either instance, we have given to the United States government the power to choose what becomes digitized, that is, the power to choose what knowledge becomes preserved and accessible. Just as medieval scriptoria copied documents to preserve them against those who would censor and destroy (Gergova, 2006, p. 38), a virtual scriptorium, created without outside funding, could fulfill the same role today, reserving to the digital librarian the power over knowledge.

"YOU MUST MAINTAIN STANDARDS"

Medieval scriptoria observed standardized conventions of manuscript production, such as placement of colophons and use of the various types of scripts, yet each manuscript maintained individuality while transferring knowledge from the scribe to the reader. Similarly, the digital librarian must observe standards to ensure the transfer of knowledge to the reader while not letting a slavishness to standards prevent digitization. This and the next section discuss standards frequently used to forestall digitization projects: standards relating to image quality, finding aids, formats, and organization.

When considering overall image quality and "resolution" (the amount of detail in a digital photo), the digital librarian would do well to heed the words of Psohlavec (1998, p. 22), that ordinary researchers, rather than technical experts, are the ones to make the major decisions about image quality and standards. Digital images of manuscripts can satisfy ordinary researchers because, according to Psohlavec, the human eye's properties have remained constant over the centuries from ancient scribes to contemporary scholars. "The technological possibilities of digitization are growing very quickly, hardware is getting cheaper" reaching the limits of the human eye's perceptual acuity (p. 27).

Digitization standards also apply to the finding aids, storage formats, and presentation formats of manuscript digitization projects. For example, in 1994, the Bulgarian National Library digitized two manuscripts (Moussakova, 2006). Yet, in the following 12 years, technical and organizational issues have prevented most further digitization of manuscripts. Moussakova cites software incompatibilities, disagreement over format and content of metadata, disagreement over presentation format and contextual content, and unresolved questions about electronic cataloging.

Interestingly, an analogous situation occurred in the Balkans during its centuries of occupation by foreigners. Two classes of manuscripts existed. One class, produced from the somewhat privileged monastic scriptoria, maintained the highest standards of the Byzantine and Slavic manuscript tradition, for example, the 16th century *Slepchevo Gospel* (see Figure 1 above and Figure 4 below).

Figure 4. A page from "Gospel, Slepchevo monastery, 16th century," HACI collection.

The other class of manuscripts was created by scribes from the disadvantaged scriptoria located in remote towns and villages (see Figure 5 below). They followed standards as best they could, using what materials they had, writing in the spoken vernacular language without models and standards to guide them (Mutafchieva, 1964, pp. 12–13). Examples of the latter include *damaskins* (collections of stories written in the vernacular), and the *Istorija Slavjanobolgarskaja* (*Slavo-Bulgarian History*, Hilendarski, 1762).

Figure 5. Pages from a 17th century prayer book manuscript, town of Lukovit, Bulgaria.

Thus, while some people will defer digitization for fear of not meeting standards, the effective digital librarian will act. For example, the first author of this paper took a digital camera to HACI in 2002 and digitized representative portions of Slavic manuscripts. Today, with better equipment, these pages could be digitized more quickly and at a higher resolution, but fast or slow, the job was done, and a need for higher resolution has not been demonstrated. Further, had those pages not been digitized in 2002, they would not have appeared on the Web for researchers worldwide to access, and most researchers have judged them *good enough*. The lesson here is simply to start, simply to do something acceptably, rather than to do nothing exquisitely. To liberate the knowledge of the world, the intellectual insurgent of today requires only a digital camera and a DVD writer. One further requirement for successful digitizing, organization, appears in the next section.

"TOO MUCH INFORMATION IS AS BAD AS TOO LITTLE"

The concern over digitization standards also manifests itself with respect to *organization* of manuscript images on the Web. If a virtual scriptorium were to exist on the Web, with thousands of pages of digital photos of manuscripts, how would a researcher find any particular photo? The answer to this problem lies in the discipline of librarianship, the goal of which is "to bring human beings and recorded knowledge in as fruitful a relationship as it is humanly possible to be" (Shera, p. 30). In other words, the insurgent with a camera must employ at some point the skills of a librarian to organize and provide access to the intellectual content of digitized images.

An extremely small-scale example of the virtual scriptorium exists on the first author's Web sites, in which the manuscript images are organized by topic and searchable by keywords (see Nikolova-Houston, 2002; 2003; 2004). This organization for provision of access requires thought and time, and critics of digitization are correct in raising the "need for organization" objection. However, the digital search and organization need be done but once, whereas without the virtual scriptorium, *each researcher* must conduct a separate search through the physical manuscripts. Further, if this objection of "too much information" prevents the capture and publishing of manuscript images, the digital librarian will have abrogated the choice of the repertoire of the world's knowledge to someone else.

Figure 6. A damaged manuscript in the HACI collection.

"HOW CAN YOU KNOW WHAT TO DIGITIZE?"

Two primary factors determine which manuscripts to digitize. The first involves the expected usage of the manuscripts, and the second involves the physical condition of the manuscripts (see Figure 6 above). No one can foresee future research needs, so the digital librarian must examine past usage to develop an idea of expected usage. In the case of the HACI manuscripts, the HACI usage records for 1990–2001 revealed which manuscripts received the heaviest use. Then, a preservation survey identified the manuscripts most susceptible to damage through handling. The director of the institution assisted in the selection of the manuscripts to digitize, based on his specialized knowledge of the collection. Other selection criteria appear in the literature of digitization, for example, the comprehensive decision matrix presented in Hazen et al. (1998). As with the question of digitization standards, the digital librarian faces one of two prospects in manuscript selection: thoughtful lack of action, or action undertaken with incomplete information. The choice between these two prospects becomes a personal decision, a balancing act conducted by every digitizer. Judging by the paucity of medieval Slavic manuscript images on the Web, there would seem to be room for more action.

"YOUR EQUIPMENT WILL BE OBSOLETE IN TWO TO FIVE YEARS"

This objection, eloquently expressed in Dobreva (2003) as the "Achilles and the Tortoise Paradox of Zeno of Elea" (cf. Wikipedia, 2006a), presents a valid cautionary note to the digital librarian. The 20th century contains many episodes in which irreplaceable information has been lost through the obsolescence of the equipment necessary to recover or process it (cf. CLIR, 2005). The CPARLG (1996) estimated the life cycle of digital equipment at two to five years. Microsoft (2006) supports its consumer software for three to five years. This short lifespan presents a mandate to the digital librarian to maintain familiarity with the technology of digitization, to "migrate" (re-format) the digitized data for new equipment when necessary, and to maintain data and metadata in formats that are as widely used and as simple as possible. For example, the extremely simple ASCII (American Standard Code for Information Interchange) was standardized in 1967 and continues to be understandable today, 40 years later, in spite of revisions (Wikipedia, 2006c). The looming spectre of equipment obsolescence should not deter the digital librarian who a) remains abreast of advances in digital technology, and b) chooses formats for their simplicity and for their relative ubiquity.

Two other reasons exist for digitizing in apparent defiance of this objection. First, the digital "capture" comprises the most difficult component of the digitization process. Once an image is captured, a computer can convert it from one format to another in a negligible amount of time, compared with the time required for the original capture. Second, the technology ALWAYS will be ahead of the digital librarian. A faster computer or larger memory device ALWAYS will exist in someone's warehouse, even as you buy the currently fastest or largest model "on the shelf." You will NEVER catch up with current digitization technology, unlike Achilles and the tortoise. That being the case, the digital librarian who waits for the ultimate technology will never commence a digitization project. Start now with what you have, heed the cautions, and let the future take care of itself.

"WHAT MAKES YOU THE EXPERT ABOUT DIGITIZING MANUSCRIPTS?"

The field of medieval manuscript scholarship contains experts, many of them outstanding and innovative scholars. Their personal knowledge base exceeds that of experts of any previous era. Yet, most of these subject experts have not created digital works or libraries and thus have restricted their expertise to their own personal practice in authoring and presenting scholarly treatises. Undoubtedly, these scholars know more than most digital librarians about manuscripts. Yet, how much subject knowledge is required to digitize manuscripts?

Future generations will judge the expertise of experts by any remaining documents, rather than by expertise contained in personal knowledge. On this basis, the publishing digital librarian WILL be the expert to future generations, simply because digital documents one day will be the only accessible documents. Do you doubt it? Then remember, please, the television series "Star Trek." In the episode "A Piece of the Action," Captain Kirk asks for information about Chicago mobs of the 20th century. Does the Enterprise librarian pull the ancient volume *Chicago Mobs of the Twenties* off the shelf? Or does the librarian consult the ship's electronically stored copy? You can guess the answer, even if you never saw the show. Someday, *all* books and manuscripts (except for recreational books such as the books you curl up with in bed) that do not reside in museums will be accessed digitally. Those who publish digitally today will be the *de facto* experts of the future.

However, the act of publishing, per se, is not enough. A Web site that does not satisfy a need for information will remain unused. Similarly, a Web site that is difficult to use will remain unused. Mooers (1960, p. 204) has postulated that "An information retrieval system will tend not to be used whenever it is more painful and troublesome for a customer to have information than for him not to have it." The digital librarian need not be an expert in Web design, however, to create usable Web sites. "Participatory design" (PD) is a technique in which the users of a Web site assist in its construction. PD originated in Scandinavia in the 1970s as a way to empower workers by involving them in the design of tools and artifacts (Greebaum & Kyng, 1991; Spinuzzi, 2005). At first appearances, PD sounds like user-centered design, but PD is design *by* users, while user-centered design is design *for* users (Iivari, 2004).

The PD Web site by CPSR (2000) presents a comprehensive introduction to PD, so we present only an outline, here. Traditionally, PD occurs in several stages. During the first "discovery" stage, the digital librarian gains the confidence of the users of a Web site, explores their working practices, and studies their goals, values, and needs. Further context comes from examination of the visual and textual sources used in the users' practice. In the second "evaluative" stage, the participants explore and evaluate the Web site to be designed, focusing on its strengths and weaknesses, and telling of positive experiences with similar sites. The third "prototyping" stage involves "brainstorming" with the users as they suggest ideas,

Figure 7. A museum setting, the National Library of Norway, Oslo. Photo by the first author, August, 2005.

sketch concepts, and envision future use and developments in the field. Finally, the participants evaluate the new design and approve the final version.

The HACI manuscript Web sites were improved through a PD project. Users found the resulting Web sites easier to use and more pleasant to view (Nikolova-Houston, 2005). While we never will eliminate the profession of digital librarian, PD can make digital libraries easier to use. When that ease of use exceeds the ease of use of traditional paper and ink libraries, the digital libraries will become the *de facto* libraries of the future, establishing the digital librarian as the *de facto* authority on manuscripts.

"YOU HAVE NO RIGHT TO REPRODUCE THIS MATERIAL"

Can information be treated as if it were physical property? Wikipedia (2006b) presents a concise history of this debate as it applies to electronic media. Many who *want* information, say "no" (e.g., Barlow, 2004). Many who *have* information, for example, many traditional publishers, say "yes." Digital librarians, as mediators between those who want information and those who have information, must learn and comply with the laws of the countries in which they operate and to negotiate for rights. In the case of the HACI manuscripts, the institution permitted the digitization, viewing digitization as another way to facilitate their twin mandates of preservation and access. The digital librarian faced with a curator making the argument, "you have no right to publish this material," would do well to remind the curator of the underlying mission of libraries, museums, and archives, to disseminate knowledge, not to hoard it.

"WHO CARES ABOUT MEDIEVAL MANUSCRIPTS?"

"Why were the Middle Ages called the Dark Ages?" our daughter challenged us one day. We started to lecture her, and she interrupted impatiently: "No! Because there were so many knights! Do you understand? Because of the (k)nights!" Seriously though, one of the earliest and most important art historians, Giorgio Vassari (1511–1674), viewed the Middle Ages as the Dark Ages (Trachtenberg, 2001). He also labeled Byzantine art as "ugly and clumsy" (Gombrich, 1987). Due to Vassari's lack of understanding of the deeply religious and philosophical symbolism of medieval and Byzantine art, he viewed them only through the narrow lens of form, style, color, and aesthetics. For four centuries, Vassari's view propagated the perception of the East as the poor, ugly, clumsy, and backward margin of the prosperous, powerful, and illuminated West. Apparently, Vassari and his disciples ignored the role that Byzantine and then Slavic manuscripts played in preserving classical Western civilization during the Middle Ages and the role that Byzantine and Slavic manuscripts played in transmitting that knowledge to Renaissance Europe.

Today, as the digital age develops, Vassari's 16th century judgment still affects collection development and the availability of resources in libraries. Slavic resources wither in the margins of library collections while French and English literary genres flourish to occupy entire floors. In 2001, the Web contained no sites with images of Slavic manuscripts (Nikolova-Houston, 2001). Today, it has very few (e.g., Nikolova-Houston 2002, 2003, 2004). Slavic scholars grieve about this "clear gap" in Slavic cultural heritage on the Web (e.g., Dobreva, 2003), citing obsolete data formats and tools, linguistic difficulties, lack of digitized manuscripts, lack of financial support, and copyright issues. Some cite the wide variety of computer hardware and software that prevents standardization (Miltenova, 2002). Regardless of the reason, Slavic manuscripts and materials about Slavic manuscripts do not appear in libraries or on the Web with anything approaching the frequency of Western manuscripts. The effective digital librarian will see such a lack as a challenge and not allow such obstacles, whether they be the legacy of Vassari's prejudice or not, to dictate the future content of the digital world.

"WHAT WILL HAPPEN TO YOUR EFFORTS WHEN THE RESEARCH CLIMATE CHANGES?"

As Heraclitus demonstrated, change is the only constant. Yes, research needs will change. However, electronic texts allow continual redesign, a necessary feature for a field growing in unpredictable directions, such as digital manuscripts. New resources, new online tools and devices, and new software continually emerge. Digital publishers and librarians will find that online sources are much easier to modify than traditional printed material, so once again, digitize and let the future take care of itself.

Figure 8. Manuscript storage at HACI, before facilities restoration and document re-housing. Photo by the first author, summer, 2002.

Similarly, pedagogy and its use of Web-based resources will continue to change. If digital librarians use PD (participatory design) to create and modify online educational resources, they will maintain a position in the academic community simply by serving the needs of those who use the digital libraries. Although many university faculty still do not trust online sources (Nikolova-Houston, 2005), the PD "marketing strategy" of giving customers a role in designing the product convinces users that the online sources they design can be trusted for use in the most rigorous academic teaching and research. By meeting change with change, the digital librarian will continue to fulfil the mission of conjoining the human mind with the documentary record.

CONCLUSION AND RECOMMENDATIONS

Knowledge is out there, stored in the pages of manuscripts locked away in dusty archives. It will remain there, unused, unless you take your digital camera, digitize the images, and post them in a Web-based virtual scriptorium. You may not create the perfect library; you may not have sufficient permissions; your work soon may require reformatting. Yet, whether or not you digitize, these problems will persist. Digitize now, and they may be overcome.

REFERENCES

ALA & SAA (American Library Association & Society of American Archivists). (1994). *ALA-SAA joint statement on access: Guidelines for access to original research materials*. Retrieved August 6, 2010, from http://www.archivists.org/statements/alasaa.asp

ALA (American Library Association). (1995). *Code of ethics of the American Library Association*. Retrieved August 6, 2010, from http://www.ala.org/ala/aboutala/offices/oif/ifgroups/cope/Code%20of%20Ethics%202008.pdf

Barlow, J. P. (1994). The economy of ideas: A framework for patents and copyrights in the digital age. (Everything you know about intellectual property is wrong.). *Wired*, 2(03). Retrieved August 6, 2010, from http://www.wired.com/wired/archive/2.03/economy.ideas_pr.html

CLIR (Council on Library and Information Resources). (2005). *Into the future: On the preservation of knowledge in the electronic age*. Retrieved August 6, 2010, from http://www.americanfilmfoundation.com/order/into_the_future_choose.html

CPARLG (Commission on Preservation and Access and Research Libraries Group, Inc.). (1996, May 1). *Preserving digital information: Report of the task force on archiving of digital information*. Retrieved August 6, 2010, from http://www.clir.org/pubs/reports/pub63watersgarrett.pdf

CPSR (Computer Professionals for Social Responsibility). (2000). *Participatory design*. Retrieved August 6, 2010, from http://cpsr.org/prevsite/program/workplace/PD.html/

Dobreva, M. (2003). *Mediaeval Slavonic written cultural heritage in the E-world: The Bulgarian experience*. Retrieved August 6, 2010, from http://www.ncd.matf.bg.ac.rs/casopis/02/d005/download.pdf

ECPA (European Commission on Preservation and Access). (1997). *Digitization as a means of preservation?* Retrieved August 6, 2010, from http://www.clir.org/pubs/reports/digpres/digpres.html

Gergova, A. (2006). *Knizhovno-dokumentalno nasledstvo (Book-documentary heritage)*. Sofia: Sv. Kliment Ohridski.

Gombrich, E. (1987). The values of the Byzantine tradition: A documentary history of Goethe's response to the Boisserée collection. In G. P. Weisberg (Ed.), *The documented image*. Syracuse, NY: Syracuse University Press. Retrieved August 6, 2010, from http://www.gombrich.co.uk/showdoc.php?id=23

Greebaum, J., & Kyng, M. (1991). *Design at work: Cooperative design of computer systems*. Hillsdale, NJ: Lawrence Erlbaum.

Hazen, D., Horrell, J., & Merrill-Oldham, J. (1998). Selecting research collections for digitization. *Microfilm and Imaging Review*, *27*(3). Retrieved August 6, 2010, from http://www.clir.org/pubs/reports/hazen/pub74.html

Hilendarski, P. (1762, 2000). A Slavo-Bulgarian History. In K. Topalov, B. Hristova, & N. Voutova (Compilers). Sofia, Bulgaria: St. Cyril and St. Methodius National Library.

Iivari, N. (2004). Enculturation of user involvement in software development organizations: An interpretive case study in the product development context. In *Proceedings of the third Nordic conference on human-computer interaction*. New York: ACM Press.

Microsoft. (2006). *Microsoft support lifecycle*. Retrieved April 18, 2010, from http://support.microsoft.com/gp/lifepolicy

Miltenova, A. (2002). The Sofia Corpus of data on Slavic manuscripts. *Slavic and East European Information Resources*, *3*(2/3), 81–86.

Mooers, C. N. (1960). Mooers' law; or, why some retrieval systems are used and others are not. *American Documentation*, *11*(3), 204.

Moussakova, E. (2006). The digitalisation of the special collections in St. Cyril and St. Methodius National Library. 1st Colloquium of Library Information Employees of the V4+ Countries: "Libraries in the

Knowledge Society". Retrieved May 1, 2010, from http://www.svkbb.sk/colloquium/zbornik/data/moussakova.pdf

Mutafchieva, V. (1964). *Da se znae (Let it be known)*. Sofia: Izdatelstvo na Otechestvenia front.

Nikolova-Houston, T. (2001). The Internet and the virtual scriptorium of Slavic medieval manuscripts: Preservation and access. In H. Achleitner & A. Dimchev (Eds.), *Libraries in the age of the Internet*. Sofia, Bulgaria: Union of Librarians and Information Services Officers.

Nikolova-Houston, T. (2002). *Slavic medieval treasures from Bulgaria. "Preservation."* Retrieved August 6, 2008 from http://www.ischool.utexas.edu/~slavman

Nikolova-Houston, T. (2003). *Byzantine medieval hypertexts*. Retrieved August 6, 2008 from http://www.ischool.utexas.edu/~slavman/hypertexts

Nikolova-Houston, T. (2004). *Slavic medieval treasures*. Retrieved August 6, 2008 from http://www.ischool.utexas. edu/~slavman/manuscripts

Nikolova-Houston, T. (2005). Using participatory design to improve websites. *Computers in Libraries, 25*(9), 20–25. Retrieved August 6, 2010, from http://www.infotoday.com/cilmag/oct05/nikolova-houston.shtml

Psohlavec, S. (1998). Digitization of manuscripts in the National Library of the Czech Republic. *Microfilm and Imaging Review, 27*(1), 22.

Shera, J. H. (1970). *Sociological foundations of librarianship*. New York: Asia Publishing House.

Spinuzzi, C. (2005). The methodology of participatory design. *Technical Communication, 52*(2), 163–174.

SSA (Social Security Administration). (2005). *National average wage index*. Retrieved April 18, 2010, from http://www.ssa.gov/OACT/COLA/AWI.html

Trachtenberg, M. (2001). Desedimenting time: Gothic column/paradigm shifter. *Res, 40*, 5–24.

Wikipedia. (2006a). *Zeno's paradoxes*. Retrieved August 6, 2010, from http://en.wikipedia.org/wiki/Zeno's_paradoxes

Wikipedia. (2006b). *Information wants to be free*. Retrieved August 6, 2010, from http://en.wikipedia.org/wiki/Information_wants_to_be_free

Wikipedia. (2006c). *ASCII*. Retrieved April 18, 2010, from http://en.wikipedia.org/wiki/ASCII

Tatiana Nikolova-Houston and Ron Houston
School of Information
University of Texas at Austin, USA

HEATHER JOSEPH

15. SPARC

Creating Innovative Models and Environments for Scholarly Research and Communication

SPARC (the Scholarly Publishing and Academic Resources Coalition) occupies a unique space in the scholarly communications landscape. It was formed in 1997 as an initiative of the Association of Research Libraries, and given an explicit charge: to serve as a catalyst for community action in correcting imbalances in the scholarly publishing system, and to create a more open system of scholarly communication. Its formation was spurred in large part by the long-time trend of spiraling journal subscriptions costs, which have driven the cost of scholarly journals (especially in science, technology, and medicine) to levels that are unsustainable for many libraries. This has had the effect, over time, of inhibiting the scholarly community's ability to *access*, *share*, and *use* information – a situation that slows the advancement of research and scholarship and that is directly at odds with the needs of scholars and the academy.

SPARC places a high premium on collaboration, working with a wide variety of stakeholders to advance its mission. Structurally, SPARC is a membership organization, with its core consisting of an alliance of 221 academic and research libraries in the USA and Canada. These libraries run the gamut – from the large, research-intensive libraries to smaller liberal arts colleges. Over the past few years, SPARC has expanded to include an additional 600 libraries in its counterpart organizations, SPARC Europe and SPARC Japan.

While SPARC was born (at least in part) out of a sense of the library community's frustration with the status quo, its agenda focuses on identifying and advancing opportunities for positive change. It works to identify and develop new models of scholarly communication that utilize digital technology to expand access and use of scholarly research, while helping to reduce financial pressure on the library community. Consequently, SPARC has had a deep interest in advancing the understanding and implementation of open access to scholarly research results – both in the form of primary peer-reviewed literature as well as digital data of all kinds.

One of the greatest challenges that SPARC faces is to actively advance the viability and acceptance of open access models for both publishing and archiving the results of scholarly research, while acknowledging that change will occur differently in various disciplines. SPARC recognizes that, in some areas, the community may be best served (at least in the short term) by affordable subscription-supported publishing solutions. Consequently, SPARC's programs aim at building

R. Rikowski (ed.), Digitisation Perspectives, 245–249.

a broader understanding of opportunities for change in *all* fields, and place an emphasis on identifying areas of common advantage to all stakeholders in the scholarly communications community.

From a programmatic standpoint, SPARC has found it very effective to deploy a pragmatic, three-tiered approach to creating change. Its programs center on identifying and advancing strategic opportunities in three key areas: education, incubation, and advocacy. It is, of course, an ongoing challenge to keep a robust agenda of relevant, related activities in the works for each of these program areas at all times, but doing so (more or less!) successfully is central to SPARC's ability to continue to make progress.

For a better understanding of how SPARC works to advance its agenda, we can look at the three program areas in turn and, along with each one, examine a key current issue that SPARC is grappling with and explore the kind of initiatives that SPARC has deployed in response.

SPARC's first key program area is *Education*. Since its inception, SPARC has created a series of campaigns designed to both illuminate the issues and challenges facing the scholarly communications community, and – just as critically – to outline the opportunities inherent in these challenges to create positive change. These campaigns have spanned topics that range from introducing the community to basic issues of the commercialization of scholarly information and the alarming trend of serials price increases in its 'Create Change' (www.createchange.org) campaign, to the introduction of the concept and potential implementation of Open Access (www.arl.org/sparc/openaccess).

SPARC's most recent educational campaign is an effort geared toward authors. This critical initiative is designed to raise awareness of the fact that the creators of scholarly works (i.e. the authors) can determine the scope of the ultimate distribution and re-use of their articles. SPARC's Author Rights campaign (www.arl.org/sparc/author/) underscores the need for scholars to be aware of their rights as authors and to make informed decisions concerning what rights they choose to sign over to a publisher in exchange for article publication. It raises the idea that copyright transfer need not be an 'all-or-nothing' proposition for an author, but rather is a contract which can and should be negotiated to ensure that the needs of both parties are adequately met.

As with SPARC's other educational campaigns, Author Rights combines brochures and a website to illustrate the issue and provide a starting point for librarians, faculty, and administrators to begin a conversation on the topic with their constituencies. This is an especially important strategy. These tools provide an opportunity for important stakeholders – authors and publishers – to engage in a productive dialogue on the importance of broad dissemination of scholarship and of the value of the scholarly community being allowed to actively use and build upon that scholarship. While operating within and respecting the subscription-access environment, the campaign nonetheless raises key constructs that help illustrate the potential benefits of open access.

The Author Rights campaign also provides supporting tools – including a legal addendum for authors to use in conjunction with standard copyright transfer forms – which expand the applicability and utility of this approach. Author Rights is illustrative of the significant and ongoing challenge that SPARC, as an organization tasked with initiating action, faces – to provide not only materials to deepen the community's understanding of an issue, but also the tools and incentive to take action.

SPARC's second key program area is *Incubation* of new business and publishing models – understanding that it is critical to experiment with new models in order to generate experience and real data to build upon. SPARC has, since its inception, made a practice of 'putting its money where its mouth is' – providing resources, funding and support for projects and initiatives that advance changes benefiting scholarship and academe. One of SPARC's very first initiatives was to create a series of partnership programs to highlight emerging alternatives in the scholarly publishing arena.

The *Alternative* program supports lower-cost, competitive subscription access journals as an alternative for academic disciplines formerly dependent on high-priced journals. The *Leading Edge* program supports ventures that demonstrate open access or otherwise innovative business models. And on a larger scale, the *Scientific Communities* program supports development of non-profit projects that serve the needs of a discrete scientific community by aggregating peer-reviewed research and other content. Perhaps the best-known initiative to arise from this program is BioOne (www.bioone.org), a successful collaboration between libraries and publishers that works to keep not-for-profit publishers independent and viable by providing a mechanism for digitization and electronic dissemination of journal content.

BioOne is a notable illustration of SPARC's strategy for several key reasons. First, it recognizes the important role that not-for-profit publishers play in the community, and actively supports them by providing a previously unavailable option for expanding their reach and relevance in the digital world. It also provides a very important demonstration of a novel way to fund an alternative venture. To launch BioOne, SPARC successfully raised more than $1 million in what amounted to community venture capital investments in the form of pre-subscription commitments from SPARC member libraries. This money was then used to create the technical platform, recruit and digitize content, and staff the project.

Because this capital was explicitly viewed as an investment by both parties, the libraries who provided the start-up money experienced a significant return – they received access to a new collection of previously undigitized, high-quality biological science journals and, over a five-year period, were repaid their initial investment in the form of yearly discounts to the list subscription price of the BioOne database.

BioOne also contributed directly to another underlying aim of SPARC; as it developed and adapted its novel business model, it took pains to transparently share data about which elements of its business plan worked successfully – and which elements did not. This willingness to share data is a substantial benefit to the community, informing other ventures facing similar development challenges.

In SPARC's third key area, *Advocacy*, SPARC maintains a robust program to encourage policy changes that enhance opportunities for advancement of scholarly communications. SPARC's early advocacy efforts took place mainly at the local institutional level and centered on raising awareness of scholarly communications issues within the library community. However, as librarians became increasingly well versed in the challenges facing the community, opportunities emerged to advocate for change on a much larger scale. During the past several years, SPARC has greatly expanded its advocacy program to encourage the development of local, national and international policies that explicitly recognize that dissemination is an essential, inseparable component of the scholarly process.

Currently, SPARC's advocacy program is focused on policies aimed at a specific subset of research results – those that are produced as a direct result of federal funding. SPARC began actively advocating for 'Public Access' polices – policies that encourage timely, free access to the results of research conducted using public funds – through its support of a proposed policy announced in 2003 by the National Institutes of Health (NIH) (http://publicaccess.nih.gov/).

The goals of this proposed policy are expansion of access to the results of NIH-funded research, the anticipated subsequent resulting acceleration of the scientific process as well as discovery and innovation, and the establishment of a permanent, freely available archive of these results. All of these goals are directly aligned with SPARC's vision. At the time of the NIH announcement, SPARC began an active campaign to raise awareness among its members of the potential benefits of such a policy.

As the discussion and debate over this proposed policy intensified, SPARC's public access advocacy activities also expanded. To this end, SPARC helped establish the Alliance for Taxpayer Access (ATA), which brings together the library community with patient advocacy organizations, consumer groups, public interest groups, universities, students and other interested organizations which support the goal of public access to federally funded research results.

In the three years following the initial introduction of the NIH policy, SPARC has expanded its focus to supporting a number of legislative and policy proposals promoting the adoption of government-wide public access policies, including the Federal Research Public Access Act, the Canadian Institutes for Health Research public access policy, the Research Councils UK public access policies, and several others.

These advocacy activities have raised the profile of issues of concern to SPARC members and the larger library community. The advocacy program has also created a deep political interest in exploring alternatives to the status quo where, just a few short years ago, none existed.

In looking to the future, a major challenge for SPARC is to remain sufficiently agile so the organization can continue to identify emerging trends and new strategic opportunities. For example, more informal modes and methods of communicating scholarly results are now emerging. The integration of digital technology into nearly every aspect of the daily workflow of scholars and researchers has begun to produce new channels of communication that do not fit neatly into the category of 'journal' or 'pre-print' or even 'email communication'. These new mechanisms include blogs and wikis that spring up organically around a topic or an experiment and collaborative annotations on a web page. These advances are the natural result of scholars using digital technology in ways that they independently determine best serve their immediate needs and the needs of their community.

The new mechanisms are wildly diverse, but they share common traits. They spring up quickly, are extremely flexible, and lend themselves to open and easy collaboration. Perhaps most notably, they can be maddeningly ephemeral. There are already signs that such characteristics are straining the boundaries of the academic community's collective traditional approach to dealing with scholarly communication.

As these new forms of scholarly communication appear (and disappear) over increasingly short cycles of time, they will present challenges to the community to decide how they are used, how they are evaluated, how they are valued, how they are supported and how they are preserved. In short, they require the scholarly community to re-evaluate everything we have learned and reapply it to new forms of communications – time and time again.

Heather Joseph
Executive Director of the Scholarly Publishing and Academic Resources Coalition
Washington, DC, USA

YEHUDA KALAY

16. IMPACTS OF NEW MEDIA ON SCHOLARLY PUBLISHING

INTRODUCTION

This chapter summarizes a few key results of a workshop, held in the University of California Berkeley in June 2006, organized by the Center for New Media and supported by Elsevier, the leading publisher of scholarly journals. The workshop focused on the following questions: How will scientific publishing be affected by New Media? How will the new means of production, dissemination, and consumption of information impact scientific publishing? How will they affect the social, cultural, legal, and economic modalities of its practice? How will they affect the practitioners and the institutions that rely on it? How will they affect society at large? The chapter discusses the results of the workshop in terms of how New Media affect personal information behavior, research group behaviour, and issues affecting scholarly communication generally.

SCHOLARLY PUBLISHING

Over the past decade we have been witnessing a technological revolution affecting most intellectual activities involving the production, dissemination, and consumption of information. Known as New Media, this revolution encompasses a number of converging technologies for the creation, representation, and communication of information, based on the paradigm of computation. Like other technological revolutions, New Media were born from a confluence of technological innovations that resonated with perceived needs in representation and communication of information. New Media proceeded swiftly to become the primary, if not exclusive, media for writing and reading scholarly papers, communicating with fellow researchers worldwide, searching for information, and a myriad of related activities. The impacts of New Media on scholarly publishing are manifested through the World Wide Web, blogs, wikis, open source, podcasts, RSS feeds, and many other applications. They directly impact dissemination practices, revenue models, and archiving methods, and – indirectly – tenure and promotion procedures in academic institutions. More broadly, they impact the nature and quality of information itself. It is of no surprise, therefore, that the impacts of New Media have become the subject of study in many disciplines. Hence, a critical assessment of the technical, professional, social, and ethical implications of New Media on scholarly publishing is urgently needed.

Historical precedents have taught us that the effects of technological revolutions are never limited to one domain alone.[1] They always bring about social, cultural, economic, political, and legal changes as well. Moreover, the impacts of a

R. Rikowski (ed.), Digitisation Perspectives, 251–263.

technological revolution are difficult, if not impossible, to assess while the revolution has yet to run its course: it often takes a perspective of time to understand and assess its impacts. Consider, for example, the second industrial revolution, which started after World War II. It was based on the inventions of the semiconductor, the integrated circuit, and the computer.[2] They transformed mechanical industries into information-based industries, where knowledge is the new capital, rather than the physical assets of the past. Not only has this revolution led to the development of new types of products, services, and modes of production, but it has also changed organizational structures, including the roles played by employers, employees, customers, and suppliers. In this so-called 'New Economy' the value of products no longer depends on the amount of material resources necessary to produce them, but rather on the amount of knowledge required to design them. One of the largest current industries – the software industry – requires no raw materials and produces no tangible goods. Information itself has become the product.[3] Moreover, Henry Ford's celebrated 'mass production' process has been transformed into a process of 'mass customization', where the consumers, with the help of manufacturers, can customize, to a smaller or greater extent, the products they purchase. This relatively new mode of production is already on its way to be replaced with 'mass personalization', where the production of one-of-a-kind, highly customized products, combining the effort of multiple manufacturers, is technically and economically feasible.[4]

New Media has thus swiftly begun to create new applications, while shaking up existing methods and practices. This trend, shared by all technological revolutions, is causing an 'identity crisis' in many of the practices affected by it, precipitated by the uncertain status of the New Media in relation to established, known media, and their social, cultural, legal, and economic practices. Not only is their place in society still ill defined, but their ultimate meaning and impact are not well understood.

Consider, for example, the World Wide Web, which epitomizes (but is not the only example of) the New Media revolution. It was first conceived as a means of sharing documents among scientists, hence such terms as 'web page' and 'web browser'. But it quickly proved to be no poor cousin of paper documents: it could combine different types of media, make them interactive, and afford collaboration like no other medium could in the past. As such, it has the power to shape and affect old media and their practices in unforeseen ways. Netscape Communications Corp. (founded in 1994, disbanded in 2003) was the first to develop methods that enabled two-way communication, such as getting information from consumers. It led to a rapid diffusion and growth in the use of the Web by companies, for electronic commercial transactions; and to its use by ordinary people for swapping data, music, pictures, videos, or simply personal information through file-sharing, wikis, and blogs.

One of the obvious areas that appears to be posed for change due to New Media is scientific publishing. But just how New Media will affect it is not yet clear.

Scientific publishing in the Western world began in the fifteenth century, as a result of a number of social forces and technological advances, including the invention of the movable type printing press in Europe and the development and improvement of postal services. These technological advances resonated with the changing attitudes in the scholarly community, which was shifting its focus at that time from the writings of the Ancients to new discoveries based on observation and experimentation. Knowledge was becoming empirically based, and scholars were actively sharing their new experimental results by way of personal correspondence.

That approach suffered from disruptions and interpersonal disputes (consider, for example, Newton and Leibniz's mutual accusations of plagiarism[5]). In some situations, secrecy was maintained, using coded scripts to ensure that priority in discovery could be established and competitors were kept away from each other's developments. The need to regularize these correspondences was recognized in 1660 by the Royal Society in London, and in 1665 by the French Academy of Sciences. The French were the first to publish a scientific journal, the Journal des Sçavans, which was followed five years later by the British Philosophical Transactions of the Royal Society, or Phil. Trans. (still published today).

Since then, scientific journals have become the standard means for both disseminating scientific knowledge and for building scientific careers: top journals draw the highest quality submissions, which reinforces their reputations, which in turn enhances the status of the scientists who publish therein, creating a positive feedback loop. Their content, validated through a peer-review process, becomes part of society's cultural capital – the expert-validated repository of trustworthy knowledge. As a form of 'capital', this repository has value. It is subject to protection, sale, as well as theft and falsification. It can be lost, and it can be exchanged for monetary and other rewards (e.g. tenure, promotion, fame, etc.).

The advent of the Internet, along with discontent over the slow pace and high cost of accessing this capital, prompted attempts to replace paper publishing with electronic forms of dissemination, along with different economic models for sustaining the process (e.g. charging the authors who benefit from being published, rather than the readers). This form of publishing also makes the information eminently searchable, linkable, and allows for immediate feedback by the readers, wiki-style. But it also has the risk of devaluing the information, if it is self-published without the benefit of peer review. The traditional peer-review institutions – the scientific journals – may lose their monopoly on publishing the information, and along with it their revenue models that sustain the review and publishing process. The attendant loss of archiving may render older publication inaccessible, and the loss of tracking bibliographic citations may hamper tenure and promotion cases.

There are two ways to assess these positive/negative changes: one is to view them as *forcing a square peg into a round hole* – implying that the use of the new technology is misdirected, or at least poorly fits the processes that have traditionally comprised scholarly publishing. The second way describes them as a state of transformation, where the new technology is viewed through the obsolete and 'backward' lens of the practice it is changing, much like the automobile was viewed as a *horseless carriage* in the early days of the twentieth century. It implies a lack of appreciation for the emerging potentials of technology to change the task to which it is applied.

The 'square peg in a round hole' view explains the problems arising from adapting a new technology to existing practices. In the case of scholarly publishing, these include validation, copyright issues, revenue models, acceptance, archiving, and more. Underlying this view is the assumption that the dysfunction can be resolved by 'rounding the peg' so it better fits the current practice.

The 'horseless carriage' view of technology is much more complicated, and therefore more difficult to assess. It views the new technology as a means to alter the practice itself. Using the term 'horseless carriage' to describe the automobile showed a failure to recognize that the practice of travel had been dramatically changed. It failed to anticipate the emergence of freeways, suburbs, drive-throughs, shopping malls, and a myriad of other associated social, cultural, environmental, economic, legal, and other changes.

New Media is the modern-day 'horseless carriage' of scholarly publishing: it holds the potential to change scholarly publishing in much more fundamental ways than simply substituting electronic paper for physical copy. It has the potential to change not only how knowledge is communicated, but also what is knowledge, how it is produced, and how it is used.

Technologies such as the Internet, cell phones, computer games, iPods, camera phones, RSS feeds, podcasts, wikis, and blogs have already altered the traditional modes of publishing afforded by traditional media models: they allow practically anyone to publish his/her work to a worldwide audience. They are altering the unidirectional flow of information, effectively blurring the difference between authors and readers. The consequent convergence of knowledge production and consumption, coupled with the introduction of new forms of information and the means to access them, create an unprecedented potential for new individual and social practices in knowledge production and consumption – the engine that fuels scientific research.

How will the new means of production, dissemination, and consumption of information impact scientific publishing? How will they affect the social, cultural, legal, and economic modalities of its practice? How will they affect the practitioners and the institutions that rely on them? How will they affect society at large?

The complexity of these questions precludes finding answers in any one academic discipline alone, or in any one segment of society involved in scientific scholarship. Rather, the answers – in as much as they exist at this early stage of the lifecycle of this technological revolution – can only be found by interrogating as many stakeholders as possible.

The Center for New Media at the University of California Berkeley has been explicitly formed for such purposes: to make it possible to convene experts, representing different disciplines, for the purpose of investigating this and related issues from many different points of view. This approach, of course, does not guarantee answers: it only provides a mechanism to search for them.

To address the issue of the impacts of New Media on scientific publishing, the Center for New Media at UC Berkeley teamed up with Elsevier – one of the premier scientific publishers in the world – to convene a series of workshops, titled 'Information Dynamics Workshops', as a forum that will help to reveal the opportunities and implications for scholarly publishing made possible by New Media.

The first Information Dynamics Workshop was held in June 2006, convening 30 scholars representing 15 different disciplines. Three topics were chosen for investigation:

1. *Personal information behaviour*: the impact of new media on the personal information practices of academics (gathering, filtering, customizing, personalizing, and disseminating information);
2. *Research group behaviour*: the impact of New Media on research and scholarly communication within a research group in specific disciplines;
3. *Issues affecting scholarly communication generally*: how the new forms of publication, digital archiving, and other technologies are perceived across all researchers and media.

It is impossible, of course, to condense six hours of intense deliberations into one short account. In the following, a (necessarily) condensed summary of the deliberations of this panel will attempt to shed light on some of the key issues identified under each one of the three main themes.

PERSONAL INFORMATION BEHAVIOUR

It was noted earlier that scientific publishing forms the backbone of the knowledge production and verification process in general, and the tenure and promotion system in academic institutions in particular. Top journals build their reputation by drawing quality submissions, and in turn lend credence to the information itself and status to the scientists who published it. This positive feedback loop is built on the perceived mutual benefit to the authors and to the publishers. Authors contribute content and participate in the requisite peer-review process, free of charge. Publishers add value to the process by collecting, managing, printing, disseminating, archiving, and tracking the content, recouping their investment by charging their readership subscription fees.

This scientific publishing model (with certain variations) has been subject to much criticism of late, especially on the part of the academic institutions who must pay for both content creation (the salaries of the contributing scholars), and for content acquisition, in the form of escalating journal subscription fees. Propositions to change the status quo have, so far, been inadequate, for lack of a suitable alternative to the current scholarly publishing model.

At first glance, the advent of New Media, especially the Internet, appears to offer a potentially viable alternative to the current model: it allows scholars to self-publish their work, on personal or institutional websites, and readers to access that body of knowledge, at no (or a small) charge, thus bypassing the publishers. But while economically viable, this approach ignores many of the social and cultural aspects of scholarly publishing, in particular knowledge accreditation, knowledge tracking and archiving, and their role in building scientific societies and personal careers. As such, it demonstrates both the 'square peg' and the 'horseless carriage' faces of introducing New Media into an established practice: the technology can facilitate some aspects of the practice, but ignores, perhaps even harms, its other less obvious aspects.

Addressing this issue raises, first and foremost, the questions of what exactly is scholarly publishing, and what is its role in society. Is it a *distribution technology*, which transfers knowledge from an author to a reader? Or is it a social *communication process*, which collaboratively is responsible for the creation, validation, and archiving of the cultural capital known as 'knowledge'? These questions are similar to the misconceptions that accompanied the invention of the railroads late in the seventeenth century, and the automobile early in the twentieth century: both perceived themselves as means of transportation, responsible for carrying people and goods from point A to point B. They ignored their larger impact on shrinking both temporal and spatial distances, thereby connecting places that, until then, were too far apart to have any meaningful relationship,[6] introducing along the way such novel concepts as standardized time, suburbs, freeways, shopping malls, and drive-throughs, as well as some undesired consequences like pollution, increased energy consumption, and drive-by-shooting. Similarly, scholarly publishing is not merely about distributing papers: it is as much about the social creation and guardianship of knowledge as it is about its distribution. In the current model, the publishers play the role of gatekeepers, who organize and manage, through the peer review process, the social institutions that endow knowledge with credibility, and transform it into the cultural capital it has become.

The introduction of New Media into this practice, by substituting one form of distribution (paper) with another (digital), cannot, in and of itself, adequately deal with all aspects of scholarly publishing. To fully appreciate the impact of New Media on personal information behavior, therefore, requires rethinking the knowledge validation process as well, without which it will lose its credibility, therefore its value.

Several attempts are under way to try to address this aspect of scientific publishing. They include Wikipedia,[7] Creative Commons,[8] and the Open Source Initiative,[9] among others. These efforts substitute the centralized editorial curatorship with a widely distributed model, relying on the social awareness of the authors and their critics instead of a self-selected body of scholars to review, verify, and if necessary correct the information. They invest in authenticating the individual agency of the scholar, instead of the institutional agency of the editorial board. The result is a democratically constituted collection of information, much of it lacking the proper sources that the scientific community considers necessary for an article to be considered 'high quality'.

The absence of an accredited 'seal of approval' prompted the emergence of other measures of valuation. Some rely on the number of links (much like Google's search engine prioritizes the web pages it displays on the screen). Some rely on popularity, much like Amazon.com ranks books according to the number of copies they sell. Some rely on a kind of 'voting' system, much like sellers of goods on e-Bay are qualified for their reliability.

These (and other) measures provide viable alternatives to the centralized editorial model, in terms of associating value with the information. But they raise questions regarding the difference between popularity and credibility: is a paper that has been downloaded by hundreds of readers more 'valuable' than one that sports a seal of approval given to it by a small, hand-picked, review panel? Should the opinion of a few 'experts' count more than the perceived social value accorded to the work by its users?

Interestingly, these attempts at 'squaring the peg' (i.e. providing a means to overcome the loss of credibility due to self-publishing) ignore the social aspects of New Media itself: its ability to track not only the data itself, but also the metadata. By cross-linking articles and other scholarly works with the biographical data of their creators, New Media can provide a personalized authentication mechanism, instead of the institutional one. Such metadata is already the basis of Amazon.com's *recommender* system, as well as Yahoo!'s various social networking applications.

Can these capabilities of New Media be harnessed to substitute for the loss of organized gate keeping, a function now provided by scientific publishers? Or will it lead to the dystopian future envisioned for newspapers and television newscasts, whose diminishing audience is forcing them to devolve into superficial tabloids rather than practise cutting edge journalism?[10] Can individuals assume the gate-keeping authority? If so, will that be a matter of popularity, or substance? To paraphrase NBC Nightly News anchor Brian Williams, New Media has the potential to democratize information (by giving everyone the power to disseminate their work), but at what cost to knowledge?[11]

RESEARCH GROUP BEHAVIOUR

New Media impinge on another important role of scientific journals: providing an organized means for finding relevant information. Bound journal volumes, or journal websites (e.g. Science Direct[12]), provide a managed, organized clustering and indexing mechanism for scholarly publications, based on their content. Commercial search engines like Google, on the other hand, use non-contextual means to determine which pages should be retrieved in response to a query, such as key words. Hence, they may miss scholarly articles which are contextually related to the query, but do not match exactly the specified search criteria. If the user who formulates the query is unaware of related but differently phrased search strings, relevant information may not be retrieved. Put differently, a search engine returns the *sought* information, not necessary the *appropriate* information.

By clustering related information, traditional journals, therefore, fulfil a social networking function, in addition to accrediting and archiving the information. They provide a mediated forum where much, if not all the information pertaining to some subject matter can be found, even when the user who seeks the information is not aware of it.

Yet, while providing a managed forum to find relevant information, journals do a poor job of facilitating the use of that information, especially as far as discussion among the users of the information is concerned. Traditional publishing takes much too long, relative to the shelf-life of much of the published information, and responses to it by knowledgeable readers take even longer. That is why conferences are increasingly substituting for journal publications: while most afford a somewhat less rigorous peer-review process than edited journals (due to the need to maintain a certain level of attendance and economic viability), they afford an immediate response and unmediated intellectual exchange related to the publication.

Online publishing, in the form of blogs and wikis, provides an affordance similar to conferences, except that they never stop. They allow for a dialogue between authors and readers: an instantaneous collaboration that has the power to build a 'society' of scholars, complete with debates, sidebars, and cliques. It affords individuals the ability to be connected to their research community on a daily basis, not through publications and conferences and other forms of infrequent interaction, but through blogs, wikis, email, Instant Messenger, and voice messaging.

Digital media affords another, indirect way of communal feedback, through annotating and adding comments to published works. Like physical books, which are often marked up by their readers (to the chagrin of librarians), this annotation creates a kind of communal trace of people's engagement with the subject. It may be distracting or enlightening, depending on one's point of view (and who made the mark in the first place). It allows communal research to progress much faster and more pervasively than older models of feedback have allowed (e.g. letters to the editor, or direct but private communication with the author).

Scholarly communities gain a different dimension online: they may involve people who are active in some research, those who are peripherally active, and casual visitors, depending on the frequency they visit a website – not unlike a (physical) conference, but with much-expanded semantics. A tagged site keeps a visible trace of the participants who visited it. They can be contacted directly, if desired, to expand on the information they left at the site, creating new research communities who might otherwise have never formed, aligning people as they haven't had been able to align before. Physical journals provide a similar function, of course, but in a time-shifted manner: it can take up to two years for a paper to be published in a journal, which in some technical fields corresponds to a five generations gap.

As a result, the pace of invention itself is changing. It is far removed from the 360 years old model, when the scholar might have been working in his own lab, sending letters back and forth – which would take weeks – using a low bandwidth and slow rate of communication.

The ability to cross-reference and cross-link the information makes it eminently searchable. It allows information to be consumed in a manner that is different from how it was produced, or disseminated. A researcher might begin reading a paper, but jump directly to the full text of a cited reference, which may prove more relevant to her or him than the originating paper. At its best, such tagging creates a tangible record of a subject's (or object's) social history. It can help one better understand the value of the subject, much like the reviews provided by Amazon.com help readers evaluate a book far beyond the publisher's description of the work. At its worst, however, chasing the reference chain may come at the expense of the authors whose work is used as a jumping off point to the work of others. This may make more productive use of a researcher's time, at the expense of his or her work: the results of the research, when published, may be used by other scholars as a jumping off point to others.

In a New *York Times* article, Kevin Kelly[13] describes the 'library of the future', where each word in each book is 'cross-linked, clustered, cited, extracted, indexed, analysed, annotated, remixed, reassembled …', creating one universal 'very, very, very large single text: the world's only book'.[14] But such a massively interconnected text may also lose its coherent, discrete identity, in favour of a meandering 'choose your own adventure' through knowledge, becoming a textual cacophony instead of a beautiful symphony.

ISSUES AFFECTING SCHOLARLY COMMUNICATION GENERALLY

Journals and books limit the kinds of scholarship they can communicate to a few types of media (text and static images). Films add another dimension, at the expense of the ability to change and modify the content on the basis of reviewers' comments. But scholarly production is not limited to these few forms of representation afforded by media: art, music, performances, and other forms of interactive scholarship are as valuable as text and images. Attempts to fit them into the traditional modality of scholarship are, perhaps, the epitome of trying to fit a square peg in a round hole.

Elsevier and other publishers, as well as many researchers, have attempted to do just that, only to discover that, in the case of scholarly publishing, the media is, indeed, the message.[15] For example, learning history from a book is fundamentally different from physically visiting an ancient site, which itself is (or would have been) a different experience than visiting the site when it was still in use, rather than in a state of ruin. Digital media make such interactive, performative experience possible. Historically inspired video games are a case in point. But they introduce a myriad of issues which 360 years of scholarly publishing has never had to deal with: issues of narrative structure, authenticity, user interfaces, and bandwidth are a few of them. It is a very different kind of authorship to describe an ancient civilization in words than to depict it in an interactive, participatory manner.[16] And, of course, as the forms of scholarly communication are rapidly transforming, so are the forms of archiving this new media production.

Rather than emulating older technologies and practices of publishing the same material, the Internet's multimedia capabilities could be used to communicate the information itself, which the paper describes. The Internet's interactivity could be used to allow the viewer to participate in and experience the scientific experiments themselves, witness and participate in cultural rituals, or attend some historically significant event. Such participatory engagement might affect the production of knowledge and its communication. Scientific publishing might become more like choreographing a play, or directing a movie, than reporting on one.

The difficulty of creating non-text content (e.g. video), and the difficulty of editing it compared to text, are monumental, and scholars trained in biology or computer science are not equipped to negotiate them, much like movie directors and composers are not trained in scientific scholarship. And even if they are, they are often limited to producing continuous, linear narratives of video and other types of media, rather than the non-linear, interactive, immersive media afforded by the Internet and by video games.

Bringing them together, for the purpose of producing the kind of scholarship afforded by New Media, requires nothing less than rethinking the educational systems that are now available to students. Few courses exist that teach students how to communicate via the interactive, immersive medium of video games, and those that exist are considered to be outside the 'core' studies of most academic disciplines, relegated to 'entertainment' or 'media arts' rather than 'scholarship'. Developing such courses of study is a new academic discipline in and of itself, drawing upon and combining topics currently taught in such diverse disciplines as education, philosophy, art, technology, social sciences, drama, journalism, architecture, and many more.

CONCLUSION

According to Kelly,[17] from the Sumerian clay tablets till now humans have 'published' at least 32 million books, 750 million articles and essays, 25 million songs, 500 million images, 500,000 movies, 3 million videos, TV shows and short films and 100 billion public web pages. Until very recently, all but the web pages were stored in libraries and archives all over the world. If fully digitized, this material would fill 50 petabytes of storage – the size of a small library, at current compression rates.[18] Tomorrow, it will fit in an iPod. This astonishing feat of New Media pales, however, compared to its much more significant accomplishment: providing access to all this information from anywhere on the planet (and, presumably, beyond).

More significant yet, *access* itself has been redefined: since anyone with access to the Web can add to this information at will, the boundaries between authors and readers have been blurred, along with established models of knowledge validation and valuation.[19] The traditional authentication institutions – the scientific journals – are losing their monopoly on publishing the information. New methods that purport to replace them are much more efficient, but far too mechanistic, relying on quantitative, rather than qualitative measures: they confuse popularity with quality, seeing value when none exists, moving from a scholarship that is structured by authority to one that is structured by participation.

Still, the abilities to digitize and access information represent only the 'square peg' part of the New Media revolution affecting scholarly publishing. Rather, it is New Media's ability to cross-link, cluster, extract, index, remix, and reassemble information that represents its 'horseless carriage' aspect: the ability to create 'new' information, which has not even been touched by human hand, let alone human intellect.[20] How will this massive new authorship affect humanity's common knowledge base?

As scholarly publishing is migrating online, the Web is becoming the new arena for scholarly discourse. It is changing personal information behavior, group information behaviour, even the nature of what was considered scholarly information itself. Along the way it is also changing corporate behavior, forcing centuries-old scholarly publishers like Elsevier to adopt new publishing models, while looking for new economic models that can sustain them.

The ability to mix and match all forms of digitized information – text, images, sound, and video – in one publication is changing the nature of scholarly production. But simply embedding video clips in 'traditional' publications is not enough. New media changes the *content* of the publication and the way it is authored, how it is distributed, and how it is consumed from a linear narrative into a non-linear one, which can be explored interactively and experientially. So far few scholars have mastered such production abilities, in part because the educational systems that acculturate them into their respective professions have yet to learn how to do so. As they learn how to teach the new modes of production, educational institutions will also have to learn to evaluate such scholarly production as part of their tenure and promotion procedures.

Without such system-wide changes, authors will fall back on the security of the traditional publishing format, which is both easier and more acceptable, relinquishing the new affordances of the media to non-scholarly applications, such as massively multiplayer online games (MMOGs).

Can the Web, and other New Media technologies, transform scholarly publishing from the old model to the new one? Clearly, they can, and they have already begun to do so. However, like all technological revolutions at the time of their first introduction into an existing practice, they have been following the 'square peg' metaphor: emulating old methods and practices, with the attendant dysfunctions due to the misalignment between the affordances of the new technologies and the old practices. They have, for example, raised questions about knowledge creation and authentication, the role old publishing institutions (journals, books) can play under the new system, how the new information will be archived so it can be accessed in the future, copyright issues, and many more.

A more productive way of examining the impacts of New Media on scholarly publishing will come by viewing the transformation through the 'horseless carriage' point of view: not merely as a technological revolution, but as a wholesale social reorganization, affecting the very core of human knowledge, the modes of its production, validation, and dissemination, and shifting the locus of knowledge production from institutions to individuals, complete with relocation of authority over knowledge authentication and valuation. Along the way, it threatens the very notion of knowledge itself, the belief system – and the institutions that support it – which have been carefully built up over the past four centuries.

We are witnessing one of those moments in history when a fundamental technological revolution is bringing about major changes in social organization, communication, and knowledge production. As such, this is not a matter of technology: it is a matter of reconfiguring a system of knowledge production that has configured itself in the last 360 years to work in a particular way. Clearly, a single workshop cannot capture the many dimensions of this revolution. It can only address some key issues, often raising more questions than it can answer. We plan to continue this discussion through subsequent workshops, termed 'Information Dynamic Workshops', which will provide not only added opportunities to examine the evolving practices of scholarly publishing, but also offer an opportunity to examine our assumptions and predictions over time.

ACKNOWLEDGEMENTS

The ideas expressed in this chapter are the author's alone, but they are based on the opinions and discussion of the participants in the *First Information Dynamics Workshop*, held at the University of California, Berkeley, in June 2006. Participants included: Ruzena Bajcsy, Anthony Burke, Alissa Centivany, Y.S. Chi, Irene Chien, Marc Davis, Ahmed El Antably, Bauni Hamid, Gary Handman, Diane Harley, Karen Hunter, Yehuda Kalay, Thomas Kalil, Cecilia Kim, Gokce Kinayoglu, Juddson King, Catherine Koshland, Kathy Kulhmann, Selina Lam, Thomas Leonard, Peter Lyman, Jasna Markovac, Christy McCarthy, Gregory Niemeyer, Kris Paulsen, Irene Perciali, Richard Rinehart, Pamela Samuelson, AnnaLee Saxenian, and Therese Tierney. The Workshop was a joint venture between the Berkeley Center for New Media, and Elsevier.

NOTES

1 See, for example, J.M. Diamond (1999) *Guns, Germs, and Steel: the fates of human societies*. New York: W.W. Norton.

2 R. Kurzweil (1990) The Second Industrial Revolution, in *The Age of Intelligent Machines*. Cambridge, MA: MIT Press.

3 M. Castells (1996) *The Rise of the Network Society*, vol. 1. Oxford: Blackwell.

4 See, for example, M.M. Tseng & F.T. Piller (2005) *The Customer Centric Enterprise: advances in mass customization and personalization*. New York: Springer.

5 See, for example: C. Boyer (1968) *A History of Mathematics* (2nd edn). New York: John Wiley & Sons.

6 R. Solnit (2004) *River of Shadows: Eadweard Muybridge and the technological Wild West*. New York: Penguin.

7 Wikipedia is a web-based, free-content encyclopedia project, written collaboratively by volunteers, allowing most articles to be changed by almost anyone with access to the Web, raising questions of reliability and accuracy, as well as concern for uneven quality and inconsistency, systemic bias, and preference for consensus or popularity over credentials.

8 The Creative Commons is a non-profit organization devoted to expanding the range of legally available creative works for others to build upon and share, which current copyright laws might otherwise prohibit. Using a mechanism known as Creative Commons Licenses, the Creative Commons enables copyright holders to grant some of their rights to the public while retaining others through a variety of licensing and contract schemes. Their intent is to counter the effects of what Creative Commons considers to be an increasingly restrictive distribution culture, dominated by traditional content owners in order to maintain and strengthen their monopolies on cultural products such as scientific papers, music, and movies.

9 The Open Source Initiative, founded in February 1998, is an organization dedicated to promoting open source software (computer software whose source code is available under a copyright license that permits users to study, change, and improve the software, and to redistribute it in modified or unmodified form).

10 See: http://www.robinsloan.com/epic/ – a fictional account which describes the demise of the *New York Times* in the year 2014 due to the rise of 'GoogleZone' – the personalized publishing product of the merger between Google and Amazon.

11 In his op-ed in the December 2006 issue of *Times*, Williams writes that 'we've made the media more democratic [by letting everyone post their opinion online], but at what cost to our democracy?'

12 Science Direct is Elsevier's database of 2000 full text journals, in a wide range of subject areas, including sciences, health, business and management and social sciences. For most journals, coverage is from volume 1, no. 1.

[13] K. Kelly (2006) 'Scan This Book!' *New York Times*, May 14.

[14] The Internet Archive, founded in 1996, is a non-profit organization that aims to build an Internet library, with the purpose of offering cross-linked, permanent access for researchers, historians, and scholars to historical collections that exist in digital format. Located in the Presidio, in San Francisco, it includes texts, audio, moving images, and software as well as archived web pages in its collection.

[15] To paraphrase Marshall McLuhan's famous edict.

[16] See, for example, Y.E. Kalay & P. Grabowicz (2006) Oakland Blues: virtual preservation of Seventh Street's 1950s Jazz Scene, *3DVisA Bulletin*, Issue 1, September, http://www.viznet.ac.uk/3dvisa/

[17] Kelly, 2006.

[18] By comparison, the famed third century BC *Library of Alexandria* in Egypt, once the largest library in the world, is estimated to have stored at its peak 400,000 to 700,000 parchment scrolls (Wikipedia).

[19] Consider, for example, the enormous popularity – and banality – of MySpace and YouTube, attesting to the pent-up desire to 'publish'.

[20] Raj Reddy (1995) The Universal Library: intelligent agents and information on demand, *Lecture Notes in Computer Science*, 1082, 27–34.

REFERENCES

Kuhn, T. S. (1962). *The structure of scientific revolutions*. Chicago: University of Chicago Press.

Resnick, M. (1995). New paradigms for computing, new paradigms for thinking. In A. DiSessa, C. Hoyles, & R. Noss (Eds.), *Computer & exploratory learning* (pp. 31–34). Berlin: Springer-Verlag.

Yehuda E. Kalay
Faculty of Architecture and Town Planning
Israel Institute of Technology

PART VI: FUTURISTIC DEVELOPMENTS OF DIGITISATION

TOM PETERS

17. MEETING AND SERVING USERS IN THEIR NEW WORK (AND PLAY) SPACES

OVERVIEW

The goal of this chapter is to explore – at a certain level of abstraction – the public services components of digital and virtual libraries, with an emphasis on the experiences, needs, and expectations of the end-users, especially how the proliferation of personal, portable computing appliances for information, communication, and entertainment has changed how people interact with and think about these fundamental human activities.

A distinction is being made between digital and virtual libraries. Digital libraries have been in existence for decades. They usually began with a focus on digitized content, often tied to a collection at some particular library. The earliest digital libraries were more like self-serve and find-as-find-can repositories for digital content. Associated metadata services and public services were slower to develop. The metadata and service components of digital libraries often emerged after a critical mass of digitized content had been achieved. Digital libraries currently are primarily web-based. Although sound, images, and moving images have made some inroads on web-based information transfer, most digital libraries remain intensely alphanumeric in character, and the user's interaction with the content primarily is two-dimensional.

Virtual libraries are newer than digital libraries. Virtual libraries typically exist in three-dimensional virtual worlds, also known as multi-user virtual environments, or MUVEs. The Alliance Second Life Library 2.0 project (in the popular world called Second Life) is an example of a virtual library. Virtual libraries often come into existence via public services, such as reference services, orientation tours, workshops, book discussion groups, and lecture series. Collections, and metadata about those collections, have been slower to develop. Early development of virtual libraries has seen a triumph of the two E's – events and exhibits – over traditional collection development. As virtual libraries evolve and develop, they may never place heavy emphasis on collections. The virtual libraries of the future may be more about events, exhibits, and immersive three-dimensional information experiences than about amassing large collections of discrete digital objects.

Some metadata services work and preservation strategy development for virtual libraries is already being done. A group of volunteer cataloging librarians interested in and active in Second Life has been meeting in-world to discuss metadata needs for the types of information created, contained, and used in virtual worlds in general and virtual libraries in particular. In August 2007 the Library of Congress funded a project spearheaded by the University of Illinois at Urbana-Champaign (UIUC) to undertake some metadata and preservation work related to virtual worlds,

R. Rikowski (ed.), Digitisation Perspectives, 267–273.

interactive fiction, and older video games. Partners with UIUC on this project include Stanford University, the University of Maryland, Rochester Institute of Technology, and Linden Lab, the creator of the Second Life virtual world. This initiative is part of the Preserving Creative America program, which in turn is part of the National Digital Information Infrastructure and Preservation Program (NDIIPP).[1]

With the proliferation of digital and virtual libraries, it seems safe to conclude that the 'spaces' where people live, learn, work, and play continue to expand. Each of these new spaces requires some sort of computing device to access them. Each space can be understood as an ecosystem where learning, entertainment, and information experiences in general are created, shared, and enhanced.

When most people think of computers, they think either of the traditional desktop models, or perhaps of a laptop computer. The real future in computing devices, however, may be in the ultra portable line. PDAs (personal digital assistants) were the harbingers of that trend. Mobile phone technology has continued to improve and has subsumed many of the functions formerly relegated to PDAs. Ultra portable music players, commonly called MP3 players, have been phenomenally successful portable computing appliances. In the second quarter of 2007 alone, Apple reported sales of nearly 10 million units of its line of iPod portable MP3 players.[2]

A general trend in media is that wherever sound extends, video soon follows (radio broadcasts were followed by television broadcasts, for example, and music videos added a visual layer to soundtracks). This seems to suggest that portable video appliances may soon supplant portable music devices as a popular consumer information/communication/entertainment appliance. Portable gaming devices may be the sleeper category here. There are lots of gamers in the general population, and their love for and use of games does not seem to wane as they grow older. There seems to be no end in sight to the types and brands of both personal, portable, handheld information/communication/entertainment devices, including mobile phones, portable audio players, portable video appliances, portable gaming devices, and a rich array of computing devices designed for pre-teen use that are almost too rich and varied to attempt to tag or classify.

Because the computational bar for accessing *virtual* libraries is still quite high, most library work being done in virtual worlds is being done on desktop and laptop computers. As the computational bar for accessing *digital* libraries already is much lower, the demand for being able to access digital library resources and services on personal, portable information/communication/entertainment devices already is high.

Let us boldly venture onto a thin, new branch and proclaim that in the future virtual libraries will be more about services and community building than they will be about collections per se. This does not mean that collections will lose all value and usefulness. Rather, in the dawning era when we are awash in digital information, information objects, and rich information environments, it will be the services that support the exploration, appreciation, and use of information that will distinguish excellent information organizations from humdrum ones.

Although the Library 2.0 movement continues to be much discussed, debated, and challenged, one general trend already discernable is that the 'users' of new social networks and information systems are much more actively engaged in using the resource and in adding value to it. Librarianship has always struggled with settling on an acceptable name for people who use libraries. They have been called patrons, clients, customers, and just plain users. These users are becoming co-creators of shared information ecosystems on the web and in virtual worlds.

GENERAL CHARACTERISTICS OF THE NEW INFORMATION WORKSPACES

Many of the new information workspaces are highly personalized. The designers and manufacturers of portable gadgets encourage their owners to personalize the look and content contained on them. Of course, the appearance and behavior of avatars in virtual worlds such as Second Life are highly personalized, but so too is one's perspective on that environment. To take a mundane example, in a typical formal teaching environment the instructor stands in front of the class of students. In virtual worlds such as Second Life, the instructor-avatar can stand in front of the assembled student-avatars, but the instructor's perspective can actually be situated at the back of the class, or hovering above the entire assembly, or wherever the instructor wishes to have a vantage point. The distinctive perspectives of teachers and students begin to blur.

The portability of current and foreseeable future devices is amazing and will have a profound effect on how students and instructors think about classrooms, libraries, and other places for work, research, and study. In the days when the real world had no viable competition for our task-oriented attention, learning in a classroom or lab situation generally involved a highly structured curriculum and syllabus, as well as a very formal learning space. Now that we all have been to 'Paris' and seen and experienced how rich and interactive formal learning environments can be in virtual worlds, traditional real-world classrooms often seem like passive sensory-deprivation chambers. There have been some attempts to break down the structure and formality of formal higher education in the real world, but those attempts pale in comparison to the prevailing structures, expectations, and mores of higher education in virtual worlds.

Libraries in the real world also have highly structured layouts and methods for organizing and categorizing information and information objects. Actual use of real-world libraries by students, researchers, and scholars, however, tended to be relatively unstructured, open-ended, and driven by personal need and preference. If a library user wishes to find one good book on a topic of interest, and then browse the stacks nearby looking for other good books on that topic, he or she is welcome to pursue that course. If, on the other hand, a library user wishes to use the online catalog and other online information resources from a remote location (i.e. outside the physical confines of the library – visiting the library only when absolutely necessary to retrieve needed material), he or she is welcome to pursue that course. As an information space, a real-world library is highly structured, but how a library is actually used is not dictated and prescribed in the same way that formal learning in real-world classroom environments often is.

In the real-world library, the impact and effects of usage of the structured information space on that space are minimized. If a user pulls a book off the shelf and leaves it on a nearby table, eventually some library staff member comes along and returns the book to its proper location. If a user writes marginalia in a book and is caught doing it, she or he is fined. The point is that in real-world libraries, usage does not modify the underlying structure of the information very much, and the system does not really encourage such modification.

As digital and virtual libraries emerged and continue to develop, several of these real-world assumptions about how classrooms, labs, libraries, and other learning spaces should work are being challenged and changed. Digital and virtual libraries have the potential to become much more participatory than their real-world counterparts. Users already are encouraged to tag information objects with words and phrases that complement the more formal thesaurus terms and subject headings that are applied by librarians after consulting various lists. Users also are encouraged to write reviews of works, create links between one work and another, etc. Initiatives such as 'LibraryThing' and the 'My Library' features of Google Book Search seem to point toward a future where use of the bibliosphere is much more communal and participatory, where users and usage add significant value and complexity to the overall bibliosphere.[3]

The largest, most far-reaching potential change that virtual libraries offer to the use of information is the prospect of transforming human interaction with information from a predominantly two-dimensional model to a predominantly three-dimensional model. Especially in three-dimensional virtual environments, information interaction is becoming an immersive experience, not a flat, two-dimensional interaction with discrete information objects. Initially, the three-dimensionality of virtual libraries seems to exist primarily to provide a comforting familiarity to the people who visit these strange new worlds. Eventually, however, the three-dimensionality may become the most innovative, exciting, and worthwhile aspect of a new type of information experience.

In a blog post to the ALA *TechSource* blog, Peters stated that the primary promise of librarianship in Second Life and other virtual worlds is an immersive, three-dimensional information experience:

> Until three-dimensional virtual worlds came into existence, most human interaction with information was two-dimensional. Nearly all interaction with printed information is two-dimensional. Screens of various types (the canvas of a painting, a motion-picture screen, a TV screen, and a computer screen) can give the viewer a sense of depth, but rarely have we utilized that virtual sense of depth to create immersive three-dimensional information experiences. Second Life and virtual worlds in general may inaugurate a long revolution whereby human beings increasingly come to interact with information in immersive three-dimensional spaces. The molecules and works of art in Second Life you can fly around and through now are just the harbingers of things to come. Recreations of entire civilizations in an historical period, such as what Caledon does for the Victorian era and what Renaissance Island does for Elizabethan England, are fast becoming massively multi-disciplinary areas

> where avatars are interacting with an entire environment, not just a series of discrete digital objects.[4]

In the new learning environment, students are not placed in classrooms so that they experience few distractions as teachers try to instruct and students try to learn. This is the dawning age of multi-tasking, even 'multi-worlding', in which an individual is actively engaged in two or more worlds at the same time. The lines between work, learning, and entertainment are blurring. Students, professors, researchers, and others are using these new information spaces in virtual worlds and on personal, portable information/communication/entertainment appliances to pursue all their interests, from the sublime to the ridiculous. This situation is not new.

The idea that learning and edification cannot be inherently enjoyable is fairly recent, probably within the past three hundred years. Before then, many of the leading minds of the day agreed that 'to teach and delight' were the simultaneous, co-equal goals of even the loftiest literature and other cultural events and products.

CHALLENGES

When it comes to creating public services for digital libraries and virtual libraries, a fundamental question quickly surfaces: What types of services are needed? Brewster Kahle of the Internet Archive and the Open Content Alliance has stated, 'Let's build services in the digital world analogous to the services we perform in the analog world'.[5] That is a common human reaction when confronting a new technology that offers new affordances. The potential problems with merely replicating in digital and virtual realms the library public services that we all know and love from the real, analog world are numerous. First, many library public services are labor-intensive and thus expensive to deliver and difficult to scale up. Students at colleges and universities often want the library and its service points to be open day and night, every day, but the costs of doing so are prohibitive. The largely volunteer reference service on Info Island in the Alliance Information Archipelago in Second Life has been quite successful, in part because it has replicated the real-world model of providing a reference service. The avatars in Second Life who use the reference service really like the fact that they are interacting with a 'real' avatar, not just some question-answering bot. But this model is as difficult to fund, staff, sustain, and scale up in a virtual world as it is in the real world. The fact that it currently is a largely volunteer service may be masking the price that eventually will need to be paid somehow, unless some other reward structure – other than wages and salaries – can be devised and accepted by all participants as sufficient cause to contribute their time and talent to such a service.

On July 23, 2007 at the ALA *TechSource* 'Gaming, Learning, and Libraries Symposium' in Chicago, John Kirriemuir gave a talk about the adoption of Second Life as a teaching, research, and service venue for higher and further education in the United Kingdom. During the spring and early summer of 2007 he conducted a survey of higher and further educational activities involving UK academics, departments, colleges, universities, and related organizations. His final report, published by the Eduserv Foundation, noted:

> ...that a growing number of UK academic institutions, departments and groups are at different stages of [Second Life] development ... over 40 UK Universities and Colleges ... have a building, land or island on the grid, many appearing in the last few weeks and not yet open for public visiting while they are being developed.[6]

During an interview the author conducted with Kirriemuir on July 22, 2007, he indicated that the 2007/08 academic year will be the crucial test for higher education activities in Second Life involving UK institutions.

Higher education is not yet ready to bet the farm on virtual worlds as learning and teaching environments, but they do see some advantages in virtual worlds over other currently available distance education environments. The next few years will be the crucial test of the ability of virtual worlds to deliver in a sustaining, satisfying way the types of higher education and higher learning that are needed.

CONCLUSION

To bring robust, sustainable, usable, and useful public services to digital libraries and virtual libraries, we need to begin actively planning and experimenting for the day fast approaching when most information workers, including students and teachers, will be connected to the Internet – or whatever succeeds the Internet – most of the time, unless they consciously choose to be living offline. Both individually and collectively, they will be using a wide variety of personal, portable information/communication/entertainment devices. We may be facing a future in which no single portable device or even device type comes to dominate the marketplace. Libraries will be expected to deliver services to them all.

Most students, teachers, researchers, and knowledge workers also will be active users of several virtual worlds, including, of course, the real world. They will want to share information and insights across these multiple worlds. Learning and information seeking may become significantly more participatory. Rather than teach to the test, most teachers – and students – will be expected to add value to the gestalt learning experience. In most online and virtual communities of the future, the residents will add more value to the information system than will the librarians. As Josh Knauer noted during a talk about library innovation he gave at the Alliance Library System Innovation Day: 'If *they* build it, they will come'.[7] In online and virtual information environments, the best way a library can serve a community is by helping the community to serve itself.

What we need is some gumption, a willingness to fail early and often, and an inherent commitment to be attuned to the needs of the people we serve. Brewster Kahle has summarized the situation, the need, and the possibility both succinctly and aptly:

> It doesn't require grants. It does require some creativity, a lot of slack to try it out, and the realization that there is a lot at stake. We have to recognize that it's not only possible but it is our responsibility to bring digital services to the world.[8]

NOTES

1 Peters, T. (2007). Library of Congress to preserve games, virtual worlds. *Smart Libraries Newsletter, 27*(9), 6.

2 Crum, R. (2007, July 26). Apple profit surges on Mac and iPod sales. *MarketWatch*. Retrieved October 8, 2007, from http://www.marketwatch.com/news/story/apple-stock-surges-macipod/story.aspx?guid=F79C14C2-8B7C-47B7-AAE0-5AD7FD8E1D11

3 See, for example, http://www.librarything.com and http://books.google.com/googlebooks/mylibrary/. [Accessed April 18 2010].

4 Peters, T. (2007). My three die. A post made to the ALA. *TechSource* Blog on 11 August 2007. Retrieved October 8, 2007, from http://www.techsource.ala.org/blog/2007/08/my-three-die.html.

5 Albanese, A. R. (2007). Scan this book! In the race to digitize the public domain, is the future of the library at stake? An interview with the open content alliance's Brewster Kahle, *Library Journal, 132*(13), 32–35. Retrieved October 8, 2007, from http://www.libraryjournal.com/article/CA6466634.html.

6 Kirriemuir, J. (2007, July 16). *A July 2007 'Snapshot' of UK higher and further education developments in second life*. Eduserv Foundation, 20. Retrieved October 8, 2007, from http://www.eduserv.org.uk/upload/foundation/sl/uksnapshot072007/final.pdf.

7 Knauer, J. (2007, October 5). Innovation, social networking, and the information commons. A presentation at Alliance Library System Innovation Day.

8 Albanese. (2007). *op. cit.*

Tom Peters
TAP Information Services
Missouri, USA

LORI BELL, MARY-CAROL LINDBLOOM, TOM PETERS
AND KITTY POPE

18. VIRTUAL LIBRARIES AND EDUCATION IN VIRTUAL WORLDS

Twenty-First Century Library Services

The Gartner Group predicts that by 2011, 80% of those who use the Internet and Fortune 500 companies will be involved in virtual worlds. This is estimated to be 50–60 million people (Gartner Group Press Release, 2007). From April 2006 to July 2007, the virtual world of Second Life increased from 180,000 accounts to over 8 million, growing an average of 30% a month. The ultimate virtual world may or may not be Second Life; however, with the rapidly increasing use of programs like Second Life, World of Warcraft, and other worlds, virtual worlds are here to stay in one form or another. We think libraries need to be there too. Many individuals involved in virtual worlds may not be traditional library users. By putting ourselves where the users are, there is a great opportunity to increase use of the bricks and mortar library and to promote library services and materials. In this chapter we will discuss the virtual world of Second Life, what libraries are doing in Second Life, the successes and challenges of the project, partnerships with education, and why libraries are relevant in these worlds.

WHAT IS SECOND LIFE?

Second Life is a virtual world entirely built and owned by its residents, or users. New participants discover a vast digital continent, teeming with people, entertainment, and opportunities. After exploring, individuals might decide to buy land, purchase a home, or start a business. Users can buy a small piece of land on the mainland starting at 512 square meters or a private island which is equal to 65,000 square meters. In Second Life, residents are surrounded by the creations of fellow residents. Because residents retain the rights to their digital creations, they can buy, sell, and trade with other residents. Everything you can imagine (and some you cannot) can be found in Second Life. There are museums, nineteenth-century worlds where residents dress in period clothing and live in Victorian homes, immersive learning environments such as an Egyptian tomb, and Star Trek futuristic realms. The Alliance Second Life Library has built a Renaissance Island where users can participate in historical role-play, participate in costume, or just observe. Central Missouri State University received a grant to recreate Harlem of the 1920s complete with public library, cabarets, and other buildings and activities of the era.

Participants build an ‘avatar’, or alternate persona, to actively participate in the creation of media instead of the more passive modes of watching television or

R. Rikowski (ed.), Digitisation Perspectives, 275–285.

viewing a static web page. An avatar is their digital persona. A participant may create an avatar that resembles them in real life, or they can change the color of their hair, eyes, skin, or even be a different sex. Although some might view virtual environments as new and unproven, in fact online communities often provide new environments for mutual support and learning, in some ways embodying the evolving roles of libraries within their 'real-life' communities. Second Life goes beyond recreational gaming.

LIBRARIES IN SECOND LIFE

As is evident to academic librarians and documented in library literature, student use of academic libraries is decreasing with the advent of the Internet and online resources (Akeroyd, 2001; Luther, 2001; and others). These institutions are having to rethink the nature of collections, services, and the library as place. As college campuses, hospitals, large companies like Dell and IBM, and non-profit institutions investigate and establish their presence in virtual worlds such as Second Life and Active Worlds (Appalachian State University and Eastern University in Pennsylvania are two prime examples), the Alliance Library System decided it was important to look at this for its 259 multitype member libraries.

In April 2006, Alliance started a library in a small rented building in Second Life to investigate library services in the virtual world. Immediately, Alliance was approached by a number of other partners to provide library services and to work with organizations to develop customized resources for specific educational programs. As of July 2007, the Second Life Library, now called the Info Archipelago, has nearly 40 islands associated with it. At the core are the library islands (Info International, Infotainment, Info Island I, Cybrary City, Cybrary City 2, ALA Arts/Info Island, Renaissance Island, HealthInfo Island, Eduislands, 1, 2, 3 and 4) surrounded by partners including non-profit agencies, educational institutions, such as San Jose State University, associations such as the International Society for Technology in Education, and government agencies including the Centers for Disease Control (CDC).

As academic, non-profit, and medical organizations, as well as schools, expand their presence in Second Life, libraries, to remain viable, must do the same. Libraries should be prepared to assist virtual residents in finding and evaluating online information, giving them independence and confidence in using the Internet and providing access to high-quality information resources. As in the real world, it is important that the library reach out to these communities, and provide a location where residents can visit, learn, experience, and communicate.

WHAT RESIDENTS WANT FROM LIBRARIES

One fascinating aspect of librarianship in Second Life is that many of the fundamental questions of our profession force themselves to the forefront of the discussion. The first fundamental question we addressed was whether avatars in Second Life even wanted or needed library services. With an average of approximately 5000 avatars visiting the Information Archipelago each day, we have concluded that the answer to that question is a resounding yes.

With that fundamental question answered, a host of other fundamental questions crowd into the foreground. How many libraries are needed? If more than one, how should they be divided and distinguished from one another? Currently, across the Information Archipelago and throughout Second Life the libraries tend to be distinguished along traditional lines. Some colleges and universities have decided to create their own libraries. The Cullom-Davis Library at Bradley University is an example. There are also 'branch' libraries focused on consumer health information and a medical library for information professionals as well. We also have 'thematic' branches, such as the Victorian-themed Caledon branch library.

Are library buildings needed? Because there is no weather in Second Life (unless it is avatar-induced), inclement weather is rare. Many avatars prefer to meet and work out of doors. Nevertheless, library buildings do seem to have some use. Architecture serves different purposes in Second Life than it does in real life, and over time the form and function of the two types of architecture probably will diverge. In Second Life a library building need not bear the weight load of a collection, so the architecture can be much more open.

SIMILAR BUT DIFFERENT LIBRARY SERVICES

Surprisingly, residents *do* want books. Libraries make books available in several formats, along with a few newspapers and magazines. Not many publishers have yet entered Second Life, although the number is increasing. Penguin Books just opened in Second Life and more publishers are setting up a presence. Publishers can display works residents may view with a link to information about the book; they can recreate the book so that it can be read in Second Life; or they can have a display with a link to their website where the actual sales occur. Bantam-Dell just entered Second Life – they have a virtual Barnes and Noble like presence and in addition to displaying their works, they have authors like Dean Koontz as speakers and poetry nights.

Residents also want access to information resources. One building on Info Island I is a traditional academic library with links to Web resources on different topics on each floor. Because we do not have a large budget, if students or residents need to use a commercial database, they are usually referred to their local, off-world, library. We also have book discussions on Info Island, Caledon, our branch nineteenth-century library, and Mystery Manor.

People want reference services, which can be face to face, virtual, or by instant message. Many of the buildings and shops in Second Life are unstaffed. However, we have noticed that our visitors really like a friendly face and greeting, even if the person is not an information professional and cannot answer a question. When visitors 'teleport' to Info Island, they land at a welcome center with a calendar of events, information for new residents, and (for 40 hours per week) a reference librarian. Currently we have approximately 20 librarians volunteering two hours per week, mostly in the evening when it is busiest. We offer face-to-face (really avatar-to-avatar) reference and instant messaging services. In spring 2007 we had a trial of Question Point, but it was not heavily used. In fall 2006, approximately 30% of questions were about Second Life, 30% were about Info Island, and 30% were traditional library informational type questions. In spring 2007, reference staff were handling from 700 to over 1000 queries per month at the virtual world reference desk. This work is extremely important as we learn more about the virtual user and their needs.

We get tremendous attendance at our programs and events, which vary from well-known science fiction authors to Syracuse University's David Lankes on virtual networks to teen tech week, a re-enactment of Henry VIII, live piano performances, art shows, Jeff Bezos from Amazon, and a giant ant talking about his culture. We are also offering more continuing education for librarians. A program about MySpace attracted over 50 librarians. Programs and events are planned by different groups, such as those interested in science fiction, mysteries, and genealogy.

LEARNING AT THE LIBRARY

Visitors also love exhibits and immersive environments, which is the new learning environment where the library and museum intersect. We are looking at new ways of providing access to resources, digital collections, and new ways of presenting the information through audio and immersive environments. For example, the nineteenth-century house of Bradley University has exhibits, pictures, and slide shows about Lydia Bradley, the founder of the university. The furniture and surroundings are period. We had an exhibit about Marie Antoinette in a room called the Throne Room with period furniture, a throne, a three-dimensional effect to replicate the Hall of Mirrors in Versailles, books about Marie, and paintings of the people in her life. Marie will soon give a tour and talk about her life. Video can also be streamed in and residents can create movies/videos called machinima. There are a number of art shows in which artists share sculptures, paintings, and even photography.

People also enjoy the safety and international flavor of the archipelago. The Info Island community provides a unique opportunity for innovative folks to meet and work together – people who, in any other environment, would never get the opportunity to gather, work, socialize, and collaborate. Since collaboration is one thing that librarians do very well, it is not surprising that we have adapted to Info Island so quickly and made such amazing strides in such a very short period of time. Info Island staff are friendly and willing to assist. The many interesting things to say and do bring regular repeat visits.

THE WIKINOMICS APPLICATION TO SECOND LIFE

Wikinomics, published in 2007 and written by Don Tapscott, makes an important point which can be applied to the Alliance Second Life Library and to other collaborative efforts by non-profit organizations, educators and others in Second Life. No one company or library can keep up with all of the new developments in innovation and technology. To keep up, businesses and libraries must work together and with other organizations to remain innovative and viable. With all of the new social networking tools and the rapid growth of information, collaboration is the key to success.

This is true of library success and survival in a virtual world. As in collaborative virtual reference services, no one library, no matter how big or how many staff, has the staff or the resources to provide virtual reference services 24/7; therefore, libraries work collaboratively to provide this service. Collaboration provides more coverage, more staff, more expertise, and improved services. Although libraries are beginning to set up their own presences in Second Life, they will have to continue to work together to provide comprehensive services.

WHAT LIBRARIES ARE DOING

There are over 50 libraries with a presence in Second Life. Some of them are setting up a small building with a presence to promote their digital collections and services; others are working with their college campuses where their libraries will be located. These are some examples of what a few are doing.

Bradley University

The Cullom-Davis Library at Bradley University in Peoria, Illinois has set up a replica of the real-life library and a Lydia Moss Bradley House, a tribute to their founder. Inside the library, they have links to library resources, a slide show of the library and the campus, and contact information for library staff. The Bradley House features displays of artwork by students, a slide show of the Presidents of Bradley, a horology collection (the study of the science and art of timekeeping, which Bradley taught at one time), slide shows and videos about Lydia Bradley, a meeting room, and other information about Bradley. In fall 2007, all five colleges at Bradley set up a presence on their campus in Second Life. Homecoming activities including a homecoming dance and a tour of the Second Life campus were held.

San Jose State University

San Jose State University Graduate School of Library and Information Science, with 1800 students, set up an island in Second Life in the Info Archipelago, to offer credit courses to their graduate students. They are the first library school to offer for-credit courses in Second Life. Because most of their students are distance learners, SJSU is using Second Life to enhance their distance learning program.

University of Illinois Graduate School of Library and Information Science

The University of Illinois Graduate School of Library and Information Science is offering 'Introduction to Virtual World Librarianship' and 'Intermediate Virtual World Librarianship'. These non-credit courses are six weeks in length and meet for two hours a week. The first five courses, available for up to 20 students in each course, filled up quickly.

CHALLENGES

The major challenge for Second Life Library currently is staffing, funding, and sustainability. A remarkable number of talented volunteers from around the world have contributed their talents and expertise in different ways, from collection development to reference and exhibit building. We are still not able to have a librarian on duty 24/7. As with many volunteer-run organizations, there is some burnout. Other things, such as real life and real jobs, take precedence over a volunteer job in a virtual world. In general, volunteer librarian-avatars respond very positively to the creative freedom they experience in Second Life.

There is a steep and long learning curve in Second Life. One has to set aside a great deal of time to learn how to move and participate. Not all bosses think Second Life is work; some remain unconvinced. A fairly new computer with high graphics capabilities is needed, as is a broadband connection. This creates a digital divide, but whenever new technologies are introduced, some people will have the resources to participate, while others will not. Although some libraries want to wait until a divide is gone or not so wide before offering a service, they can take advantage of being early adopters so they are ready as the gap lessens.

Another challenge is going to be determining what services virtual world residents want. Currently we find that exhibits and events are the most popular library services used by residents. As virtual worlds mature, will this remain the same? As more universities use Second Life as a distance learning platform, how will this impact the need for library services?

JOB SKILLS FOR VIRTUAL WORLD LIBRARIANS

Some traditional librarian skills pertain to job skills for Second Life libraries. Working in a virtual library opens up more flexible schedules and encourages working from home. Some information professionals do not have the self-discipline or interest to work from home, but many do. Reference is similar, in that whether librarians are in the virtual or the real world, they must be able to multitask well, with patrons or avatars, in person, on live chat, or through instant messaging. In the real world, librarians also have to answer phone calls. A sense of humor is required, as is the ability to be ready for anything. Outlandish behavior seems to happen with greater frequency in Second Life than in the real world.

Librarians must communicate effectively online, since in Second Life there is only text chat, although beta testing of voice communication in Second Life has begun. Some virtual worlds have audio but the librarian still does not experience the visual cues they get when talking to someone in person. A librarian working in a virtual world must be comfortable using and troubleshooting technology. Unless they have a working computer and are comfortable using it, they will not enjoy virtual world work. The virtual librarian must be ready to face constant change and learning new skills.

Librarians need to be able to help patrons troubleshoot technology and be patient, especially in these early days of library service in virtual worlds. The librarian also needs to know something about the virtual world they are working because as in the real world, patrons will want to know about the community and how to locate goods and services. The majority of the informational requests received at the reference desk are like libraries in real life – questions about the environment. Where is the bathroom, where are the computers, what hours are you open?

BENEFITS

The collaboration of librarians and others around the world has been unbelievable and phenomenal. This type of project could not be done by one library, with the existing demands of a bricks and mortar library and the web services. Yet, we believe that libraries do need a presence in virtual spaces where more and more people are gathering. We have had some authors and presenters we would never have had the opportunity to hear, because of travel expenses and time constraints, other than in Second Life. Being in a virtual world keeps libraries on the cutting edge and ensures their survival. A referral to the local library for a non-user may help increase usage in the bricks and mortar library.

Second Life is not for everyone. There have been numerous debates and opinions, negative and positive, about this project and whether or not librarians should be in Second Life at all. Time will tell. One fruit the project will bear is information which will help libraries should this be a future direction education and others move into. More and more library services are being offered virtually or through the Web. To keep up with this, librarians need to do their best to keep up their technology and learning skills to remain viable and make the library an interactive, effective and innovative institution.

EDUCATION IN SECOND LIFE

Although different figures are bandied about concerning the number of academic institutions in Second Life, there are at least 150 academic institutions in Second Life, and many more instructors from other institutions working on their own without institutional support. Educators are looking at Second Life as a new distance learning platform on its own or in conjunction with the open source learning management system called Moodle. Blackboard has also expressed interest in integrating Second Life in its distance learning product. There are more than 3700 educators who subscribe to and participate in the SLED Second Life Education listserv. They are working together and with librarians to create dynamic, interactive learning experiences for students in Second Life. In addition to hearing the professor and reading the assigned text, students can experience an era, live in the era, and meet people from that era. The libraries in Second Life are working with educators on one such immersive environment to improve the learning and the library experience.

RENAISSANCE ISLAND AND THE VILLAGE OF READING PRIMLEY

In February 2007, Alliance Library System received the donation of an island to create an immersive Renaissance education area and library. The goal of the project was for librarians to partner educators to create an Elizabethan area where students, instructors, and other Second Life residents could experience and live a life like in Tudor times. Renaissance Island's Parish of Reading Primley features shops, cottages, a large manor house called Lagswell, a bulwark, galleon, gardens, a market square, a church, tavern, town green, a resident musician, poet, and the Globe Theatre. We probably have some explaining to do as to why there is a Globe Theatre in our parish – one of these days the truth will be known. As with many Tudor towns, there has been a problem with sheep.

The parish was constructed along the river Thames, a very long time ago, in pre-Roman Britain. There was a Roman presence, however, which can still be seen in some of the old roads. The river serves many purposes for the thriving community, both practical and recreational. In February, some of the more adventurous residents may even be found ice skating!

The parish reflects the growing peace and prosperity of the Tudor period – after all, the five Tudor monarchs – Henry VII, Henry VIII, Edward VI, Mary, and Elizabeth – died in their own beds. That there was relative peace is also evidenced in the manor house and gardens, as well as in the growing number of merchants and tradesmen, whose shops line the market square. Visitors and students will note how tightly the shops are packed together, and that often the shop owners live above their place of business. The types of shops one might find in the parish include a bakery, which provides the most pleasant of aromas on the entire island – outside of the kitchen garden, of course; cloth and clothing shops, and printing. Our parish is also fortunate to have a resident musician specializing in recorder music, and a poet.

The market square also boasts a market cross, hundreds of years old – they say 500 – which granted the village permission to conduct weekly markets. Monks used to preach from there on market day, but since the introduction of the new religion, no one has done that for awhile. The square also sports a livestock pen and platform for auctions.

The village streets are primarily dirt, except for those paved Roman ones. The parish is fortunate to have streets that are in such good shape – most villages are challenged by much more mud and manure than in Reading Primley. The men of the parish spend a certain number of days each year on road maintenance, and unlike in some communities, in Reading Primley they do wonderful work.

Adjoining the town and its shops are cottages, many of which are arranged around a green. The Parish of Reading Primley has made a conscious effort to keep from being overrun by sheep, as has happened elsewhere. It is beneficial, though, to have some sheep grazing on the green, as this space is used for such community gatherings as meetings, archery and fencing practice, and bowls. The green includes a well. If you look closely, you may see coins in it. If you make a wish, then toss in the coin and the coin lands face up, your wish will be granted; if not, you might wish to try again.

The parish also includes a church, which survived the big change. Churches generally lacked pews, but services were mercifully short, though by the end of Elizabethan times they had grown in length to the point that seating had to be added.

On the other side of the church lies the manor house, known as Lagswell Hall. The house is based upon a number of real-world structures including Haddon Hall, Stokesay Castle, and Penshurst Place. The manor was constructed by master builder Aldo Stern and contains an excellent library, chapel, numerous fireplaces, and Long Hall. Visitors may obtain a note card to learn more about the history and construction of the Manor. Lagswell Hall also hosts Her Majesty during the Queen's Progresses through this section of Her country.

One of the two featured gardens of the parish is at Lagswell Hall: Minerva's Knot Garden. Named to honor one of the island's esteemed gardeners rather than the Roman goddess, it is reflective of the knot gardens that appeared in the middle of the fifteenth century in Tudor England. Such gardens were formal in design – some very complicated – containing borders of compact, clipped hedges. Such gardens reflected the period of relative peace and stability that followed the Reformation. Knot gardens also demonstrated the owners' prosperity and education. Indeed, houses were no longer built as fortresses, but included windows. Knot gardens and other landscaping were positioned where they could be viewed from the house's windows or from mounts, which were small, human-engineered hills. The Tudors followed Italian influence in creating their gardens, mirroring the alignment of the house and creating a harmony of line and proportion. Sundials and statues were once more used as garden ornaments, as in Roman times.

The Globe Theatre is one of the showcase buildings on Renaissance Island. The theatre has been authentically created by an experienced Second Life builder, Charlene Trudeau. She consulted with resident Shakespearean scholar, Dolgorusky Umarov, whose specialty includes the Globe Theatre. Talks, meetings, readings, dances, and plays are some of the events that can be held there.

The Parish of Reading Primley is also fortunate to be guarded from any threats of invasion by the 'trayned men at arms' associated with the blockhouse, which many of us refer to as the 'bulwark'. Our bulwark is typical of the small, riverside fortifications that existed in Elizabethan times. As part of the island's defense, we are in possession of our very first galleon!

RENAISSANCE ISLAND AND EDUCATION

Renaissance Island is an interesting mix of Tudor England enthusiasts, educators, and students. The island offers an immersive learning and teaching environment. Some of the citizens speak in the dialect of the day and are attired in period clothing. There is help available for those wishing to learn the language of the day; there are also library resources available on a variety of pertinent topics. Additional resources are embedded in the actual buildings and some of the parish objects. There are several educators affiliated with the island who are exploring ways to best use Renaissance Island to enhance learning experiences for their students. At least some colleges and universities are suggesting or requiring their faculty to explore ways of incorporating new technologies into their teaching methods and pedagogy. For faculty teaching the literature or history of this period, Renaissance Island could help meet such instructional objectives.

OPPORTUNITIES FOR STUDENTS

There are many ways for instructors and students to use Renaissance Island. Minimally, it is a great place for a class to visit for an immersive experience. They (through the instructor's avatar) could walk around the Globe, wander down a parish street, visit the gardens, bulwark, and manor house, etc.

The island is very much a work in progress. Authenticity is encouraged and sought, but we have characterized it as a 'journey to authenticity'. The island provides an opportunity for educators to offer their students an exercise in critical thinking. What is out of place? Challenge your students to find them. For example, at one time we had a bale of hay on the island. Of course, the process of baling had not yet been developed, so it was deleted.

At one point, the day after the opening of the Globe, a Tudor scholar happened to stop in the manor house only to discover, much to his dismay, a set of waltz dance balls. The balls had been placed there for the dance that accompanied the opening and were not normally there. Second Life residents love to dance, and so as part of the opening we wanted to offer some dancing. We tried to stay away from hip-hop and other extremely contemporary dances, but included some waltzes, jigs, slow dances, etc. A journey to authenticity, indeed! At this time, a friend of the parish is scripting some period dances, including the pavane, galliard, and branle.

Beyond a chance to walk on Tudor streets, enter a period church, tavern, manor house, the Globe, there are opportunities for greater student involvement. The library could always house additional resources. If students wrote excellent papers on such topics as religion in Tudor England, burial practices, food and beverages, women, etc. it would all be welcome. Second Life offers a multimedia experience.

Students could also research a notable figure of the day and portray that person for an hour-long program. If they have had a research project, they could present a program on their topic for Second Life residents. Students could do an exhibition. They could set up a period shop. If they are already in Second Life and have developed scripting or building skills, they could do something utilizing those skills, in conjunction with our building team. The residents and managers of Renaissance Island want to see the parish used to promote education and are amenable to most ideas.

It is critically important that the students, like all residents of Second Life, be familiar with Linden Lab's community standards of behavior as well as those operating on Renaissance Island, and conduct themselves accordingly. It is also recommended that instructors provide an overview of Second Life for their students, and spend time examining the best practices in education materials that are available through http://www.secondlife.com. Educators are encouraged to join the Second Life Educators (SLED) mailing list. Depending on the type of student project, it may be necessary to obtain clearance through your institution's review board.

Renaissance Island's virtual community of the parish of Reading Primley can serve as the basis for educators, students, residents, and visitors to engage in a quality learning, role-playing, and immersive environment to explore the world of Tudor England. Just as Second Life itself is a '3-D virtual world entirely built and owned by its residents', Renaissance Island is built and imaged by its citizens and friends.

It is a living, growing, evolving world that has the ability to enrich and to be enriched by everyone who wishes to participate in some capacity, be it education or as a Tudor aficionado.

CONCLUSION

We believe that virtual worlds such as Second Life are the next phase of the Internet. Just as libraries had to jump on the bandwagon of the early graphical web in the 1990s, they need to create an effective presence in virtual worlds to investigate what kinds of library services will work and how they can work together to benefit and serve users. It is also important that libraries work closely with other educators and collaborate with groups. No one library can do everything themselves – collaboration will be key in establishing virtual world presences for libraries.

REFERENCES

Akeroyd, J. (2001). The future of academic libraries. *Aslib Proceedings, 53*(3), 164-172.

Gartner Group Press Release. (2007). *Gartner Group says 80 percent of active Internet users will have a 'Second Life' in the virtual world by the end of 2011*. Retrieved August 6, 2007, from http://www.gartner.com/it/page.jsp?id=503861

Further Information about 'Second Life': Alliance Library System and OPAL (Online Programming for All Libraries) (http://www.opal-online.org/) provide selected OPAL programs in an online virtual reality game called 'Second Life' – http://www.secondlife.com/. 'Second Life' includes book discussions, training sessions and an outreach program to people that might not otherwise use the library. It has over 10 million residents and is continually growing. For more information see 'Second Life' in *The Shifted Librarian*, 12 April 2006. Retrieved May 11, 2010 fro http://www.theshiftedlibrarian.com/archives/2006/04/12/second_library.html

Lori Bell, Mary-Carol Lindbloom and Kitty Pope
Alliance Library System

Tom Peters
TAP Information Services

CONCLUSION

When working on a book project, one has different and specific aims. The objectives in my first two books were more singular, as well as being more political and theoretical than this book.

There were a number of different aims in bringing together this digitisation book. The first was to focus on a very important trend that is taking place before our eyes today; namely, the digitisation of various resources. This process will, and indeed is, changing the map for us all, making information much more easily and readily available, and altering the way in which we engage with each other. However, we must also remain level-headed about it. Not everyone can benefit from all this; and the developing world, in particular, lags behind; the digital divide is, indeed, very real. Neither can it cure all our ills. Rather, technology is a tool that can help us; it cannot do the work for us, it cannot think for us; it cannot produce a better world for us. All of this is still very much in the hands and minds of humans.

The second aim was to bring together the works of various academics and information professionals who are experts in the digitisation field; important works that can hopefully offer some new insights. The final aim was to cover the topic in both some breadth and depth and to assist the reader when considering the future of digitisation and how she/he would like it to develop. Hopefully, this will also inspire and encourage people to be more pro-active in the field.

Thus, hopefully, the book will provide a source of inspiration for further research, leading to some more effective ways to proceed with the digitisation process. Also, that it will be possible to do this within a framework that can be used for good rather than ill, and for the benefit of many.

CONTRIBUTORS

Lori Bell has worked in a variety of library settings, most recently as Director of Innovation at the Alliance Library System, USA. Bell is a graduate of Western Illinois History (B.A. History), University of Illinois, USA, Graduate School of Library and Information Science (M.S.) and has a certificate in Distance Learning from the Department of Instructional Design and Technology at Western Illinois University. She is a lecturer at San Jose State University School of Library and Information Science and an adjunct lecturer at University of Illinois Graduate School of Library and Information Science.

Peggy Cabrera is Assistant Librarian at San Jose State University, USA and library liaison to the Environmental Studies, Global Studies, Humanities and Kinesiology departments at SJSU. Peggy Cabrera is interested in research on citation indexing research to enable students to learn how to search more effectively. She has also written on recruiting and training librarians from diverse backgrounds to the field of library and information science.

Paul Catherall is a librarian currently working at University of Liverpool, UK. He has worked in E-Learning and technical support roles over a number of years and his current role involves providing library services to students studying online. Paul Catherall also worked for several years at North East Wales Institute of Higher Education (NEWI), UK (now Glyndŵr University) as a Web Developer, Information and Student Services and as a College Lecturer in Information Communications Technology. He is also undertaking a PhD within the area of E-Learning and is a graduate of Glyndŵr University, *formerly NEWI* (B.A.) and John Moores University (M.A. Dist). In addition, Paul Catherall is an associate of the Higher Education Academy and a Chartered member of Chartered Institute of Library and Information Professionals (CILIP). Paul has been active in various CILIP affiliated groups, including the Career Development Group and is a member of the Editorial Board of the e-journal *Information for Social Change*. Paul has authored various published journal articles and texts including a stand-alone book *Delivering E-Learning for Information Services in Higher Education* (Chandos, 2005).

Susan Copeland is the Senior Information Adviser (Research) at Robert Gordon University in Aberdeen, UK. She is a graduate of the University of St Andrews (MA, Ancient and Mediaeval History), the University of Sheffield (M.Phil, Archaeology) and the University of Strathclyde (PhD, Information Science). She obtained her Postgraduate Diploma in Librarianship from the University of Wales and worked in public and school libraries before moving into the Higher Education sector. Copeland is a member of the Board of Directors of the Networked Digital Library of Theses and Dissertations (NDLTD) and a member of the DART-Europe Board. She has given presentations at conferences in Europe, Australia and North America and, in 2008, she co-chaired the 11th International Symposium on Electronic Theses and Dissertations.

Isaac Dunlap is a Professor and Information Systems Coordinator at Western Illinois University Libraries, USA. Dunlap is a graduate of Campbell University (B.A. History), Southern Baptist Theological Seminary, Louisville, KY (M.Div.), and the University of North Carolina at Greensboro (MLIS). He is the author of numerous articles on information technology and the book "Open Source Database Driven Web Development: A Guide for Information Professionals" (Oxford: Chandos Publishing, 2006). A frequent speaker at national and regional forums on library technology, Dunlap is an active web applications developer. His research interests include web accessibility, and current trends in technology and academic libraries.

Dieu Hack-Polay is a Senior Lecturer in International Human Resources Management at London South Bank University, UK. He holds a doctorate (EdD) in educational leadership and management and a PhD in Sociology. His research interest includes comparative education, human resource management and migrant labour. Hack-Polay is a fellow of the Higher Education Academy and has published articles in several journals.

Ron Houston has, since 1987, directed and taught for the non-profit educational corporation "Society of Folk Dance Historians," an archive and library of information pertaining to the history and practice of recreational international folk dancing. He received from the University of Texas at Austin, USA the BA (Psychology), BBA (International Business), BS (Geology), MLIS (Archival Enterprise), and Ph.D. (Information Science). In addition to folk dance history, he investigates and writes about societal injustice, compelled (non-volitional) nonuse of information, and the Retroductive Recognition of Absence (RRA) research methodology.

Heather Joseph is the Executive Director of the Scholarly Publishing and Academic Resources Coalition (SPARC), USA, founded by the Association of Research Libraries in 1997. She is responsible for SPARC's overall program development; leads advocacy efforts to support open access to scholarly research; negotiates partnerships with scholarly publishers; and represents the interests and values of SPARC to the stakeholders in scholarly communication. Before joining SPARC in 2005, Heather Joseph served as President and Chief Operating Officer for BioOne, a scholarly e-publisher that helps small scholarly societies in the biological sciences remain competitive while maintaining academic friendly access policies. For her work in successfully launching and establishing BioOne, Heather Joesph was awarded the 2002 Association of Learned and Professional Society Publishers' Award for Services to Not-for-Profit Publishing.

Yehuda E. Kalay is the Dean of the Faculty of Architecture and Town Planning at the Technion, Israel Institute of Technology. Prior to this, for 18 years he was a Professor of Architecture at the University of California, Berkeley, USA, where he also co-founded and directed the Berkeley Center for New Media, from 2004 to 2007. Professor Kalay holds a B.Arch (professional) and MSc (research) degrees in Architecture from the Technion (Israel), and PhD in Architecture from Carnegie Mellon University (Pittsburgh, PA). Prior to his tenure at Berkeley, for 10 years Kalay taught in the departments of architecture and computer science at the State University of New York at Buffalo. He is a founding member and past president of *ACADIA* (Association for Computer Aided Design in Architecture), and former co-Editor-in-Chief of *Automation in Construction*, an international refereed journal (Elsevier, UK). Kalay's research focuses on digital and collaborative design. He has published over 100 scholarly papers and eight books, the most recent of which are *Collaborative Working Environments for Architectural Design* (Palombi, 2009), *New Heritage: Cultural Heritage and New Media* (Routledge, 2008), and *Architecture's New Media* (MIT, 2004).

Mary-Carol Lindbloom executive director of the South Central Regional Library Council, holds an M.L.S. from Syracuse University, USA, and a B.A. in Anthropology from St. John Fisher College. She serves on the planning team for My Info Quest SMS text reference service, chairs its marketing committee, and has been involved with four collaborative virtual reference programs. She was project director for the world's first academic library virtual reference initiative, *Ready for Reference*. Her venture into the virtual world of Second Life began in 2006. In 2007 she became a Coordinator of Renaissance Island, a sim offering learning opportunities and events in an immersive environment, based on Tudor, Britain. She has continued to work with educators, students, and Second Life residents on Renaissance Island, which SCRLC now sponsors. She has worked in academic, public, hospital, consortial, and museum library settings and serves on three school library system advisory councils.

Kate Littlemore is the Academic Support Manager for the Schools of Arts and Applied Sciences at the University of Northampton, UK, where she works in the Department of Information Services, which is a converged library and IT service. She has over 10 years experience in a variety of Information Management settings, is a chartered member of CILIP (the Chartered Institute of Library and Information Professionals) and is currently undertaking her PG Certificate in Teaching in HE.

Dr Jia Liu was an Associate Professor at the Department of Information Management, Peking University, Beijing, China. From 2004 until 2006, she had been a Research Fellow of the Alexander von Humboldt Foundation (AvH Foundation), Germany. During that period, hosting in the Lower-saxony State and Goettingen University Library, she implemented a project on the subject of metadata and its applications in the digital library. Later, with two resumed fellowships from the AvH Foundation, she conducted two other projects on digital reference service in Germany. After that, as a Visiting Scholar, she visited the Faculty of Information Studies, University of Toronto, Canada. Her main research interests are metadata, digital library and digital reference services. Dr Liu has published 45 journal papers and 5 monographs in the mainland of China, Taiwan, the United States, Germany and the United Kingdom in either Chinese or English. She is the author of *Metadata and Its Applications in the Digital Library,* Libraries Unlimited, USA, 2007 and *Evaluation of the World-Wide Reference Service in the Libraries,* Chandos Publishing: Oxford, 2007.

Mengxiong Liu is Professor and Engineering Librarian at San Jose State University, USA. Her teaching and research focuses on human information seeking behaviour, reference and instructional service assessment, and digital libraries. She has published numerous research articles in scholarly journals, conference proceedings, and book chapters. Dr. Liu is an active speaker at national and international professional conferences, and has been invited to lecture in the libraries and academic institutions worldwide. In addition to teaching and research, she has been actively involved in professional organizations, such as the American Library Association (ALA) and the ethnic librarians associations. More recently, she received the Fulbright Senior Specialist Award and completed her Fulbright trip to Uruguay.

Tatiana Nikolova-Houston is a successful manuscript illumination and calligraphy artist in Austin, Texas, USA. She received the BS and MS (Landscape Architecture) from the Forestry Institute in Sofia, Bulgaria; the BS from the Institute of Christian Studies in Austin, Texas; the MS from Abilene Christian University in Abilene, Texas; and the MLIS and Ph.D. (Information Science) from the University of Texas at Austin. In addition to creating artwork, she continues to investigate, write, and lecture about issues pertaining to medieval manuscripts; issues such as preservation, conservation, history, forensic analysis, and marginalia.

M. Paul Pandian obtained his PhD from Karnatak University, Dharwad, India and an Associateship in Documentation and Information Science from the Documentation Research and Training Centre, Indian Statistical Institute, Bangalore, India. He is currently Head of the Library and Information Resource Centre at the Institute of Mathematical Sciences, Department of Atomic Energy, Chennai, India where he has successfully implemented an RFID-based system for the library recently. He was previously the Head of the Library and Information Resource Centre at the Indian Institute of Management, Indore, India and a member of the core team that was responsible for the setting up of a campus-wide information system for the IIM. He has also worked as a scientist at the INFLIBNET Centre, University Grants Commission, India where he was responsible for developing the online union catalogues of participating libraries at INFLIBNET. As a course coordinator at INFLIBNET, he also designed and developed course materials for a six-week residential course on the applications of computer and communication technologies in libraries for library executives and information scientists. He has in addition contributed several research articles on the topic of library and information science to a number of journals and presented papers at national and international conferences.

Tom Peters is the CEO of TAP Information Services, USA (www.tapinformation.com), a small company he founded in 2003 to help libraries and other organizations innovate. Tom has worked previously at the Committee on Institutional Cooperation (CIC, the academic consortium of the Big Ten universities and the University of Chicago), Western Illinois University in Macomb, Northern Illinois University in DeKalb, Minnesota State University at Mankato, and the University of Missouri at Kansas City. Tom Peters did his undergraduate work at Grinnell College, where he majored in English and philosophy. He earned his library science degree at the University of Iowa. His second master's degree (in English) was completed at the University of Missouri at Kansas City. His library experience includes reference service, library instruction, collection management, and administration. His current interests include downloadable digital audio book services (e.g., www.unabridged.info), mobile library initiatives (e.g., www.myinfoquest.info), eReading on portable devices, library services in virtual worlds (e.g., Second Life), and online programming using web conferencing software (e.g., www.opal-online.org). Tom Peters is fond of both visual reading (on paper and on his Blackberry) and auditory reading.

Kitty Pope has been Executive Director of the Alliance Library System, USA since January 2004. She earned her MA in Library Science from the University of Western Ontario, Canada. She has worked in a variety of library settings all over the world. In 2007, Kitty Pope was named the winner of the ALA/Information Today Library of the Future Award for her coordination of libraries in the virtual world in Second Life. She and co-worker Lee Logan were also winners of the ALA ASCLA Leadership Award in 2007 for the multitype library system certification program they developed.

Ruth Rikowski is a Commissioning Editor for Chandos Publishing, Oxford, UK Freelance Editor, Chandos Publishing, Oxford. She is an Associate of the Higher Education Academy and a Chartered Librarian. Ruth Rikowski is the author of *Globalisation, Information and Libraries* (Oxford: Chandos Publishing, 2005) and the editor of the book *Knowledge Management: social, cultural and theoretical perspectives* (Oxford: Chandos Publishing, 2007). She has also written numerous articles and given many talks; focusing in particular on the topics of globalisation, knowledge management and information technology. In addition, Ruth Rikowski is on the Editorial Board of *Policy Futures in Education* and *Information for Social Change*. The Rikowski website, 'The Flow of Ideas' can be found at www.flowideas.co.uk and her blog, 'Ruth Rikowski Updates' is at http://ruthrikowskiupdates.blogspot.com/. Ruth also circulates a newsletter to over 400 subscribers.

Leburn Rose is Acting Academic Registrar and former Head of the Department of Mathematics, Statistics and Foundation Studies at London South Bank University, UK. His current research interest is in the development of strategies for technological and infrastructural development in West African countries, specifically Nigeria. He is deeply committed to his specialist subject area of management education, which spans subject areas such as technology management, information management, business process management, and knowledge management, and marketing. He has wide experience of the Higher Education sector, and has represented London South Bank University as an academic ambassador in a wide range of countries in Europe, Africa and in the Caribbean.

Alan Rosling is the Academic Support Manager for the Schools of Health and Business at the University of Northampton, UK, where he works in the Department of Information Services, which is a converged library and IT service. He is a qualified teacher with extensive experience in teaching information skills. He also teaches Information Management in the Northampton Business School and supports students in developing their study skills at both undergraduate and post-graduate levels. Rosling is a Fellow of the Higher Education Academy.

Melissa Terras is the Senior Lecturer in Electronic Communication in the Department of Information Studies, University College London, UK, and the Deputy Director of the UCL Centre for Digital Humanities. With a background in Classical Art History and English Literature, and Computing Science, her doctorate (University of Oxford) examined how to use advanced information engineering technologies to interpret and read the Vindolanda texts. She is a general editor of DHQ (Digital Humanities Quarterly) and Secretary of the Association of Literary and Linguistic Computing. Her research focuses on the use of computational techniques to enable research in the arts and humanities that would otherwise be impossible.

Tony Ward is an architect, builder and critical pedagogue. Born in England, he has taught there (Portsmouth, Kingston and the A.A.), in America (University of California, Berkeley) and New Zealand (Auckland University) where for twenty years he directed the Community Design Studio, working with his students in real-world situations for marginalised communities. His life's work has been devoted to social equity and justice across cultural boundaries. Much of his work in New Zealand has been with the Maori community. In 1999 he completed his PhD in Critical Education Theory, then in 2001 he joined the Maori University of Te Whare Wananga o Awanuiarangi as Director of Programme Development writing and implementing new degree programmes (5) framed in Maori language, pedagogy and tikanga (traditional customs). He was the only non-Maori senior member of the academic staff. He is currently the Wiepking Distinguished Visiting Professor at Miami University in Oxford, Ohio, USA, appointed by three departments – Architecture, Psychology and Educational Leadership. His extensive website (www.TonyWardEdu.com) is a free educational resource with downloadable essays, articles and projects. He is currently writing a book on The Ward Method of creative consensus-building and social transformation.

INDEX

Lightning Source UK Ltd.
Milton Keynes UK
10 February 2011

167249UK00001B/33/P